T0321727

Digital Psychology's Impact on Business and Society

Muhammad Anshari
Universiti Brunei Darussalam, Brunei

Abdur Razzaq
Universitas Islam Negeri Raden Fatah Palembang, Indonesia

Mia Fithriyah
Indonesia Open University, Indonesia

Akmal Nasri Kamal
Universiti Brunei Darussalam, Brunei

A volume in the Advances in Human
and Social Aspects of Technology
(AHSAT) Book Series

Published in the United States of America by
IGI Global
Information Science Reference (an imprint of IGI Global)
701 E. Chocolate Avenue
Hershey PA, USA 17033
Tel: 717-533-8845
Fax: 717-533-8661
E-mail: cust@igi-global.com
Web site: http://www.igi-global.com

Library of Congress Cataloging-in-Publication Data

Names: Anshari, Muhammad, 1977- editor.
Title: Digital psychology's impact on business and society / Muhammad
   Anshari, Abdur Razzaq, Mia Fithriyah, and Amkal Nasri Kamal, editor.
Description: Hershey, PA : Engineering Science Reference, [2023] | Includes
   bibliographical references and index. | Summary: "Digital psychology is
   a field of study that focuses on the impact of information and
   communication technology on the human mind, behavior, conscious and
   unconscious motivation, feelings, thoughts, attitudes, emotions, among
   other things. Indeed, digital psychology influences businesses to
   fine-tune their strategies and practices, resulting in the emergence of
   innovative business models and disruptive innovation. As a result, this
   study will evaluate not only individual strategies, but also those of
   businesses, organizations, and even nations"-- Provided by publisher.
Identifiers: LCCN 2022039762 (print) | LCCN 2022039763 (ebook) | ISBN
   9781668461082 (hardback) | ISBN 9781668461099 (paperback) | ISBN
   9781668461105 (ebook)
Subjects: LCSH: Information technology--Economic aspects. | Information
   technology--Psychological aspects. | Information technology--Social
   aspects.
Classification: LCC HC79.I55 D56 2023 (print) | LCC HC79.I55 (ebook) |
   DDC 303.48/33--dc23/eng/20220930
LC record available at https://lccn.loc.gov/2022039762
LC ebook record available at https://lccn.loc.gov/2022039763

This book is published in the IGI Global book series Advances in Human and Social Aspects of
Technology (AHSAT) (ISSN: 2328-1316; eISSN: 2328-1324)

British Cataloguing in Publication Data
A Cataloguing in Publication record for this book is available from the British Library.

All work contributed to this book is new, previously-unpublished material.
The views expressed in this book are those of the authors, but not necessarily of the publisher.

For electronic access to this publication, please contact: eresources@igi-global.com.

Advances in Human and Social Aspects of Technology (AHSAT) Book Series

ISSN:2328-1316
EISSN:2328-1324

Editor-in-Chief: Mehdi Khosrow-Pour, D.B.A., Information Resources Management Association, USA

MISSION

In recent years, the societal impact of technology has been noted as we become increasingly more connected and are presented with more digital tools and devices. With the popularity of digital devices such as cell phones and tablets, it is crucial to consider the implications of our digital dependence and the presence of technology in our everyday lives.

The **Advances in Human and Social Aspects of Technology (AHSAT) Book Series** seeks to explore the ways in which society and human beings have been affected by technology and how the technological revolution has changed the way we conduct our lives as well as our behavior. The AHSAT book series aims to publish the most cutting-edge research on human behavior and interaction with technology and the ways in which the digital age is changing society.

COVERAGE

- Cyber Behavior
- Cyber Bullying
- End-User Computing
- Technology and Freedom of Speech
- Cultural Influence of ICTs
- Human Development and Technology
- Public Access to ICTs
- Technology and Social Change
- Information ethics
- ICTs and human empowerment

IGI Global is currently accepting manuscripts for publication within this series. To submit a proposal for a volume in this series, please contact our Acquisition Editors at Acquisitions@igi-global.com or visit: http://www.igi-global.com/publish/.

Titles in this Series

For a list of additional titles in this series, please visit:
http://www.igi-global.com/book-series/advances-human-social-aspects-technology/37145

Handbook of Research on Implementing Digital Reality and Interactive Technologies to Achieve Society 5.0
Francesca Maria Ugliotti (Politecnico di Torino, Italy) and Anna Osello (Politecnico di Torino, Italy)
Information Science Reference • © 2022 • 731pp • H/C (ISBN: 9781668448540) • US $295.00

Exploring Ethical Problems in Today's Technological World
Tamara Phillips Fudge (Purdue University Global, USA)
Information Science Reference • © 2022 • 385pp • H/C (ISBN: 9781668458921) • US $240.00

Technological Influences on Creativity and User Experience
Joshua Fairchild (Creighton University, USA)
Information Science Reference • © 2022 • 305pp • H/C (ISBN: 9781799843542) • US $195.00

Machine Learning for Societal Improvement, Modernization, and Progress
Vishnu S. Pendyala (San Jose State University, USA)
Engineering Science Reference • © 2022 • 290pp • H/C (ISBN: 9781668440452) • US $270.00

The Digital Folklore of Cyberculture and Digital Humanities
Stamatis Papadakis (University of Crete, Greece) and Alexandros Kapaniaris (Hellenic Open University, Greece)
Information Science Reference • © 2022 • 361pp • H/C (ISBN: 9781668444610) • US $215.00

For an entire list of titles in this series, please visit:
http://www.igi-global.com/book-series/advances-human-social-aspects-technology/37145

701 East Chocolate Avenue, Hershey, PA 17033, USA
Tel: 717-533-8845 x100 • Fax: 717-533-8661
E-Mail: cust@igi-global.com • www.igi-global.com

Table of Contents

Detailed Table of Contents

Chapter 1
    Fatma Ince, Mersin University, Turkey

Due to the complexity of human psychology, well-being depends on many factors, so it is helpful to consider different aspects in a multidisciplinary way. However, it is still unclear how these factors, which are the keys to a better life, will be affected by digital transformation. There are both challenges and opportunities in areas such as work-life balance, social connections, civic engagement, and governance. From this point of view, in this chapter, firstly the digitalization process, then the concepts of psychological adjustment and digital well-being, are mentioned.

Chapter 2
    Ida Haizatultasha Zaqreen, Universiti Brunei Darussalam, Brunei
    Sheirene Diana Hong, Universiti Brunei Darussalam, Brunei
    Nur Hayati Mohd Daud, Universiti Brunei Darussalam, Brunei

The number of smartphone users has steadily risen over the last few years and smartphones have apparently become an unavoidable part of daily life; and with that, concerns have progressively risen worldwide in regards to users' physical and psychological well-being when using smartphones for extended periods of time. This study looked at the relationship between smartphone use and physical well-being, as well as the role of emotion regulation in the relationship between smartphone usage and functional impairment. This research sheds light on the harmful relationship between excessive smartphone use and the user's physical and mental health. The findings show that smartphone usage plays an important role in individuals' everyday lives. As a result, the influence on physical and psychological well-being should be discussed further in order to prevent the negative consequences of smartphone usage.

Chapter 3

*Ivona Huđek, Faculty of Economics and Business, University of
Maribor, Slovenia*
*Karin Širec, Faculty of Economics and Business, University of Maribor,
Slovenia*

This chapter relates to digital transformation and its impact on the labor market, with a focus on the emergence of new business models characterized by less reliance on physical elements-the "gig economy." As a result, new forms of work such as freelancers are taking an increasingly large share of the labor market, characterized by self-directed and independent career development. Although global leaders face the challenge of harnessing this trend and promoting its economic benefits while ensuring an inclusive society by preventing social polarization in labor markets, findings suggest that social protection and appreciation for new forms of work are still low. Using 200 Slovenian freelancers, the authors examine demographic characteristics, motivation for freelancing, and their subjective well-being. Accordingly, the implications for policymakers are to invest more effort in creating a supportive ecosystem that is open not only to "standard" but also to new contemporary and digitally enabled careers.

Chapter 4

Pelin Yolcu, University of Dicle, Turkey

A digital footprint is simply defined as the trace of users' online activities. Another definition explains the digital footprint as the trace left by the online and offline activities of users electronically in electronic media (database, server, etc.). Social media shares, web pages visited, e-mails sent, and online games played are some of the parts that make up the digital footprint. In short, the records of the interaction between the individual and the virtual electronic world constitute the digital footprint. In this direction, the aim of this study is to determine the digital footprint awareness of university students and to determine their general views on the digital footprint, and the time they spend in electronic tools and environments.

Chapter 5

Nuroul Widad Khalid, Universiti Brunei Darussalam, Brunei

A smartphone is a gadget with a variety of features that reside in the capacity of a machine. It is a gadget that can be described as a minicomputer due to its specific size and its different features, such as a PC or a computer device. The objectives of this chapter are to discuss the positive and negative impact of COVID-19 smartphone dependency on employees' job performance at the workplace. Job performance can be defined as the "total expected value" to the organisation of the discrete behavioural episodes that an individual carries out over a standard period of time. The positive and negative impact of COVID-19 smartphone dependency will be discussed and demonstrated using the Ishikawa diagram.

Chapter 6

In the age of COVID-19, couriers are one of the jobs that have been categorised as essential; while other jobs have changed to working from home if they can, couriers and other essential workers still need to carry out their tasks as usual in order to maintain a semblance of normalcy for others. Yet, problems previously experienced by couriers have instead been made worse by COVID-19, such as the prevalence of overwork becoming more common as the demand of online shopping increases. As a result, job burnout has become more pronounced in this new norm. In view of this, exploratory research was conducted by reviewing various literature surrounding job burnout and courier work in the context of the COVID-19 pandemic. The findings are then analysed using Ishikawa's fishbone diagram, which are then categorised into four interlinked themes of environmental, psychological, physical, and financial factors. Afterwards, a discussion was made to further detail the extent of these factors towards job burnout, with recommendations being made to potentially remedy these factors.

Chapter 7

Every aspect of one's life, from educating oneself through YouTube to finding a suitor on dating apps, shows how intertwined one's life is with digitalisation. COVID-19 has only allowed it to proliferate further. This chapter examines how different digitalisation policy initiatives in Brunei during COVID-19 have enabled the creation of a digital Islamic society through an Islamic governance perspective. A digital ethnographic approach was employed, and data were drawn from three sources: 1) document analysis, 2) social media, and 3) observation. Analysis was carried out using the Maqāṣid collaborative framework. Results from the study show that a digital Islamic society is currently being shaped in Brunei in all aspect of the Maqāṣid of the Sharia.

Chapter 8

Financial technology (FinTech) has become more ubiquitous in an era of accelerating internet technology and rising e-commerce. With the increasing digitisation of the marketplace, smartphones are now used not only for communication but also as a means of payment in a number of countries. Several initiatives have been undertaken to accelerate the digital transformation of the business, including the use of digital wallets by young adults. Given the scarcity of research examining FinTech adoption from a human behaviour perspective, this study will examine the elements that motivate people to use digital wallets. Three major themes were theoretically derived using a qualitative technique and Maslow's hierarchy of needs as the research instrument. The main reasons why young adults use digital wallets were found to be "youth digitalization," "technological anxiety," and a "positive attitude toward technology use."

Digital psychology has affected human behavior, including in the educational sector. The advancement in digital exposure opens the possibility of learning in online-based systems. For years, this new shift has been considered to bring more advantages for people. Recently, this way of learning has been adopted by law schools as an impact of the pandemic in Indonesia. Forecasting the benefits of this digitalized education mechanism, this change is expected to last after the COVID-19 pandemic. Not only does offering help, but the change also raises some challenges and opportunities, including the potential markets for the higher education business, particularly law schools. This chapter analyzes challenges and opportunities to show how the digital world impacts legal education, its current development, and its future projection in Indonesia. This analysis applies qualitative methods supported by secondary data and information.

This chapter aims to explore the digital transformation in higher education institutions, especially in regards to the increased use of e-learning in recent years by identifying the parties who are affected by the transformation and the challenges people may face in implementing the use of e-learning. By using the CATWOE analysis technique, it identified that the main parties that are affected by this transformation into e-learning are the students and teachers of higher education institutions and to an extent the institutions themselves. Furthermore, through the construction of the fishbone diagram, it identified the main issues of implementing e-learning: cost, internet connectivity, lack of interaction, suitability of e-learning, and lack of knowledge. As the parties affected and challenges have been identified, this study can be used to improve e-learning processes in the future.

Chapter 11

The advancement of technology has increased the usage of the internet and social media platforms like Facebook, Twitter, WhatsApp, and Instagram. Many people face health and psychological issues due to overuse of social media. So, there is a need to promote techniques of a healthy lifestyle for the people, especially the youth. After studying the ill effects of social media and excessive phone usage by the youth, the authors have tried to use heartfulness to reduce the impact of the digital world on their physical and mental health. If we can train our minds properly, we can avoid unwanted thoughts and focus inward. But we have to know the correct techniques to train our minds. The heart plays a very important role so by meditating on the heart one can control their thoughts. It happens only through heartfulness meditation practice. Meditation helps us to improve sleep quality and sound sleep gives us a healthy lifestyle. By regular practice of heartfulness meditation, one can have better awareness and self-control by which the health of an individual remains good.

Chapter 12

This chapter addresses digital footprints and how they can affect today's modern world, whether it be on the behaviour of humans, effects on society and governments, or even a person's ability to maintain their security or privacy. There is a possibility that leaving a digital footprint, regardless of the information that individuals post online, can have both positive and negative effects. The greater a person's digital footprint is, the more active they are in their interactions on the internet. It is necessary to bring attention to the matter at hand, which is the concept behind digital footprint being put into practise. It discusses digital footprints in a variety of contexts, such as real-life examples that illustrate how a digital footprint can have an impact in the actual world.

Preface

Having access to data is beneficial to a wide range of organizations, including individuals, businesses, organisations, and nations. People generate data at their own will, developing habits, patterns, and behaviours in the process. As a consequence of the data that they produce, their psychological characteristics will be better exposed, which could be used to improve decision-making. Organizations are motivated by the ability to collect and assess as much data as they possibly can from the general public or prospective consumers in order to gain a deeper understanding of the psychological characteristics of these individuals and increase the likelihood that they will buy the goods or services being offered by the organisation. As a result, there has been a great deal of debate about the use of data from the perspectives of individuals, organizations, the general public, and the government.

The edited book "Digital Psychology's Impact on Business and Society" examines the strategies of individuals as well as those of businesses, organisations, and even countries. This reference work is ideal for policymakers, psychologists, business owners, managers, industry professionals, researchers, scholars, practitioners, academicians, instructors, and students because it covers topics such as digital transformation and well-being, smartphone habits and behaviour, digital wallet usage among youth, and digitization in education. This book is organized into ten chapters addressing key issues in Digital Psychology's aspects. Let's present a summary of the collection of ten chapters of this book.

Chapter 1, titled "The Digital Transformation and Well-Being," by Fatma Ince, states that because human psychology is so complex, a person's happiness is dependent on a variety of different things, and it's helpful to examine various things from different fields of study. However, it is still unknown how the digital transition will impact these aspects, which are essential to living a better life. In areas like work-life balance, social connections, civic engagement, and government, there are both issues and ways to solve them. From this point of view, this section discusses first the process of digitalization, then about psychological adjustment, and finally digital well-being.

Chapter 2, titled "Smartphone Habits and Behaviour: A Review on Issues in Relation to the Physical and Psychological Well-Being of Users," by Ida Haizatultasha Zaqreen, Sheirene Diana Hong, and Nur Hayati Mohd Daud, affirms that the number of smartphone users has rapidly risen in recent years and has become an inevitable part of daily life. Concerns have risen worldwide about users' physical and psychological well-being when using cellphones for lengthy periods of time. This study examined the association between smartphone use and physical well-being, as well as the influence of emotion control. This study shows how excessive smartphone use can affect physical and mental health. The findings reveal that smartphone use is common. The impact on physical and mental health should be discussed extensively to prevent smartphone-related harm.

Chapter 3, titled "The Impact of Digital Transformation on Freelancer Well-Being: Insight From Slovenia," by Ivona Huđek and Karin Širec, discusses digital revolution and its impact on the labour market, focusing on the "gig economy" and its less tangible business structures. Freelancers and other self-directed workers are growing their share of the labour market. Global leaders must exploit this development and promote its economic benefits while minimising social divisiveness in labour markets. However, social protection and respect for new kinds of work remain low. The authors study 200 Slovenian freelancers' demographics, motivation, and well-being. Policymakers should invest more in developing a conducive ecosystem for "standard" and emerging digitally enabled occupations.

Chapter 4, titled "Are We Followed in the Digital World?" by Pelin Yolcu, states that a digital footprint is a user's online activity trail. Digital footprint is the record of online and offline user activity in electronic media (database, server, etc.). Digital footprint includes social media shares, website visits, e-mails written, and online games played. Digital footprints are the recordings of an individual's electronic interactions. This survey aims to identify university students' digital footprint awareness and their thoughts on the time they spend in technological tools and surroundings.

Chapter 5, titled "The Positive and Negative Impact of COVID-19 Smartphone Dependency on Employee Job Performance," by Nuroul Widad Khalid, discusses a smartphone is a device having a variety of features that exist within a machine's capabilities. It is a device that can be classified as a minicomputer due to its size and functions, similar to a personal computer or computer device. This chapter's aims are to examine the positive and negative effects of COVID-19 smartphone dependency on employee job performance. An individual's job performance can be defined as the "total expected value" to the organisation of the discrete behavioural episodes he or she demonstrates over a standard time period. Using an Ishikawa diagram, the positive and negative effects of COVID-19 smartphone dependency will be explained and shown.

Chapter 6, titled "Delivery Workers, COVID-19, and Job Burnout," by Nur Hazirah Mohd Sufian, states that couriers are one of the essential jobs in the age of COVID-19; while other jobs have transitioned to working from home if they can, couriers and other vital workers still need to carry out their tasks as usual. COVID-19 has made carriers' problems worse, such as overwork as online shopping demand rises. This new norm has increased job fatigue. Exploratory research was undertaken by reviewing job burnout and courier work in the context of COVID-19. The findings are categorised into environmental, psychological, physical, and economical components using Ishikawa's Fishbone Diagram. After discussing the extent of these issues, proposals were made to fix them.

Chapter 7, titled "A Digital Ethnographic Account of a Digital Islamic Society During COVID-19: An Islamic Governance Perspective," by Hamizah Haidi, states that From educating oneself on YouTube to finding a date on dating apps, digitalization has permeated every element of modern life. Covid-19 just let it spread. This chapter discusses how digitization policy actions in Brunei under Covid-19 have created a digital Islamic society from an Islamic Governance perspective. Data was obtained via document analysis, social media, and observation using a digital ethnographic approach. Maqid was used for analysis. The report demonstrates that Brunei is shaping a digital Islamic society in all aspects of Sharia Maqid.

Chapter 8, titled "Maslow's Hierarchy of Needs and Digital Wallet Usage Among Youth," by Iffah Haziyah Rumaizi, Muhammad Anshari, Mohammad Nabil Almunawar, and Masairol Masri, states that in an era of accelerating internet technology and expanding e-commerce, FinTech has become more prevalent. In some nations, smartphones are utilised not just for communication but also as a form of payment. Young adults are using digital wallets to speed the business's digital transformation. Due to the lack of human behaviour research on FinTech adoption, this study will analyse what motivates consumers to utilise digital wallets. Using qualitative research and Maslow's Hierarchy of Needs, three key themes were identified. "Youth digitalization," "technological anxiety," and a "positive attitude toward technology use" are why young adults adopt digital wallets.

Chapter 9, titled "The Digitization in Legal Education: Picturing and Projecting Indonesia's Experience," by Zuhda Mila Fitriana and Eka Nanda Ravizki, states that digital psychology affects human behaviour, including education. Digital exposure advances online learning. This shift has been regarded beneficial for years. As a consequence, in Indonesia, legal schools have recently adopted this method of education. This modification is likely to last after the COVID-19 pandemic. The move increases problems and opportunities for higher education businesses, especially law schools. This article examines how the digital world affects legal education, its current progress, and its future projections in Indonesia. It uses qualitative methodologies supplemented by secondary data and information.

Chapter 10, titled "Digital Transformation in Higher Education Institutions," by Siti Nurbarizah Haji Mohammad Azari, discusses the digital transformation in higher education institutions, especially as it relates to the increased use of e-learning in recent years. This will be done by figuring out who is affected by the change and what problems people may face when putting e-learning into practice. Using the CATWOE analysis method, it was found that the main people affected by this change to e-learning are higher education students, teachers, and, to some extent, the institutions themselves. Also, by making the fishbone diagram, it was possible to figure out what the main problems were with implementing e-learning: cost, lack of internet connectivity, lack of interaction, e-learning not being the right fit, and lack of knowledge. Since the people who are affected and the problems that need to be solved have been found, this study can be used to make e-learning better in the future.

Chapter 11, titled "Heartfulness Meditation: A Technique to Reduce the Health Impacts of Digital Psychology," by Anjum Nazir Qureshi Sheikh and Manisha Urkude, affirms that the growth of technology has boosted the use of the internet and social media platforms like Facebook, Twitter, WhatsApp, and Instagram. Social media overuse causes health and mental concerns for many. It's important to promote a healthy lifestyle, especially among youth. After examining the negative effects of social media and phone use on kids, we tried to employ heartfulness to improve their physical and mental health. Train your mind to ignore undesirable thoughts and focus within. Mind training requires the right techniques. By meditating on the heart, you can regulate your thoughts. Only through heartfulness meditation. Meditation improves sleep quality and promotes a healthy lifestyle. By regularly practising heartfulness meditation, one can gain awareness and self-control, improving health.

The last chapter of the book, titled "Digital Footprint and Human Behavior: Potential and Challenges," by Adi Putra Pg Rosman, informs about digital footprints and their impact on the contemporary world, whether it be on human behaviour, effects on society and governments, or a person's capacity to retain security or privacy. Leaving a digital imprint, independent of the material that individuals put online, may have both beneficial and bad repercussions. The greater an individual's digital footprint, the more engaged they are in their online interactions. It is vital to draw attention to the issue at hand, which is the implementation of the principle underlying digital footprint. It addresses digital footprints in a number of scenarios, including real-world examples illustrating the influence a digital footprint can have in the real world.

Muhammad Anshari
Universiti Brunei Darussalam, Brunei

Abdur Razzaq
Universitas Islam Negeri Raden Fatah Palembang, Indonesia

Mia Fithriyah
Indonesia Open University, Indonesia

Akmal Nasri Kamal
Universiti Brunei Darussalam, Brunei

Acknowledgment

Alhamdulillah, all praise be to Allah (SWT) for giving us the strength to complete this book in the midst of the COVID-19 pandemic. We are grateful to all the contributors to this book for their valuable contributions. We would like to thank the reviewers for taking the necessary time and effort to review the manuscript. We sincerely appreciate all your valuable comments and constructive feedback, which helped improve the quality of the chapters. Last but not least, the editors also acknowledge the guidance and assistance provided by IGI Global.

Chapter 1
Digital Transformation and Well–Being

Fatma Ince
ⓘⅅ https://orcid.org/0000-0002-0628-5858
Mersin University, Turkey

ABSTRACT

Due to the complexity of human psychology, well-being depends on many factors, so it is helpful to consider different aspects in a multidisciplinary way. However, it is still unclear how these factors, which are the keys to a better life, will be affected by digital transformation. There are both challenges and opportunities in areas such as work-life balance, social connections, civic engagement, and governance. From this point of view, in this chapter, firstly the digitalization process, then the concepts of psychological adjustment and digital well-being, are mentioned.

INTRODUCTION

The radical changes in the past have irreversibly affected human life and managed to call the period when it took place a revolution. These periods of change, known as industrial revolutions, have brought a new world order by differentiating business life, lifestyles, and all habits. Nowadays, this rapid change in digitalization gains more momentum than before and forces people to adapt to concepts that were not in their nature before. Although all developments contribute to improving life, their effects on human psychology are more complex than expected. Psychological states, which are the combined effect of more than one factor, show an interactive and complex structure so that the individual can say I feel good (Cohen & Sherman, 2014). For this reason, it is not possible to easily understand the concepts of human

DOI: 10.4018/978-1-6684-6108-2.ch001

psychology such as well-being, personality, and emotion. Complex systems with interrelationships help to understand how difficult some concepts are, otherwise they have the potential to cause chaos.

Technology is not expected to affect everyone at the same rate, but it is a known fact that it somehow takes place in everyone's life. In today's metaverse developments, it is crucial to study and understand human behavior concerning technology, as the lines between cyberspace and reality are increasingly blurred. And the greater the overlap between individuals and machines, the greater the need to develop such disciplines as cyberpsychology. It is thought that the Internet has an effect on mental health in various aspects such as shortening the attention span, multitasking, technology addiction, exposure to fake information, bullying, loneliness, depression, or cheating (Lam & Peng, 2010). As a result, emerging research fields such as cyberpsychology aim to empower people to make the internet a safer and better place. Thus, there is a need for studies that bring together the internet and people in terms of controlled growth, and prevention of mental and physical harm (Lam & Peng, 2010). For this reason, the need for research, action plans, and strategies that connect people to the internet to prevent mental and physical harm by growing in a controlled way is increasing day by day. Guidance is invaluable at an early age when habits begin to develop and when school life is new.

For digital transformation to take place healthily, multidisciplinary perspectives examining the interaction between humans with technology and efforts to provide psychological well-being should be taken into account by decision-makers and global companies that have the power to shape society. Because the developments experienced produce serious outputs in both directions, positive and negative, it is necessary to ensure controlled progress in terms of human and social psychology (Korunovska & Spiekermann, 2019). Digital well-being concerns individuals' subjective well-being in a social environment where digital media are omnipresent. A general framework is developed to integrate empirical research toward a cumulative science of the impacts of digital media use on well-being. It describes the nature of and connections between three pivotal constructs: digital practices, harms or benefits, and well-being (Büchi, 2021). Focusing on the complex relationships with digital applications, their harms and benefits, and dimensions of well-being, the concept explains the nature of the situation and the consequences of interaction.

By prioritizing descriptive validity and formal theory development, digital wellbeing studies have the potential to mediate positive increases in individual well-being outcomes with a certain regularity. While the structural rules of the digitalized society are shaped by public and private governance mechanisms such as competition policy (Just, 2018). Dominant digital intermediaries such as social media platforms also manage daily individual practices. Digitalization and interconnected technological innovations together determine the conditions under which social, political, and economic relations are carried out. In this respect, the subject also attracts the attention of institutions and organizations that conduct extensive research, such as the OECD, due to its power to influence the future (Van-Zanden et al., 2014). Aiming to challenge how policymakers and society as a whole think about progress, the institution notes that the results are still uncertain as it explores dimensions that are key to a better life. Depending on the steps to be taken, there are both risks and opportunities in areas such as work-life balance, social connections, governance, and civic engagement.

Some countries, such as Finland, are also taking up the issue intending to lead the next industrial revolution. It exhibits a strategic perspective by addressing all dimensions of innovation, from investing in information technologies to making necessary infrastructure preparations, multidisciplinary studies, and R&D projects (Annanperä et al., 2021). The issue, therefore, plays a crucial role in every dimension, from its impact on human psychology to its potential to shape the future. Such issues, which focus on complex relationships, should be examined from a wide perspective and at different scales, from micro to macro effects. Because of the complexity of psychological factors, it is insufficient to produce solutions based on a single dimension, so there is a multidimensional well-being structure. It is unclear what role digitalization will play in this complex structure. That's why it's important to research well-being for a better life because understanding human nature is the most fundamental key to sustainable success with human-technology harmony. In the chapter, for a comprehensive presentation, the subject of trends in the digital era is initially discussed with the following content; technological points of digital transformation, and digital technologies toward industry 6.0. Then the subjects of cyberpsychology with adaptation to innovation, and promoting social prosperity with trust are highlighted. Digital well-being with some points to ponder is lastly mentioned before the conclusion and future research suggestions. Thus, the crucial dimensions of well-being are exhibited in the age of change that emphasizes technology and human harmony.

METHODOLOGY

In this study, a holistic literature review is conducted using a systematic review. As a summary of the literature that uses reproducible methods to systematically explore, critically evaluate and synthesize a particular topic, a systematic review is important to lay the groundwork for new studies. The method of gathering all available evidence on a specific topic to answer a particular research question proceeds by narrowing the available resources based on certain criteria. The process both allows for scoping reviews and a simplified approach to systematic review within time constraints.

The method as one of the explanations of reason helps to clarify the essentials. The difference in views, styles, and topics can be expressed by the author, and this is an advantage in presenting a diversity of approaches to understanding systematic reviews. It provides rigor, insight, and completeness to identify all appropriate studies by extracting the necessary data (Chalmers & Altman, 1995). In this context, the effects of digital transformation and accompanying technologies on well-being and other socio-cultural factors within the scope of industrial revolutions are examined with a holistic approach in this chapter.

TRENDS IN THE DIGITAL ERA

The digital era, which characterizes the transition from an industrial economy to a knowledge-based economy, in which computers or other technological devices are used as communication tools, is witnessing many developments concerning business and social life. Digital and post-digital terms are used commonly, while technology is divided into four main ages pre-mechanical, mechanical, electromechanical, and electronic. From the individual to the nations, in the age of mass entrepreneurship and innovation, socio-economic change is seen as inevitable at all levels. The rapidly increasing online shopping and global logistics networks during the last pandemic period are among the most prominent developments where cyber developments will go beyond physical borders. This process, in which all sectors, especially education, health, logistics, agriculture, and media, rapidly adapt to change, accelerates the adoption of new business and working models with remote working models or hybrid preferences without being physically present at the workplace (Ince, 2021a). In all developments with a social aspect, it is necessary to pay attention to delicate balances to offer sustainable, solutions as a result of the mutual interaction of people, nature, and technology. Since the difficulties arising from change and transformation are like the process, the solutions developed need to be evaluated well. Considering all these issues, first of all, the digital dimension of the transformation and then the industrial revolutions that await humanity today and in the future are mentioned in this title. Addressing digitalization with all its dimensions from different perspectives reveals the aspect that affects human psychology more clearly.

Technological Points of Digital Transformation

Digital Transformation, which is defined as the process of developing and finding solutions to social and sectoral needs with the integration of digital technologies and the change in workflows or culture accordingly, provides the necessary tools for institutions to keep up with the changing competition. The reflection of this transformation in the business world is seen as the process of using modern technology to create or change existing business processes, culture, and customer experiences. This reimagining of business and social life in the digital age, while offering new solutions, sometimes leading to radical steps, normally progressing cumulatively, gives a new impetus to human-technology interaction (Matt et al., 2015). This transformation, which transcends traditional sales-oriented customer service activities, offers innovations that focus on business or corporate-individual interaction. The gradual incorporation of new technology into all processes offers interested parties the opportunity to reconsider their current business models and habits. This situation, which enables the opening of sectors that were not possible before, requires some basic elements to be taken into account while taking human interaction to a different dimension.

Process transformation is one of the first elements to consider. This phase may involve radical updates, requiring changing elements of a business' processes to achieve new goals. It is necessary for outputs such as modernization of operational methods, adaptation to new technologies, savings, and increases in system efficiency. This move, which includes major and radical changes in business process management, requires moving away from the usual type and following similar steps. Only in this way, does digital transformation, which means the holistic transformation of employees, working environments, ways of doing business, strategy, culture, leadership, and technological infrastructure, come to the fore in parallel with the intense use of digital technologies. Talent management, a business strategy and HR (Human Resources) policy implemented by businesses to attract, develop and retain talented employees, is an essential part of new and rapidly evolving digital workplaces. The prevalence of such work environments, which traditionally do not have physical boundaries, where work is mostly done in virtual environments, where technology is used intensively, and where digital business models and ways of doing business are adopted, are the prominent indicators of digitalization. As new problems create new solutions, one of the benefits of digitalization is digital talent hunting (Schwarzmüller, 2018). The need for employees who know digital technologies with the skills and abilities to use them in the workplace increases the need for qualified personnel, forcing employees to develop.

The workplace environment, the way the work is done and the technologies used constitute an important part of individual and social well-being from the perspective of the employee's psychology. The qualifications of the job are as pivotal as the income obtained for financial growth, development, and welfare in economic and individual terms. Job qualifications and person-job (PJ) fit are as pivotal as income for financial growth, development, and well-being in economic and individual terms. To adopt an approach with a multidimensional perspective that takes into account both the individual and the organization, effective process management is needed in organizations that want to be the leader of change by proactively reacting beyond adapting to change (Akanni & Oduaran, 2022). To decide on the basic strategy, a target is first determined that includes answers to some critical questions. First of all, by answering the question of what is the factor that causes the need for change, it should be understood whether it is a renewal of the system or a radical step. The answer to the question of what process is required for a new organizational structure and which steps should be adapted determines the scope of strategic alignment and synergy (Ince, 2021b). After determining the goals of the transformation, the second step is to establish the basic criteria, which are all measurable planning variables such as cost, time, and budget. Third, a roadmap should be created that offers a set of alternative strategies and the best solution. Third, a roadmap should be created that offers a set of alternative strategies and the best solution. The final step in process transformation is to implement the plan, monitor, and keep the process under constant control (Baiyere et al., 2020). Alongside process transformation, business model transformation can be regarded as one of the advances or imperatives driven by digital change.

The business model transformation has reached the level where conveniences can be seen in daily life. Digitalization effects can be mentioned in almost all sectors such as video, photo or film sharing, transportation services, and logistics networks. With the new generation of taxis, people can make reservations from their smart devices while listening to music on their devices. Every individual can shop online with personalized advertising, insurance, and product options, insure their vehicle remotely, and even instruct the IoT-enabled devices in their smart home to communicate with each other. So that when they go home, the desired room temperature, safety measures, and other conditions can be provided (Hale, 2021; Ince, 2021c). Examples can be multiplied in many sectors such as health, education, and tourism, but the main issue here is that many companies are following digital technologies to transform their traditional business models. By reinventing and adding to existing success models, organizations can go through a renewal process that offers significant new opportunities for growth. The competition of enterprises in the rapid entry into the world of Metaverse is one of the digital steps that try to take maximum advantage of the inevitable technological change.

Domain transformation is one of the other elements to consider for the change due to digitalization. This area, which has enormous potential, is the identification of new products and services based on core capabilities and the allocation of new competitive areas. The most common example of this perspective, which offers new value creation opportunities, is Amazon's entry into the big data business in the cloud using its comprehensive portfolio distribution infrastructure. The company, while needing storage to keep up with the global scale by providing basic computing services to newly established or growing businesses, has stepped into cloud systems and turned the situation into a business opportunity (Bugiotti et al., 2012). From this example, it can be suggested that businesses undergoing digital transformation should pay attention to the new opportunities for domain transformation that they find themselves in with the inclusion of new technology. Focusing on processes whose essential qualities are mastered to achieve synergy can alleviate the pains of change such as culture shock or difficulty in adaptation.

Cultural or organizational transformation, one of the indispensable elements of the human-centered perspective, reminds organizations that a successful digital transformation requires more than just updating technology or redesigning products. Human capital, one of the most dynamic elements of strategic alignment, has the power to directly affect success. In this process, it is not enough to find talented employees, they also need to be worked in organizational harmony. Leadership, transparency, and a clear vision can help in this process (Ince, 2023a). Concerns should be reduced by openly sharing with employees in a participatory approach the potential risks, why they should be taken, and the gains that can be made. A comprehensive collaborative effort is a useful tool for culture to understand, embrace and advance digital transformation from slow adoption of digital technologies to loss of competitiveness, failure, or performance degradation, negative effects can have knock-on or butterfly effects. This process, which has the potential to create a domino effect, can easily get away from synergy and create an environment of chaos that puts sustainability at risk (Larjovuori et al., 2018; Ince, 2022a). Therefore, technology should not be taken as a stand-alone variable, but instead, both technology-human compatibility and organization-human compatibility should be considered. The success of organizational structures that bring people together in a complex compatibility relationship is directly dependent on cultural elements. The digital culture, which deals with the concepts of technology and the internet, which affects this function of the culture that shapes the behavior, thought, and communication style in society, is also a part of the organizational transformation. This culture, which encourages an external rather than internal orientation, has a structure that prefers to be participatory rather than coercive. To benefit from the experiences of older generations who were not born in the digital age, there must be processes that contain them (Ince, 2022b). Actions rather than plans can be at the forefront with practices that encourage courage for innovative steps (Wokurka et al., 2017). The collaborative perspective is an indication that individual efforts alone are not enough and that group dynamics must be well-adjusted for change. These basic elements of digital culture are the locomotive elements in the sustainability of change and transformation.

For long-term investment, a culture that empowers employees helps optimize operations, and where talent can be showcased must be created, as innovation in services and products alone will not be enough. Only in this way can customers be attracted permanently, because human capital can easily reveal its innovative side with technology support. Considering the developments experienced by the sectors in terms of technology and artificial intelligence (AI), it is understood that this issue will continue to progress by keeping it up-to-date. The global partnerships and race of tech giants to buy each other means that the artificial intelligence era will be more than ever and be embedded in processors dedicated to computing, from the cloud, smartphones, PCs, self-driving cars, and robots to edge IoT (Internet of Things) for use (Krishna et al., 2021). How to manage efforts in research, training, human capital development, operational synergies and the creation of new opportunities for innovative resources is another challenge (Ince, 2023b). For this reason, taking into account the management issues including organizational psychology, technology change should be tried to be achieved in structures that value people. Otherwise, digitization can create a mismatch in organizational elements, creating an anti-human practice bias.

Digital Technologies Towards Industry 6.0

Technological developments that left their mark on industrial revolutions have caused permanent and irreversible changes in human life periods. These developments, which change social life, urbanization, and all other socio-economic elements, continue at an increasing pace today. While the fourth industrial revolution is taking place, the effect of digitalization has already begun. This period, which brings people closer to technology by creating a new environment where physical, digital, and biological fields are combined, forms the infrastructure of the next periods with new technological inventions. The development of digital technologies such as machine learning, artificial intelligence, data mining, internet of things, deep learning, autonomous systems, internet of things, robotics, and blockchain are some of the developments that force all economies, industries, businesses, and individuals to transform and change (Braña, 2019; Ince, 2023c). The effects of newly developing cyber-physical technologies in terms of human-technology compatibility can be in different ways.

With the development of cyber-physical systems, some of the work from users is initiated only by machines, and some are initiated by human-machine cooperation. While the Industry 4.0 revolution causes some changes at the organizational level, it provides the redistribution of work between machines and people. This innovation also enables remote monitoring and unmanned management of business processes. This new distribution of work pushes employees to acquire different skills and requires knowledge of how to manage the digitalized business. At a different stage, machines can generate activity or data and have the power to provide more interaction. This means a technology-intensive with a human-free working model. Instrumental distribution in human-technology harmony can also occur in the direction of one aspect to take place more heavily in business or social life. If reducing human attachment means employees don't understand cyber-physical systems and become increasingly distant, the system's functioning can become harmful after a level (Harteis et al., 2020). It is not only possible for system developers to understand the process, but employees should also know what data the system collects, how it is used, and how it is included in its decision-making mechanism.

Considering such direct and other indirect effects of cyber-physical systems on the working environment and employees, it is understood that this process is not an ordinary automation or adaptation process. While the change like the work affects the employee cognitively, there are also emotional, motivational, and other psychological effects due to processes such as adapting to new systems and learning new information from the machine. As the pace of change increases and its scope expands, it challenges the adaptability of employees, businesses, and society. After the productivity-oriented rapid mechanization revolution, the people-oriented mechanization period comes. This situation, which is not sufficient to have all kinds of technological infrastructure, is an indication that sustainability cannot be achieved without digital employees, where new talents are the focus (Minh-Nhat et al., 2022). Increasing resource scarcity makes people realize that social factors are as important as economic factors in the interaction of nature, economy, and technology (Ince, 2018a).

While the existence of unmanned and smart technologies started to be discussed with Industry 4, subsequent developments show that Industry 5 is a human-oriented technology. The expectation of increased cooperation between humans and intelligent systems is that industrial automation will combine human cognitive and critical thinking abilities. Also known as the super-smart society, this era aims to offer personal services or products by focusing on mass customization by moving the cognitive system dimension to cyber-physical structures. At this point, although robots are quite successful in mass production, it is thought that human assistance is needed when they want to add something special to products. While autonomous robots are coded to perform a task routinely, work independently, and stay still, collaborative robots, also known as cobots, are coded to learn multiple tasks so they can help humans. Due to the collaborative robots in Industry 5.0, employees are not only returning to the center of industrial production, providing consumers with the personalized products they demand but also enabling employees to be more creative in their production processes (Nahavandi, 2019). While such innovations enable industrial revolutions to take place in less time, social adaptation may not occur at the same speed. Therefore, while talking about the 6th period, on the one hand, there are also societies in the automation process on the other.

Sensor robotic manufacturing with AI is considered the mainstream of thought of Industry 6, which includes ubiquitous, seamless, customer-centric, and virtualized manufacturing. It reaches the final consumer, supported by applications such as customer-oriented, highly customized products, fast data flow, and a dynamic supply chain. Sustainability-related technological revolutions with reduce, reuse, and recycle components are expected to emerge more in the future and become a fundamental element of the economy. As a dominant logic, service-dominant (S-D) logic predicts value creation in behavioral economics through exchanges between configurations of actors. As an alternative to the traditional logic of exchange, to contribute to the understanding of the co-creation of human values, people use their competencies to benefit others through the exchange of service in exchange for service and mutually benefit from the applied competencies of others. Digital twins 1.0, heterogeneous data sources, information transparency, decentralized decisions, technical assistance to support people by aggregating and visualizing information, and functional materials provide new opportunities are some of the innovations in Industry 4 (Annanperä et al., 2021).

In the 5th and 6th revolutions, it is expected that the following innovations will be adopted by making new additions to them. Human in focus, re- or de-manufacturing, zero waste or emission, digital twins 2.0 providing understanding not only about the factory processes but the whole environment, complexity increase, product complexity is increasing as a result of the adoption of advanced are some of the changes to Industry 5. Non-functional Requirement (NFR), which indicates the quality nature of a software system, is the evaluation of the system against non-functional standards that are critical to the success of the system, such as responsiveness, usability, security, and portability. Antifragility gained via the systems' designs relying on Non-Functional Requirements (NFR) thinking is expected to be more involved in the 6th revolution. Human digital twin connects manufacturing, AI optimizes the production to obtain sustainability and antifragility, and Hyperconnected factories in complex, dynamic supply chains and value networks, where data flows across different administration domains are some of the other reliable forecasts (Rahy & Bass, 2022). Although each foresight has its challenges, it can already be said that the need for digital talents specialized in information and communication technologies will increase in almost every sector. This need seems to increase especially in software and coding. Infrastructure formation, cultural change and many other adaptation requirements are discussed in the next titles.

CYBERPSYCHOLOGY AND ADAPTATION TO INNOVATION

One of the most fundamental applications in the world of marketing is customer segmentation as it enables businesses to target potential customers most accurately and cost-effectively possible. As a very crucial component of an effective marketing strategy, segmentation is a critical part of budget management as well as the starting point of providing personalized service to an individual or group. Such decisions regarding segmentation, targeting and positioning depend on this prioritization. The business adopts the marketing movement according to the consumer classification in line with the strategic decisions covering the entire organization such as business activities, processes and production. This situation makes the feelings, thoughts and behaviors of individuals and the society they live in important for the business (Wiederhold & Riva, 2013). Demographic segmentation based on age, gender, marital status, income, etc, is one of the most common audience determination methods. However, it is not uncommon for people with the same demographic profile to act in radically different ways. Further, it is not enough to meet the need of brands to seek deeper information about their target audiences within the scope of personalized services.

On the other hand, the field of psychology focuses on collecting and analyzing the somewhat more abstract characteristics of an audience, such as interests, habits, attitudes, emotions, and preferences. This information can tell the business not only which product or service the customer might buy, but also why. Psychographic data is used in areas where conditions are necessary, such as health, improving the education and activation efforts of the consumer, patient, or client. Psychographics provide businesses with a window into the motivations, values and desires of their target audiences, enabling them to look at the drivers of consumer behavior from different perspectives. In other words, psychographic segmentation is the act of identifying and classifying groups of people based on shared data points that allow brands to customize their tone and message to better connect with potential consumers or the people they are trying to reach (Deccax & Campani, 2022). In other words, the first classification focuses on physical or external factors such as age, ethnicity, race, gender, location, and employment status while the second considers psychological factors such as personality, values, motivations, attitudes, beliefs, priorities, interests and lifestyles.

The most unique aspect of this perspective is that it is based on the recognition that people are different and are often motivated by very different values, personalities, lifestyles and attitudes. On the other hand, addressing differences between groups of people in terms of perceived commonality, such as age, occupation, or status, may miss details by focusing on general data. Due to the widespread availability of publicly available data, demographic information is relatively easier to obtain than psychographic factors. Because obtaining detailed information about psychology, developing a robust psychographic segmentation model and reflecting the segments to the determined population requires a special effort and systematic study (Ince, 2022a). The fact that the interests and preferences of an audience can exceed demographic classifications necessitates psychological research. These efforts, which are of great benefit in creating a brand message that appeals to the interests and affinities of a particular audience, should also facilitate the follow-up of change.

Psychography has grown significantly in recent years due to its ability to create highly detailed audience profiles. The combination of demographic and psychographic segmentation provides success, especially in social media giants that emerged with the development of the internet. This combination of basic classifications helps brands develop relevant communications that can easily connect with their target audience, causing major social networking platforms to create feature-rich advertising platforms. First of all, general classifications made in every field such as health, education, technology, and then detailed psychological distinctions enable the customer to find the starting point and the element that gives the first momentum. The use of psychological elements for customer or user engagement and behavior change is one of the requirements for adapting to innovative developments in the digital world. Approaches that personalize participation reject the "one size fits all" perspective, assuming that people have unique personalities, motivations, and priorities (Rahimi, 2022). Innovative applications that enable digital participation are among the rapidly developing new habits of the digital age.

An increasing number of big data and psychographics studies make it necessary to examine the interaction of the internet, which is a requirement of the age, with people. Cyberpsychology, a subfield of psychology that deals with the psychological effects and consequences of computer and online technologies such as the Internet and virtual reality, includes the study of how and why people interact online (Wiederhold & Riva, 2013). The existence of such a discipline psychologically is one of the most important indicators of adapting to change and not ignoring the effects of technology on people. New issues arise as individuals become part of it, as their technology evolves into algorithmic devices that interface seamlessly with the digital personality. Given the cognitive advances, technology can make, a wise brain-based approach to cyberpsychology is helpful. Because humans are so dependent on their technology, destroying it or damaging it in some way can be synonymous with a personal attack. On the other hand, algorithmic devices can affect human psychology both positively and negatively, while threatening autonomy and privacy. One of the fields that benefit at this point is digital psychology. Cyberpsychology is also known as web psychology, digital psychology, and Internet psychology as a field of studies on the impact of digital technology and media on psychological aspects of human life such as motivation, behavior, motivation, attitude, learning, and habit (Boguszewicz et al., 2021).

Industries that understand and guide how technologies that can create positive change can be used to improve personal growth and well-being will continue to lead. Positive change in the healthcare industry means cybertherapy and can be used for clinical recovery. The common denominator shared by both poles of cyberpsychology is the emotional involvement and participation allowed by the interactive capabilities of technology. In addition, in extraordinary situations such as pandemics, education services can be reached uninterruptedly and equality in education can be provided to a certain extent with free education packages (Ince, 2020a). Of course, certain internet infrastructure is required, but for students who have problems going to school or individuals who want to improve themselves in a subject, digital solutions make it possible to make progress with various educational videos, courses, or training (Ince, 2021d). Such developments, which remove physical boundaries, also increase the awareness and literacy of individuals in health, finance, the internet, digitalization, or other issues (Ince, 2020b). Examples for different sectors can be multiplied.

The focus on suggesting specific strategies to improve each of the relevant dimensions and the use of technology to improve the quality of personal experiences associated with them qualify as positive technology. This means being individual-oriented rather than results-oriented as a result of individual preferences or needs that are part of the process of participating in decisions (Wiederhold & Riva, 2013). Cyberpsychology helps people realize the direction of cultural change and helps to understand the factors that cause behavior and attitude change through social networks. Cyberpsychology, while helping to realize the direction of cultural change, also provides an understanding of the factors that cause behavior and attitude change through social networks.

The internet, which is actively used by approximately five billion people, requires the examination of the human mind and behavior in the context of human-technology interaction due to its rapid development. Not being able to control this technology, which takes an intense place in people's lives with increasing momentum, can create harmful effects that go beyond its positive outputs. Mentioning positive technology, it is also necessary to mention the dark side of developments that are not well managed. Knowing why social networking sites and online media are so popular makes it easy to understand the psychological basis of cyberbullying. It would be insufficient to address the issue simply by doing more personal advertising and selling more for global businesses. The system, which is open to political manipulations and directions that shapes consumption trends and creates new consumption habits, needs to be handled multidimensionally (Riva et al., 2015). Discovering what motivates people online provides an understanding of the psychological underpinnings of shopping, gaming, or dating apps. On the other hand, negative situations such as the causes of cybercrime, addictive algorithms and bullying should also be understood. Therefore, cyberpsychology can be seen as one of the methods of managing change, as it includes studies that examine how people relate to online information and how organizations can best use the internet.

Technology is not expected to affect everyone at the same rate, but it is a known fact that it somehow takes place in everyone's life. In today's world of metaverse developments, it is vital to study and understand human behavior concerning technology as the lines between cyberspace and reality are increasingly blurred. When an environment of free behavior emerges in a world where brains mastered reading body language and communicating face-to-face, the questions remain as to why people behave differently from real life, how they develop online relationships, and what personality tendencies they display. A broader focus on human behavior in conjunction with emerging technologies such as artificial intelligence, virtual reality, and the Internet of Things is addressed by cyberpsychology. This area, which becomes more important as the overlap between individuals and machines increases, is also valuable in terms of drawing attention to aspects that affect mental health such as lack of attention, addiction, and the bombardment of fake information. To make an innovative development such as the Internet a safer and better place, it is necessary to achieve fruitful results. It includes social engineering, cyberbullying and online privacy dimensions to strengthen cybersecurity with psychology (Van-Schaik et al., 2017).

PROMOTING SOCIAL PROSPERITY AND TRUST

Neuroscience includes artificial vision, natural voice and eye-tracking and offers unique 3D face control measurements that allow measurement by natural human movements and detection of nearly a thousand marks of the human body. Fields that enable the production of this kind of information, such as Artificial Emotional Intelligence (AEI), are solutions for understanding and interpreting human behavior. One of the ways to promote social well-being and trust lies at the heart of developments in this field (Schuller& Schuller, 2018). It is also possible to use developments in all variables in technology both positively and negatively. Predicting human behavior can be a tool for manipulation by society or a lifesaving tool for the world of security and intelligence. Interpreting human behavior and predicting potential targets of mass destruction, especially in public places, is essential to the well-being of society. Recognizing a situation before it gets worse is crucial to ensuring public safety and protecting national security. That's why it's a key process to create information or artificial intelligence that is impartial, reliable, and not easily stolen or copied. AI technologies only show some of the possible innovations today. Emerging technologies such as robotics, machine learning, and high-tech facial recognition are indications that progress will take more unexpected dimensions. When emotional intelligence is achieved, what people think, feel, or have behavioral tendencies will become noticeable. In Autostadt's study, Hohmann, (2007) emphasizes the importance of emotions in the new age and draws attention to the concept of "Emotional Digitalization" and talks about a structure like every meter is staged with nature and technology meeting in a dialogue heavily supported by IT. These developments, which are like a double-edged sword, are seen as positive in terms of ensuring national and global security, as well as causing fears such as being watched, modern handcuffed life, and violation of freedom.

For those who deal with the subject with a technology focus, human prejudice should be destroyed and the conditions for change should be prepared. This point of view, which is thought to be used for the service of human beings, since robotic developments are already inevitable, focuses on artificial intelligence that can make objective decisions without human subjectivity. When this research area, which goes beyond the declarations or behaviors of people, is handled with a focus on security, the importance of objective decision-making emerges. The ability to read subconscious facial expressions of an individual's emotions in real-time, understand deep emotions and provide instant feedback draws attention as one of the current topics of artificial intelligence and robotics studies. While basic emotions such as anger, contempt, happiness, fear, sadness, disgust and surprise can be determined, detailed subconscious determinations cannot be made yet (Abdollahi et al., 2022).In the public sphere, feelings of trust, irritability, passion, boredom, honesty, curiosity, and depression can be discerned in detecting emotions as indicators of potential risk or threat.

Being able to recognize a single individual by analyzing the masses in open areas, shopping centers, or crowded environments such as stadiums, airports, and concert venues provides very important data as a preventive measure. Early detection of antisocial behaviors such as fear, anger, or contempt can help prevent theft, assault and other potential crimes. These technologies, which are used for prevention, such as the detection of the symptom of depression before the suicide attempt, can also facilitate the diagnosis during the treatment phase. however, it should not be forgotten that as in every development, the subconscious reactions of the person can be used in every field. Of course, the private sector can also use this information to purchase the product or to create more propensity to consume and directed demands. It may be necessary to protect these innovative solutions, created with the aim of a healthy and prosperous society, from practices such as the sale of personal information for advertising purposes or data sharing, or to restrict their use with a competitive focus to profit pressure by various legal sanctions (Prentice et al., 2020). Gaining the trust of society and maintaining this should be one of the basic principles at every stage.

In AEI technology, not only emotion detection but also grading can be done to assess risk and gain insight. That is, how angry the person is or how prone to crime or suicide can be graded as a little, medium, or high. It is a newly developed technology to learn about personality types and behavioral traits by capturing hidden signs invisible to the naked human eye. Once the necessary infrastructure for facial recognition has been established, the next step is to interpret the raw data. In addition to facial recognition, and marking of personal characteristics and emotions, crowd tracking is used as well as the detection of wanted persons. Therefore, it can be said that technologies for perceiving emotions will continue to develop (Schuller& Schuller, 2018). Through the controlled structure of smart cities, social well-being-oriented studies aim to disseminate technology (Ince, 2022c). Emotions are one of the most prominent human characteristics, and even the brain, which has evolved for thousands of years, can sometimes make mistakes, while developed algorithms may need to be sensitively focused despite all the differences. Systems such as computational empathy or Artificial Empathy (AE) also serve in the development of technologies that can detect and respond to human emotions empathetically, with applications such as companion robots or virtual agents (Bagheri et al., 2020). This system, which is based on the analysis of behaviors by interacting with the individual, has been developed to respond to situations that require empathy, such as behaving compassionately. These and similar innovations can be considered as an indication that the emotions that affect the decision mechanism are as important as the behaviors. The uncertainties and dimensions of this transformation, which present both risks and opportunities in areas such as social connections, work-life balance, governance and civic participation, should be well analyzed. While security is only one dimension of the business, other sectors that touch people should also be considered.

DIGITAL WELL-BEING: SOME POINTS TO PONDER

Digital well-being, is a concept related to the subjective well-being of individuals in a social environment where digital media is omnipresent. It provides a general framework for integrating empirical research into a cumulative science of digital media use on well-being. Three basic structures are used when explaining the connections between well-being and the digital world and the nature of the concept; digital practices, harms or benefits, and well-being. Socio-technical structural conditions shape the individual's response to digital applications and lead to certain psychological consequences. Being able to recognize the causal chain in this mutual interaction where theory and practice meet is one of the main goals of digital well-being studies (Büchi, 2020).

Despite the constant use of digital media and its addictive algorithm, it takes some control and monitoring for people to lead a good life. While the advances made in neuromarketing, which deals with deep examinations of human psychology, serve the profit-oriented sales goals of the enterprises, the social dimension of the event should also be addressed. The degree of impact on people and society varies according to the frequency of use of digital media, the way it is used, its purpose, and other factors. There are also external factors that affect access to digital content. Due to the subjective nature of the term, it is necessary to look at the different effects of online applications on human well-being without directly qualifying them as beneficial or harmful. Digital solutions used in many sectors such as daily activities, logistics, financial transactions, health, and education are an indication that the event is not limited to social media and entertainment (Ince, 2021c). Similarly, solutions offered with smart technologies can have a positive or negative effect depending on the way they are handled. While developments in the medical field show technology as an important support for human life, the use of the same developments in different sectors has the potential to end human life. There are also studies emphasizing that even video games that are considered harmful (Beattie & Daubs, 2020), because of their effects such as addiction, eye or mental disorders, and asociality have good aspects (Johannes et al., 2021). Therefore, within the scope of the contingency approach, when it is a benefit and harm, and the cause-effect relationships of all these should be studied.

Digital well-being includes proximate consequences in the form of harms and benefits, welfare analyses of distant consequences, as well as socially relevant consequences such as digital well-being, political participation, or social capital, which have a detailed digital scope of application. Digital applications that affect subjective well-being can play a decisive role in individual and social situations with the effect of additional variables such as personality or situational factors. Technologies that restrict or direct individual action may tend to spread to society through social networks. Small changes that look like micro can create a butterfly effect as triggers of complex processes over time. The digital well-being framework includes the following with its micro and macro dimensions to highlight the sociological side of digital well-being as well as psychological approaches (Büchi, 2021):

- Society at the macro level: These are factors that reduce or increase social welfare which include economic welfare, security and democratic quality; productivity, utility, collective action and innovation and vice versa political manipulation, privacy violations, and inequality.
- Individual at the micro level: These factors, as emotional or psychological elements, can reduce or increase subjective well-being; stress, misinformation, embarrassment, and vice versa, knowledge, connectedness, convenience, and benefit.

From a broad perspective, sociology can analyze the norms and differences between them that influence the appropriate choice of smart device use or digital app by social class, while psychology examines the impact of social media use on personal variables such as emotions, empathy, or conflict. This field, in which the interaction of society and individuals is seen most clearly, creates the digital tendency of society as a result of class differences, norms, and values due to the inclusion of an individual who is negatively affected by social media. Incorporating trends characterized by the use of big data that emerged with the rise of digitally networked communications into decision-making mechanisms is also necessary for several reasons; the isolated effects of digital media in society or technological isolationism, moral panics, fear of change, adaptation anxiety, cultural and ethical concerns.

Interpreting and analyzing the expected or actual results of advanced digitalization is concerned with political manipulation, privacy violations and increasing socioeconomic inequality, as well as the direction of increased efficiency, innovation and transparency. Controlled digitalization positively impacts the well-being of society when measured by economic welfare, social wealth, democratic quality, security, higher life expectancy, education and health opportunities and vice versa (Ince, 2022c). Digital applications have the opportunity to present large information in a single share than is realized. Sharing a simple photo or video can provide a variety of information about an individual's habits, social interaction, entertainment, or understanding of life. Even the environments that the individuals like or avoid, even their economic and social status can be interpreted approximately.

Today, even individuals who have no experience abroad know the lifestyle, food culture and marriage traditions of various cultures in the world, even though they do not seek information about, it because they come across it on the internet. While widespread knowledge raises the issue of reliability, it also accelerates the world's becoming a global village. While taking into account the general digital media effects, every movement that seems simple thanks to smart devices needs to be evaluated in itself. From a sociological point of view, even the simplest digital application is an action (Reichmann, 2019). Benefits and harms can be mentioned when actions have direct and indirect consequences. Desires, beliefs, and other motivations driven by social interaction are the driving forces that create this action. These aspects are very useful in terms of reflecting the complexity of the subject.

It can be assumed that a simple digital application such as photo sharing provides subjective well-being within the scope of social connectedness, depending on the personality and situation of the individual. However, correctly interpreting the cyclical structure of the causal relationship is more difficult than it seems. Even in this simple example, the mechanisms that cause mutual relations and interactions in human psychology may not be clearly explained. Because, contrary to what is believed, perhaps there may be a sharing made to compensate for the lack of moments perceived at a low level in one's inner world, beyond trying to establish a connection between people. Multidisciplinary work combining theory with research, and decisions to put them into practice to improve human well-being are therefore key.

FUTURE RESEARCH DIRECTIONS

For digital transformation to take place conveniently, studies should be carried out to provide psychological well-being with multidisciplinary perspectives examining the interaction of humans and technology. For digital transformation to take place conveniently, studies should be carried out to provide psychological well-being with various perspectives examining the interaction of humans and technology. Since the developments have produced serious outputs in both positive and negative directions, it is necessary to ensure controlled progress in terms of social psychology. It has not yet been clarified by which essential dynamics that have the power to affect society are shaped and directed. While the structural rules of the digitalized society are shaped by public and private governance mechanisms such as competition policy (Just, 2018), dominant digital intermediaries such as social media platforms also manage daily individual practices. Digitization and interconnected technological innovations are influential on all concepts arising from the nature of social, political, and economic relations, based on chain effects. For this reason, besides economic research, the political and social dimensions of the issue should also be addressed.

To cumulatively integrate the effects of digital media use on well-being with empirical research, psychological concepts that provide a general framework need to be addressed with different dimensions. Putting the results into practice makes it easier to obtain outputs that both the business world and social life can benefit from (Johannes et al., 2021). In addition to physically measuring the impact of technological tools on the human brain, obtaining interdisciplinary results by making psychological measurements supports decision processes and future predictions. Studies on social expectations as well as consumers can be a guide in learning the causes of prejudices towards digital transformation (Beattie & Daubs, 2020). Knowing the factors of deep concern can lead to a clearer understanding of adaptive innovative solutions without excluding people.

Drawing attention to innovative developments with various studies also supports the preparation process of the relevant institutions, organizations, or nations for the preparation of the necessary infrastructure. Countries that want to lead the next industrial revolution should carry out serious R&D studies in this direction and try to complete their preparations, while countries that do not want to be left behind in the competition should bring the issue to the agenda with various national strategies (Annanperä et al., 2021). These strategies, which need to be developed with a long-term public commitment, should benefit from multidisciplinary studies and include action plans to establish the necessary information infrastructure. Only in this way can social and digital well-being be increased by being a leader while shaping the future.

CONCLUSION

Sustainability is one of the vital issues that not only individuals but also institutions, nations and even all parties on a global scale should deal with (Ince, 2018b). Human's relationship with nature is constantly affected, directly and indirectly, by the industrial revolutions that systematically change social life. This mutual interaction has accelerated with the emergence of digital developments and the internet network reaching the whole world, and the revolutions have taken place in a shorter time than before. While the acceleration of change creates various new pressures on society, it forces psychology to adapt to technological applications that it does not know yet. It is quite natural for human psychology, where the instinct of survival directs the basic dynamics of life, to fear the unknown to protect itself (Cohen & Sherman, 2014). This fear is also seen in the acceptance of the digitalized world, whose physical boundaries are gradually disappearing. For this reason, it is necessary to analyze the relationship between digitalization and the factors affecting psychological well-being (Korunovska & Spiekermann, 2019).

Since the natural state of mind of the individual also affects the well-being level of the society or nation, it is not possible to distinguish the smallest unit from the other. Prejudices against change can also stem from past experiences of the industrial revolution. It is normal to experience fears of employment when organizational structures that exclude people in the transition to mechanization bring unemployment problems (Ince, 2022b). Ensuring equality in issues such as the gradual shrinking of logistics borders, increasing mobility, improvement in health services, online education over the internet, or reaching unreachable masses are among the prominent features of the new developments (Schwarzmüller et al., 2018). However, on the contrary, there are also difficulties such as those who cannot keep up with digital developments, feeling excluded, changing employment balances, and having to acquire new talents.

Digital transformation cannot be evaluated from a single point of view as only very good or very bad for humanity. There are different predictions in terms of the degree of human involvement in the theories developed for technology-human harmony. In these estimates, people are at one pole, and technology at the other, while other options are determined by the level between the two (Harteis et al., 2020). Thus, the impact of digitalization will vary according to the degree of human participation in the process. If managed well and considering the harmony of nature and humans, synergy can be achieved, otherwise, failure to achieve a balance between the parties involved may also mean that human values are forgotten. However, since global environmental problems endanger the sustainability of natural resources and pose a vital threat, it will be difficult for businesses to continue activities that do not take into account people, nature and future generations (Ince, 2018c). So, a strategic perspective on these issues, which includes legislators, administrators, politicians, and others who shape society, will help ensure progress without harming people. From this point of view, technology and human relations are discussed in terms of well-being in this chapter.

By avoiding only good or bad classifications, all the challenges that the technological revolution will bring are mentioned and the necessary infrastructure and management skills are highlighted. To understand the impact of these developments on human psychology, it is aimed to share the disciplines that deal with technology-human harmony by touching on cyberpsychology and psychographic issues both in terms of businesses and society. The section is completed with some points that need to be considered and some suggestions for digital well-being. As studies investigating the effects of technology on humans become more widespread, it will be better understood how human nature and its elements will respond to digitalization. For this reason, in today's world where change is inevitable, the well-being of the employees, society, and nature should be considered, and act without giving up on any of them.

REFERENCES

Abdollahi, H., Mahoor, M., Zandie, R., Sewierski, J., & Qualls, S. (2022). Artificial emotional intelligence in socially assistive robots for older adults: A pilot study. *IEEE Transactions on Affective Computing*, 1. doi:10.1109/TAFFC.2022.3143803

Akanni, A. A., & Oduaran, C. A. (2022). Person-job fit and work-life balance of female nurses with cultural competence as a mediator: Evidence from Nigeria. *Frontiers of Nursing*, 9(1), 81–86. doi:10.2478/fon-2022-0010

Annanperä, E., Jurmu, M., Kaivo-oja, J., Kettunen, P., Knudsen, M., Lauraéus, T., & Porras, J. (2021). From Industry X to Industry 6.0: Antifragile Manufacturing for People, Planet, and Profit with Passion. *Business Finland AIF, White Paper 5,* 1-38.

Bagheri, E., Esteban, P. G., Cao, H. L., Beir, A. D., Lefeber, D., & Vanderborght, B. (2020). An autonomous cognitive empathy model responsive to users' facial emotion expressions. *ACM Transactions on Interactive Intelligent Systems*, 10(3), 1–23. doi:10.1145/3341198

Baiyere, A., Salmela, H., & Tapanainen, T. (2020). Digital transformation and the new logics of business process management. *European Journal of Information Systems*, 29(3), 238–259. doi:10.1080/0960085X.2020.1718007

Beattie, A., & Daubs, M. S. (2020). Framing'digital well-being'as a social good. *First Monday*. doi:10.5210/fm.v25i12.10430

Boguszewicz, C., Boguszewicz, M., Iqbal, Z., Khan, S., Gaba, G. S., Suresh, A., & Pervaiz, B. (2021). The fourth industrial revolution-cyberspace mental wellbeing: Harnessing science & technology for humanity. *White Paper*. Global foundation for cyber studies and research.

Braña, F. J. (2019). A fourth industrial revolution? Digital transformation, labor and work organization: A view from Spain. *Economia e Politica Industriale*, *46*(3), 415–430. doi:10.100740812-019-00122-0

Büchi, M. (2020). *A proto-theory of digital well-being*. OSF. https://osf. io/k3e2j

Büchi, M. (2021). Digital well-being theory and research. *New Media & Society*, 1–20. doi:10.1177/14614448211056851

Bugiotti, F., Goasdoué, F., Kaoudi, Z., & Manolescu, I. (2012, March). RDF data management in the Amazon cloud. In *Proceedings of the 2012 Joint EDBT/ICDT Workshops* (pp. 61-72). 10.1145/2320765.2320790

Chalmers, I., & Altman, D. G. (Eds.). (1995). *Systematic reviews* (pp. 86–95). BMJ Publishing.

Cohen, G. L., & Sherman, D. K. (2014). The psychology of change: Self-affirmation and social psychological intervention. *Annual Review of Psychology*, *65*(1), 333–371. doi:10.1146/annurev-psych-010213-115137 PMID:24405362

Deccax, R. A., & Campani, C. H. (2022). Segmentation of current and potential investors in retirement plans to retain and capture customers. Brazilian Business Review (Portuguese Edition), 19(1). doi:10.15728/bbr.2022.19.1.2

Hale, L. A. (2021). Courtship for business model innovation: Early-stage value negotiation for the sustainability of smart homes. *Journal of Cleaner Production*, *297*, 126610. doi:10.1016/j.jclepro.2021.126610

Harteis, C., Goller, M., & Caruso, C. (2020, January). Conceptual change in the face of digitalization: Challenges for workplaces and workplace learning. In Frontiers in Education (Vol. 5, p. 1). Frontiers Media SA. doi:10.3389/feduc.2020.00001

Hohmann, C. (2007). Emotional Digitalization as Technology of the Postmodern: A Reflexive Examination from the View of the Industry. *International Journal of Technology and Human Interaction*, *3*(1), 17–29. doi:10.4018/jthi.2007010102

Ince, F. (2018a). International Businesses and Environmental Issues. In S. Idris (Ed.), *Promoting Global Environmental Sustainability and Cooperation* (pp. 86–111). IGI Global. doi:10.4018/978-1-5225-3990-2.ch004

Ince, F. (2018b). Perceptions of Environmental Sustainability Amongst Mineworkers. *Global Journal of Environmental Science and Management, 4*(1), 1–8. doi:10.22034/GJESM.2018.04.01.001

Ince, F. (2018c). Green Environment and Management: Environmental Management System (EMS). In S. Tsai, B. Liu, & Y. Li (Eds.), *Green Production Strategies for Sustainability* (pp. 100–116). IGI Global., doi:10.4018/978-1-5225-3537-9.ch006

Ince, F. (2020a). The Effects of COVID-19 Pandemic on the Workforce in Turkey. *Smart Journal, 6*(32), 1125–1134. doi:10.31576mryj.546

Ince, F. (2020b). Financial Literacy in Generation Z: Healthcare Management Students. *Smart Journal, 6*(36), 1647–1658. doi:10.31576mryj.616

Ince, F. (2021a). COVID-19 Pandemic Made Me Use It: Attitude Of Generation Z Towards E-Learning. *Smart Journal, 7*(54), 3489–3494. doi:10.31576mryj.1215

Ince, F. (2021b). Creating Synergic Entrepreneurship as Support of Sustainability: Opportunities and Challenges. In R. Perez-Uribe, D. Ocampo-Guzman, N. Moreno-Monsalve, & W. Fajardo-Moreno (Eds.), Handbook of Research on Management Techniques and Sustainability Strategies for Handling Disruptive Situations in Corporate Settings (pp. 464-486). IGI Global. doi:10.4018/978-1-7998-8185-8.ch022

Ince, F. (2021c). A Revolutionary Business Model for Global Purpose-Driven Corporations: Mobility as a Service (MaaS). In R. Perez-Uribe, C. Largacha-Martinez, & D. Ocampo-Guzman (Eds.), *Handbook of Research on International Business and Models for Global Purpose-Driven Companies* (pp. 22–42). IGI Global. doi:10.4018/978-1-7998-4909-4.ch002

Ince, F. (2021d). Opportunities and Challenges of E-Learning in Turkey. In B. Khan, S. Affouneh, S. Hussein Salha, & Z. Najee Khlaif (Eds.), *Challenges and Opportunities for the Global Implementation of E-Learning Frameworks* (pp. 202–226). IGI Global. doi:10.4018/978-1-7998-7607-6.ch013

Ince, F. (2022a). Creative Leadership: A Multidisciplinary Approach to Creativity. In Z. Fields (Ed.), *Achieving Sustainability Using Creativity, Innovation, and Education: A Multidisciplinary Approach* (pp. 30–49). IGI Global. doi:10.4018/978-1-7998-7963-3.ch002

Ince, F. (2022b). The Human Resources Perspective on the Multigenerational Workforce. In F. Ince (Ed.), *International Perspectives and Strategies for Managing an Aging Workforce* (pp. 274–297). IGI Global. doi:10.4018/978-1-7998-2395-7.ch013

Ince, F. (2022c). Digital Literacy Training: Opportunities and Challenges. In M. Taher (Ed.), *Handbook of Research on the Role of Libraries, Archives, and Museums in Achieving Civic Engagement and Social Justice in Smart Cities* (pp. 185–199). IGI Global. doi:10.4018/978-1-7998-8363-0.ch009

Ince, F. (2023a). Leadership Perspectives on Effective Intergenerational Communication and Management. IGI Global. doi:10.4018/978-1-6684-6140-2

Ince, F. (2023b). Transformational Leadership, In A Diverse and Inclusive Organizational Culture, In Perez-Uribe, R. I., Ocampo-Guzman, D., & Moreno-Monsalve, N. (Eds.). Promoting an Inclusive Organizational Culture for Entrepreneurial Sustainability. IGI Global. doi:10.4018/978-1-6684-5216-5

Ince, F. (2023c). Socio-Ecological Sustainability (SES) within the scope of industry 5.0. In M. Sajid, S. Khan, & Z. Yu (Eds.), *Implications of Industry 5.0 on Environmental Sustainability*. IGI Global. doi:10.4018/978-1-6684-6113-6

Johannes, N., Vuorre, M., & Przybylski, A. K. (2021). Video game play is positively correlated with well-being. *Royal Society Open Science*, *8*(2), 202049. doi:10.1098/rsos.202049 PMID:33972879

Just, N. (2018). Governing online platforms: Competition policy in times of platformization. *Telecommunications Policy*, *42*(5), 386–394. doi:10.1016/j.telpol.2018.02.006

Korunovska, J., & Spiekermann, S. (2019). *The effects of digitalization on human energy and fatigue: A review*. Vienna University of Economics and Business. https://arxiv.org/vc/arxiv/papers/1910/1910.01970v1.pdf

Krishna, K., Karumuri, N., Christopher, C., & Jayapandian, N. (2021, May). Research Challenges in Self-Driving Vehicle by Using Internet of Things (IoT). In *5th International Conference on Intelligent Computing and Control Systems (ICICCS)* (pp. 423-427). IEEE.

Lam, L. T., & Peng, Z. W. (2010). Effect of pathological use of the internet on adolescent mental health: A prospective study. *Archives of Pediatrics & Adolescent Medicine*, *164*(10), 901–906. doi:10.1001/archpediatrics.2010.159 PMID:20679157

Larjovuori, R. L., Bordi, L., & Heikkilä-Tammi, K. (2018, October). Leadership in the digital business transformation. In *Proceedings of the 22nd international academic mindtrek conference* (pp. 212-221). MindTrek Conference. 10.1145/3275116.3275122

Matt, C., Hess, T., & Benlian, A. (2015). Digital transformation strategies. *Business & Information Systems Engineering, 57*(5), 339–343. doi:10.100712599-015-0401-5

Minh-Nhat, H. O., Nguyen, H. L., & Mondal, S. R. (2022). Digital Transformation for New Sustainable Goals with Human Element for Digital Service Enterprises: An Exploration of Factors. In *Sustainable Development and Innovation of Digital Enterprises for Living with COVID-19* (pp. 85–103). Springer. doi:10.1007/978-981-19-2173-5_6

Nahavandi, S. (2019). Industry 5.0-A human-centric solution. *Sustainability, 11*(16), 4371. doi:10.3390u11164371

Rahimi, I. D. (2022). Ambient Intelligence in Learning Management System (LMS). In *Science and Information Conference* (pp. 379-387). Springer, Cham. 10.1007/978-3-031-10467-1_24

Rahy, S., & Bass, J. M. (2022). Managing non-functional requirements in agile software development. *IET Software, 16*(1), 60–72. doi:10.1049fw2.12037

Reichmann, W. (2019). The digitalization of the social situation—A sociological exploratory experiment. *Osterreichische Zeitschrift fur Soziologie, 44*(1), 237–255. doi:10.100711614-019-00355-2

Riva, G., Calvo, R. A., & Lisetti, C. (2015). Cyberpsychology and affective computing. The Oxford Handbook of Affective Computing, 547-558. Oxford. doi:10.1093/oxfordhb/9780199942237.013.017

Schuller, D., & Schuller, B. W. (2018). The age of artificial emotional intelligence. *Computer, 51*(9), 38–46. doi:10.1109/MC.2018.3620963

Schwarzmüller, T., Brosi, P., Duman, D., & Welpe, I. M. (2018). How does the digital transformation affect organizations? Key themes of change in work design and leadership. *Management Review, 29*(2), 114–138. doi:10.5771/0935-9915-2018-2-114

Van-Schaik, P., Jeske, D., Onibokun, J., Coventry, L., Jansen, J., & Kusev, P. (2017). Risk perceptions of cyber-security and precautionary behaviour. *Computers in Human Behavior, 75*, 547–559. doi:10.1016/j.chb.2017.05.038

Van-Zanden, J. L., Baten, J., Mira d'Ercole, M., Rijpma, A., Smith, C., & Timmer, M. (Eds.). (2014). *How Was Life?: Global Well-being since 1820.* OECD Publishing. doi:10.1787/9789264214262-en

Wiederhold, B. K., & Riva, G. (2013). The quest for active and healthy ageing: What cyberpsychology can offer. Annual Review of Cybertherapy and Telemedicine. *Positive Technology and Health Engagement for Healthy Living and Active Ageing*, *191*(3), 444.

Wokurka, G., Banschbach, Y., Houlder, D., & Jolly, R. (2017). Digital culture: Why strategy and culture should eat breakfast together. In *Shaping the digital enterprise* (pp. 109–120). Springer. doi:10.1007/978-3-319-40967-2_5

KEY TERMS AND DEFINITIONS

AEI: Artificial emotional intelligence, also known as Affective Computing, Artificial Empathy (AE), or Emotion AI, is the study and development of technologies and computers that can analyze and read human emotions and give appropriate responses by monitoring data such as body movements, facial expressions, tone of voice.

Cobot: A collaborative robot is one that, unlike its autonomous relatives, can go beyond just performing a single task, and can also learn multiple tasks to help humans.

Cyberpsychology: It is also known as web, internet, or digital psychology as a discipline that includes various studies of digital technology and media's impact on psychological aspects of human life such as motivation, behavior, motivation, attitude, learning, and habit.

Cybertherapy: Also known as "internet therapy", "virtual therapy", "e-therapy", "online counseling" or "telepsychiatry", it is a service provided online by authorized mental health professionals, not face to face.

Digital Talent: These are the skills that individuals who know digital technologies and have the skills and abilities to use these technologies in a business or social life should keep up with the age.

Digital Workplaces: They are working environments that there are no physical boundaries, work is mostly done in a virtual environment, and technology-intensive or digital business models are adopted.

Emotional Digitalization: As emotional engineering, this link is a progression that can be understood as a link between the complexity of the computer, human gestures, and aesthetics, narrowing the gap between technology and humanity.

NFR: Non-functional requirements are characteristics that define the operational capabilities and limitations of the system by evaluating the software system against dysfunctional standards such as responsiveness, usability, security, and portability.

PJ Fit: Person-job fit is defined as the compatibility between individuals and the work or tasks they perform at work.

S-D Logic: Service-dominant logic is an alternative theoretical framework in behavioral economics that explains the creation of value through the exchange of configurations of actors to mutually benefit from the practical competencies of others through the exchange of services.

Chapter 2

Smartphone Habits and Behaviour:
A Review on Issues in Relation to the Physical and Psychological Well-Being of Users

Ida Haizatultasha Zaqreen
Universiti Brunei Darussalam, Brunei

Sheirene Diana Hong
Universiti Brunei Darussalam, Brunei

Nur Hayati Mohd Daud
Universiti Brunei Darussalam, Brunei

ABSTRACT

The number of smartphone users has steadily risen over the last few years and smartphones have apparently become an unavoidable part of daily life; and with that, concerns have progressively risen worldwide in regards to users' physical and psychological well-being when using smartphones for extended periods of time. This study looked at the relationship between smartphone use and physical well-being, as well as the role of emotion regulation in the relationship between smartphone usage and functional impairment. This research sheds light on the harmful relationship between excessive smartphone use and the user's physical and mental health. The findings show that smartphone usage plays an important role in individuals' everyday lives. As a result, the influence on physical and psychological well-being should be discussed further in order to prevent the negative consequences of smartphone usage.

DOI: 10.4018/978-1-6684-6108-2.ch002

INTRODUCTION

The rapid advancement of technology is well acknowledged to have had a significant impact on our everyday activities and behaviours. Smartphones serve numerous functions for different occasions, including for work, education, and leisure, and are more capable of processing information than normal cell phones, thanks to continual technological advancements (Anshari, 2020). In the second quarter of 2021, around 313.2 million smartphones were shipped according to the International Data Corporation (IDC) worldwide quarterly mobile phone tracker. Additionally, in comparison to 2020, the data is revealed that there is a 13.2 per cent increase in smartphone users globally. This gadget includes modern technology which performs similarly to a computer, allowing multitasking, and making it simple to stay in touch with people. The availability and accessibility of a smartphone have improved everyone's lives because it allows us to connect to each other through forms of video calling, voice calling, and text messaging amongst others. Smartphones provide consumers with ongoing access to mediated communication, helping them to stay engaged in their daily lives (Mulyani et al., 2019).

Consequently, there are a variety of smartphone brands nowadays, each with its own set of functions and features, depending on the user's preferences (Low & Anshari, 2012). Smartphones, without a doubt, behave like small computers because their functionalities are comparable to those of a computer but in a smaller and more portable form. However, from the standpoint of technology addiction or problematic usage, pervasive mobile connectivity is associated with a decrease in users' well-being. The smartphone's active and online status, along with its portability and multifaceted capability, has raised concerns about its addictive potential. Although smartphone developments allow users to quickly adjust to new technology, experts suggest that they have a significant impact on their everyday communications and lifestyles over time (Line et al., 2011; Anshari et al., 2022). In light of this, a significant amount of research has linked excessive smartphone use to a variety of addiction-like behavioural and psychometric symptoms that causes issues on users' well-being. Hence, the proper use of smartphones is vital to people's lives and to society as a whole since it can contribute to the development and enhancement of society, which will result in changes and advancements.

As a result, the primary goal of this research is to determine the concerns that arise as a result of users' habits and behaviour in relation to the usage of smartphones in terms of physical and psychological well-being.

LITERATURE REVIEW

Smartphone Habits and Behavior

The most important function of a smartphone is its communication and connectivity for many people. All relationships are built on the foundation of communication. Humans have been on a hunt for new ways to communicate effectively since the dawn of humanity. Mobile phones are rapidly replacing landlines as the major means of personal communication across the world. With the access to the internet via smartphones, it has become second nature to the point where people have become overly dependent on it. It's as crucial as a social item like a mobile phone. Its use has evolved into a social phenomenon, driven by product, service, and social norm judgments. Communication has grown into a form that would have been unfathomable just a few decades ago due to the advancement of science and technology. In the twentieth century, the car was the dominating symbol of adolescent autonomy and status; in the twenty-first century, the mobile phone appears to be the predominant emblem of teenage autonomy and prestige. The cell phone, which was traditionally identified mostly with male business executives, is now connected with contemporary youth culture. It's the main mode of contact for most individuals, allowing them to be reached anywhere and at any time. That's why many attempts to change this behaviour of constantly using their smartphone have failed because this behaviour has become habitual (Anshari et al., 2015).

Excessive usage of smartphones can lead to issues with a person's physical and mental well-being, such as maladaptive behaviours, school productivity disruptions, restricted real-time social engagement, and relationship troubles (Kuss & Griffiths, 2011, Anshari et al., 2013a). It is commonly established that excessive use of smartphones contributes to the user's unfavourable physical and psychological effect as excessive and uncontrolled smartphone activity, according to Oulasvirta et al. (2011), can be related to a conflict with habitual evolution, which emerged as a consequence of repeating acts in certain contexts. As studied by Oulasvirta et al. (2011), the habitual concept of smartphone usage was driven primarily by desires for entertainment, consciousness, and to pass the time. Frequent short usage and browsing over short periods of time are habits that contribute to mobile phone addiction. The author also underlines that habits can be divided into three categories: informational, interactive, and awareness (Anshari et al., 2013b). Non-interactive components, such as the clock widget on the phone's main screen, are referred to as informational. Interactional systems, on the other hand, are those that require individuals to engage and actually respond in real-time, such as social media platform updates or messaging features. Finally, awareness refers to a circumstance in which a user refreshes his or her mailbox but finds no new emails, resulting in awareness value. As a result, depending on the user's habits, smartphones might be prevalent (Zulkarnain & Anshari, 2016).

Well-Being

Kesgin & Topuzolu (2006) describe health as a condition of total physical, mental, and social well-being, not just the absence of sickness or infirmity, as defined by the World Health Organization. In order to achieve total well-being, it is important to maintain a good balance between body, mental, and social states. Given that maintaining good well-being makes people happy, researchers have begun to look at additional aspects that might impact happiness (Saygn & Arslan, 2009; Osmanolu & Kaya, 2013; Erylmaz, 2010; Almunawar & Anshari, 2014; Almunawar et al., 2012). There are many aspects that could be related to well-being such as positive feelings and moods (e.g., contentment, happiness), the absence of negative emotions (e.g., sadness, anxiety), satisfaction with life, fulfilment, and positive functioning are all examples of well-being.

Physical Well Being

Physical well-being is defined by the capability to keep a healthy lifestyle and quality of life that allows us to do daily activities for a long time without feeling fatigued or physical stress (Anshari et al., 2019b). Furthermore, taking care of the bodies and understanding the impact of daily physical routine and behaviours towards general fitness, well-being and quality of life (Australian National University, n.d.).

Physical and Sedentary Activity

Physical activity can be defined as bodily movement produced by skeletal muscles that need energy. This includes movements during rest time, the act of going from one place to another and many others. The importance of physical activity has been emphasized by various studies and journals for the last couple of decades. Both males and females from a wide range of age gain benefits from active physical activity such as reduced premature death from stroke, heart failure, obesity, diabetes and many other deadly non-communicable diseases (Galloway & Jokl, 2000). Moreover, physical activities on a regular basis can also help improve bone health and function, reduce the risk of falling and subsequent waist and back fractures, and can improve quality of life and physical wellbeing. On the contrary, the lack of physical activity can contribute to an increased risk of death as the World Health Organization (WHO) states inactive individuals can have a 20 to 30 per cent higher chance of death compared to active persons (WHO, 2020). There are an estimated 3.2 million people globally dying each year due to diseases caused by inactive physical activity.

Causes leading to lack of physical activity can be traced to a plethora of reasons. Various studies had been made to investigate the correlations between lack of physical activity of a person and factors including laziness, lack of time, suffering from diseases, and the increasing amount of time using smartphones. The increasing smartphone usage and behaviour in a population for the past decades has become normalized due to the evolution and innovation of technology. In the United States, 91 per cent of adults were shown to own a smartphone and 64 per cent were stated to have internet accessibility (Fennel et al, 2018). Activities that were allowed to happen by using smartphones such as streaming videos, texting, playing games and using social media can be labeled as sedentary activity as it promotes inactive and "sitting" behaviour. Immoderate sedentary activity and physical inactivity are troubling as both are independently correlated with a higher risk of a plethora of health problems including metabolic syndrome, cardiovascular disease, and diabetes. Despite the fact to be well known, people still fail to increase their physical activity and reduce sedentary activity. Furthermore, it was found that a large fraction of an adult's sedentary activity was caused by using a smartphone.

A study investigating the relationship between smartphone use, sedentary behaviour and physical activity of college students in the United States shows evidence of the effect of smartphone usage and behaviour on an individual's physical health. The paper states that students with higher smartphone usage are involved in a sedentary activity for 78-145 minutes per day more than medium and low users. found out that the students that have higher smartphone usage positively correlated with a higher sedentary activity (Fennel et al, 2018). Furthermore, the study suggested that students with higher smartphone usage have no association with physical activity. However, assessing the situation, higher sedentary activity and lack of physical activity has the same effect; health problems and death.

Eyesight

Eyesight has been deemed to be the most important and complex sense (Hutmacher, 2019). This is because eyesight is a tool for gaining the vision which informs the person about the environment surrounding the individual and thus, giving information about the world. Furthermore, it gives the ability for exploration and navigation of the person in this world. Hence, losing or even a reduced degree of vision can produce a devastating result. A survey was made in the United States across all ethnic and racial groups investigating the public views regarding eyes and vision health (Scott Et al, 2016). From the survey, it was suggested that the public viewed losing eyesight to be something that has a significant impact on daily life compared to loss of limb, memory, hearing and speech. According to an article from Healthgrades (2021), causes contributing to the loss or reduced eyesight are eye trauma, clouding of cataracts, glaucoma, retinal damage due to diabetes, macular degeneration and light-induced damage to the retina. Both macular degeneration and light-induced damage to the retina can be found to be caused by excessive use of smartphones.

The desire for an efficient way to produce light results in the innovation of light-emitting diodes (LED). Coupled the blue-light LED with a phosphor to produce a white light source called white-light LED (Tosini et al, 2016). This method of producing lights for illumination had been deemed to be technologically advantageous leading to be the main choice of light production

for smartphones worldwide. However, several investigations regarding the effect of light exposure of a specific wavelength with a specific intensity towards the retina have been made and the results are shown to be damaging to the retina. Further investigation had shown that light-induced damage may even be irreversible. Moreover, the longer time; around 12 to 48 hours, the eyes are exposed to light even with less intense light exposure, retinal damage will be larger and similar results can be seen with shorter time but the higher intensity of light with a specific wavelength. The studies also state that blue-light (400-440 nm) specifically have a higher damage intensity towards the eye. Other than that, excessive smartphone usage can result in dry eye disease (DED) which is usually associated with autoimmune and inflammatory disorders (Moon et al, 2016).

Physical Pain and Migraine

Nomophobia had increased the sedentary activity and decreased physical activity of a person's daily life. The usage of smartphones demands specific muscle and bone structure that affects the physicality of an individual especially the cervical erector spinae and upper trapezius and causes neck-shoulder pain (Xie et al, 2015). Furthermore, nomophobia will make the person have a longer sedentary activity and thus staying inactive in a longer period of time which leads to a larger impact on the body region stated. Moreover, the act of texting and using smartphones with one hand requires a higher muscle demand in the shoulder, forearm and thumb compared to using both hands furthering the pain in the neck and shoulder. This leads to a higher risk of developing musculoskeletal disorders which can disturb the daily lifestyle and routine.

The addictions towards using smartphones in everyday life had caused several disturbances towards the quality of life, sleep pattern and capability of thinking. All of this had led to pain and an increasing frequency of migraine and headaches. Yasemin P. Demir & Mehmet M. Sumer (2019) discovered in their investigative paper that higher smartphone usage results in a longer time and a higher frequency of migraine the person will suffer.

Psychological Well Being

Psychological well-being is described as a person's ability to effectively communicate his contentment without letting others influence his good sentiments (Diener et al., 2003). Apart from healthy physiology, free of stress and other mental issues, psychological well-being is intimately linked to self-acceptance, positive relationships with others, autonomy, environmental mastery, purpose in life, and personal progress (Ryff, 1989). Feeling good

incorporates not just positive feelings like happiness and satisfaction, but also emotions like curiosity, engagement, confidence, and affection. From a psychological perspective, successful functioning entails realizing one's full potential, having some control over one's life, having a feeling of purpose (e.g., striving toward worthwhile objectives), and having meaningful relationships.

Individuals do not have to feel good all of the time to be happy. Painful emotions such as disappointment, failure, and sadness are a natural part of life, and being able to handle these negative or painful emotions is critical to still be considered as well-being. However, negative emotions that are severe or very long-lasting that interfere with a person's willingness to participate in everyday life could jeopardize psychological well-being. In today's generation, it is generally acknowledged that numerous factors influence people's psychological well-being, and technology innovations are one of the most significant influences on human psychology.

Smartphone Habits And Behavior Interruption
On Psychological Well Being

Technology is well acknowledged to have a significant impact on human lives. In this regard, technology which is rapidly improving day by day has emerged as one of the most important innovations in daily life. The smartphone business is undergoing massive changes and improvements, allowing for the launch of new types of smartphones with innovative features such as video calls, computers, internet access, cameras, navigation, music players, calculators, cameras, and video recording. As a result of these features, smartphones have become an indispensable part of daily life, with usage steadily increasing (Tatl, 2015; Doan & Karakuş, 2016). Every technology, however, has both benefits and drawbacks, and smartphones are no exception (Ahmed et al., 2011). Despite the benefits it has brought to people's lives, this gadget causes major concerns depending on when and where it is used (Gümüş & rgev, 2015).

According to Anshari et al (2016), young people are claimed to be more inclined to utilize social media and online messaging apps to communicate with their family and friends. This has resulted in a surge in the popularity of social networking sites, as well as an increase in the number of young people who use them. Moreover, the finding from the research noted that the older age utilizes the internet for fewer than 6 hours each day, whilst the younger ones use it almost continuously. When it comes to young people's smartphone usage, social networks, communication, gaming, video, music, and streaming are the most popular (Anshari et al., 2016; Gezgin & Cakir, 2016). Young people have developed a strong liking for using smartphones. It has been noted that students, in particular, have a proclivity to look at or pay attention to their smartphones regardless of the situation. This circumstance might be classified as smartphone addiction or obsession (Gümüş & rgev, 2015).

Smartphones have been connected to mental health difficulties on their own. For example, excessive gaming, including online gaming, has been connected to depression, lack of self- control, and low self-esteem (King & Delfabbro, 2013; Kwon, Chung & Lee, 2011; van Rooij). Additionally, social networking is a widely used feature on smartphones, particularly among teenagers (Ofcom Report, 2011). Experts have labeled social networking sites as "addiction- prone technologies" (Tarafdar et al., 2013; Turel & Serenko, 2012), with the potential for strong habit formation and pathological and maladaptive psychological dependency (Tarafdar et al., 2013). Overall, studies have found that excessive gaming, social networking, Internet browsing, emailing, phone calls, and texting are associated with stress, anxiety, and depression.

Smartphones, which are intended to improve communication and computing, have just as many bad as beneficial consequences on young people's social behaviour, learning abilities, successes, and even interactions with the environment. According to a study by Young (1998), when smartphone use becomes compulsive, it can have negative consequences in terms of economical, physical, psychological, and social elements of life. The accumulating evidence suggests that many individuals use their phones in ways that negatively impact their everyday lives and mental health (Cheever et al., 2014 & Clayton et al., 2015). Different terms have been used to characterize various types of smartphone use. These include "excessive smartphone usage," "problematic smartphone use," and "smartphone addiction," and how they may damage users' well-being. Furthermore, we primarily focus on social usage (i.e., online engagement with others) as the primary cause of problematic smartphone behaviour and accelerates habit formation (Li & Chung, 2006; van Deursen et al, 2015). Studies have indicated that excessive smartphone habits and behaviour in relation to social media can contribute to psychological well-being such as nomophobia and body dysmorphic disorder.

Phone Addiction and Nomophobia

As smartphones have grown integrated in our everyday routines (Parasuraman et al., 2017). People utilize these gadgets to participate in online activities such as accessing social networking sites, sending and receiving emails, chatting with others, searching for information,

and watching, downloading, and uploading movies (Roa, 2012). Individuals who send a large number of texts, according to Lu et al. (2011), can develop "text message dependency," becoming increasingly concerned about why they have not received a response to their message immediately, increasing feelings of isolation or neglect, and ultimately increasing anxiety. Smartphone users displayed responsiveness to pressure, which is defined as "the anticipation of the user to respond quickly to a message after receiving it," as well as accessibility pressure, which is defined as " a user will make time to check and respond to messages" whether or not the user has that time (Matusik & Mickel, 2011). According to a study by Woollaston (2014), that further supports the claims through his finding that users do in fact 'pick up' their smartphones roughly 1,500 times on average in which two-fifths of them are feeling lost without their smartphones.

As people struggle to maintain control over their smartphone usage and become reliant on them, this generates an imbalance in the amount of time they devote to various things in their life. The difficulty to abstain from using their phones, sense of anxiety when they are not using them that comes with losing or being separated from one's smartphone, as well as the worry that comes with being unable to use one's smartphone (Bian & Leung, 2015; Emanuel et al., 2015; SecurEnvoy, 2012; Yildirim, 2014) are referred as Nomophobia. It is regarded as a digital era modern phobia that is linked to problematic mobile technology use (Gezgin et al., 2017) and addiction issues (Güzel, 2018). When stressed, users are more likely to engage in unhealthy lifestyle habits in which it can lead to mental health issues and thus negatively impact users' psychological well-being.

Body Dysmorphic Disorders

Social media contains images of a variety of people (e.g., friends, family, strangers, celebrities), and it is commonly used to interact with one's peers (Hew, 2011), with research suggesting that appearance comparisons to peers may have a particularly strong influence on body image (Carey ET al, 2014). There are a number of distinguishing characteristics of social media that may play a role in any influence it has on body image. In the literature, the term "body image" has been defined in a variety of ways, including body dissatisfaction, the desire for thinness/ muscularity, and self-objectification (Fardouly & Vartanian, 2016).

In context to smartphone habits and behaviour, where users utilize their devices for online activities and socializing, may result in problematic behaviour that may affect their psychological well-being. For example, a study by Meier & Gray (2014), excessive appearance exposure on Facebook (e.g., uploading, watching, and commenting on pictures) has been linked to increased weight dissatisfaction, thin-ideal internalization, and self-objectification among female high school students. As there are more social media sites such as Instagram which are more image-based are being introduced and are gaining in popularity, particularly among young people, this further affects its users by means of comparing their look to that of others. According to a study by Kim et al (2010), excessive use of smartphones can also result in poor dietary habits, where high-risk Internet users eat smaller meals, have less hunger and skip meals. This may be due to the users following up on what they saw on the internet that ends up influencing their perception of their daily life. As a result, the influence of these image-focused platforms that were associated with its users' habits and behaviours might be seen as jeopardizing psychological well-being.

It is critical to comprehend why people could become so engrossed in these smartphone habits and behaviours that they develop high usage habits and high participation that led to low psychological well-being.

METHODOLOGY

The paper focuses on literature reviews of previous studies. Additionally, the paper will also focus on analyzing the problem and coming up with solutions that can be implemented. By widening our perspective of the problem and increasing efficiency through a problem audit, we may evaluate and address this problem through CATWOE and 5 WHYs.

CATWOE analysis is used to define and understand the perspectives of the six elements. The mnemonic stands for Customers, Actors, Transformation, World view, Owner and Environment. It is a simple checklist method to find appropriate solutions for the problem. By understanding the perspectives, it will give ideas on the impacts and responses of the elements to the founding suggestions and solutions. Furthermore, it will give clearer directions on how to approach the problems.

5 WHYs are one of Root Cause Analysis (RCA) techniques, it is a problem-solving tool that involves finding the problem's root cause, assessing it, and developing a strategy for addressing it. If the problem remains, it is likely that the real root cause has yet to be discovered. The goal of a root cause analysis is to figure out what occurred, why it happened, and what needs to be done to prevent it from occurring again.

ANALYSIS

The problem in this paper can be identified in two categories, the impact of smartphone habits and behaviours towards 1) physical well-being and 2) psychological well-being. Both of these problems will be analysed separately using the same method of CATWOE and 5 Whys analysis.

Physical Well-Being Analysis

The problem identified was the negative impacts suffered by an individual due to the excessive smartphone usage towards physical well-being. Below is the analysis made utilizing CATWOE and 5 Whys tools in the attempt to investigate the root cause analysis including suggesting solutions appropriate to be implemented. By understanding the perspective of each CATWOE, it will be easier to give clarity on the problems and solutions that will be analysed.

Table 1. CATWOE analysis of smartphone habits and behaviors in physical well-being

CATWOE	Description
Clients	Smartphone users
Actors	● Manufacturers of smartphone ● Internet provider ● Software application companies
Transformation process	Services and products that can be utilized by the users provided by smartphone companies and internet providers. This includes streaming videos, movies and series, gaming, social media, online interaction, online shopping and information searching.
Worldview	A huge fraction of the population relies heavily on smartphones for entertainment, connectivity, accessibility and convenience which causes heavy addictions towards the usage of smartphones and its services. This had led to higher statistics toward deteriorating physical health problems such as neck-shoulder pain and eyesight damage. Far more concerning matters can be said to be death by noncommunicable diseases that rise due to being inactive from a higher amount of time used for using a smartphone.
Owners	● Smartphone brand owners ● Smartphone applications company owners ● Internet provider company owners
Environmental constraints	The willpower of the addicted individual towards changing their own habits and behaviour and their own motivation to change for a better and healthier lifestyle. The increasing amount of online work forces these individuals to use their smartphones for research, writing and more. The convenience smartphone provides for its users encourages lesser natural physical activity. For example, limiting physical shopping by the increasing number of online shops that provide safe and convenient ways of purchasing products. 　The fast advancement of innovative technology that will be popular and encourage more online activity

To investigate the root cause of the problem; negatively affected physical well-being due to smartphone habits and behaviours, 5 whys methods will be utilized. The diagram of 5 whys can be seen below.

Figure 1. The 5 why's

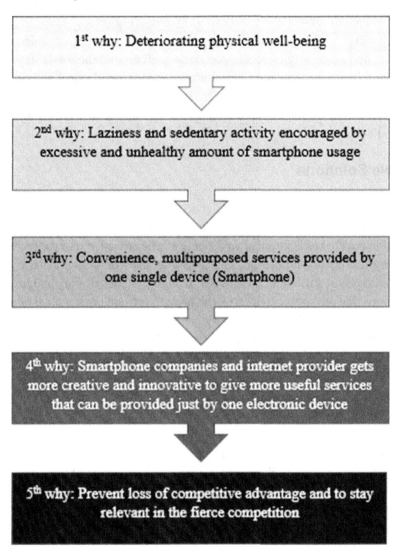

By analysing the problem by using 5 Whys, it can be seen that the fear or risk of loss of competitive advantage contribute to the push factors in creating more innovative applications, games and services that are allowed to be provided by smartphone. In addition to that, the strong will to stay relevant in the fierce business competition also leads to the companies to attempt newer ways to attract the smartphone customers including consumers of contents supplied by these companies. A survey was made in the United Kingdom shows the importance of connectivity between the seller and buyer especially in the increasing emergence of technology era for the past decades, pushing non-smartphone companies to make applications that encourage convenience in purchasing or comparing prices (Marketing Week, 2011). However, this convenience and multipurpose services provided by just one device had negatively impacted populations all around the world. It promotes laziness and increased sedentary activity while reducing physical activity due to the large fraction of time in a day used for using smartphones. Thus, as a result, it affects the physical well-being of the users, making them have negative smartphone habits and behaviours.

Possible Solutions

From the analysis, the main problem and root causes were identified. One of the main impacts of smartphone habits and behaviours is the effect on physical well-being. The degree of impact towards physical well-being can be considered as concerning as it affects physical health and eyesight. Furthermore, the worst-case scenario of these situations can be death. Thus, it is crucial to attempt in developing and implement the solutions that are appropriate, with the hope to prevent the negative impact and reduce the effect on individuals affected.

From previous studies and articles, some of the initiatives to increase physical activity, reduce sedentary activity and reduce the time used towards smartphones can be found.

I.   Increase physical activity and reduce sedentary lifestyle.

Due to the innovation of technology, it is not possible to separate oneself from technology so, for the solution to have a positive effect, there has to be a mixture of technology by using the smartphone to counter the problem caused by smartphones. For a full engagement, it was stated that the software or application developed to encourage physical activity has to own two things; objective and social connectivity (Harries et al, 2013).

A convenient and easy objective setting and performance feedback influences a person's behaviour greatly and is considered to be the key to promote physical activity and reduce sedentary lifestyle. Furthermore, the creativity behind the "apps" has to include increased difficulty to be deemed as "fun" and increase the self-satisfaction that can be achieved once the objectives are obtained and motivate the person further to engage in physical activity. In addition, the goal has to be appropriate with the individual and the need to continuously introduce new and fresh features for the "apps" to stay relevant. UbiFit and ChickClique apps are examples of applications that encourage physical activity by setting their own step-count daily.

In the modern age, the ability to show and tell friends and family through social media has become the normalized way. This shows how social connectivity is important even when showing one's achievements. In other words, telling the world about accomplishments and achievements may become some individual's source of motivators in completing the goals set in applications that encourage physical activity. In Fish'n'Steps, the users were given a fish avatar that behaves with respect to the number of steps taken by the users daily which gives a sense of accomplishment when the "fish '' is growing and behaving nicely. Furthermore, the accomplishment will be shared with friends and families who use the Fish'n Steps apps.

In recent years, the success of the online game "Pokemon Go '' has affected individuals all around the world (Althoff et al, 2016). The popularity of the game influenced people to download and try the game themselves. The idea of "Pokemon Go" was to capture "Pokemon '' which was set in different real places and get items from known places all over the countries. Furthermore, the users need to walk a certain distance to "hatch an egg". This promotes physical activity under the guise of full engagements and entertainment provided by the game. Over the period of 30 days, some users rise 1473 steps daily while playing the game which is 25 percent more than before the users play the game. Furthermore, physical activity was increased throughout all genders, ages, races and weight statuses.

II.   Reducing exposure towards light produced by smartphone

The long period of screen time from smartphone usage was shown to have negative effects on eyesight such as reduced vision and dry eye disease. Prevention measures are needed to reduce the negative effects of smartphones on eyesight. From analysing previous solutions implemented, there are two things that were done in order to prevent further light-inducing damage to the retina; introducing new features and tools that can help reduce the negative impact to the eye and features that promote the reduction of time used towards smartphone usage.

In 2016, the "Apple" company introduced true tone as a new feature of the iPad that can adjust the brightness and colour depending on the surrounding. The feature was used by the consumer well as it helps the eye and reduces the effects which lead to the feature being included in the newer phones and devices. Other than that, some companies manufactured glasses that block the toxic blue light produced by smartphones. It was also claimed that decreasing the exposure towards blue-light, also reduced the frequency of the individual getting eye strain, migraine and headaches. Furthermore, the company released newer features in 2018 to encourage screen time management by introducing "Do Not Disturb", screen time report and Downtime features. The "Do Not Disturb" feature was used to lessen interruptions in real life such as during class or meetings and hide all notifications. Screen time report is a useful tool to give understanding on the time used in front of smartphones screen and give clarity whether it is healthy or unhealthy. Downtown features offered by "Apple" will actually limit the time allowed for the individual using certain applications and games. This feature allows parents to control their children's smartphones by limiting access during certain times and choosing which applications and games are allowed for the kids.

In conclusion, most companies have started to give attention to the negative impacts of bad smartphone habits and behaviours and thus, initiated the innovation of smartphones and software to prevent further damage caused.

1. Psychological Well-Being Analysis

The problem has been identified as individuals involved in smartphone habits and behaviour develop high usage patterns and strong participation, resulting in bad psychological well-being, However, before attempting to solve any problem, it is beneficial and, in some cases, necessary to investigate the problem's origins and all related variables before deciding how to proceed after learning about the situation. With this process, the same situation from different perspectives can be reviewed. This can be accomplished through CATWOE.

Table 2. CATWOE analysis of smartphone habits and behaviour in psychological wellbeing

CATWOE	Description
Clients	Smartphone users
Actors	● Smartphone users ● Manufacturers of smartphone ● Application companies
Transformation process	Smartphone users that engage in problematic smartphone behaviour need to willingly decrease it. Smartphone applications companies can introduce applications that help with mental health etc so that people do not use it blindly.
Worldview	Smartphone habits and behaviour may persist to result in negative outcomes due to the current accessibility provided by smartphone producers and applications companies that are not properly utilized by its users. However, if this is not resolved, this may result in more severe cases in relation to health issues and well-being. Furthermore, if this problem is resolved, the use of technology such as smartphones can out-balance the negative impacts and be more towards the good side as advancement in technology can be properly used for greater purposes.
Owners	● Smartphone manufacturers ● Smartphone Application companies
Environmental constraints	It is based on the users decreasing their involvement in the use of smartphones. For example, even if smartphone producers embed "Do not Disturb" technology in their products as a way to reduce notification coming in or etc and or even if there have been initiatives such as applications that help with mental health etc introduced to allow constant use of a smartphone, it is based on the individuals to practiced it or it may result to nothing.

Several causes could also be discovered as probable causes using the 5 WHYs methodology, and these causes help to pinpoint the root cause of the problem. For example, based on the problem described before, this presents the following questions:

Figure 2. The 5 why's methodology

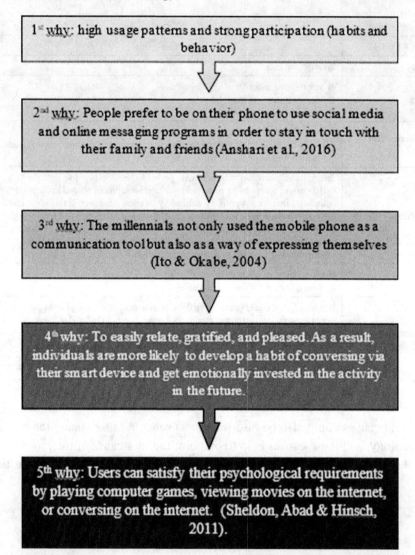

Users thought that using a smartphone was preferable for them than living normally in their everyday lives, as a method of escaping reality, because of the emptiness created by the continual isolation and alienation. The growth of mobile phone technology may be "endorsing" a better aversion than reality, which might be the main reason. Smartphones provide us with a distorted view of the world. By portraying the type of world we'd prefer to see on its screen, smartphones provide a haven from many of the controversial or disturbing aspects of reality.

Possible Solutions

After identifying the facilitators of negative effects of smartphone habits and behaviours within the layer of psychological well-being, we will identify key ingredients necessary for a successful intervention.

Phone technology businesses have a strong claim to the issue because they are the manufacturers of smartphones. Smartphone manufacturers, such as Apple and Samsung, are very interested in how their customers engage with their products. Given the surge in bad behaviour associated with their goods, it is in their best interests to assist consumers in developing positive long-term connections with technology (Salkever & Wadhwa, 2018). For example, Apple is now working on a set of features dubbed "Digital Health" that will help consumers become more mindful of their interactions with technology. However, because these capabilities are only available on the most recent versions of the iPhone, there is a clear relationship between them and a desire to increase iPhone sales (Perez, 2018).

Companies that create habit-forming technology are now attempting to undo its effects. They can help support an intervention since they have a clear stake in reducing harmful smartphone behaviour and having the ability to effectively establish a technology-based firm. In order to break behaviours, users must reclaim control over triggers in their surroundings by means of:

1. 'App Control Centre,' a centralized location where users can customize alerts for all of their applications,
2. 'Screen time management,' a feature that sends a message when a user spends more time on apps they identify as problematic. For example, "Quiet Mode" disables push notifications and reminds you to use the app responsibly. You just choose a time period for when you want the social media to be available and when you want it to remain silent to use the new function.

Last but not least, the solution lies in the users that are willing to change their habits and behaviours.

DISCUSSION

Physical Well-Being

Benefits

This study was able to highlight the issues on the negative effects of smartphone habits and behaviour on physical well-being, as well as strategies for helping users minimize the arising problematic issues on smartphone activity towards physical well-being. There are two possible solutions that were found. The first one is the implementation of software applications, where the innovation of software applications that promote physical activity, such as 'Pokémon Go' is introduced. The second possible solution would be the existence of phone's features, introduced by smartphone companies such as Apple's to reduce the harmful effect of smartphones on its user such as 'true tone', 'do not disturb' and downtime features.

Challenges

The first challenge of implementation of this software application, where the innovation of software applications that promote physical activity solutions is that it requires a certain cost, time and research. It is also difficult for the applications for the software to stay relevant for a long period of time. The second challenge for features such as the 'true tone', 'Do not disturb' and downtime features possible solution is that it is to be set manually by the users and hence they have to be willing and have the motivation to improve themselves (Razzaq et al., 2018).

Future Directions & Limitations

Although there have been several studies conducted to identify the impact of smartphone habits and behaviours towards users, further studies still need to be conducted to have a broader range of information on the relation between smartphone usage and physical well-being to further inspect and evaluate the effect of the possible solutions. Identifying whether there are existing flaws detected and if the effect is negative or positive and standardising the solutions for the implementation.

Psychological Well-Being

Benefits

This paper is able to address and support the negative outcome on psychological wellbeing as a result of smartphone habits and behaviour as well as address the solutions on how to help users reduce problematic smartphone behaviour in order to not jeopardize their relationships and their own wellbeing. Through the implementation of the analysis, several transformations carried out shows that even though the company decided to introduce technology such as "app control management" and "screen time management", this can still safe-keep their customers using their products but at the same time could help reduce smartphone habits and behaviour among the users.

Challenges

It is based on the users decreasing their involvement in the use of smartphones. For example, even if smartphone producers embed "Do not Disturb" technology in their products as a way to reduce notifications coming in, or even if there have been initiatives such as introducing applications that help with mental health which allows constant use of a smartphone, it is still based on the individuals to practised it or it may result to nothing (Hasmawati et al., 2020). We acknowledge the seeming contradiction of technological improvement on a smartphone application to curb problematic smartphone behaviour. Ideally, existing smartphone applications and the smartphone itself should be designed in a way that does not lead to problematic behaviour. It is not reasonable to expect that smartphone technology and application companies will act because their success relies on the continued sale and usage of their products. Smartphone usage is a social phenomenon deeply embedded in contemporary society which is hard to emulate and understand.

Future Directions & Limitation

The findings of this paper which were gathered from literature reviews of previous research show that there is indeed a negative outcome in psychological wellbeing as a result of smartphone habits and behaviour as well as a result of communication through social media, in which its users regard it as a way from escaping reality. As most studies surveyed the effect of psychological well-being on smartphone habits and behaviours through their own experimental method, very few studies have focused on the impact of psychological well-being on smartphone habits and behaviour based on psychiatric interviews. Hence, additional future study is needed to address unsolved parts of the problem with solid evidence to support this finding through proper experiments and data collection through mixed research approaches rather than just focusing on approaches that may be possibly biased in this research. Hence, more research is needed to clarify the ways in which smartphone habits and behaviours may affect psychological well-being.

CONCLUSION

Smartphones are phone devices with cutting-edge technologies that go beyond the basic functionality of phones. Smartphone usage is crucial to people's lives and society. According to the study, it is seen that excessive use of smartphones has resulted in sedentary activity and to combat these issues, a suggested solution is to create an app to encourage more physical activity. Additionally, another solution is to provide 'true tone', 'Do not disturb' and 'downtime' features to reduce further harmful effects. As for the concerns in regards to the psychological aspects of well-being, users have regarded smartphones as a way of escaping reality and to this, a suggested solution is to use digital health apps to monitor illness, health risks and promote

wellness. In addition, using functions such as an app control centre, and screen management time is also suggested as a solution to alert users of your excessive time spent on smartphones. As a recommendation, it is suggested that it is important for an individual to be mindful of the digital use of smartphones. Whereby individuals need to raise awareness about how their smartphones are being utilized and set clear goals on the purpose of using smartphones for the transitions into the digital era.

To conclude, the purpose of this study is to learn about the impact of smartphone user habits and behaviours on well-being. The research's major conclusion suggests that there are indeed issues detected in the correlation between smartphone habits and behaviours and users' physical and psychological well-being. The two analytical methodologies can connect to the objective of this research by analysing the data based on existing literature reviews from previous studies. It clearly indicates the possible problem of extended smartphone usage using the CATWOE analysis approach, as well as the RCA method, which offers an idea on how to cope with the ongoing concerns. Additionally, with the alarming increase of over-reliance on smartphone usages among consumers, it is necessary to conduct ongoing and comprehensive research to determine if a smartphone is beneficial to consumers or detrimental to their physical and psychological well-being.

REFERENCES

Ahad, A. D., Anshari, M., & Razzaq, A. (2017). Domestication of smartphones among adolescents in Brunei darussalam. [IJCBPL]. *International Journal of Cyber Behavior, Psychology and Learning, 7*(4), 26–39. doi:10.4018/IJCBPL.2017100103

Ahmed, Imy & Ramzan, Muqadas & Qazi, Tehmina & Jabeen, Shaista. (2011). An investigation of mobile phone consumption patterns among students and professionals; is there any difference?. *European Journal of Economics, Finance and Administrative Sciences,* 136-143.

Almunawar, M. N., & Anshari, M. (2014). Empowering customers in electronic health (e–health) through social customer relationship management. *International Journal of Electronic Customer Relationship Management, 8*(1-3), 87–100. doi:10.1504/IJECRM.2014.066887

Almunawar, M. N., Anshari, M., & Younis, M. Z. (2015). Incorporating customer empowerment in mobile health. *Health Policy and Technology, 4*(4), 312–319. doi:10.1016/j.hlpt.2015.08.008

Almunawar, M. N., Wint, Z., Low, K. C., & Anshari, M. (2012). Customer expectation of e-health systems in Brunei Darussalam. *Journal of Health Care Finance, 38*(4), 36–49. PMID:22894020

Althoff, T., White, R.W., & Horvitz, E., (2016), Influence of Pokemon Go on Physical Activity: Study and Implication. *Journal of Medical Internet Research, 18*(12).

Anshari, M. (2020, March). Workforce mapping of fourth industrial revolution: Optimization to identity. *Journal of Physics: Conference Series, 1477*(7), 072023. doi:10.1088/1742-6596/1477/7/072023

Anshari, M. & Alas, Y., Hardaker, G., Jaidin, J., Smith, M., & Abdullah, A. D. (2016). Smartphone habit and behaviour in Brunei: Personalization, gender, and generation gap. *Computers in Human behaviour. 64,* 719- 727. doi:. doi:10.1016/j.chb.2016.07.063

Anshari, M., Alas, Y., & Sulaiman, E. (2019b). Smartphone addictions and nomophobia among youth. *Vulnerable Children and Youth Studies, 14*(3), 242–247. doi:10.1080/17450128.2019.1614709

Anshari, M., Alas, Y., Yunus, N., Sabtu, N. I., & Hamid, M. H. (2015). Social customer relationship management and student empowerment in online learning systems. *International Journal of Electronic Customer Relationship Management, 9*(2-3), 104–121. doi:10.1504/IJECRM.2015.071711

Anshari, M., Almunawar, M. N., Lim, S. A., & Al-Mudimigh, A. (2019a). Customer relationship management and big data enabled: Personalization & customization of services. *Applied Computing and Informatics*, *15*(2), 94–101. doi:10.1016/j. aci.2018.05.004

Anshari, M., Almunawar, M. N., Low, P. K. C., & Al-Mudimigh, A. S. (2013a). Empowering clients through e-health in healthcare services: Case Brunei. *International Quarterly of Community Health Education*, *33*(2), 189–219. doi:10.2190/IQ.33.2.g PMID:23661419

Anshari, M., Almunawar, M. N., Low, P. K. C., Wint, Z., & Younis, M. Z. (2013b). Adopting customers' empowerment and social networks to encourage participations in e-health services. *Journal of Health Care Finance*, *40*(2), 17–41. PMID:24551960

Anshari, M., Almunawar, M. N., & Masri, M. (2022). Digital Twin: Financial Technology's Next Frontier of Robo-Advisor. *Journal of Risk and Financial Management*, *15*(4), 163. doi:10.3390/jrfm15040163

Apple, (2018), ios 12 introduces new features to reduce interruptions and manage Screen Time. *Apple Newsroom*. https://www.apple.com/newsroom/2018/06/ios-12-introduces-new- features-to-reduce-interruptions-and-manage-screen-time/

Australian National University. (n.d), *Physical Wellbeing,* ANU. https://www.anu. edu.au/covid-19-advice/health-wellbeing/strategies-for-wellbeing-at- home-or-on-campus/physical-wellbeing

Bian, M., & Leung, L. (2015). Linking loneliness, shyness, smartphone addiction symptoms, and patterns of smartphone use to social capital. *Social Science Computer Review*, *33*(1), 61–79. doi:10.1177/0894439314528779

Carey, R. N., Donaghue, N., & Broderick, P. (2014). Body image concern among Australian adolescent girls: The role of body comparisons with models and peers. *Body Image*, *11*(1), 81–84. doi:10.1016/j.bodyim.2013.09.006 PMID:24148894

Cheever, N. A., Rosen, L. D., Carrier, L. M., & Chavez, A. (2014). Out of sight is not out of mind: The impact of restricting wireless mobile device use on anxiety levels among low, moderate and high users. *Computers in Human Behavior*, *37*, 290–297. doi:10.1016/j.chb.2014.05.002

Clayton, R. B., Leshner, G., & Almond, A. (2015). The Extended iSelf: The Impact of iPhone Separation on Cognition, Emotion, and Physiology. *Journal of Computer-Mediated Communication*, *20*(2), 119–135. doi:10.1111/jcc4.12109

Demir, Y. P., & Sumer, M. M. (2019). Effects of smartphone overuse on headache, sleep and quality of life in migraine patients. *Neurosciences*, *24*(2), 115–120. doi:10.17712/nsj.2019.2.20180037 PMID:31056543

Diener, E., Oishi, S., & Lucas, R. E. (2003). Personality, culture, and subjective well–being. *Annual Review of Psychology*, *54*(1), 403–425. doi:10.1146/annurev.psych.54.101601.145056 PMID:12172000

Doğan, U., & Karakuş, Y. (2016). Lise Öğrencilerinin sosyal ağ siteleri kullanımının yordayıcısı olarak çok boyutlu yalnızlık. *Sakarya Üniversitesi Journal of Education*, *6*(1), 57–71. doi:10.19126uje.40198

Emanuel, R., Bell, R., Cotton, C., Craig, J., Drummond, D., & Gibson, S. (2015). The truth about smartphone addiction. *College Student Journal*, *49*(2), 291–299.

Eryılmaz, A. (2010). Ergenlerde öznel iyi oluşu artırma stratejilerini kullanma ile akademik motivasyon arasındaki ilişki. *Klinik Psikiyatri*, *13*, 77–84.

Fardouly, J., & Vartanian, L. (2016). Social Media and Body Image Concerns: Current Research and Future Directions. *Current Opinion in Psychology*, *9*, 1–5. doi:10.1016/j.copsyc.2015.09.005

Fennel, C., Glickman, E. L., Lepp, A., Kingsley, J. D., & Barkley, J. E. (2018). The Relationship between Cell Phone Use, Physical Activity, and Sedentary behaviour in United States Adults above College-age. *International Journal of Human Movement and Sports Sciences*, *6*(4), 63–70. doi:10.13189aj.2018.060401

Galloway, M. T., & Jokl, P. (2000). Aging Successfully. *The Importance of Physical Activity in Maintaining Health and Function*, *8*(1), 37–38. PMID:10666651

Gezgin, D. M., Sumuer, E., Arslan, O., & Yildirim, S. (2017). Nomophobia prevalenc among pre- service teachers: A case of Trakya university. *Trakya Üniversitesi Egitim Fakültesi Dergisi*, *7*(1), 86–89. https://dergipark.org.tr/en/pub/trkefd/issue/27304/287423/.

Gezgin, D. M., Cakir, O., & Yildirim, S. (2016). *The Relationship between Levels of Nomophobia Prevalence and Internet Addiction among Adolescents* [*Ergenler arasında Nomofobi Yaygınlık Düzeyinin İnternet Bağımlılığı ile İlişkisi*] [Paper presented]. The 3rd International Eurasian Educational Research Congress, Muğla, Turkey.

Gümüş, İ., Harries, T., Eslambolchilar, P., Stride, C., Rettie, R., & Walton, S. (2013). *Walking in the Wild – Using an Always-On Smartphone Application to Increase Physical Activity*. Springer.

Güzel, S¸. (2018). Fear of the age: Nomophobia (No-Mobile-Phone). *Journal of Academic Perspective on Social Studies*, *1*(1), 20–24. http://dergipark.gov.tr/japss/issue/43202/519609/. doi:10.35344/japss.519609

Hasmawati, F., Samiha, Y. T., Razzaq, A., & Anshari, M. (2020). Understanding nomophobia among digital natives: Characteristics and challenges. *Journal of Critical Reviews*, *7*(13), 122–131.

Healthgrades. (2021). *Vision Loss*. Health Grades. https://www.healthgrades.com/right- care/eye-health/vision-loss

Hew, K. (2011). Students' and teachers' use of Facebook. *Computers In. Human Behavior*, *27*(2), 662–676. doi:10.1016/j.chb.2010.11.020

Hutmacher, F. (2019), *Why Is There So Much More Research on Vision Than on Any Other Sensory Modality?* NCBI. https://www.ncbi.nlm.nih.gov/pmc/articles/PMC6787282/

International Data Corporation (IDC). (2021). *Second quarter report 2021*. IDC. https://www.idc.com/promo/smartphone-market-share

Kim, Y., Park, J. Y., Kim, S. B., Jung, I. K., Lim, Y. S., & Kim, J. H. (2010). The effects of internet addiction on the lifestyle and dietary behaviour of Korean adolescents. *Nutrition Research and Practice*, *4*(1), 51–57. doi:10.4162/nrp.2010.4.1.51 PMID:20198209

King, D. L., & Delfabbro, P. H. (2013). Issues for dsm-5: Video-gaming disorder? *The Australian and New Zealand Journal of Psychiatry*, *47*(1), 20–22. doi:10.1177/0004867412464065 PMID:23293310

Kuss, D. J., & Griffiths, M. D. (2011). Online social networking and addiction—A review of the psychological literature. *International Journal of Environmental Research and Public Health*, *8*(9), 3528–3552. doi:10.3390/ijerph8093528 PMID:22016701

Kwon, J.-H., Chung, C.-S., & Lee, J. (2011). The effects of escape from self and interpersonal relationship on the pathological use of internet games. *Community Mental Health Journal*, *47*(1), 113–121. doi:10.100710597-009-9236-1 PMID:19701792

Li, S.M., & Chung, T.M. (2006). Internet Function and Internet Addictive behaviour. *Computers in Human behaviour, 22*(6), pp. 1067–1071.

Line, T., Jain, J., & Lyons, G. (2011). The role of ICTs in everyday mobile lives. *Journal of Transport Geography*, *19*(6), 1490–1499. doi:10.1016/j.jtrangeo.2010.07.002

Low, K. C. P., & Anshari, M. (2013). Incorporating social customer relationship management in negotiation. *International Journal of Electronic Customer Relationship Management, 7*(3-4), 239–252. doi:10.1504/IJECRM.2013.060700

Lu, X., Watanabe, J., Liu, Q., Uji, M., Shono, M., & Kitamura, T. (2011). Internet and mobile phone text-messaging dependency: Factor structure and correlation with dysphoric mood among Japanese adults. *Computers in Human behaviour, 27*(5), 1702- 1709

Marketing Week. (2011), Smart ways to attract smartphone shoppers. Marketing Week. https://www.marketingweek.com/smart-ways-to-attract-smartphone-shoppers/

Matusik, S. F., & Mickel, A. E. (2011). Embracing or embattled by converged mobile devices? Users' experiences with a contemporary connectivity technology. *Human Relations, 64*(8), 1001–1030. doi:10.1177/0018726711405552

Meier, E., & Gray, J. (2014). Facebook Photo Activity Associated with Body Image Disturbance in Adolescent Girls. *Cyberpsychology, Behavior, and Social Networking, 17*(4), 199–206. doi:10.1089/cyber.2013.0305 PMID:24237288

Moon, J.H., Kim, K.W., & Moon, N.J., (2016), Smartphone use is a risk factor for pediatric dry eye disease according to region and age: a case control study. *BMC ophthalmology, 16*(1), 1-7.

Mulyani, M. A., Razzaq, A., Sumardi, W. H., & Anshari, M. (2019, August). Smartphone adoption in mobile learning scenario. In *2019 International Conference on Information Management and Technology (ICIMTech)* (Vol. 1, pp. 208-211). IEEE. 10.1109/ICIMTech.2019.8843755

Örgev, C. (2015). Önlisans öğrencilerinin akıllı cep telefon kullanmalarının başarı ve harcama düzeylerine olası etkileri üzerine bir çalışma. *ISCAT/Akademik Platform,* 310-315. http://kritik-analitik.com/ISCAT2015_bildiriler/C1-ISCAT2015ID65.pdf

Osmanoğlu, D. E., & Kaya, H. İ. (2013). Öğretmen adaylarının yükseköğretime dair memnuniyet durumları ile öznel iyi oluş durumlarının değerlendirilmesi: Kafkas Üniversitesi örneği. *Sosyal Bilimler Enstitüsü Dergisi, 12,* 45–70.

Oulasvirta, A., Rattenbury, T., Ma, L., & Raita, E. (2012). Habits make smartphone use more pervasive. *Personal and Ubiquitous Computing, 16*(1), 105–114. doi:10.100700779-011-0412-2

Parasuraman, S., Sam, A. T., Yee, S. W. K., Chuon, B. L. C., & Ren, L. Y. (2017). Smartphone usage and increased risk of mobile phone addiction: A concurrent study. *International Journal of Pharmaceutical Investigation, 7*(3), 125–131. https://doi.o rg/ doi:10.4103/jphi.jphi_56_17

Perez, S. (2018). Apple to Launch its Own 'Digital Health' Features in iOS 12. *TechCrunch.* https://techcrunch.com/2018/06/01/apple-to-launch-its-owndigital-health-features-in- ios- 12-says-report/

Razzaq, A., Samiha, Y. T., & Anshari, M. (2018). Smartphone habits and behaviors in supporting students self-efficacy. *International Journal of Emerging Technologies in Learning, 13*(2), 94. doi:10.3991/ijet.v13i02.7685

Roa, A. (2012, October 5). One of 3 Filipinos can't live without cell phones–survey. *The Inquirer.* http://technology.inquirer.net/18168/one-of-3-filipinos-cant-live-without-cell-phones- survey#ixzz5JLeeJKWO/

Ryff, C. D. (1989). Happiness is everything or is it? Explorations on the meaning of psychological well- being. *Journal of Personality and Social Psychology, 57*(6), 1069–1081. doi:10.1037/0022-3514.57.6.1069

Salkever, A., & Wadhwa, V. (2018). How Tech Companies Can Make Their Products Less Addictive. *Medium.* https://medium.com/s/story/how-tech-companies-can-make-their-products-less-addictive

Saygın, Y., & Arslan, C. (2009). Üniversite öğrencilerinin sosyal destek, benlik saygısı ve öznel iyi oluş düzeylerinin incelenmesi. *Selçuk Üniversitesi Ahmet Keleşoğlu Eğitim Fakültesi, 28,* 207–222.

Scott, A. W., Bressler, N. M., Ffolkes, S., Wittenborn, J. S., & Jorkasky, J. (2016). *Public Attitudes About Eye and Vision Health, 134*(10), 1111–1118.

SecurEnvoy. (2012). 66% of the population suffer from Nomophobia the fear of being without their phone. *SecurEnvoy.* http://www.securenvoy.com/blog/2012/02/16/66-of-thepopulation-suffer-from nomophobia-the-fear-of-being-without-their-phone/

Tarafdar, M., Gupta, A., & Turel, O. (2013). The dark side of information technology use. *Information Systems Journal, 23*(3), 269–275. doi:10.1111/isj.12015

Tatlı, H. (2015). Akıllı telefon seçiminin belirleyicileri: üniversite öğrencileri üzerine bir Uygulama [The determinants of smartphone choice: An application on university students]. *Çankırı Karatekin Üniversitesi İktisadi ve İdari Bilimler Fakültesi Dergisi,* 1-19. doi:10.18074/cnuiibf.233

Tosini, G., Ferguson, I., & Tsubota, K. (2016), Effects of blue light on the circadian system and eye physiology. NCBI. https://www.ncbi.nlm.nih.gov/pmc/articles/PMC4734149/

Turel, O., & Serenko, A. (2012). The benefits and dangers of enjoyment with social networking websites. *European Journal of Information Systems*, *21*(5), 512–528. doi:10.1057/ejis.2012.1

Van Deursen, A.J.A.M., Bolle, C.L., Hegner, S.M. & Kommers, P.A.M. (2015). Modeling Habitual and Addictive Smartphone behaviour: The Role of Smartphone Usage Types, Emotional Intelligence, Social Stress, Self-Regulation, Age, and Gender. *Computers in Human behaviour, 45*(1), pp. 411-420.

Woollaston, V. (2014). How often do you look at your phone? The average user now picks up their device more than 1,500 times a week. *Daily Mail*. http://www.dailymail.co.uk/sciencetech/article-2783677/How-YOU-look-phone-Theaverage-user-picks- device-1-500-times-day.html

World Health Organization. (2020), *Physical activity.* WHO. https://www.who.int/news-room/fact-sheets/detail/physical-activity

Xie, Y., Szeto, G. P. Y., Dai, J., & Madeleine, P. (2016). A comparison of muscle activity in using touchscreen smartphone among young people with and without chronic neck– shoulder pain. *Ergonomics*, *59*(1), 61–72. doi:10.1080/00140139.2015.1056237 PMID:26218600

Yakamoz, Y., Kesgin, C., & Topuzoğlu, A. (2006). Sağlığın tanımı; başa çıkma. *İstanbul Kültür Üniversitesi Dergisi, 3*, 47-49.

Yildirim, C. (2014). Exploring the dimensions of nomophobia: Developing and validating a questionnaire using mixed methods research [Graduate Thesis]. Graduate Theses and Dissertations, 14005 https://lib.dr.iastate.edu/etd/14005/.

Young, K. S. (1998). Internet addiction: The emergence of a new clinical disorder. *Cyberpsychology & Behavior*, *1*(3), 237–244. doi:10.1089/cpb.1998.1.237

Zulkarnain, N., & Anshari, M. (2016, November). Big data: Concept, applications, & challenges. In *2016 International Conference on Information Management and Technology (ICIMTech)* (pp. 307-310). IEEE. 10.1109/ICIMTech.2016.7930350

Chapter 3

The Impact of Digital Transformation on Freelancer Well-Being:
Insight From Slovenia

Ivona Huđek

(iD) https://orcid.org/0000-0001-6400-9950
Faculty of Economics and Business, University of Maribor, Slovenia

Karin Širec
Faculty of Economics and Business, University of Maribor, Slovenia

ABSTRACT

This chapter relates to digital transformation and its impact on the labor market, with a focus on the emergence of new business models characterized by less reliance on physical elements-the "gig economy." As a result, new forms of work such as freelancers are taking an increasingly large share of the labor market, characterized by self-directed and independent career development. Although global leaders face the challenge of harnessing this trend and promoting its economic benefits while ensuring an inclusive society by preventing social polarization in labor markets, findings suggest that social protection and appreciation for new forms of work are still low. Using 200 Slovenian freelancers, the authors examine demographic characteristics, motivation for freelancing, and their subjective well-being. Accordingly, the implications for policymakers are to invest more effort in creating a supportive ecosystem that is open not only to "standard" but also to new contemporary and digitally enabled careers.

DOI: 10.4018/978-1-6684-6108-2.ch003

INTRODUCTION

The development of digital technology and its integration into businesses in the late 20th century created new revenue and value-creation opportunities and changed the way businesses operate and how they deliver value to their customers. Although digitalization primarily impacts businesses and is reflected in GDP growth, job creation, and innovation, digital transformation also has broader societal implications (OECD, 2018) such as quality of life and access to services (Mergel et al., 2019). Mediation through and reliance on digital technologies, particularly digital platforms, has led to the emergence of the gig economy, which is experiencing tremendous growth in a variety of industries and regions and is a significant and expanding phenomenon that is rapidly reshaping aspects of the economy and society-the labor market (Barnes et al., 2015; 2019; Goos et al., 2014; Rhein, et al., 2018; Wood et al., 2018).

The digitalization of the labor market is accompanied by the emergence of new framework conditions for work, such as the increasing differentiation and flexibilization of labor market segments. Lucio and MacKenzie (2017) note that ICT-enabled mobile work (workers can do their jobs from anywhere and at any time, supported by modern technologies), portfolio work (where freelancers work for a large number of clients and do small jobs for each of them), crowd employment (where an online platform brings employers and workers together), and collaborative employment (where self-employed workers, or micro-enterprises work together in some way to overcome size constraints and professional isolation) are new forms of employment that have emerged as a result of digitalization.

These broad new forms of employment constitute the gig economy and have multiple implications for working conditions and the labor market. In contrast to traditional careers characterized by hierarchical advancement, organizational career management, and low mobility, many individuals are becoming more mobile and self-directed in their careers. International statistics (Section 2.2) show the rising trends of new, digitally enabled forms of work, which simultaneously impose questions about the digital preparedness of the economy for new forms of employment and the socio-psychological well-being of citizens.

Furthermore, career success today is no longer based (only) on objective measures of success (e.g., financial performance or progress), but also on subjective assessments (e.g., work-life balance, well-being, or personal growth) that are linked to a person's internal career anchors, making "psychological success" the most important indicator of career success. An increasingly diverse workforce, the growing importance of other areas of life such as "quality time with family and friends," and increasing individualization, value-based careers, independent career management, and personal responsibility are leading to an approach in which individuals do not rely primarily on organizations for their career development, but take responsibility for their own career management (Baruch, 2004; Savickas, 2011).

In this sense, the focus of this chapter on digitally related forms of work – the freelancers. Freelancers are workers who manage flexible working arrangements and belong to the category of self-employed without employees who use their potential to apply for temporary jobs or projects. In addition, they pay their own income tax, have full control over where they work (they work remotely), do not receive benefits from companies, typically work with multiple clients and projects simultaneously, and set their own rates-whether they charge by the hour or per project (Darlington, 2014). Since the gig economy is a relatively unexplored field of research, this chapter contributes to the study of the gig economy phenomenon and its characteristics in the small economy - Slovenian labor market. Therefore, the authors pose the questions:

What are the motivations of Slovenian freelancers for such a career, and does this new form of work reflect their well-being?

This chapter aims to answer the above research questions. A sample of 200 Slovenian freelancers is used to determine their reasons for pursuing such careers. In addition, their subjective well-being is measured in terms of job and career satisfaction, life satisfaction and income satisfaction. In doing so, the data and findings on the motivation are compared to other international reports and findings on freelancers (Upwork, 2019, 2021; Malt & EFIP, 2018. In addition, other academic research that has already addressed the well-being of freelancers (Fraser & Gold, 2001; Van den Born & Van Witteloostuijn, 2013; Van der Zwan et al., 2020) are used for comparison and conclusions are drawn for future policy proposals. As EU member states implement national strategies for digital transformation, the study results shed light on the unique characteristics and challenges that foster freelancing in Slovenia.

Therefore, this chapter represents a significant contribution to science in the following respects:

- in terms of the sample studied, i.e. the group of freelancers,
- in terms of variables: the study includes motivation and subjective well-being variables relevant to freelancers' careers,
- in terms of research design, which includes primary data collected through questionnaires with freelancers,
- in terms of the usefulness of the data for national policy making (as there is no literature on the characteristics and shortcomings of freelancers in Slovenia) and international comparisons.

In terms of structure, the chapter begins with an introduction to the interrelated trends: technological and social, that are impacting labor by creating new business systems such as the gig economy. In the gig economy, short-term jobs are mostly performed by independent contractors, or freelancers, who are the focus of the study presented in the applied part of the chapter. The final part of the chapter discusses the implications for policymakers arising from the findings and provides recommendations for future research and concluding considerations.

BACKGROUND

Digital Transformation

The development of science, mainly information and communication technologies, have promoted information exchange and global competitiveness, which in turn has encouraged entrepreneurship and innovation (IMF, 2000) and the emergence of the new economy as a transition from a manufacturing and commodity-based economy to one that uses technology to produce new products at a pace that a traditional manufacturing economy could not keep up with. This process has shaped the end of the 20th century and the beginning of the 21st century, changing how people do business and live. The industrial age, which was dominated by analogue technologies, is being replaced by an innovation-driven age of knowledge and creativity, dominated by digital technologies. For the future and prosperity of the economy, this is one of the most important business trends.

Digital transformation was first proclaimed in the 1990s, when high-tech tools, particularly the internet and increasingly powerful computers, began to enter consumer and business markets, making them digital and creating new subsectors that include the gig economy, sharing economy, streaming economy, Cloud computing, Big Data, artificial intelligence, etc. (Kenton, 2020). In everyday communication, many terms are encountered from the digital world, especially digitalization. For a better understanding, Figure 1 illustrates the pyramid of digital transformation, which shows that digital transformation is not possible without digitalization as adoption process and foundational digitization.

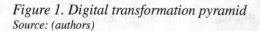

Figure 1. Digital transformation pyramid
Source: (authors)

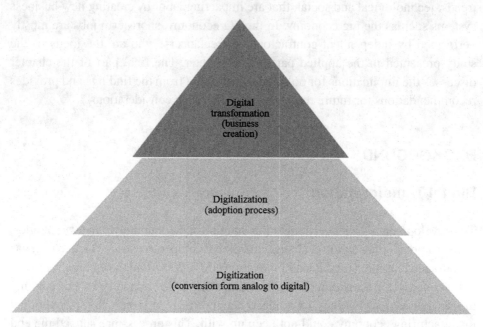

Accordingly, digitization refers to the process of turning an analogue signal into a digital form (computer-readable format) understood by computer systems and electronic devices (Brennen & Kreiss, 2016b). In other words, various forms of information content, such as sounds or images, are converted into a single binary code that facilitates digital computer processing, storing and transmitting data.

Digitalization represents a far-reaching socio-technical process. It implies the integration of digital technologies into aspects of daily social life, including smartphones, e-government, smart homes, e-health, and smart cities (Brennen & Kreiss, 2016b). Digitalization in business mainly refers to the improvement and transformation of business activities, processes and models through the use and adoption of digital technologies and the broader use and context of digitized data converted into intelligence and adequate knowledge (while digitization refers more to record).

Finally, digital transformation refers to the strategies or processes that go beyond the application of digital technologies and imply a profound change in the business environment (strategy, culture, technology, customers, workforce), which consequently affects the new paths for revenue and value creation (Karimi & Walter, 2021).

The Impact of Digitalization On The Labor Market

One of these effects is the emergence of a new phenomenon, namely the gig economy. The gig economy (also known as the "collaborative economy" or "platform economy") is often defined as the economic and social activities enabled by online platforms (Schwellnus et al., 2019), and recently this type of work has been taking an increasingly large share of the labor market. With the introduction of digital infrastructures (Warner, & Wäger, 2019) - platforms serve as intermediaries between buyers and sellers (Velu, 2015) - many activities and forms of work can be easily performed and offered remotely (online). In the gig economy, these short-term tasks or projects within specific activities are performed by individual self-employed workers (Tran & Sokas, 2017), so-called independent professionals (contractors), better known as freelancers. As a result of digitalization, many workers can perform their tasks in a more efficient and fragmented way, creating new jobs and improving old jobs in the labor market (Cahuc & Postel-Vinay, 2002).

Due to advances in technology and connectivity that allow gig workers to penetrate markets worldwide, a 2016 McKinsey Global Institute study showed that 20-30% of the workforce in the USA and EU-15 countries is part of the gig economy. This equates to up to 162 million working-age people in the USA and EU-15 who are self-employed in some form. In Europe, according to estimates from the COLLEEM survey on platform work (Pesole et al., 2018), in 14 EU member states, an average of 10% of the adult population has used online platforms to perform some type of work activity.

In addition, the Online Labour Index (OLI) shows that in 2020, there were 163 million registered user accounts of online platforms worldwide, of which 8.6% have worked at least once and 2.0% have either completed at least 10 projects or earned $1,000 during their freelance career. As for Slovenia, there is no research on the gig economy there yet. Looking at Slovenia's neighbouring countries included in the survey, according to the COLLEEM survey (Slovenia was not included), there were platform workers from Italy (13.5%), Croatia (12.1%), and Hungary (8.9%). Portugal had the most of them (15.7%) and Finland the least (6.9%). In 2020, Malt and the Boston Consulting Group (BCG) jointly conducted a survey of more than 2,324 respondents in three countries (France, Germany, Spain) to better understand the dynamics of freelancing in Europe. According to the survey, freelancers are mainly male (65%), over 40 years old and highly educated (> 75% have a 3-year university degree) and more than 80% of respondents work in technology/data, communications/marketing and web/photo/sound design.

Careers As Movement Through Social Space And Driven By The Person Rather Than The Organization

It appears that technological and economic changes have the most important impact on the business world, especially in terms of entrepreneurship and the labor market. More flexible and global labor markets being formed, provide opportunities for individualisation and diversification of labor relations. Therefore, new ways of doing business and working are emerging, consequently affecting individuals' development process on the path of experience and work for one or more organisations – the career (Baruch & Rosenstein, 1992).

According to Patton & McMahon (2006) careers are determined by the social context in which individuals live. As such, they shed light on the relationships between the individual and broader society – organisations, authorised institutions, family, friends, etc. Thus, individuals' careers not only influences organisational performance (Altman & Baruch, 2016), but also personal identity, health, and well-being (Christie & Barling, 2006; Valcour, 2007; Davis et al., 2014). In addition, from an economic perspective, it is important to understand careers because they reflect the following three categories: physical and mental labor used to produce goods and services, human capital reflecting the knowledge and skills that enable people to create, and entrepreneurship as the ability to bring resources together to make a better product or service (Khapova & Arthur, 2011).

Moreover, with new technology, our opportunities and needs grow. Careers occur in a social context (work, home, friends, leisure). Responsibilities for caring for children and the elderly increase, as do job demands (Greenhaus & Kossek, 2014). Faced with these multiple obligations, many people express the need to balance their work with other areas of their lives (Newman, 2011). They no longer stick to one particular organization, there are increasing opportunities to move between organizations and occupations. Work and life are merging, allowing people to make career decisions based on their personal circumstances. As a result, individuals have more responsibility for their career decisions and outcomes. Individuals are therefore more willing to invest in their professional competencies.

To understand "new" careers, from a theoretical perspective, the Boundaryless career perspective (DeFillippi & Arthur, 1994; Arthur & Rousseau, 1996; Sullivan & Arthur, 2006) could be used. According to proponents of the Boundaryless career perspective, career actors are responsible for their own careers, including the development of their competencies (Forrier et al., 2009). Career actors are assumed to be both psychologically and physically mobile. When these actors take advantage of their purported mobility, they are engaging in career management, and this perspective therefore emphasizes the individual's independence from the employer.

Accordingly, the discussion of responsibility for career development has shifted from an organisation-centred to an individual-centred view (Roper et al., 2010). As a result, the focus of career theorists has shifted from the traditional concept of career to understanding the new concepts of career. Today, people are expected to become increasingly mobile and self-directed in terms of their careers, as opposed to traditional careers characterized by hierarchical advancement, organizational career management, low mobility, and full-time employment with a single employer (Greenhaus, et al., 2008). Table 1 compares traditional and contemporary career paradigms.

Table 1. Traditional vs. contemporary paradigms

Traditional	**Contemporary**
Office	Virtual space
Perceived success = career ladder	Success = valued skills
Authority	Influence
Manager/management	Leader/Leadership
Entitlement	Marketability
Loyalty to company	Loyalty to work and self
Salaries and benefits	Contracts and fees
Job security	Personal freedom and control
Identity = job, position, occupation	Identity = contribution to work, family and community
Attention to bosses and managers	Attention to clients and customers
Employees	Vendors, entrepreneurs, team members
Retirement	Self-employment – second career

Source: (adopted from Jarvis, 2003)

Accordingly, traditional office workplaces are being replaced by virtual spaces, such as online work platforms or other applications. Success is no longer just moving up the hierarchical ladder, but changing careers, retraining, and changing specialties frequently, leading to an internal sense of accomplishment (Baruch, 2004; Savickas, 2011). Career development becomes leadership. Leadership means taking action, taking risks, and learning something new (Redekopp, 2006). When employees have the required competencies, they are no longer a resource available to the company, but are seen as inherently entrepreneurial individuals who sell their skills to the company and contribute significantly to its success (Jacobsson, 2003). The primary responsibility for career lies with the individual. As a result, the autonomy of the individual is increasing (Raksnys et al., 2015), as is autonomy in career development and striving for a work-life balance. The delivery of reliable, high-quality services relies on contact-based contracts as nonstandard work arrangements replace full-time employment. To perform such work, one must be confident and self-assured and know how to present and sell one's knowledge (marketability) (Jarvis & Keeley, 2003). With the increasing individualization and self-determination of careers, the category of self-employment and modern (growing) freelance careers in business and academia is gaining more and more attention. The following subchapter presents the demographic characteristics of Slovenian freelancers as well as their reasons for choosing such a career and their perceptions of subjective well-being.

DIGITALLY ENABLED FORM OF WORK- A CASE OF SLOVENIAN FREELANCERS

The empirical study was conducted with a random sample of Slovenian freelancers. To ensure the largest possible response rate, respondents were randomly selected from a list of the GVIN Dun & Bradstreet database, from channels of online work platforms, and from online groups of self-employed persons. In order to obtain a representative sample of freelancers, this research was guided by the theoretical findings and definitions of freelancers. Thus, the study was initially limited to respondents who fall into the entrepreneurial category of self-employed without employees, as freelancers work for themselves (Van den Born & Van Witteloostuijn, 2013).

The questionnaire and final list of freelancers were forwarded to an external contractor who conducted the survey. The external contractor provided a random survey.

In addition, the sample was limited to those who work remotely from home, coworking spaces, or anywhere else where they have access to the necessary resources and who have worked with at least two clients in the past 12 months (Darlington, 2014). Finally, the sample was limited to respondents who freelanced more than 21 hours per week. There were 342 responses to the original survey. After establishing certain limitations for the purposes of the study, 200 valid responses were obtained. Data collection took place from late July 2020 to mid-September 2020.

Basic Characteristics of Slovenian Freelancers

This section describes the characteristics of the freelancers in the study sample based on the control variables included in the study, namely: gender, age, education level, place of work, channels of job search, weekly working hours and business sector.

The following figures illustrate the structure of the sample according to the main control variables selected.

In terms of gender, there is gender gap. There are more male than female freelancers, as shown in Figure 2.

Figure 2. Gender aspect of the respondents (n=200)
Source: (authors)

Traditional	Contemporary
Office	Virtual space
Perceived success = career ladder	Success = valued skills
Authority	Influence
Manager/management	Leader/Leadership
Entitlement	Marketability
Loyalty to company	Loyalty to work and self
Salaries and benefits	Contracts and fees
Job security	Personal freedom and control
Identity = job, position, occupation	Identity = contribution to work, family and community
Attention to bosses and managers	Attention to clients and customers
Employees	Vendors, entrepreneurs, team members
Retirement	Self-employment – second career

In relation to age, the highest number of Slovenian freelancers fall into the 35-44 age group (30.0%), followed by the 45-54 age group (27.9%), while the lowest number are within the 65 and over age group (5.5%) and the 18-24 age group (1.5%), as shown in Figure 3.

Figure 3. Age groups of the respondents (n=200)
Source: (authors)

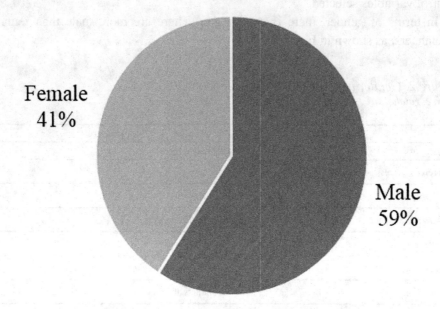

In terms of the level of education (Figure 4), the highest percentage of Slovenian freelancers have completed the second stage of tertiary education (42.2%), while the smallest percentage of them have completed specialized education (9.5%).

Figure 4. The level of education of the freelancers (n=200)
Source: (authors)

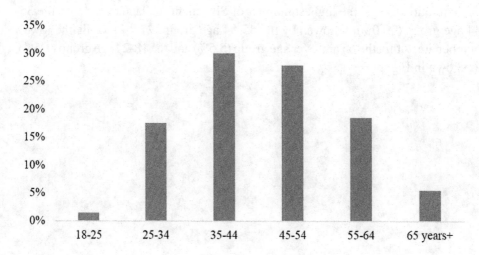

From the survey results presented in Figure 5, it can be seen that respondents mainly work from home. 58% of respondents work from home (regardless of the situation during the pandemic COVID-19), followed by 40% who work in coworking spaces (rented offices), while only 3% work anywhere, provided they have access to the necessary resources.

Figure 5. Place of work (n=200)
Source: (authors)

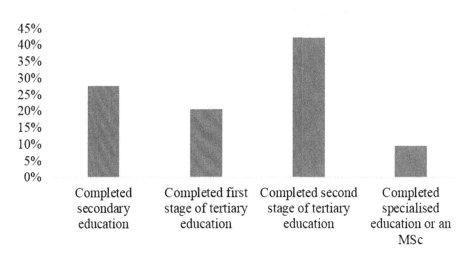

Due to technological advances and the increasing presence of the online labor platforms, Slovenian freelancers still rely more on acquaintances and recommendations than on job search through platforms, but the difference is very small. Figure 6 shows that 48% of respondents find a job through word of mouth (referral), followed by online labor platforms (41%). Slovenian freelancers search for jobs only to a very small extent via social media (6%), specialized newspapers (3%) and HR agencies (2%).

Figure 6. Job search channels (n=200)
Source: (authors)

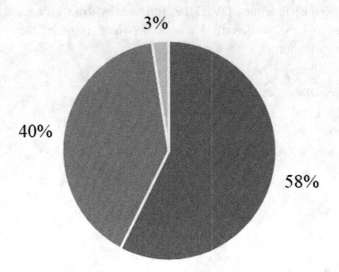

3%

40%

58%

■ Work from home   ■ Coworking space   ■ Anywhere

Looking at the weekly working hours in Figure 7, almost half of the respondents work more than 40 hours per week.

Figure 7. .Weekly working hours as a freelancer (n=200)
Source: (authors)

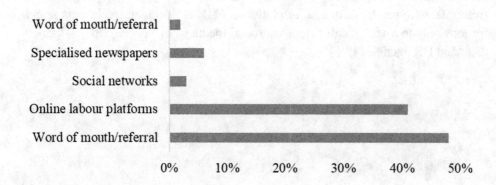

In terms of the type of business sector (Figure 8), according to standard classification, more than 80% of freelancers in Slovenia work in the professional, scientific, technical, information and communication sectors. These types of activities usually include software development, design and multimedia, website development, network and information systems development, writing, and translation.

Figure 8. Business sector (n=200)
Source: (authors)

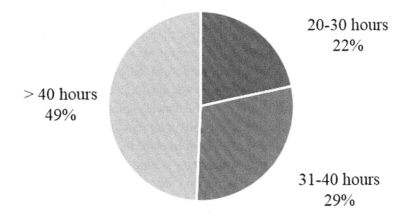

Motives for Freelancing

Furthermore, the study examines the motives that drive freelance careers among Slovenian freelancers. It is investigated whether the motives for freelancing differ or whether most freelancers pursue the same goal. Motivation is an important career factor because it is the product of a person's expectation that a certain effort will lead to an intended performance and that this performance will produce a certain desired outcome for the person (Vroom, 1964). In other words, motivation explains the reasons why someone acts in a certain way. In the academic literature on entrepreneurship, research shows that a person's motives for an entrepreneurial venture range from socioeconomic characteristics, necessities because of the unemployment, market uncertainty, and opportunity, to greater job satisfaction, social status, profit, innovation, independence, self-actualization, and learning (Block & Wagner, 2010; Deli, 2011; Binder & Coad, 2013; Carter et al., 2003; Giacomin et al., 2011, Rebernik & Širec, 2021). Accordingly, it is obvious that the motives are very diverse, which is why many of them are interrelated and complementary.

In addition, the entrepreneurship literature often distinguishes more generally between so-called opportunity and necessity entrepreneurship, i.e., between pull and push motivational factors for choosing an entrepreneurial career (Van Der Zwan et al., 2016). Pull factors generally induce people to engage in entrepreneurial activities. They refer to aspirations or personal preferences for a particular lifestyle, e.g., flexibility, autonomy, higher income, work-life balance, and the ability to work from home, while push factors refer to external forces with negative connotations, e.g., job dissatisfaction, difficulty finding a job, inadequate salary, or inflexible work schedules that drive people to become entrepreneurs out of necessity in order to survive.

This polarization can also be seen with respect to freelance careers. On the one hand, some freelancers choose this profession for reasons of flexibility, work-life balance, autonomy, and professionalism. They work on a project basis and enjoy a high degree of independence and autonomy (Smeaton, 2003). In contrast, there is the second type of freelancer. This type of freelancer typically has fewer skills and is paid less due to underemployment or non-employment (Kitching & Smallbone, 2012). In addition, there are a large number of freelancers who fall between the two types of freelancers described above and enjoy a high degree of freedom in their work, but have to work especially hard to find the next 'gigs'. Moreover, Kitching and Smallbone (2012) report that the number of freelancers is likely to increase as unemployment rises.

For the purposes of this study, Slovenian freelancers' motives for freelancing were identified using a 10-item questionnaire from the first European Survey of Freelancers (Malt & EIPF, 2019), which included questions on entrepreneurial aspirations, flexibility, and extra earning opportunities and necessity. The questionnaire included the statements (reasons for becoming a freelancer), and freelancers could express their agreement or disagreement on a 7-point Likert scale (1: strongly disagree, 7: strongly agree). The statements defining freelancers' motivation are presented in Table 2 along with the results of the descriptive statistics.

Table 2. Descriptive statistics of motivation variables

Motivation (MOTIV)	Mean	Std. error	Std. deviation statistics	Skewness		Kurtosis	
				Statistic	Std. error	Statistic	Std. error
(MOTIV_v1) To have more flexibility (including working from home).	5.86	0.123	1.745	-1.691	0.172	1.867	0.342
(MOTIV_v2) To be able to choose my own projects.	5.93	0.105	1.491	-1.699	0.172	2.606	0.342
(MOTIV_v3) To realize my own business ideas/be entrepreneurial.	5.82	0.108	1.519	-1.454	0.172	1.718	0.343
(MOTIV_v4) To learn new skills.	5.66	0.103	1.451	-1.293	0.172	1.69	0.342
(MOTIV_v5) To explore new passions, career or business opportunities.	5.45	0.116	1.638	-1.032	0.172	0.361	0.343
(MOTIV_v6) To have a better work/life balance.	5.47	0.127	1.793	-1.02	0.172	-0.099	0.342
(MOTIV_v7) To earn more money.	4.95	0.128	1.804	-0.646	0.172	-0.483	0.343
(MOTIV_v8) To provide backup in case I lose my main job.	3.17	0.161	2.27	0.54	0.172	-1.253	0.343
(MOTIV_v9) I could not find a suitable job as an employee.	2.53	0.151	2.136	1.1	0.172	-0.313	0.343
(MOTIV_v10) I was made redundant (or expected to be).	1.48	0.096	1.351	3.136	0.172	9.151	0.343
MOTIV_average	5.17	0.068	0.951	-0.822	0.174	1.713	0.346

Source: (authors)

As can be seen in Table 2, when asked to express their agreement or disagreement with the statements what their reason for freelancing is, the freelancers mostly agreed with the statement MOTIV_v3 *Being able to choose my own projects* (mean: 5.93; std. error: 0.105; std. deviation: 1.491). They also highly agreed with the following statements: (MOTIV_v1) *Having more flexibility (including working from home)* (mean: 5.86; std. error: 0.123; std. deviation: 1.745) and (MOTIV_v3) *Being able to realize my own business ideas/being entrepreneurial* (mean: 5.82; std. error:

0.108; std. deviation: 1.519). The respondents, least agreed with the statement that they chose a freelance career (MOTIV_v10) *because they were made redundant (or expected to be)* (mean: 1.48; std. error: 0.096; std. deviation: 1.351). In addition, the dispersion of responses (std. deviation) is greatest for the statement (MOTIV_v8) *To provide backup in čase I lose my main job* (std. deviation: 2.27), which means that agreement with this statement varies the most in relation to the responses received.

Table 2 also shows the basic statistics for the motivation (MOTIV_average) variable. The formed variable is based on the total assigned estimates for all ten claims calculated on the number of claims. As can be see, the average freelancer's agreement rate with motivation statements was 5.17 (std. error: 0.068; std. deviation: 0.951) indicating that freelancers in average agree more or less with the claims. Also, the coefficient of asymmetry (-0.822) (skewness) indicate that the distribution of MOTIV_average is left asymmetric, while the kurtosis coefficients with positive value (1.713) indicates a peaked distribution (Bastič, 2006, p.7).

Moreover, Figure 9 illustrates that pull factors (motives for autonomy, flexibility, learning and entrepreneurship) prevail more among Slovenian freelancers than push factors (underemployment, unemployment).

Figure 9. Motives for freelancing
Source: (authors)

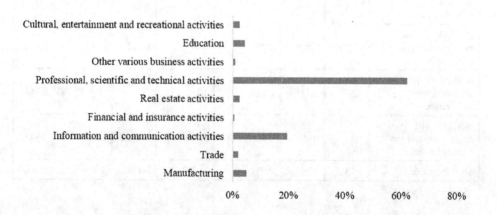

These findings on the motivation of Slovenian freelancers are also in line with the results of the First European Freelance Study (2019), a study based on a survey of almost 1,000 European freelancers, where 76.6% of the participants were freelancers by choice (Malt & EIPF, 2019). The main reason for taking up freelancing was flexibility (46.80%), followed by being able to choose their own projects (37.40%), working from a location of choice (36.9%), being their own boss

(35.6%), and having a better work-life balance (28.40%). These findings are also in line with studies on freelancers in the US. According to the Freelancing in America study (Upwork, 2019), 46% of freelancers believe that freelancing promotes work flexibility. In addition, 71% of freelancers believe that freelancing gives them the ability to do their work from any location.

These findings on the reasons for freelancing also point to the advantages, the positive side of freelancing, in the sense that a freelance career offers more freedom, autonomy, flexibility, new learning opportunities, etc. However, they also raise the question of satisfaction with such a career, which on the other hand is characterized by insecurity, temporary work and questionable social protection for such new careers. In an analysis by Peters et al. (2020), job autonomy emerged as the single most important factor in career satisfaction among female freelancers, confirming the theoretical framework that assumes that when levels of job autonomy are relatively high, intrinsic work motivation can be catalysed, which is reflected in higher levels of career satisfaction. Lo Presti et al. (2018) also suggest that freelancers' control over their work can lead to higher levels of work commitment, and ultimately to a more positive assessment of having achieved, or being able to achieve, work-related values, which is then reflected as higher levels of career success.

Therefore, the following sections examine the subjective success of freelancers. Indeed, there is still a dearth of scholarly work on the perceived benefits of freelance careers. However, researchers have begun to investigate the subjective well-being of self-employed groups and freelancers (Van Stel and Van der Zwan, 2020; Van der Zwan et al., 2020) and the drivers of freelance career (Van den Born and Van Witteloostuijn, 2013).

Subjective Well-Being

The relationship between self-employment and entrepreneurship on the one hand and subjective well-being on the other is a topic of growing scientific interest. The subjective aspect of well-being captures a person's subjective satisfaction with his or her life (Veenhoven, 2012) and is usually measured by the person's evaluation of his or her life domains. According to Erdogan et al. (2012), the following domains of subjective well-being are distinguished in the literature: life satisfaction, job satisfaction, health satisfaction, income satisfaction, leisure satisfaction, satisfaction with health, etc.

Previous findings on self-employment and subjective well-being have traditionally been focused mainly on self-employed individuals' satisfaction with their jobs/ work. There is a clear evidence that the self-employed are significantly more satisfied with their jobs than employees explained by the non-monetary rewards that self-employment offers (Benz and Frey, 2008; Blanchflower, 2000; Binder & Blankenberg, 2020).

The first study to consider freelancers as a subgroup of the self-employed in terms of their life satisfaction and its domains is the study by Zwan et al. (2020). Until then, the life satisfaction literature did not distinguish between freelancers, other self-employed, and employers. They used a respondent self-assessment to define the sample. Respondents were asked whether they were employed or self-employed, and a follow-up question asked the self-employed to indicate whether or not they had employees and whether they were freelance or otherwise self-employed (e.g., operated a business or professional practise, worked for themselves, subcontracted, or were otherwise self-employed). The results suggest the following. Freelancers are significantly more satisfied with their free time than other self-employed individuals, employers, and salaried workers because freelancers are better able to balance their work life with their personal or family life due to their flexibility (as they tend to work from home). Freelancers also score significantly better than salaried workers in terms of life and job satisfaction, but not better than other self-employed persons and employers. This can also be explained by the fact that employers have experienced a higher degree of autonomy (Benz & Frey, 2008). Freelancers are as satisfied with their health as other self-employed workers and employers. Moreover, the significantly lower income satisfaction of freelancers compared to employers found in this study confirms the uncertainty and risk of freelancing (Zwan et al., 2020, p.12). The analysis shows that freelancers are on par with other groups of self-employed people in terms of subjective well-being, despite the uncertainty and risk associated with their project-based work.

The findings of Zwan et al. (2020) draw attention. Indeed, the high leisure, life, and job satisfaction of freelancers compared to salaried workers could contribute to the attractiveness of a freelance career and be an option for salaried workers and a possibility for other self-employed workers. The possibility of changing careers could be an important message to be conveyed by governments focusing on the current issue of improving the work-life balance of citizens. On the other hand, the financial concerns of freelancing might discourage people from pursuing freelance careers. From these considerations, there is a need to further examine the factors that influence subjective success outcomes, i.e., job/career satisfaction, life satisfaction, and income satisfaction, in order to better understand success drivers of freelancers as a new subgroup of the self-employed and to facilitate their entrepreneurial ventures.

The subjective well-being of Slovenian freelancers was examined in terms of job and career, income and life satisfaction. Overall job satisfaction is defined as a pleasant or positive emotional state resulting from one's evaluation of one's job or job experiences. A limitation of using job satisfaction as an indicator of career success is that a person may be very satisfied with his or her current job even though he or she is dissatisfied with his or her career. And the other way around. Although high job satisfaction may contribute to the impression that one has a successful career, it is clear that career success cannot be reduced to job satisfaction. Job satisfaction has traditionally been measured using the three-part scale developed by Judge et al. (1994) (Cronbach alpha=0.78), while career satisfaction is usually measured using the widely used Greenhaus et al. (1990) career satisfaction scale (Cronbach alpha=0.85). Although such standardized measures of career success generally have an acceptable degree of internal consistency, these characteristics are not necessarily sufficient to provide a valid assessment of individual respondents' career success. In our case job/career satisfaction was measured using the combined career and job satisfaction scale adapted from Calhoun (2015), based on studies by Bray and Howard (1980), Judge and Bretz (1994), and Greenhaus et al. (1990). Sample items were "I am satisfied with the progress I have made toward meeting my overall career goals" and "I am satisfied with the progress I have made toward meeting my goals for advancement." In addition, a single measurement item was used to measure income satisfaction, which was also used in the work of Sutherland (2013), Falco et al. (2015), and Reuschke (2019).

In addition, the life satisfaction dimension (also referred to as life success) is also important because, according to Judge and Bretz (1994), adding life satisfaction also recognizes the importance of work-life balance (Greenhaus & Beutell, 1985). The Satisfaction with Life Scale (SWLS) was originally developed by Diener, et al. (1985) and was intended as a brief assessment of a person's general sense of satisfaction with his or her life as a whole and has good psychometric properties (Pavot & Diener, 1993). In this study, this particular dimension was measured using the shorter version (Cronbach alpha= 0.70) of the 4-item scale proposed by Gattiker and Larwood (1986). Sample items were "I am satisfied with my life overall" and "I am enjoying my non-work activities."

Therefore, the research examined Slovenian freelancers' subjective well-being measuring financial (income satisfaction) and non-financial aspect (job and career satisfaction and life satisfaction). The results of descriptive statistics are showed in Table 3.

Table 3. Descriptive statistics of subjective well-being dimensions

Subjective success	Mean	Std. error	Std. deviation statistics	Skewness		Kurtosis	
				Statistic	Std. error	Statistic	Std. error
Financial aspect of subjective well-being	5.29	0.093	1.312	-0.883	0.173	0.961	0.344
Non-financial aspect of subjective well-being	5.94	0.062	0.854	-1.893	0.175	7.226	0.349

Source: (authors)

Figure 10 shows that, on average, freelancers are satisfied with the financial aspect of subjective well-being (income satisfaction). On a 7-point Likert scale, the mean value of income satisfaction is 5.29 (std. error: 0.093; std. deviation: 1.312). However, freelancers' satisfaction with non-financial aspects of subjective well-being (job and career satisfaction, life satisfaction) on the 7-point Likert scale is higher, 5.94 (std. error: 0.093; std. deviation: 1.312), confirming previous studies. Figure 10 also shows that the mean score for life satisfaction is 6.095 (std. error: 0.083; std. deviation: 1.169), while the mean score for job and career satisfaction is slightly lower at 5.815 (std. error: 0.08; std. deviation: 1.139). It can be concluded from the coefficients of asymmetry (-0.692) (skewness) that the distribution of the financial and non-financial aspects of subjective well-being are left asymmetric, while the kurtosis coefficients with positive values indicate a peaked distribution (Bastič, 2006, p.7).

Figure 10. Mean scores of subjective well-being dimensions
Source: authors

Motivation (MOTIV)	Mean	Std. error	Std. deviation statistics	Skewness		Kurtosis	
				Statistic	Std. error	Statistic	Std. error
(MOTIV_v1) To have more flexibility (including working from home).	5.86	0.123	1.745	-1.691	0.172	1.867	0.342
(MOTIV_v2) To be able to choose my own projects.	5.93	0.105	1.491	-1.699	0.172	2.606	0.342
(MOTIV_v3) To realize my own business ideas/be entrepreneurial.	5.82	0.108	1.519	-1.454	0.172	1.718	0.343
(MOTIV_v4) To learn new skills.	5.66	0.103	1.451	-1.293	0.172	1.69	0.342
(MOTIV_v5) To explore new passions, career or business opportunities.	5.45	0.116	1.638	-1.032	0.172	0.361	0.343
(MOTIV_v6) To have a better work/life balance.	5.47	0.127	1.793	-1.02	0.172	-0.099	0.342
(MOTIV_v7) To earn more money.	4.95	0.128	1.804	-0.646	0.172	-0.483	0.343
(MOTIV_v8) To provide backup in case I lose my main job.	3.17	0.161	2.27	0.54	0.172	-1.253	0.343
(MOTIV_v9) I could not find a suitable job as an employee.	2.53	0.151	2.136	1.1	0.172	-0.313	0.343
(MOTIV_v10) I was made redundant (or expected to be).	1.48	0.096	1.351	3.136	0.172	9.151	0.343
MOTIV_average	5.17	0.068	0.951	-0.822	0.174	1.713	0.346

Examining the subjective dimensions of success seems particularly relevant, as the challenge of achieving a balance between job, career, and personal life (family) may have implications for social policy. Moreover, incorporating life satisfaction into models of career success may reveal the state of affairs in a given country and encourage the government to improve the policy implications of social protection and well-being.

SOLUTIONS AND POLICY RECOMMENDATIONS

According to the results, freelancing can be an attractive labor market option for employees who want to combine their professional lives with their nonprofessional lives in a satisfying way. The possibility of changing careers could be an important message to be conveyed by governments and companies focused on the current issue of improving working conditions and work-life balance for their citizens.

The analysis shows that freelancers exhibit high levels of subjective satisfaction despite the uncertainty and risk associated with their project-based work. Many people now choose gig work over traditional employment models because they find more flexibility, autonomy and personal fulfilment in it than in full-time employment with a single employer. However according to the additional, international results of the survey of European freelancers, more than half of the respondents felt that "freelancers should be better recognised and supported by policy makers" and 37% expressed simplification of administrative procedures as one of their top two concerns (Malt & EIPF, 2019).

In such a challenging environment, the need for career guidance services for people at different stages of life becomes increasingly important. Therefore, policies to support effective transitions into and through the labor market should take into account that workers increasingly need additional skills, knowledge, and understanding of the labor market under current economic conditions. In addition, policymakers must also be able to consider internal, deeper psychological constructs that drive people to make particular career choices by identifying individual aspirations and desires. Therefore, policymakers should create innovative learning environments to facilitate better career choice and development and respond appropriately to technological, social, and economic trends (European Commission, 2019).

First of all, policymakers should ensure that workers are equipped with the right skills. More than ever, educational institutions should work hand-in-hand with the corporate sector to prepare young people for a rapidly changing work environment by fostering their entrepreneurial competencies along with digital skills. Therefore, the gig economy could be more inclusive of young people, but not only of them, but also of women, as such work arrangements allow more flexibility in balancing work and family life.

In addition, career choices are often made without being properly informed or knowing all the options. In this sense, the establishment of an effective career guidance service within the employment agencies tailored for new forms of work would be very beneficial for societies and their citizens.

In addition, policymakers in some OECD countries have expressed concern about the quality of self-employment and the potentially aggravating features of the gig economy. Policymakers must support the growing gig worker sector and give them the opportunity to work while being socially secure. The European Commission has also recognized this and has proposed an EU directive (European Commission, 2021) to update and adapt current legislation to gig workers in order to secure contracts, guaranteed minimum wages, sick leave and paid vacations. The goal of the European Commission's proposed directive is to end bogus self-employment in the European Union. Some member states are not waiting for directives from the European Union, but have already joined forces to democratize self-employment and bureaucracy and extend existing social security coverage to non-standard workers, such as Spain and France. Spain has introduced a legal status called *Autonomo* for freelancers for 2023. France has already introduced a much-simplified status in 2011 like microenterprise, which allows a freelancer to obtain a registration number in less than two days and charge clients up to EUR 70,000 per year with limited taxation, with the aim of stimulating the growth of the talent economy in France (Malt, 2021). In addition, France, for example, also requires platforms to cover the cost of accident insurance for the self-employed (United Nations, 2022). Policy debate has been spurred. However, the legal framework in Slovenia, as in other parts of the world, is not designed to ensure flexibility and social security at the same time. Attempts to fit this new reality into the outdated legal framework are leading to various measures, ranging from social dialogue at the European and national levels to worker protection and legislative measures on the platform economy. This requires a move away from one-size-fits-all solutions to tailored measures that consider the unique opportunities and challenges of different types of new forms of work.

FUTURE RESEARCH DIRECTIONS

The study has several limitations that lead to recommendations for further research. First, there is still too little literature on freelancers in a national context. Based on the findings of this chapter, it is clear that the characteristics and influencing factors associated with digitally enabled careers such as freelancing deserve more attention from authors and designers of labor, social, and economic policy, as the segmentation of such a workforce and theoretical background, along with empirical evidence, represent an important research priority for understanding the future of work.

To gain more comprehensive insight into freelance careers, future research could aim to develop a conceptual model that combines internal (such as personality traits, motivation, human and social capital) and additional external factors, i.e., ecosystem perceptions of readiness and support for such new careers, consideration of government programmes, and support from the legal system. Further implications of potential moderators influencing these relationships could be explored. In addition, different relationships could be explored based on control variables (e.g., gender, age, education). Such models would also reflect the use of more complex methods such as partial least squares structural equation or regression analysis that many other programmes such as WarpPLS, SPSS, AMOS, or SmartPLS use.

Van den Born and Van Witteloostuijn's study is the first large-scale quantitative study of freelancers' career drivers. It also improves the understanding of modern career success by bridging the gap between career and entrepreneurship literature. In addition, the model incorporates the external environment. This model could be used and adapted for the careers of freelancers in small businesses in Slovenia. Based on this, it would be possible to identify shortcoming of the freelancers and differences in the implementation of policies and the creation of an appropriate external environment for freelancers, thus providing a broad overview of appropriate approaches to enhance their careers.

Other research possibilities include investigating to what extent Slovenian companies involve freelancers in their entrepreneurial activities and whether companies use business projects that are exclusively targeted at freelancers in order to explore the economic value of freelancers to an economy.

In addition, there are clear opportunities for future research to expand the measurement instrument to include new constructs in freelancers' career development and to conduct in-depth interviews to gain better insight.

In addition, the study is a cross-sectional study. A longitudinal design would reflect the impact of individual perceptions on specific aspects over time and would most likely reveal much stronger relationships, which would also provide an opportunity to expand the scope of the research.

CONCLUSION

In summary, the results on digitally enabled forms of work specifically for Slovenian freelancers show that they are mostly between 35 and 44 years old, are mainly male, have a high level of education, work from home, find their job mostly through references and online work platforms, mostly work more than 40 hours per week, and that more than 80% of freelancers in Slovenia work in the fields of science, technology, information and communication. Moreover, Slovenian freelancers are most fond of the flexibility of their work. Moreover, they have shown that their job and career, as well as their income, bring a high level of satisfaction and ultimately life satisfaction. Therefore, the statements that working hard, working for an organization, working fixed hours, and having a steady job promote career well-being are not in line with today's career trends. Therefore, policy makers should make more efforts to recognize the specifics of the gig economy, especially freelancing as a new market trend, as a model that impacts society and the future of work, in order to create appropriate conditions for the future creation of new value in the (digital) market.

ACKNOWLEDGMENT

This research was supported by the Slovenian Research Agency [research core funding No. P5–0023].

REFERENCES

Abele, A. E., & Spurk, D. (2009). How do objective and subjective career success interrelate over time? *Journal of Occupational and Organizational Psychology*, *82*(4), 803–824. doi:10.1348/096317909X470924

Advisory Gropup, A. R. C. 2020. *What is Digitization, Digitalization, and Digital Transformation?* ARCweb. https://www.arcweb.com/blog/what-digitization-digitalization-digital-transformation

Altman, Y., & Baruch, Y. (2012). Global self-initiated corporate expatriate careers: A new era in international assignments? *Personnel Review*, *41*(2), 233–255. doi:10.1108/00483481211200051

Arthur, M. B., & Rousseau, D. M. (1996). The Boundaryless Career as a New Employment Principle. In M. B. Arthur amd D. M. Rousseau (eds.) The Boundaryless Career, pp. 3-20. Oxford University Press.

Audrin, C., & Audrin, B. (2022). Key factors in digital literacy in learning and education: A systematic literature review using text mining. *Education and Information Technologies*, *27*(6), 1–25. doi:10.100710639-021-10832-5

Barnes, S. A., Green, A., & De Hoyos, M. (2015). Crowdsourcing and work: Individual factors and circumstances influencing employability. *New Technology, Work and Employment*, *30*(1), 16–31. doi:10.1111/ntwe.12043

Baruch, Y. (2004). Transforming careers: from linear to multidirectional career paths: organizational and individual perspectives. *Career Development International*, *9*(1), 58–73. doi:10.1108/13620430410518147

Baruch, Y. (2006). Career development in organizations and beyond: Balancing traditional and contemporary viewpoints. *Human Resource Management Review*, *16*(2), 125–138. doi:10.1016/j.hrmr.2006.03.002

Baruch, Y., & Rosenstein, E. (1992). Human resource management in Israeli firms: Planning and managing careers in high technology organizations. *International Journal of Human Resource Management*, *3*(3), 477–495. doi:10.1080/09585199200000161

Benz, M., & Frey, B. S. (2008). The value of doing what you like: Evidence from the self-employed in 23 countries. *Journal of Economic Behavior & Organization*, *68*(3-4), 445–455. doi:10.1016/j.jebo.2006.10.014

Binder, M. (2018). *The way to wellbeing. A multidimensional strategy for improving wellbeing of the self-employed.* Center for research on self-employment. http://crse.co.uk/sites/default/files/The%20Way%20to%20Wellbeing%20Full%20Report_0.pdf

Binder, M., & Blankenberg, A. K. (2020). Self-employment and subjective well-being. Handbook of Labor, Human Resources and Population Economics, 1-25.

Blanchflower, D. G. (2000). Self-employment in OECD countries. *Labour Economics*, *7*(5), 471–505. doi:10.1016/S0927-5371(00)00011-7

Block, J. H., & Wagner, M. (2010). Necessity and Opportunity Entrepreneurs in Germany: Characteristics and Earnings Differentials. *Schmalenbach Business Review*, *62*(2), 154–174. doi:10.1007/BF03396803

Bray, J. H., & Howard, G. S. (1980). Methodological considerations in the evaluation of a teacher-training program. *Journal of Educational Psychology*, *72*(1), 62–70. doi:10.1037/0022-0663.72.1.62

Brennen, J. S., & Kreiss, D. (2016a). Information society. *The international encyclopedia of communication theory and philosophy*, 1-8.

Brennen, J. S., & Kreiss, D. (2016b). Digitalization. *The international encyclopedia of communication theory and philosophy*, 1-11.

Brynjolfsson, E., & Kahin, B. (Eds.). (2002). *Understanding the digital economy: data, tools, and research.* MIT press.

Cahuc, P., & Postel-Vinay, F. (2002). Temporary jobs, employment protection and labor market performance. *Labour Economics*, *9*(1), 63–91. doi:10.1016/S0927-5371(01)00051-3

Calhoun, J. (2015). *Antacedents and Consequences of Lodging Employees' Career Success: An Application of Motivational Theories* [Doctoral dissertation, Auburn University, USA].

Carter, N. M., Gartner, W. B., Shaver, K. G., & Gatewood, E. J. (2003). The Career Reasons of Nascent Entrepreneurs. *Journal of Business Venturing, 18*(1), 13–39. doi:10.1016/S0883-9026(02)00078-2

Chen, C. L. (2019). Value creation by SMEs participating in global value chains under industry 4.0 trend: Case study of textile industry in Taiwan. *Journal of Global Information Technology Management, 22*(2), 120–145. doi:10.1080/1097 198X.2019.1603512

Christie, A., & Barling, J. (2006). Careers and health. Encyclopedia of career development, 1, 158-62.

Darlington, N. (2014). Freelancer vs. Contractor vs. Employee: What Are You Being Hired As. *Freshbooks.* https://www.freshbooks.com/ blog/are-you-being-hired-as-an-employee-or-freelancer

Davenport, T. H. (2005). *Thinking for a living: how to get better performances and results from knowledge workers.* Harvard Business Press.

Davis, S. N., Shevchuk, A., & Strebkov, D. (2014). Pathways to satisfaction with work-life balance: The case of Russian-language internet freelancers. *Journal of Family and Economic Issues, 35*(4), 542–556. doi:10.100710834-013-9380-1

De Vos, A., & Van der Heijden, B. I. (2017). Current thinking on contemporary careers: The key roles of sustainable HRM and sustainability of careers. *Current Opinion in Environmental Sustainability, 28*, 41–50. doi:10.1016/j.cosust.2017.07.003

DeFillippi, R. J., & Arthur, M. B. (1994). The boundaryless career: A competency-based perspective. *Journal of Organizational Behavior, 15*(4), 307–324. doi:10.1002/job.4030150403

Deli, F. (2011). Opportunity and Necessity Entrepreneurship: Local Unemployment and the Small Firm Effect. *Journal of Management Policy and Practice, 12*(4), 38–57.

Deutschkron & Pearce. (2019). Sixth annual "Freelancing in America" study finds that more people than ever see freelancing as a long-term career path. *Buisnesswire.* https://www.businesswire.com/news/home/20191003005032/en/Sixth-annual-%E2%80%9CFreelancing-America%E2%80%9D-study-finds-people .

Diener, E. D., Emmons, R. A., Larsen, R. J., & Griffin, S. (1985). The satisfaction with life scale. *Journal of Personality Assessment, 49*(1), 71–75.

Diener, E. D., Emmons, R. A., Larsen, R. J., & Griffin, S. (1985). The satisfaction with life scale. *Journal of Personality Assessment, 49*(1), 71–75. doi:10.120715327752jpa4901_13 PMID:16367493

European Commission. (2010b). *A Digital Agenda for Europe*. European Commission. https://eur-lex.europa.eu/LexUriServ/LexUriServ.do?uri=COM:2010:0245:FIN:EN:PDF

European Commission. (2015b). *A Digital Single Market Strategy for Europe*. EC.https://eur-lex.europa.eu/legal-content/EN/TXT/PDF/?uri=CELEX:52015DC0192&from=FI

European Commission. (2019). *Digital Economy and Society Index (DESI) 2019*. EC. https://data.consilium.europa.eu/doc/document/ST-10211-2019-INIT/en/pdf

European Commission. (2021). *Commission proposals to improve the working conditions of people working through digital labour platforms*. EC. https://ec.europa.eu/commission/presscorner/detail/en/ip_21_6605

European Commission. (2021d). *Commission proposals to improve the working conditions of people working through digital labor platforms*. EC. https://ec.europa.eu/social/main.jsp?langId=en&catId=89&newsId=10120&furtherNews=yes

European Commission. (2019). High-Level Expert Group on the Impact of the Digital Transformation on EU Labor Markets. EC. https://www.voced.edu.au/content/ngv:82994

Falco, P., Maloney, W. F., Rijkers, B., & Sarrias, M. (2015). Heterogeneity in subjective wellbeing: An application to occupational allocation in Africa. *Journal of Economic Behavior & Organization*, *111*, 137–153. doi:10.1016/j.jebo.2014.12.022

Forrier, A., Sels, L., & Stynen, D. (2009). Career mobility at the intersection between agent and structure: A conceptual model. *Journal of Occupational and Organizational Psychology*, *82*(4), 739–759. doi:10.1348/096317909X470933

Fraser, J., & Gold, M. (2001). 'Portfolio workers': Autonomy and control amongst freelance translators. *Work, Employment and Society*, *15*(4), 679–697.

Gallup (Firm). (2018). The gig economy and alternative work arrangements. *Gallup's Perspective*.

Gattiker, U. E., & Larwood, L. (1986). Subjective career success: A study of managers and support personnel. *Journal of Business and Psychology*, *1*(2), 78–94. doi:10.1007/BF01018805

Giacomin, O., Janssen, F., Pruett, M., Shinnar, R. S., Llopis, F., & Toney, B. (2011). Entrepreneurial Intentions, Motivations and Barriers: Differences Among American, Asian and European Students. *The International Entrepreneurship and Management Journal*, *7*(2), 219–238. doi:10.100711365-010-0155-y

Grant, J., & Schofield, M. (2007). Career-long supervision: Patterns and perspectives. *Counselling & Psychotherapy Research*, *7*(1), 3–11. doi:10.1080/14733140601140899

Greenhaus, J. H., & Beutell, N. J. (1985). Sources of conflict between work and family roles. *Academy of Management Review*, *10*(1), 76–88. doi:10.2307/258214

Greenhaus, J. H., Callanan, G. A., & DiRenzo, M. (2008). A boundaryless perspective on careers. Handbook of organizational behavior, 1, 277-299.

Greenhaus, J. H., & Kossek, E. E. (2014). The contemporary career: A work–home perspective. *Annual Review of Organizational Psychology and Organizational Behavior*, *1*(1), 361–388. doi:10.1146/annurev-orgpsych-031413-091324

Greenhaus, J. H., Parasuraman, S., & Wormley, W. M. (1990). Effects of race on organizational experiences, job performance evaluations, and career outcomes. *Academy of Management Journal*, *33*(1), 64–86. doi:10.2307/256352

Gvin Dun & Bradstreet. (2019). [Data set]. https://accounts.bisnode.si/Authenticat e/?product=0&language=en-US&returnUrl=https%3a%2f%2faccounts.bisnode.si %2fHome%2f%3fproduct%3d0%26language%3den-US

Hayes, H. (2004). The role of libraries in the knowledge economy. *Serials*, *17*(3), 231–238. doi:10.1629/17231

International Monetary Fund (IMF). (2000). Globalization: Treats or opportunity. *IMF Publications*. https://www.imf.org/external/np/exr/ib/2000/041200to.htm#II

IPSE. (2020). The Cost of COVID: How the Pandemic Is Affecting the Self-Employed. IPSE. https://www.ipse.co.uk/resource/the-cost-of-covid.html

Isaksson, A. J., Harjunkoski, I., & Sand, G. (2018). The impact of digitalization on the future of control and operations. *Computers & Chemical Engineering*, *114*, 122–129. doi:10.1016/j.compchemeng.2017.10.037

Jacobsson, K. (2003). European Politic for Employability: The Political Discourse on Employability of the EU and the OECD. In C. Garsten, & K. Jacobsson. (eds.). Learning to Be Employable. New Agendas on Work, Responsibility, and Learning in a Globalizing World. Palgrave Macmillan.

Jarvis, P. S. (2003). *Career Management Paradigm Shift: Prosperity for Citizens*. Windfalls for Governments.

Jarvis, P. S., & Keeley, E. S. (2003). From vocational decision making to career building: Blueprint, real games, and school counseling. *Professional School Counseling*, *6*(4), 244–250.

Jenkins, K. (2017). *Exploring the UK freelance workforce in 2016*. Small Business Research Centre.

Judge, T. A., & Bretz, R. D. Jr. (1994). Political influence behavior and career success. *Journal of Management*, *20*(1), 43–65. doi:10.1177/014920639402000103

Judge, T. A., Higgins, C. A., Thoresen, C. J., & Barrick, M. R. (1999). The big five personality traits, general mental ability, and career success across the life span. *Personnel Psychology*, *52*(3), 621–652. doi:10.1111/j.1744-6570.1999.tb00174.x

Karimi, J., & Walter, Z. (2021). The role of entrepreneurial agility in digital entrepreneurship and creating value in response to digital disruption in the newspaper industry. *Sustainability*, *13*(5), 2741. doi:10.3390u13052741

Kenton, W. (2020). 3-D Printing. *Investopedia*. https://www.investopedia.com/terms/1/3dprinting.asp

Khapova, S. N., & Arthur, M. B. (2011). Interdisciplinary approaches to contemporary career studies. *Human Relations*, *64*(1), 3–17. doi:10.1177/0018726710384294

Kitching, J., & Smallbone, D. (2012). Are freelancers a neglected form of small business? *Journal of Small Business and Enterprise Development*, *19*(1), 74–91. doi:10.1108/14626001211196415

Kunda, G., Barley, S. R., & Evans, J. (2002). Why do Contractors Contract? The Experience of Highly Skilled Professionals in a Contingent Labor Market. *Industrial & Labor Relations Review*, *55*(2), 234–261. doi:10.1177/001979390205500203

Lee, K. H., Slattery, O., Lu, R., Tang, X., & McCrary, V. (2002). The state of the art and practice in digital preservation. *Journal of Research of the National Institute of Standards and Technology*, *107*(1), 93. doi:10.6028/jres.107.010 PMID:27446721

Lo Presti, A., Pluviano, S., & Briscoe, J. P. (2018). Are freelancers a breed apart? The role of protean and boundaryless career attitudes in employability and career success. *Human Resource Management Journal*, *28*(3), 427–442. doi:10.1111/1748-8583.12188

Locke, E. A., Sirota, D., & Wolfson, A. D. (1976). An experimental case study of the successes and failures of job enrichment in a government agency. *The Journal of Applied Psychology*, *61*(6), 701–711. doi:10.1037/0021-9010.61.6.701

Malt, Q. D. (2021). Overview of the European Freelance Industry. *Medium*. https://medium.com/@reshaping_work/overview-of-the-european-freelance-industry-c464b2497960

Malt & EFIP. (2019). The state of European Freelancing in 2018 – results of the first European freelancers' survey. *Malt*. https://news.malt.com/en-gb/2019/02/12/the-state-of-european-freelancing-in-2018-results-of-the-first-european-freelancers-survey-2/

Malt and Boston Consulting Group. (2021). Freelancing in Europe. *Malt*. https://web-assets.bcg.com/77/62/07a1c84f4be6b671ca10ec16f6f1/malt-bcg-freelancing-in-europe-2021.pdf

Martínez Lucio, M., & MacKenzie, R. (2017). The state and the regulation of work and employment: Theoretical contributions, forgotten lessons and new forms of engagement. *International Journal of Human Resource Management, 28*(21), 2983–3002. doi:10.1080/09585192.2017.1363796

McKinsey Global Institute. (2016). Independent work: Choice, necessity, and the gig economy. *Mckinsey*. https://www.mckinsey.com/featured-insights/employment-and-growth/independent-work-choice-necessity-and-the-gig-economy

.Musek, J. (2017). The general factor of personality: Ten years after. *Psihologijske teme, 26*(1), 61-87.

Muszyński, K., Pulignano, V., & Domecka, M. (2022). *Self-employment in the platform economy and the quality of work. Problems and challenges during the COVID-19 pandemic. Draft for comment.* OECD.

Newman, K. L. (2011). Sustainable careers. *Organizational Dynamics, 40*(2), 136–143. doi:10.1016/j.orgdyn.2011.01.008

Ng, T. W., & Feldman, D. C. (2014). Subjective career success: A meta-analytic review. *Journal of Vocational Behavior, 85*(2), 169–179. doi:10.1016/j.jvb.2014.06.001

OECD. (2018). *Good Jobs for All in a Changing World of Work: The OECD Jobs Strategy.* OECD Publishing.

OECD. (2019). *The missing entrepreneurs 2019: policies for inclusive entrepreneurship.* OECD Publications Centre.

OECD. (2021a). Digital trade. *OECD*. https://www.oecd.org/trade/topics/digital-trade/

OECD. (2021b). *Model Reporting Rules for Digital Platforms: International Exchange Framework and Optional Module for Sale of Goods.* OECD.

OLI. (2020). The Online Labor Index. *OLI*. https://ilabor.oii.ox.ac.uk/how-many-online-workers/

Partington, R. (2019). *Gig economy in Britain doubles, accounting for 4.7 million workers. The Guardian.* https://www.theguardian.com/business/2019/jun/28/gig-economy-in-britain-doubles-accounting-for-47-million-workers

Partners, M. B. O. (2021.) The great realization. *MBO Partners.* https://www.mbopartners.com/state-of-independence/ .

Patton, W., & McMahon, M. (2006). The systems theory framework of career development and counseling: Connecting theory and practice. *International Journal for the Advancement of Counseling*, *28*(2), 153–166. doi:10.100710447-005-9010-1

Pavot, W., & Diener, E. (1993). The affective and cognitive context of self-reported measures of subjective well-being. *Social Indicators Research*, *28*(1), 1–20. doi:10.1007/BF01086714

Pesole, A., Brancati, U., Fernández-Macías, E., Biagi, F., & Gonzalez Vazquez, I. (2018). *Platform workers in Europe.* Publications Office of the European Union.

Peters, P., Blomme, R., De Jager, W., & Van Der Heijden, B. (2020). The impact of work-related values and work control on the career satisfaction of female freelancers. *Small Business Economics*, *55*(2), 493–506. doi:10.100711187-019-00247-5

Raksnys, A. V., Valickas, A., & Valickiene, R. P. (2015). Transformation of career concept and its effect on career management in organizations. *Human Resources Management & Ergonomics*, *9*(2), 117–128.

Rasdi, R. M., Ismail, M., Uli, J., & Noah, S. M. (2009). Career aspirations and career success among managers in the Malaysian public sector. *Research Journal of International Studies*, *9*(3), 21–35.

Rebernik, M. & Širec, K. (2022). *Vzdržljivost podjetniške aktivnosti: GEM Slovenija 2021.* Maribor: Univerzitetna založba. doi:10.18690/um.epf.3.2022

Redekopp, D., Hache, L., & Jarvis, P. (2006). Blueprint for life/work design. National Life/Work Centre, Canada Career Information Partnership & Human Resources Development Canada.

Reuschke, D. (2019). The subjective well-being of homeworkers across life domains. *Environment and Planning A. Economy and Space*, *51*(6), 1326–1349.

Rhein, T. and Walwei, U. (2018). Forms of Employment in European Comparison. *IAB-Forum.* https://www.iabhttps://www.iab-forum.de/en/forms-of-employment-in-european-comparison/forum.de/en/forms-of-employment-in-european-comparison/.

Right, O. G. S. (2016). *Assessing and Anticipating Changing Skill Needs.* Organisation for Economic Co-Operation and Development OECD.

Roper, J., Ganesh, S., & Inkson, K. (2010). Neoliberalism and knowledge interests in boundaryless careers discourse. *Work, Employment and Society, 24*(4), 661–679. doi:10.1177/0950017010380630

Roy, G., & Shrivastava, A. K. (2020). Future of gig economy: Opportunities and challenges. *IMI Konnect, 9*(1), 14–27.

Sapsed, J., Camerani, R., Masucci, M., Petermann, M., Rajguru, M., Jones, P., & Sussex, W. (2015). *Brighton fuse 2: Freelancers in the creative, digital, IT economy.* AHRC.

Savickas, M. L. (2011). Reshaping the story of career counselling. In *Shaping the story* (pp. 1–3). Brill Sense.

Schwab, K. (2016). The fourth industrial revolution. *Cologny: World Economic Forum.*

Schwellnus, C., Geva, A., & Pak Mathilde, V. R. (2019). Gig economy platforms: boon or bane? Organisation for Economic Co-operation and Development. *Economics department working papers*, 1550.

Seibert, S. E., & Kraimer, M. L. (2001). The five-factor model of personality and career success. *Journal of Vocational Behavior, 58*(1), 1–21. doi:10.1006/jvbe.2000.1757

Spajic, D. J. (2022). The Future of Employment - 30 Telling Gig Economy Statistics. *Small Biz Genius.* https://www.smallbizgenius.net/by-the-numbers/gig-economy-statistics/#gref

Spurk, D., Hirschi, A., & Dries, N. (2019). Antecedents and outcomes of objective versus subjective career success: Competing perspectives and future directions. *Journal of Management, 45*(1), 35–69. doi:10.1177/0149206318786563

Sullivan, S. E., & Arthur, M. B. (2006). The evolution of the boundaryless career concept: Examining physical and psychological mobility. *Journal of Vocational Behavior, 69*(1), 19–29. doi:10.1016/j.jvb.2005.09.001

Sutherland, J. (2013, October). Employment status and job satisfaction. In *Evidence-based HRM: a Global Forum for Empirical Scholarship* (Vol. 1, pp. 187-216). Emerald Group Publishing Limited. 10.1108/EBHRM-08-2012-0008

Tran, M., & Sokas, R. K. (2017). The gig economy and contingent work: An occupational health assessment. *Journal of Occupational and Environmental Medicine, 59*(4), e63–e66. doi:10.1097/JOM.0000000000000977 PMID:28244887

United Nations. (2021). *Digitally enabled new forms of work and policy implications for labor regulation frameworks and social protection systems.* UN. https://www. un.org/development/desa/dspd/2021/09/digitally-enabled-new-forms-of-work-and-policy-implications-for-labor-regulation-frameworks-and-social-protection-systems/

Upwork. (2019). Sixth annual "Freelancing in America" study finds that more people than ever see freelancing as a long-term career path. *Upwork.* https://www.upwork.com/press/releases/freelancing-in-america-2019

Upwork. (2021). Upwork Study Finds 59 Million Americans Freelancing Amid Turbulent Labor Market. *Upwork.* https://www.upwork.com/press/releases/upwork-study-finds-59-million-americans-freelancing-amid-turbulent-labor-market

Valcour, M. (2007). Work-based resources as moderators of the relationship between work hours and satisfaction with work-family balance. *The Journal of Applied Psychology, 92*(6), 1512–1523. doi:10.1037/0021-9010.92.6.1512 PMID:18020793

Van den Born, A., & Van Witteloostuijn, A. (2013). Drivers of freelance career success. *Journal of Organizational Behavior, 34*(1), 24–46. doi:10.1002/job.1786

Van der Zwan, P., Hessels, J., & Burger, M. (2020). Happy free willies? Investigating the relationship between freelancing and subjective well-being. *Small Business Economics, 55*(2), 475–491. doi:10.100711187-019-00246-6

Van der Zwan, P., Thurik, R., Verheul, I., & Hessels, J. (2016). Factors influencing the entrepreneurial engagement of opportunity and necessity entrepreneurs. *Eurasian Business Review, 6*(3), 273–295. doi:10.100740821-016-0065-1

Van Stel, A., & Van der Zwan, P. (2020). Analyzing the changing education distributions of solo self-employed workers and employer entrepreneurs in Europe. *Small Business Economics, 55*(2), 429–445. doi:10.100711187-019-00243-9

Veenhoven, R. (2012). Happiness: Also known as "life satisfaction" and "subjective well-being." In *Handbook of social indicators and quality of life research* (pp. 63–77). Springer. doi:10.1007/978-94-007-2421-1_3

Vroom, V.H. (1964). Work and motivation. *Wiley.*

Warner, K. S., & Wäger, M. (2019). Building dynamic capabilities for digital transformation: An ongoing process of strategic renewal. *Long Range Planning, 52*(3), 326–349. doi:10.1016/j.lrp.2018.12.001

Wood, A. J., Lehdonvirta, V., & Graham, M. (2018). Workers of the Internet unite? Online freelancer organisation among remote gig economy workers in six Asian and African countries. *New Technology, Work and Employment, 33*(2), 95–112. doi:10.1111/ntwe.12112

KEY TERMS AND DEFINITIONS

Digital Transformation: a broad sociotechnical process that implies the integration of digital technologies into aspects of daily social life. It refers to strategies or processes that go beyond the application of digital technologies and involve a profound change in the business environment.

Gig Economy: a working arrangement characterized by short-term tasks or projects within the scope of specific activities that are carried out by individual self-employed persons, usually via a digital platform.

Freelancers: workers who manage flexible working arrangements and belong to the category of self-employed without employees, who use their potential to apply for temporary jobs or projects. They have full control over where they work, receive no benefits from companies, pay their own taxes, usually work with multiple clients and projects at the same time, and set their own prices - whether they charge by the hour or per project

Motivation: explains the reasons why someone acts in a certain way. Motivation is an important career factor because it is the product of a person's expectation that a certain effort will result in an intended performance and that this performance will produce a certain desired result.

Subjective Well-Being: a person's subjective satisfaction with his or her life, usually measured by assessing his or her life domains (life satisfaction, job satisfaction, health satisfaction, income satisfaction, leisure satisfaction, satisfaction with health, etc.)

Career: development process of the individual on the path of experience and work for one or more organizations.

Chapter 4
Are We Followed in the Digital World?

Pelin Yolcu

(iD) https://orcid.org/0000-0002-7235-4671
University of Dicle, Turkey

ABSTRACT

A digital footprint is simply defined as the trace of users' online activities. Another definition explains the digital footprint as the trace left by the online and offline activities of users electronically in electronic media (database, server, etc.). Social media shares, web pages visited, e-mails sent, and online games played are some of the parts that make up the digital footprint. In short, the records of the interaction between the individual and the virtual electronic world constitute the digital footprint. In this direction, the aim of this study is to determine the digital footprint awareness of university students and to determine their general views on the digital footprint, and the time they spend in electronic tools and environments.

INTRODUCTION

The online environment is cultural because everything is digitized or the images, sounds and objects we encounter are part of the internet or digital has a role in their creation (Burnham, 2018). Everything produced in this environment since the early days of the internet can be considered a digital culture element. When it is recalled that Williams, as mentioned above, states the three levels of culture that characterize the elite culture witnessed or recorded by those living at that time or the intersection of the two, digital culture is also witnessed by people living in this time and space but also included in the network. It is seen that being on the network means leaving

DOI: 10.4018/978-1-6684-6108-2.ch004

a footprint on the network, and since all data is recorded, it also covers the second level. Thumim (2012) states that digital culture also includes situations where digital technologies are not accessed or used. According to her, digital technology includes but is not limited to the internet, which shapes the production and consumption of images, sounds and texts within the culture. For example, the digitization of culture does not mean that there will be no more pencil-on-paper drawings; it also means that such a drawing now has the potential to be scanned and circulated with digital technology (Thumim, 2012). Digital culture can be traced back to when the internet first emerged, when computers were founded with electronic chips, when differential analyzers, transistors or integrated circuits were invented, and even to Leibniz's mathematics, where the origins of digital are based. However, what is the object of study in this study is the period when, together with personal computers, the World Wide Web and browsers, the period when it became widespread among ordinary users, out of the framework of the military, university, computer geeks and computer engineers when ordinary people began to participate in this production. However, digital culture is a set of cultural, social and political processes (Thumim, 2012). Digital culture can not only be reduced to technological developments but the significant effects on the social and political environment are seen.

This network culture, which was accelerated by the United States government's decision to establish a secure network during the Cold War period and the establishment of ARPANET (advanced research project agency network) in 1969 after various stages, presents us with a wide range of data today. The culture created by this environment, which generally seems to have been established only for military purposes, was nourished by many different veins (Poe, 2014). Storing, categorizing and sharing the acquired information, which started in the 16th century, is essential in this historical process. In this sense, reference cannot be made to a military origin alone. Technological inventions accelerated by the excitement of the Cold War era and supported by power institutions were also fed by countercultures and geek cultures (Poe, 2014). "As We May Think" (1945), written by Vannevar Bush, profoundly influenced many scientists who laid the foundation for the formation of digital, and Dream Machines/ Computer Lib (1974), written by Ted Nelson, who found the hypertext (linked text), provided a broad vision on the thinkers of the period. Tim Berners-Lee, who created the World Wide Web and wrote HTML (hypertext markup language), Marc Andreesen and Eric Bina, creators of Mosaic, the first web browser, have been essential mediators of participation in digital culture.

The emergence of the internet has restructured the information and communication environment. Like publishing that emerged at the beginning of the 20th century and the printing press 500 years ago, the internet has introduced new ways of producing, acquiring and sharing what people need to know. It has changed the way old media are used. It has reshaped broad social relations, including the unintended consequences of basic social activities such as work, learning, travelling, consuming, making friends, and managing. The internet has not and probably will not displace traditional media, but it has restructured public information and communication ecology (Coleman and Ross, 2010). The claim that technology affects different aspects of our culture may be simplified and deterministic, but it is not entirely wrong. We can state that all technologies interfere with and change the living environment of human beings to a certain extent and therefore change the conditions of existence of different cultures. This change does not happen with technological logic. This change depends on how society accepts it, uses it and regulates it, so it can be said that technology affects and reflects specific social changes. When technology is communication technology, its impact is even more important because its use can change our communicative and cultural patterns (Uzelac, 2008). The digital revolution has affected all our communication structures unlike other technological revolutions.

For example, while the printing press has affected the media distribution dimension of cultural communication, photography, and the still image dimension of cultural communication, the computer-mediated revolution has affected all communication layers such as acquisition, manipulation, storage and distribution. It has also restructured all its forms (Manovich, 2001). The digital culture environment was called by different names when the network included with the internet first started to form slowly. One of them is cyberculture. Cyber Culture is the sum of cultural products developed and exchanged through the Internet (Ardèvol, 2005). Cyberculture is the culture in which the machine plays an important role; It covers many concepts such as communication networks, programming and software, artificial intelligence, virtual reality, artificial life and human-machine interface (Lister et al., 2009, p. 317). Bell (2001) briefly defines cyberculture as "the lived culture made by people, machines and stories in everyday life". The concept (Jones, 1997), which has also been used as virtual culture in some studies, will discussed as digital culture in this study.

BACKROUND

Information and Communication Technology

Information and communication technologies are one of the most influential forces of social change. Thanks to these technologies, rapid changes are experienced in life. With these changes, primary living spaces and relationship styles are rapidly changing. Social institutions are affected in different ways in this process. The reflections of this new situation have been using new tools and practices in schools. The use of new online environments and tools has made it necessary for individuals to have new knowledge and skills, and new literacy concepts have emerged. These literacies have also brought about new situations that users should be aware of. One of these new situations is the issue of digital identities, which is formed with the penetration of digital technologies into every stage of social life and is closely related to the type and content of the online activities users perform. The field of this digital word that enters people's lives is not as concrete as it seems.

The concept of digital can be defined as a computer language (İspir et al., 2013). İspir et al. State that the development of digital language dates back to the 19th century. Every letter and symbol has a code in the digital language, which is considered to be founded by the mathematician Gootfried Wilhelm's discovery of the arithmetic system consisting of 0 and 1. All work is done with coding in this language. The concept of digital has become an important part of daily life in the context of skills to be possessed in the 21st century. Many new words have been derived from the concept of digital, such as digital story, digital literacy, digital citizenship, digital competence, digital ethics, and digital garbage. Digital environments have started to meet personal needs such as shopping, banking, debt payments, socializing, social sharing and games online or offline, especially with the widespread use of the internet. Thousands of records are created during these processes. In this process, the user may not be aware of the situation. The process of creating and storing the records of all transactions made in the digital environment is discussed and evaluated with the term "digital footprint" in the literature. Digital footprints were previously used to identify an activity performed by an institution or individual online. However, this situation has become more inclusive later as the trace left behind when institutions or individuals interact online (Bodhani, 2012).

Lambiotte and Kosinski (2014), who have a similar view of the concept of a digital footprint, also state that individuals leave their digital footprints in electronic databases with their online or offline activities, and these electronic records are defined as digital footprints. Digital footprints literature also includes evaluation of computer evidence (Sommer, 1998), opportunities and challenges for online social research (Golder, 2014), and records of interaction between the human and cyber world (Wang, et al.; Liu & Zhou, 2017). According to the literature on digital footprint, there are two types of footprints, passive and active. Passive traces are left by interacting with an infrastructure that provides input to location records, such as a mobile telephone network, while active traces are provided by the users themselves when location data is used in photographs, messages and sensor measurements (Girardin et al., 2008).

Social and societal intelligence research aims to reveal individual and group behaviours, social interactions and community dynamics by examining people's web applications, static infrastructure, and digital traces when interacting with mobile and wearable devices (Zhang, Guo & Yu, 2011). These footprints are collected and analyzed to reveal human behaviour patterns and community dynamics. In this process, large-scale social and social information processing technologies; A new research field called "social and community intelligence (SCI)" has emerged, which explores "digital footprints" in order to reveal individual, group and societal models (Zhang, Guo, Li & Yu, 2010).

Digital footprint life is the experience of every text, sound, image and information left by the person, consciously or unconsciously, in the digital environment. Studies examining the issue of digital footprints show that by following the digital footprints of the determined people, much personal information such as that person's view of the world, political view, religious belief, personality traits, education and address information can be accessed (Garfinkel, 2010; Kosinski, Stillwell & Graepel, 2013). ; Madden, Fox, Smith & Vitak, 2007). This shows that individuals witness various experiences in the digital environment. Experience (TDK, 2018) is defined as what remains in the person after what has been experienced, seen, heard and acquired. Social shares made on behalf of a person without his knowledge, opening a website on his behalf, bringing up the posts he made before in digital environments, revealing the subject of a search operation made by the person as an advertisement later, revealing the created and kept personal profiles, Revealing the posts that are hidden from others can be given as an example of this situation.

According to the literature, young individuals also use technology much more intensively than expected (Bennett, Maton & Kervin, 2008; Margaryan, Littlejohn & Vojt, 2011; Tapscott, 2008; C, Autio & Sapienza, 2001). In line with this determination, it can be said that young users mostly leave a digital footprint. In this context, it can be argued that raising the digital footprint awareness of young users is essential. In some studies dealing with the digital footprint issue, it was observed that the study groups mainly consisted of young individuals. For example, Camacho, Minelli, and Grosseck (2012) worked with higher education students, while Özbek, Çoklar, and Gündüz (2016) worked with high school students. Camacho et al. (2012) focused on critical questions about discovering the effects underlying higher education students' perception of digital identity, personal development, and social relationships.

Meanwhile, she states that knowing how her identity is shaped will enable students better to understand the nature of their social and cultural experiences. The article deals with epistemological perspective issues such as identity construction, impression management, friendship, network structure and privacy awareness. An undergraduate student can produce content on any subject and have the knowledge and skills to easily transmit that content to another place in an online environment. The student may be competent to produce digital content and send that content somewhere.

However, this may be related to their awareness of their responsibilities regarding the functioning of this process or their correct orientation. In the research study of

Camacho et al., in which 135 undergraduate students participated, critical questions about digital identity, personal development, social relations and lifelong learning were highlighted. This research has important implications for how the digital environment shapes students' identity and how students perceive the situation. The aim of the research carried out by Özbek et al. (2016) is to determine the digital footprint awareness of high school students and their experiences on this subject. Three hundred sixteen high school students participated in the study. As a result of the research, it was seen that the digital footprint awareness of the students was high, and their negative experiences in this regard were low. Although gender was not found to be important in terms of digital footprint awareness, it was concluded that the gender variable was important in terms of digital footprint experiences. Accordingly, it has been observed that men have more negative experiences in the digital context. In addition, while internet use self-efficacy is not essential for both dimensions, education, one of the primary internet use purposes, is an essential factor only in terms of digital footprint awareness. It was observed that students who stated that they used the internet for educational purposes had higher digital footprint awareness.

Today, the internet has become an integral part of our lives and has permeated all moments of our daily activities such as work, communication, shopping and personal life. Various types of online activities are offered, such as online shopping, e-mail, forum, blog, digital gaming, digital banking, e-commerce, and digital learning. While individuals perform these actions on the internet, they also leave their digital footprints behind. Therefore, they begin to worry about digital Privacy with the thought that they are watched every second, every moment, and the underlying concern of this concern is that the individual may be harmed economically and socially by sharing personal information. As organizations collect and analyze more and more data about users, individuals become more cautious and more reluctant to share their data. So much so that some users even try to share their personal information incorrectly or incorrectly to reduce the risk of misuse of personal information (Santhanam, 2008).

Digital literacy is more than the ability to use a digital device or software and includes specific skills in the digital environment. These skills, defined as digital literacy skills, refer to the cognitive, sociological and emotional skills necessary for users to work effectively in the digital environment. In order for users to understand the digital world, benefit from its opportunities, use technology effectively and efficiently, be aware of its risks, and be protected from the threats and dangers of the environment, they need to be digitally literate (Eshet-Alkalai, 2004: 93). According to the social, emotional dimension, one of the digital literacy dimensions developed by Ng (2012: 56), a digitally literate individual can use the internet safely knowing her responsibilities. Individuals who use the internet for communication, socialization and learning know how to protect their security and Privacy by keeping their personal information confidential. A digitally literate individual is also based on internet ethics and knows how to keep personal information confidential, protect personal security, and deal with threats when threatened. In this context, the area that overlaps with the social-emotional and technical dimensions of digital literacy shows the ability to navigate social networks effectively and to use the digital world sensitively for social interactions.

DIGITAL LITERACY

Since Paul Gilster (1997) first defined digital literacy, the term has emerged with a different dimension every day. Gillen defines digital literacy as "the ability to understand and use information in multiple formats", emphasizing critical thinking as well as information and communication technology skills. On the other hand, a comprehensive definition of digital literacy has been tried to be made in many commissions and academic studies. Gillen (2009) states that many definitions are based on definitions targeting specific audiences and emerge from different historical contexts. It is crucial to put the concept of digital literacy in a historical context. For example, literacy 3,000 years ago could have meant being a compelling speaker who could use the tools of rhetoric. On the other hand, Guttenberg brought a new dimension to literacy and redefined it to include reading and writing, where meaning is shared through language. The fact that production and distribution became more manageable with the development of image technology emphasized the importance of how to look at images with the concept of visual literacy, and it was understood that images have a communicative meaning.

With the emergence of the internet and social media, literacy has gained a new dimension (Martin, 2008). These new technologies require a new set of skills, competencies, and strategies, such as searching, finding, and evaluating information. This new concept of literacy has created the need for the technical skill set necessary to maximize knowledge potential. Digital literacy can be seen as a framework consisting of skills, knowledge, and ethics (Calvani et al., 2008). It has been emphasized that digital literacy has three dimensions: cognitive, socio-emotional, and technical. While some authors emphasize cognitive and socio-emotional aspects, others focus on technical skills (Eshet-Alkalai, 2004). Digital literacy is literacy through technology, that is, not only the ability to read and write but also the ability to shape those skills in the course of one's own life. It has been suggested that there are differences in shaping these skills among those born at different times (Lankshear & Knobel, 2008). Marc Prensky (2001) tried to explain the terms "digital natives" and "digital immigrants" to describe behavioural differences between generations.

Princeky argues that those who grew up with access to digital technology everywhere think differently from previous generations who came to technology later in life.

Generation Z youth are born into an interactive, on-demand digital culture in which they are accustomed to messaging, mobile internet, and social networks. Although many theorists object to this distinction, today's generation Z seems to be able to interact effortlessly with anything digital. However, although it is true that this generation of young people is born into technology and developed some of their skills, research shows that students do not know how to benefit from technology (O'Brien & Scharber, 2008). Although there are differences between generations, the general population lacks digital literacy skills, and it is emphasized that uncritical consumption can be dangerous, given the often misleading nature of online information (Ng, 2012). Today, where the number of pages on the internet exceeds a trillion, Mitchell Kapor interprets digital literacy as the critical use of technology by comparing getting information from the internet to getting a drink from a fire hydrant (Futurelab, 2010). It involves educating students to move from passive consumers of information to active producers, both as individuals and as part of a community.

Finding things on the internet is essential, but knowing how a search engine like Google ranks these results, and a basic understanding of Google's business model, are essential to understanding the impact technology has on our daily lives. Similarly, digital skills include taking advantage of the opportunities offered by information and communication technologies and using them in education and business in a critical and innovative way. Digital skills also include being critical of resources and evaluating content. To put it more clearly, it is stated that it is necessary for the individual to continuously develop their digital skills in the process of becoming digitally capable and critical citizens (Erstad, 2007).

Renee Hobbs (2010) defines digital literacy as a set of life skills necessary for full participation in the information society. These skills are;

1. To be able to analyze and evaluate information
2. To be able to create information and take Social Action
3. Ability to use new digital tools and create and share content
4. To have the competence to apply social responsibility and ethical principles

Although the competencies that digital literates should possess are discussed under different subheadings in different studies, these competencies can be grouped under five main headings: information, communication, content creation, security and problem solving (Ferrari, 2013). It is stated that waiting to improve our digital literacy skills will be a luxury for humanity. Because the nature of literacy is changing in the digital age, we do not have a decade to catch up with this change

(Hicks & Turner, 2013). This change similarly changes our perceptions of Privacy. Increasing developments in information technologies ensure that everything being done today is carried out faster, more flexibly and more efficiently. At the same time, information technologies reveal things that have not been seen before or do things in different ways (Çelik and Sökmen, 2018). The universal spread of the internet leads to a universal increase in the amount of usage. Research and statistics show that internet and social media use has become widespread today. According to the 2020 2nd Quarter World Internet, social media and mobile usage statistics report published jointly by "We Are Social" and "Hootsuite", there are 4.57 billion internet users and 3.81 billion social media users in the world.

While an increase of 301 million was observed in internet users compared to the same period of the previous year, this figure was 304 million in social media users, and it was determined that internet users use the internet for an average of 7 hours a day. According to this report, the most visited sites worldwide were Google, Youtube, Facebook, Baidu and Twitter, respectively. The most used social media sites were Facebook, Youtube and Whatsapp. Social media attracts people's attention in different digital environments. With the usage privileges it offers, it covers an essential part of the users' daily lives.

Thanks to the various ways of communication it offers, it causes it to be used for hours a day. Spending much time during the day also causes social media addiction. As a result of social media addiction, individuals provide general communication through social media without giving importance to face-to-face interaction and communication (Güler et al., 2019). Social media allows the sharing of content created by users with mobile and web-based technologies by creating interactive environments (Eryılmaz and Zengin 2014). In addition, it has become popular among internet users in terms of its advantages, such as continuous development, multi-use, and virtual sharing. In addition to personal information, pictures and photographs can be shared, a job can be found, and the natural world can be experienced in the digital environment (Vural and Bat 2010). At the same time, through social media tools, individuals have acquired an atmosphere where they can freely express their thoughts, thoughts and comments about products and services (Mazıcı et al., 2017).

Digital footprints are traces and records people leave on their activities on the internet. With the ever-increasing use of social media, digital footprints emerge where individuals can access massive data sets such as age, gender, location, etc. (Azucar et al., 2018). In addition, the digital footprint creates the identity of people on the online platform. The constant increase in the desire to share on social media and digital platforms has led researchers to activities such as digital footprints or revealing people's opinions from shares. In recent years, security investigations can be done in this direction. Using digital footprints to predict personality traits accurately could represent a fast, cost-effective alternative to surveys and reach larger populations that could be useful for academic, health-related and commercial purposes. Regarding academic research, the development of automated procedures for measuring personality will allow to reach larger samples and obtain measures that are potentially less prone to social desirability bias. Moreover, personality traits have also been shown to act as a potential risk and protective factor for many health-related outcomes (Widiger and Oltmanns 2017).

The digital footprint, which is difficult to change, consists of people's movements on the internet, their sharing on virtual platforms, their internet history and search engine results. People's existence in the digital environment, their way of expressing themselves and their sharing are turning into digital footprints (Thompson, 2012). Digital footprint awareness is being able to distinguish positive or negative for possible situations that may be encountered in the future as a result of online activities. The information that people access can be identity, address, bank account information, photos that require confidentiality, and all kinds of information about the person. When it comes to malicious people, it is very natural for people to be exposed to situations that they cannot predict. Accordingly, limiting the sharing of private information, not providing confidential information, and knowing the sanctions of cookies on websites will provide awareness. Briefly, digital footprint awareness; can be defined as knowing what the digital footprint of individuals is and being able to manage their online activities (Acele, 2020).

It is a fact that in recent years, more time has been spent on the internet with all devices, genius mobile phones. Therefore, as a result of this situation, digital activities have also increased. These activities can be counted as sharing, online payment transactions, information activities, etc. It is crucial for all users that these activities are carried out safely. In similar studies in the literature, it is possible to reach the conclusion that young individuals are more active on the internet compared to other age groups. Due to such reasons, it is thought that revealing the level of knowledge of social media users on this subject will create a positive development regarding their general awareness of social life, and it is crucial in this respect. Considering the possibility that internet interactions of young individuals in the literature may affect their lives, it is thought that this study will make significant contributions.

Risks on the Internet

Çubukçu and Bayzan (2013) state that the importance of internet security is increasing day by day. Although there are many conveniences and contributions brought by technology and the internet, which have an important place in people's lives, there are also risks arising from not using the internet correctly and effectively or from its unconscious use. The unconscious use of the internet can be defined as the fact that individuals do not know how much they can trust the information on the internet, that is, how to protect themselves from cyber traps. When it comes to the unconscious use of the internet, people's lives become more complex, and their personal information can be endangered. Information Technologies and Communications Authority (BTK, 2016) risks on the internet; access to false or harmful information, cyberbullying, cyber fraud, sharing of personal information and identity theft, malware, phishing, pornography/child abuse and prostitution, illegal gambling, internet addiction, health problems, online and offline communication with strangers, violence/hate / racist activities, use of weapons and substances, copyright infringement. The groups most likely affected by these risks are children and young people who have not yet acquired digital literacy skills, including internet and information literacy.

The business world now needs and prefers individuals with digital literacy skills. While traditionally having literacy is the ability of an individual to read and write the language shared in a particular culture, digital literacy includes reading and writing digital texts together with the process of accessing information, organizing, analyzing, interpreting, evaluating, transmitting and producing information using digital technologies (Akkoyunlu & Yilmaz Soylu, 2010). A digitally literate individual knows how information and communication technologies affect the world and can use digital technologies for this purpose. Minimizing the risks that individuals who have not acquired digital literacy skills may face can be possible by raising awareness of individuals about correct and effective internet use. In order to take these risks under control, these risks should be identified, and the causes of the risks should be determined. When the studies in the literature are examined, it is seen that the most common risks are cyberbullying and cyber traps.

Cyberbullying has become a social problem in recent years. This concept has emerged due to the bullying behaviours encountered in daily life appearing on the internet. Cyberbullying, first defined by Belsey (2007), is a repetitive hostile behaviour intentionally committed by a group or person aimed at harming the other person by using information and communication technologies. Patchin and Hinduja (2006) defined cyberbullying as deliberate and repeated harm through an electronic text tool. As can be seen from the definitions, behaviours such as abusive texts and e-mails, offensive messages, pictures or videos, imitating others online, excluding, humiliating, unpleasant gossip and chatting include cyber bullying (Milosevic, 2016).

Behaviours such as taking pictures of victims of cyberbullying with a camera, sharing their images on social media without their knowledge and consent, sending humiliating, sarcastic, threatening, sexual harassment or violent messages via e-mail or message, and preparing defamatory and humiliating web pages for the victim are also included. (Basturk Akca, Sayımer, Balaban Tuesday, and Ergün Başak, 2014). Another danger encountered in unconscious internet use is cyber traps. Cyber traps can also be called cyber fraud and cyber theft. The Cyber trap is scamming people over the internet. Receiving messages such as "you won a holiday", "you won a phone call" by asking for your identity information, and requesting participation in the competition with pop-up windows can be given as examples of cyber traps (Keşf@ Conscious Internet Movement Project, 2017).

Young people and children can be careless about protecting their privacy, avoid using the internet safely and take risks without realizing it. In the study conducted by Odabaşı et al. (2015), 9% of the young people did not mind following the instructions in an e-mail stating that they had won a gift, 16% did not mind participating in the competition if a reliable company's name was mentioned in a competition advertisement on the internet, 18%. On the other hand, if a chain e-mail is received from a person they trust, they have revealed that they think the e-mail is reliable. Cyber traps threaten individuals and prevent them from using the internet correctly and effectively. Therefore, it is necessary to educate and raise students' awareness on this subject. Another issue that needs to be addressed is that individuals know that the online user profile, that is, the digital footprint, is significant in the cyber world and the effective and efficient use of the internet because another threat posed by the risks on the internet for the future and reputation of individuals is that they leave negative footprints on the digital identities of both the people who cause these risks and the victims of these risks.

Digital Footprint

The trace or clue individuals leave on the internet is defined as a digital footprint. The e-mail messages shared by the individual, the uploaded or downloaded files (text, video and digital images, etc.), and the use of social networking environments are the traces that individuals leave online (Hewson, 2013). Therefore, any activity done online leaves a trace, and this trace creates a digital footprint. Mouse and keyboard clicks made without thinking and inexperience can be an obstacle for young people in their future business life or university admission (O'Keeffe, Clarke-Pearson, & Council on Communications and Media, 2011). The digital footprint, which is not easy to change, consists of individuals' interactions with the screen, sharing in the digital environment, internet archives and search engine results (Thompson, 2012). The digital footprint, which is not easy to change, consists of a combination of individuals' interactions with the screen, sharing in the digital environment, internet archives and search engine results (Thompson, 2012).

Due to the rapid growth in online social media, users' online digital footprints are also increasing (Malhotra, Totti, Meira, Kumaraguru, & Almeida, 2012). Digital footprints contain essential information about the lives of individuals and can sometimes be used against them. Managing the digital footprint of the individual correctly is essential both for using the internet correctly and effectively and for being a conscious digital citizen. In other words, to be a good digital citizen is to leave a positive digital footprint. Individuals are in a conference room connected to the world by a public address system that can record and distribute everything they say in the internet world. It will be more accurate to ensure that what is said and done in a system that the whole world listens to is more exciting and positive in terms of creating a positive identity (Digital Citizenship Adventures, 2017).

Kuehn (2012) argues that digital footprint and reputation are formed in two ways. The first of these is active, and the active digital footprint is the articles written by the individual on the blogs, the photos he shared, the videos and all kinds of shares. The other is passive, and the passive digital footprint is the shares that others create about a person other than themselves. All of these are permanent due to the nature of the Internet (Kuehn, 2012). In addition to controlling what is shared about them, individuals should regularly monitor what is said and shared about them. First, it should be started by determining what the content is about. Then, an alert can be created to notify when something about the person is published via Google (Hengstler, 2017). Madden, Fox, Smith, and Vitak (2007) grouped adults according to the steps they took to limit their online footprint. These groups and their properties are described below.

Confident Creators: They make up 17% of adults online. They say they are not worried about the accessibility of their online information and are actively uploading content but still taking steps to limit their personal information.

Anxious and Mindful: 21% of adults online are in this group. They take steps to limit their online information and are cautious about their online information.

Worried on the Edge: Although they may be concerned about how much information is available about themselves on the internet, they do not actively limit their online information. They are 18% of online adults.

Fearless and Inactive: The group makes up 43% of online adults. They are not concerned about their personal information and do not take steps to limit the amount of information that can be found about them online.

Individuals who use the internet safely and effectively, know the importance of digital citizenship, act following the rules and principles of digital citizenship, are aware of risks such as cyberbullying, cyber harassment and cyber traps, do not engage in such behaviours, empathize in their online behaviours, and use strong passwords in their accounts. Are individuals with a positive digital footprint and reputation.

Purpose of the Research

The purpose of this research is to measure the level of digital footprint awareness of university students, to find out what they pay attention to when leaving a digital footprint on the internet, and to determine whether this affects their Privacy. The study will contribute by pioneering other studies on this subject.

METHOD

Research Pattern/Model

The research was created in a qualitative design. Qualitative research can be defined as research in which qualitative data collection methods such as observation, interview and document analysis are used, and a qualitative process is followed to reveal perceptions and events in a natural environment in a realistic and holistic way (Yıldırım & Şimşek, 2006).

Working Group

This study was conducted with 20 students at Dicle University in Diyarbakir, Turkey. 10 (50%) of the participants are girls, and 10 (50%) are boys. The average age of the participants is ten 20.95.

Data Collection Tool

In the research, the participants' views on their digital footprint awareness were obtained by using the interview form. While developing the interview form, relevant literature and expert opinions were used. In the research, the standardized open-ended interview was used in terms of structure. Interviews were audio-recorded. In addition, the interviews were conducted with their permission in order not to cause ethical problems.

Analysis of Data

The conversations were transcribed for analysis. Content analysis was used to analyze the data obtained from the participants. The content analysis enables the creation of a certain framework by making sense of the raw data obtained and the concretization of codes and categories by arranging them after the emerging situation becomes clear (Yaman, 2010). In other words, the main purpose of content analysis is to reach concepts and relationships that can explain the collected data (Yıldırım & Şimşek, 2006). In parenthetical coding, the first letter represents the initials of the name, the letter in parentheses next to the first letter represents the gender of the participant, and the number next to it represents the student's age. While reporting the results of the research, direct interview quotations were included. The natural speech of the students is quoted. Validity was ensured by making one-to-one quotations from students for themes and codes (Patton, 1997). In the transfer of the quotations, the students are numbered from 1 to 20, and the indicators (F and E) representing the gender of the student are shown in parentheses as male or female. S1E (student 1, male) and S2F (student 2 female). The questions to be answered in the study are listed below.

1) Do you know what a digital footprint (Digital footprint concept) is?
2) Does the digital footprint phenomenon bother you?
3) Do you think the digital footprint phenomenon affects your Privacy?
4) Does the recording of your data and every action you take on the internet cause you to be careful while sharing or give up sharing?
5) Do you think you are being followed in the virtual world?

Table 1. Digital footprint awareness chart

SN	Students	Knowing what a digital footprint is	Disturbed by the digital footprint	Thinking that your digital footprint is affecting your Privacy	Be careful while sharing	Those who think they are being followed in the virtual world
1	S(K) 20	x	-	-	x	x
2	C (E) 19	x	x	x	x	x
3	K (K) 18	-	-	-	x	x
5	B (K) 22	x		x	x	x
6	P (E) 19	x	-	-	x	x
7	A (K) 35	x		-	x	x
8	T (E) 23	x	-	-	x	x
9	G(K) 18	x	x	-	x	x
10	R(E) 19	x	-	x	x	x
11	A (K) 21	x	x	-	x	x
12	E(E)21	x	-	-	x	x
13	Ç(K)24	x	-	x	x	x
14	H(E)18	x	-	-	x	x
15	N(K) 22	x	-	-	x	x
16	S(E)19	x	-	-	x	x
17	N(K) 25	x	x	x	x	x
18	M(E)19	x	-	-	x	x
19	P(K)18	x	-	-	x	x
20	F(E) 18	x	-	-	x	x
	Total	20	4	5	20	20

Looking at the data in Table 1, it is seen that all of the students know what "Digital footprint" (Digital footprint concept) is. Some students explained the concept of "Digital footprint" as follows: "I think every recording and sharing to virtual applications is a digital footprint. Moreover, I think this digital footprint is not lost but recorded (R (K) 19). "Digital footprints are traces that we investigate during internet use. I think that these are recorded" G(F) 18. "I think the virtual footprint is a system that records all the actions we take in the virtual environment" A (F) 35.

Four of the students stated that they were uncomfortable with the "digital footprint" phenomenon and expressed the situation as follows: "Yes, this situation bothers me because although we use our account privately on Instagram, it is possible to see the private account with certain applications, and an individual who wants to use social media privately does not want the things he shares to be hidden," G(F) 18.

Those who say that they are not disturbed by the phenomenon of "digital footprint" expressed themselves as follows: "No, it doesn't bother us because we live in the age of technology, and it's normal for those who bring this technology to us to be aware of us. Just as the transactions we make in our lives are recorded (traffic ticket, work-life history, criminal history), it is normal to record the records and shares we make digitally in one place" M (M) 19. "No, it doesn't bother me because I think it's perfectly normal and something that should happen" R(M) 19. "It does not bother me because I think this phenomenon is under my control" A (F) 35.

When 5 of the students answered yes to the question "Do you think the digital footprint phenomenon affects your privacy?" the rest said that their Privacy was not affected by this situation and made the following comments: "No, I do not think so because my posts on social media are already appealing to an audience, I think our privacy is in our own hands." "cannot affect my privacy as long as I am in control" A (F) 35.

All of the students, Does recording your data and every action you take on the internet cause you to be careful while sharing or give up on sharing? They answered yes to the question and said: "Yes, I feel compelled to restrict myself. Even though there is freedom of expression, I think we should keep some of our thoughts to ourselves M (M) 19. "Of course, it happens because as we see today, people can be punished for bad words said in a post made in the past" R(M) 19. "Yes, it causes, I think supported penalties are applied on this issue" G(F) 18.

All of the students, Do you think you are being followed in the virtual world? He answered yes to his question: "Yes, I do because social media is such a large platform that we interact with a lot of people. Among these people, it is possible that there are people who carefully look at our posts and wait for our next post. This is actually a tracking system. After all, we can see what the people we interact with are doing through social media" M (M) 19. "I'm thinking because I'm going to give an example from the events happening around us again. There are many people who are punished for their sharing. How come we are punished if we are not being followed" R(E) 19.

"Yes, I definitely think because Sometimes, when I say the slightest thing, a lot of things about that product appear on Social Media and on my home page, so I believe that we are followed" G(F) 18. "I think I'm being followed because after every action I search for, something else comes up" A (F) 35.

CONCLUSION

In the digital world, which is rapidly becoming online, people do almost all of their work over the internet. While performing these works or sharing their thoughts, they leave a trace in the digital environment. In other words, it is recorded which site they visit or what kind of shares and likes they make. In this system, which we call digital footprint, this study was conducted to determine to what extent people are aware of the possible consequences of their activities on the internet. Internet technologies, which are widely used all over the world, have become a part of life. This technology has gone beyond being a necessity in people's lives and has become one of the indispensable elements of life. In addition to its many benefits, it has also brought risks and irreversible mistakes from its unconscious use. The irreversible mistakes that affect the future are a part of people's digital footprints and are included in their identities as digital citizens. The formation of the digital footprint starts with a mouse click or a keyboard key. These traces that make up the digital identity affect the future lives of individuals positively or negatively. In both business and social life, the traces of individuals can be followed and lead to some decisions.

For this reason, it is explained in detail that it is essential to manage the digital footprint consciously with the research. This study it is aimed to examine the awareness of "Digital Footprint" from the perspective of university students. For this purpose, questions were developed by the researcher. The first conclusion reached in the study is that the digital footprint awareness of higher education students is very high. On the other hand, the concept of "digital footprint" is a concept known and used by higher education students. The lives of university students in the digital environment are primarily in the form of the searches they make in the digital environment as advertisements in different environments. Digital footprint awareness of students does not differ according to gender. It is thought that this study will make significant contributions to the digital footprint literature, as it is a newly examined subject.

FUTURE RESEARCH DIRECTIONS

In this context, the works to be planned from now on:

- Data can be collected from higher education students on a departmental basis, and their digital footprint awareness or experiences can be looked at according to the departments.
- Digital footprint awareness or experiences of high school students, who are prospective higher education students of the future, can be examined according to their high school types.
- Digital footprint awareness or experiences can be examined using different variables.

REFERENCES

Acele, B. (2020). *Investigation of Digital Footprint Concepts of Information Technology Teachers and Teacher Candidates.* [Unpublished Master Thesis, Institute of Education Sciences, Hacettepe University].

Akkoyunlu, B. & ve Yılmaz S. M. (2010). A study on teachers' numerical competencies. *Turkish Librarianship, 24*(4), 748–768.

Ardèvol, E. (2005, Aralık). Cyberculture: Anthropological perspectives of the internet. Using anthropological theory to understand media forms a practices workshop. *European Association of Social Anthropologists (EASA) Media Anthropology Network.* https:// eardevol.files.wordpress.com/2008/10/cyberculture.pdf

Azucar, D., Marengo, D., & Settanni, M. (2018). Predicting the Big 5 Personality Traits from Digital Footprints on Social Media: A Meta-Analysis. *Personality and Individual Differences, 124*, 150–159. doi:10.1016/j.paid.2017.12.018

Baştürk Akca, E., Sayımer, İ., & Balaban Salı, J., & ve Ergün Başak, B. (2014). Causes and types of cyberbullying and the place of media literacy education in preventive studies. *Electronic Journal of Professional Development and Research, 2*, 17–30.

Bell, D. (2001). *An introduction to cybercultures.* Routledge.

Belsey, B. (2007). Cyberbullying: A real and growing threat. *ATA Magazine, 88*(1), 14–21.

Bennett, S., Maton, K., & Kervin, L. (2008). The 'digital natives debate: A critical review of the evidence. *British Journal of Educational Technology, 39*(5), 775–786. doi:10.1111/j.1467-8535.2007.00793.x

Bodhani, A. (2012). Digital footprints step up. *Engineering & Technology, 7*(1), 82–83. doi:10.1049/et.2012.0125

Burnham, C. (2018). *Does the internet have an unconscious?: Slavoj Zizek and digital culture.* Bloomsbury.

Bush, V. (1945). As we may think. *Atlantic Monthly, 176*(1), 101–108.

Calvani, A., Cartelli, A., Fini, A., & Ranieri, M. (2008). Models and instruments for assessing digital competence at school. *Journal of e-Learning and Knowledge Society, 4(*3), 183-193.

Camacho, M., Minelli, J., & Grosseck, G. (2012). Self and identity: Raising undergraduate students' awareness of their digital footprints. *Procedia: Social and Behavioral Sciences, 46*, 3176–3181. doi:10.1016/j.sbspro.2012.06.032

Çelik, K. & ve Sökmen, A. (2018). The Effect of Perceived Performance on Satisfaction of E-Learning Users. *Electronic Turkish Studies, 13*(21), 73–92.

Chen, C., Chen, X., Wang, L., Ma, X., Wang, Z., Liu, K., & Zhou, Z. (2017). MA-SSR: A memetic algorithm for skyline scenic routes planning leveraging heterogeneous user-generated digitalfootprints. *IEEE Transactions on Vehicular Technology, 66*(7), 5723–5736. doi:10.1109/TVT.2016.2639550

Coleman, S. & ve Ross, K. (2010). The media and the public "Them" and "Us" in media discourse. Wiley-Blackwell.

Çubukçu, A., ve Bayzan, Ş. (2013). Digital citizenship perception in Turkey and methods to increase this perception with conscious, safe and effective internet use. *Middle Eastern & African Journal of Educational Research, 5*, 148–174.

Digital Citizenship Adventures. (2017). Managing your digital footprint. *Google.* https://sites.google.com/site/digcitizenshipadventures/managing-your-digital-footprint

Erstad, O. (2007). Conceiving digital literacies in schools-Norwegian experiences. In *3rd International workshop on Digital Literacy*, Crete, Greece.

Eryılmaz, B. & ve Zengin, B. (2014). Consumer for Hospitality Businesses in Social Media A Study on Approaches. *Journal of Business Science, 2*(1), 147–167.

Eshet-Alkalai, Y. (2004). Digital Literacy: A Conceptual Framework for Survival Skills in the Digital Era. *Journal of Educational Multimedia and Hypermedia*, *13*(1), 93.

Ferrari, A. (2012) Digital Competence in Practice: An Analysis of Frameworks. A Technical Report. *The Joint Research Centre of the European Commission.*

Futurelab. (2010) Digital Literacy. *National Foundation for Educational Research.* http://www2.futurelab.org.uk/resources/documents/handbooks/digital_literacy.pdf

Garfinkel, S. L. (2010). Digital forensics research: The next 10 years. *Digital Investigation*, *7*, 64–73. doi:10.1016/j.diin.2010.05.009

Gillen, J. (2009). Literacy Practices in Schome Park: A Virtual Literacy Ethnography. *Journal of Research in Reading*, *32*(1), 57–74. doi:10.1111/j.1467-9817.2008.01381.x

Gilster, P. (1997). *Digital literacy.* John Wiley & Sons.

Girardin, F., Calabrese, F., Dal Fiore, F., Ratti, C., & Blat, J. (2008). Digital footprinting: Uncovering tourists with user-generated content. *IEEE Pervasive Computing*, *7*(4), 36–43. doi:10.1109/MPRV.2008.71

Golder, S. A., & Macy, M. W. (2014). Digital footprints: Opportunities and challenges for online social research. *Annual Review of Sociology*, *40*(1), 40. doi:10.1146/annurev-soc-071913-043145

Hengstler, J. (2017). Managing your digital footprint: Ostriches v. eagles. *Education for a Digital World*, *2*(1), 89–139.

Hewson, K. (2013). What size is your digital footprint? *Phi Delta Kappan*, *94*(7), 14–22. doi:10.1177/003172171309400704

Hobbs, R. (2010) Digital and Media Literacy: A plan of Action, 2010. *The Aspen Institute.*

Information Technologies and Communications Authority. (2016). The risks and harms of the internet. *BTK.* https://internet.btk.gov.tr/internetin-riskleri-ve-zararlari-detay-61.html

İspir, B., Birsen, H., Binark, F. M., Özata, F. Z., Bayraktutan, G., Öztürk, M. C., & Ayman, M. (2013). *Digital communication and new media.* Web-Ofset.

Jones, S. G. (Ed.). (1997) Virtual culture: Identity & communication in cybersociety. Sage.

Keşf Conscious Internet Movement Project. (2017). Information Notes. *Kesfet Project*. http://www.kesfetprojesi.org/kesfet/iceriklist/kesfet-projesi/bilgi-notlari

Kosinski, M., Stillwell, D., & Graepel, T. (2013). Private traits and attributes are predictable from digital records of human behaviour. *Proceedings of the National Academy of Sciences of the United States of America, 110*(15), 5802–5805. doi:10.1073/pnas.1218772110 PMID:23479631

Kuehn, L. (2012). Manage your digital footprint. *Our Schools / Our Selves, 21*(2), 67-69.

Lambiotte, R., & Kosinski, M. (2014). Tracking the digital footprints of personality. *Proceedings of the IEEE, 102*(12), 1934–1939. doi:10.1109/JPROC.2014.2359054

Lankshear, C., & Knobel, M. (2008). *Digital literacies: concepts, policies and practices*. Peter Lang.

Li, X., & Santhanam, R. (2008). Will it be disclosure or fabrication of personal information? An examination of persuasion strategies on prospective employees. *International Journal of Information Security and Privacy, 29*(4), 91–113. doi:10.4018/jisp.2008100105

Lister, M., Dovey, J., Giddings, S., & Grant, I., & ve Kelly, K. (2009). New media is a critical introduction. Routledge.

Lynn Thompson, T. (2012). I am deleting as fast as possible: Negotiating learning practices in cyberspace. *Pedagogy, Culture & Society, 20*(1), 93–112. doi:10.1080/14681366.2012.649417

Madden, M., Fox, S., Smith, A., & Vitak, J. (2007). Digital footprints: Online identity management and search in the age of transparency. *Pew/Internet & American Life Project*.

Malhotra, A., Totti, L., Meira, W., Kumaraguru, P., & Almeida, V. (2012). Studying user footprints in different online social networks. *Proceedings of the 2012 International Conference on Advances in Social Networks Analysis and Mining (ASONAM 2012)*, (pp. 1065-1070). 10.1109/ASONAM.2012.184

Manovich, L. (2001). *The language of new media*. The MIT Press.

Margaryan, A., Littlejohn, A., & Vojt, G. (2011). Are digital natives a myth or reality? University students' use of digital technologies. *Computers & Education, 56*(2), 429–440. doi:10.1016/j.compedu.2010.09.004

Martin, A. (2008). Digital Literacy and the "Digital Society". In C. Lankshear & M. Knobel (Eds.), *Digital Literacies: Concepts, Policies and Practices* (pp. 151–176). Peter Lang.

Milosevic, T. (2016). Social media companies' cyberbullying policies. *International Journal of Communication, 10*, 5164–5185.

Nelson, T. (1974). *Dream machines/Computer lib*. The Distributors.

Ng, W. (2012). Can we teach digital natives digital literacy? *Computers & Education, 59*(3), 1065–1078. doi:10.1016/j.compedu.2012.04.016

O'Brien, D., & Scharber, C. (2008). Digital Literacies Go to School: Potholes and Possibilities. *Journal of Adolescent & Adult Literacy, 52*(1), 66–68. doi:10.1598/JAAL.52.1.7

O'Keeffe, G. S., & Clarke-Pearson, K. (2011). The impact of social media on children, adolescents, and families. *Paediatrics, 127*(4), 800–804. doi:10.1542/peds.2011-0054 PMID:21444588

Odabaşı, F., Varank, İ., Yıldırım, S., Koyuncu, F., Dönmez, O., & ve Şumuer, E. (2015). *Conscious internet use research.* http://www.kesfetprojesi.org/source/Bilincli_internet_Kullanim%20Arastirmasi.pdf

Özgür Güler, E. Veysíkaraní, D. ve Keskín, D. (2019). A Study on Social Media Addiction of University Students. *Çağ University. Journal of Social Sciences, 16*(1), 1–13.

Patchin, J. W., & Hinduja, S. (2006). Bullies move beyond the schoolyard. A preliminary look at cyberbullying. *Youth Violence and Juvenile Justice, 4*(2), 148–169. doi:10.1177/1541204006286288

Patton, M. Q. (1997). *How to use qualitative methods in evaluation.* SAGE Publications.

Poe, M. T. (2014) Contact history. Islık.

Prensky, M. (2001). Digital Natives, Digital Immigrants Part 1. *On the Horizon, 9*(5), 1–6. doi:10.1108/10748120110424816

Sommer, P. (1998). *Digital footprints: Assessing computer evidence. Criminal Law Review, 12, 61-78. Tapscott, D. (2008). Grown up digital: How the next generation is changing your world.* McGraw-Hill.

Tanyeri, E. M., Koçak, P., & Altıncık, H. (2017). A Comparative Analysis On The Use Of Social Media As A Public Relations Tool: Online Shopping Sites. *The Journal of Academic Social Science, 5*(60), 523–536.

Thompson, T. L. (2012). I am deleting as fast as possible: Negotiating learning practices in cyberspace. *Pedagogy, Culture & Society*, *20*(1), 93–112. doi:10.1080 /14681366.2012.649417

Thumim, N. (2012). *Self-representation and digital culture*. Springer. doi:10.1057/9781137265135

Uzelac, A. (2008). How to understand digital culture: Digital culture- a resource for a knowledge society? A. Uzelac ve B. Cvjeticanin (Ed.) Digital Culture: The Changing Dynamics içinde (7-21). Croatia: Institute for International Relations.

Vural, Z. ve Bat, M. (2010). Social Media as a New Communication Medium: A Research on Ege University Faculty of Communication. *Journal of Yasar University*, *5*(20), 3348–3382.

Widiger, T. A., and Oltmanns, J. R. (2017). Neuroticism Is A Fundamental Domain of Personality with Enormous Public Health Implications. World Psychiatry; Official Journal of the World Psychiatric Association (WPA), 16(2), 144–145. doi:10.1002/ wps.20411

Yaman, E. (2010). Teaching staff exposed to mobbing organizational culture and climate perceptions. *Educational Sciences: Theory and Practice*, *10*(1), 567–578.

Yıldırım, A., & Şimşek, H. (2006). *Qualitative research methods in the social sciences*. Distinguished Publishing.

Yli-Renko, H., Autio, E., & Sapienza, H. J. (2001). Social capital, knowledge acquisition, and knowledge exploitation in young technology-based firms. *Strategic Management Journal*, *22*(6-7), 587–613. doi:10.1002mj.183

Zhang, D., Guo, B., & Yu, Z. (2011). The emergence of social and community intelligence. *Computer*, *44*(7), 21–28. doi:10.1109/MC.2011.65

ADDITIONAL READING

Barnes, S. (2006). A privacy paradox: Social networking in the United States. *First Monday*, *11*(9). https://firstmonday.org/htbin/cgiwrap/bin/ojs/index.php/fm/article/ view/1394/1312. doi:10.5210/fm.v11i9.1394

Clark, J. R. (2010). Social media and Privacy. *Air Medical Journal*, *29*(3), 104–107. doi:10.1016/j.amj.2010.02.005 PMID:20439026

Gross, R., & Acquisti, A. (2005, November). Information revelation and Privacy in online social networks. In *Proceedings of the 2005 ACM workshop on Privacy in the electronic society ACM*. 10.1145/1102199.1102214

Kosinski, M., Stillwell, D., & Graepel, T. (2013). Private traits and attributes are predictable from digital records of human behaviour. *Proceedings of the National Academy of Sciences of the United States of America*, *110*(15), 5802–5805. doi:10.1073/pnas.1218772110 PMID:23479631

Lyon, D. (2003). *Surveillance as social sorting: Privacy, risk, and digital discrimination*. Psychology Press.

Tuten, T. L. (2008). *Advertising 2.0: social media marketing in a web 2.0 world*. Greenwood Publishing Group.

Yang, H. C. (2014). Prior Negative Experience, Online Privacy Concerns and Intent to Disclose Personal Information in Chinese Social Media. *International Journal of E-Business Research*, *10*(2), 23–44. doi:10.4018/ijebr.2014040102

KEY TERMS AND DEFINITIONS

Digital: All tools and devices with an automatic working principle, not a mechanical one, are defined digitally.

Digital Footprint: A digital footprint is a library that records the steps of all individuals on the internet. As a result of various processes performed in digital environments, many traces are left consciously or unconsciously. The traces left in the data infrastructure form part of the digital footprint in the online environment.

Privacy: Privacy is the sum of all the feelings and thoughts that one does not want to share with others in their living space and private life. In democratic societies, all individuals are given the right to Privacy. The person can share his/her information with others only at his/her request.

Social Media: Social media is an interactive communication platform that users search for, use and produce content on the internet.

Digital Literacy: Digital literacy refers to an individual's ability to find, evaluate, and communicate information through typing and other media on various digital platforms. It is evaluated by an individual's grammar, composition, typing skills and ability to produce text, images, audio and designs using technology.

Digital Citizenship: refers to using information technologies ethically, critically and safely regularly.

Chapter 5
The Positive and Negative Impact of COVID–19 Smartphone Dependency on Employee Job Performance

Nuroul Widad Khalid
Universiti Brunei Darussalam, Brunei

ABSTRACT

A smartphone is a gadget with a variety of features that reside in the capacity of a machine. It is a gadget that can be described as a minicomputer due to its specific size and its different features, such as a PC or a computer device. The objectives of this chapter are to discuss the positive and negative impact of COVID-19 smartphone dependency on employees' job performance at the workplace. Job performance can be defined as the "total expected value" to the organisation of the discrete behavioural episodes that an individual carries out over a standard period of time. The positive and negative impact of COVID-19 smartphone dependency will be discussed and demonstrated using the Ishikawa diagram.

INTRODUCTION

Over the last few decades, technological advancements have made it possible to transition from basic communication tools like the telephone to advanced wireless mobile devices, also known as 'smartphone' (Cheever, Rosen, Carrier & Chavez, 2014). A smartphone is a gadget with a variety of features that reside in the capacity of a machine. It is a gadget that can be described as a minicomputer due to its specific

DOI: 10.4018/978-1-6684-6108-2.ch005

size and its different features, such as a PC or a computer device. Users can use different software, such as online searching, emails, downloads, gaming and more (Carroll & Heiser, 2010; Razzaq et al., 2018 cited in Anshari et al., 2020). Today, it is considered unusual for one to not have a smartphone in this digital era where people worldwide are virtually connected (Anshari & Lim, 2017). One could send a text message from across the world, and it would be delivered in a matter of seconds so long as the phone has an internet connection. Smartphones offer great resources and convenience to people while at the same time, facilitating the accomplishment of tasks and achieving widespread success in today's society (Bartwal & Nath, 2019).

With smartphones being ubiquitous, it has become a norm to bring one's smartphone to the workplace as individuals develop dependency on their devices. Such dependency has long raised the question by researchers and employers on whether smartphones provide employees benefits or harm in the workplace (Anshari et al., 2019a; Mulyani et al., 2019). The number of smartphone users drastically increased with the emergence of the COVID-19 pandemic due to restricted mobility in society in order to contain the spread of the virus. For some employees around the world, working from home was the ideal solution to make ends meet in the midst of the pandemic. As a result, they rely more on their smartphones to perform work matters especially for those with limited access to a laptop or personal computer. For some period of time, working from home became a norm and organizations adopted different strategies and methods in helping employees perform and deliver their work. Today, most employees have gone back to physical work with lockdown restrictions being lifted. However, employees' dependency of smartphones during the lockdown period may still be apparent and persist as it has become a norm, embraced into their daily routine (Anshari et al., 2019b; Razzaq et al., 2018). The dependency can be argued to impact employees' working lives as they bring their smartphones with them back to work.

Thus, the aim of this paper is to discuss the positive and negative impact of COVID-19 smartphone dependency on employees' job performance at the workplace. Job performance can be defined as the 'total expected value to the organization of the discrete behavioral episodes that an individual carries out over a standard period of time' (Motowidlo & Kell, 2012). Also, the positive and negative impact of COVID-19 smartphone dependency will be discussed and demonstrated using the Ishikawa diagram.

LITERATURE REVIEW

The term 'Smartphone' was coined several years ago, but its definition has evolved. It started when people only had mobile phones, also known as cellular phones.

Smartphones are wireless communication systems that can receive and send optical or analog shortwave signals (Rouse, 2007). As a result, people can communicate with one another through these devices. Later, there were innovations and evolutions of the cell phone that made it smarter; gradually, people began calling it a 'smartphone'. The critical difference between a mobile phone and a smartphone is that "a smartphone is a mobile phone that provides more sophisticated processing capacity and accessibility than a contemporary basic feature phone (Litchfield, 2010, as cited in Pitichat, 2013). Also, the internet improves the capabilities of the smartphone. In his essay "Defining the Mobile," Litchfield describes the smartphone as a device that " runs an open (to new apps) operating system and is permanently connected to the internet" (Litchfield, 2010, as cited in Pitichat, 2013). This statement can be said to be accurate as a smartphone with internet access enables people to do many things with it.

Furthermore, the population of smartphone users has increased in recent years. According to the Internet and American Life Project at Pew Research Center, almost half of all American adults own a Smartphone. The number of Smartphone users in the United States has increased by 11% from 35% in 2011 to 46% in 2012, while the number of users who use other mobile phones has decreased by 7% from 48% in 2011 to 41% in 2012 (Smith, 2012). This figure demonstrates that regular mobile phone users shift their behavior from regular cell phones to smartphones (Pitichat, 2013; Anshari et al., 2019b). Workplaces exhibit the same patterns, with more people owning Smartphones. According to Forrester Research, approximately 350 million workers own Smartphones in 2016, with 57 per cent of these users, or approximately 200 million people, bringing the smartphones to work (Chen, 2012; Anshari & Almunawar, 2021). Similarly, mobile users aged 18 to 24 years old rose by 18 per cent between 2011 and 2012, increasing from 49 per cent to 67 per cent (Smith, 2012). They are the young generation workforces, who may have smartphones that constantly link their lives to their workplaces (Anshari & Alas, 2015; Hasmawati et al., 2020). As a result, companies must closely consider how to handle smartphone problems as they become more widespread (Pitichat, 2013).

With smartphones being ubiquitous, it is no surprise that some employees develop a dependency on their devices (Almunawar et al., 2018). The effect of smartphones on the workplace is a controversial subject. Some academics contend that smartphones greatly enhance the workplace by facilitating internal and external communication and collaboration and allowing for agile job organization and real-time knowledge exchange (Kossek & Lautsch, 2012; Lanaj, Johnson, & Barnes, 2014 cited in Li & Lin, 2019; Almunawar et al., 2015). On the other hand, others claim the contrary, stressing the unintended adverse effects for workers (Derks & Bakker, 2014; Derks, Duin, Tims, & Bakker, 2015; Perlow, 2012 cited in Li & Lin, 2019). For example, several studies have shown that people who are heavily reliant on smartphones at work find it difficult to distance themselves physically from their jobs and their phones, resulting in extreme anxiety and stress (Derks & Bakker, 2014; Perlow, 2012 cited in Li & Lin, 2019; Anshari et al., 2022). Over the last few years, there has been a significant increase in research on smartphone addiction. One prominent perspective regards mobile addiction as a form of harmful behavioral addiction (H. I. Chen, Chen, & Lee, 2015; Lapierre & Lewis, 2016; Park, Kim, Shon, & Shim, 2013; Anshari et al., 2021). Most technological addiction reports explore the manifestation of a variety of psychological and behavioral signs, such as withdrawal, preoccupation, and a sense of being out of control (Bian & Leung, 2015 cited in Li & Lin, 2019; Almunawar et al., 2020).

Nomophobia

The deliberate addictive component of smartphones has a psychological impact on individuals, and this can be observed with the growing number of individuals with nomophobia. Nomophobia can be understood as a modern age phobia that has been added to our lives as a by-product of people's dependency on mobile information and communication technologies, particularly smartphones (Yildirim & Correia, 2015). The word nomophobia, or no mobile phone phobia, is an abbreviation for non-mobile-phone phobia, which was first coined in a 2008 survey by the UK Post Office to explore the anxieties of mobile phone users suffering from it (SecurEnvoy, 2012, cited in Yildirim & Correia, 2015). Individuals with nomophobia experience distress, anxiety, and discomfort if they do not have access to their smartphone when needed (Ahmed et al., 2019, Farooqui et al., 2018 & King et al., 2013 cited in Rodríguez-García et al., 2020). The term can also be understood as the 'fear of feeling disconnected from the digital world' (Al-Balhan et al., 2018, cited in Rodríguez-García et al., 2020). According to Ali et al., (2017) and Yildirim & Correia, (2015), there are four main reasons why individuals experience nomophobia: (1) fear or nervousness of not being able to communicate with others; (2) fear of not being able to connect; (3) fear of not having direct access to information; and (4) fear of renouncing the convenience of mobile devices. By having such fears, it is common to see people with smartphones glued to their hands. Some people wake up with their phone next to them, bring it to the bathroom, have their meals while scrolling through their phones and even drive cars while checking their phones.

Muench & Muench (2020) contended there are many instances of daily life where people can constantly be seen using their smartphone. It is used in any case imaginable: on public transportation or at home, as a primary operation or as a second screen when watching TV. Although its primary purpose is to communicate, it may also be used for work-related activities, knowledge access, or entertainment. There are also fashion trends, such as the smartphone neck-strap, that allow users (primarily women) to keep their mobile close at hand. Such trends facilitate direct smartphone access without taking it out of pockets or bags, which can exacerbate one's nomophobia. The smartphone's status as a pervasive and multi-functional mobile device is mirrored in everyday use time, which in the United States was an average of 3 hours and 35 minutes in 2018 (Statista, 2020). Thus, it can be argued that smartphones are becoming an extended body part of human beings. With nomophobia being widespread in the modern world, there is a growing concern about the excessive dependency of smartphones, and this concern should be extended to the workplace.

COVID-19 and Smartphone Dependency

The COVID-19 has disturbed daily practices and appeared one of the most critical health and economic threats since World War II (WHO, 2020). Most countries have declared a state of emergency to break the chain of community dissemination of the deadly virus, which has transformed the way we live. Stay-at-home and work-from-home methods are commonly recommended around the world as the most successful approaches to avoid infection at both the personal and community levels (Cacioppo et al., 2015, as cited in Ratan, Zaman, Islam & Hosseinzadeh, 2021). As a result of self-isolation, people are increasingly dependent on their smartphones to remain connected. Smartphones open up new avenues for people to participate in various online activities such as social networking, video gaming, browsing the internet, etc. According to a recent global survey, approximately 70% of internet users, especially the young generation worldwide, were using their smartphones or electronic devices more directly due to the coronavirus outbreak (Sebire, 2020, as cited in Ratan et al., 2021). Such results imply that COVID-19-related lockdown policies can lead to excessive use of smartphones. Alsalameh et al., (2019) stated that smartphone overuse had been related to impaired physical and psychological well-being and musculoskeletal pain in the spine, lower back, and shoulders, as well as depression and anxiety. This can result in the troublesome use of a smartphone (Sohn, Rees, Wildridge, Kalk & Carter, 2019) which may hack the brain's "reward scheme" to engage one in activities that s/he was employed in before the lockdown period (Haynes, 2018). As a result, even though the lockdown effect is removed, there is a strong likelihood that the resulting harms will persist in the form of multiple mental health conditions (Ratan et al., 2021; Anshari et al., 2021).

However, the blame cannot simply be placed on the individual for their smartphone dependency during the pandemic require businesses to display BruHealth QR code at entry points the public is strongly advised to download the BruHealth app (Kon, 2020). The general public is reminded to scan the QR code with the BruHealth app while approaching or leaving premises. The public is also encouraged to take the BruHealth application seriously, as it will aid the Ministry of Health in contact tracing if the infection spreads. The Ministry of Health will take disciplinary action against anybody who fails to follow the orders and guidelines given (Kon, 2020). Thus, in compliance with the government and to avoid fines, people need to bring their phones and have them ready to scan whenever they are out.

With the increasing number of global cases and deaths, it is vital to communicate time-sensitive information to the public. COVID-19 is a new infectious disease, and community members need extensive knowledge of COVID-19 symptoms, mechanisms of transmission and disease prevention precautions. As a result, successful public health coordination is crucial in tackling the COVID-19 pandemic (Finset, Bosworth, Butow et al., 2020, as cited in Li, Guan, Hammond & Berry, 2021). Social media has been extensively used by public health authorities to share health information due to its success and ease of acceptance by community members (Neiger et al., 2012; Ramanadhan et al.; 2013 & Conrad et al., 2020 as cited in Li, Guan, Hammond & Berry, 2021). An excellent example of a social media platform is TikTok. TikTok, a short-form mobile video app that allows users to make videos lasting 15–60 seconds and sharing them with the TikTok community, is an emerging social media platform. TikTok has risen exponentially in popularity since its inception in 2017. The COVID-19 pandemic is most likely responsible for the rise in TikTok downloads. People spend more time on mobile devices during quarantine or lockdown searching for new entertainment activities and ways to stay connected, which fuels TikTok downloads. The app's exponential growth gave the public health authorities a platform to educate the public about COVID-19 knowledge; users have readily accessible information, which allows them to stay aware and take appropriate precautions (TikTok, 2020, as cited in Li, Guan, Hammond & Berry, 2021). Thus, users can use TikTok to search and share information on COVID-19 (Tilchen, 2020, as cited in Li, Guan, Hammond & Berry, 2021).

As human beings are social beings, and with the lockdown and quarantine imposed, individuals still need to satisfy their need to connect or communicate with others. On the surface, social isolation during the latest COVID-19 pandemic continues to conflict with people's fundamental need to communicate with others. A study conducted by David & Roberts (2021) found that social distancing is adversely linked to social relationships. The more individuals emotionally isolate themselves from others, the more socially isolated they become. Despite the value of social interaction, a lack of social connection was observed to be associated with higher recorded levels of stress and depression and lower perceived well-being (Rosli et al., 2022).

Interestingly, David & Roberts (2021) learned that using smartphones moderate the relationship between social distancing and social interaction. Increased mobile use enhances an individual's perceived social interaction, which is linked to improved psychological well-being. This observation is fascinating in light of the often-criticized effect of smartphone use on relationships and social connections before the pandemic (Roberts & David, 2016, cited in David & Roberts, 2021). Researchers agree that although using smartphones to communicate with others is not as successful as face-to-face contact (Ahn & Shin, as cited in David & Roberts, 2021), it tends to be a feasible choice during a public health epidemic as the ongoing COVID-19 pandemic. Thus, COVID-19 took societies' privileges in forming new and maintaining relationships with others, but devices such as smartphones allowed people to communicate and connect virtually. Public health authorities were able to disseminate information and news on COVID-19 through social media platforms. Thus, it is expected for individuals to rely on their smartphones during the pandemic, which is still ongoing today. However, for those countries that are able to contain and control the community spread of the virus, social life has resumed, and people are practicing the 'new normal'. It can be assumed their dependency on smartphones have become a part of this 'new normal'. Thus, with people physically going back to work, the question of whether their heavy dependency on smartphones as a result of the pandemic could positively or negatively impact their job performance remains.

Smartphone Dependency at the Workplace

A large body of research indicates that the smartphone phenomenon has a negative effect on workplaces (Bozeman, 2011; Ebelhar, 2009; Rush, 2011; Smith, 2012; The Economist, 2012, as cited in Pitichat, 2013). The critical issue is that excessive smartphone use can lead to addiction and nomophobia, which has a negative impact on performance at work. A smartphone is intertwined with people's lives; it has become an essential part of everyday life. Smartphone consumers are utterly obsessed with their smartphones. Some people, for example, treat their smartphones in the same manner, they treat their pets; they call them and buy gadgets to make them look stylish (Bozeman, 2011, as cited in Pitichat, 2013). As a result, some researchers or managers believe that workers do not dedicate their full time and energy to their jobs but instead rely on their smartphones, reducing productivity.

Furthermore, heavy smartphone usage disconnects people from reality. People are always holding their smartphones in their hands. They carry smartphones to a group or social gathering and use them to avoid socializing with others, or they neglect people entirely around as they use their smartphones (Bozeman, 2011, as cited in Pitichat, 2013).

Furthermore, smartphones can cause tension in employees. As workers use their smartphones to work on tasks at work, they often bring pressures from their jobs into their private lives at home, making it difficult for them to distinguish their work from their non-work lives (The Economist, 2012, as cited in Pitichat, 2013). Extra hours worked, including being continuously available by smartphone or the fear of having to be so, can have detrimental effects, such as workplace-related stress (Rush, 2011, as cited in Pitichat, 2013). Also, some employees carry personal matters to work, which may negatively affect their job performance. Likewise, using a smartphone at work can undermine corporate etiquette. Several concerns have been posed about office ethics due to people bringing their smartphones into business meetings, which may be distracting because the smartphones may disrupt the meeting (Ebelhar, 2009, as cited in Pitichat, 2013). Duke & Montag (2017) conducted research on smartphone addiction, daily interruptions and self-reported productivity where participants were administered smartphone addiction scale (SAS). The study found mild relationships between smartphone addiction analyzed by SAS ratings and variables correlated with the smartphone's distracting nature. More specifically, there was a modest association between higher SAS scores and participants showing reduced productivity due to mobile time spent at work and people spending less time working without interruption from the smartphone. There was also a significant association between SAS scores and the number of work hours missed due to smartphone use and a negative relationship between higher SAS scores and the number of hours actively working in the preceding seven days. While research may suggest that smartphone users' negative consequences in the workplace, the number of smartphone users is growing (Smith, 2012). Thus, corporate leaders cannot ignore the smartphone, which is here to stay; instead, they must find ways to handle and use smartphones to positively impact workplaces (Pitichat, 2013).

Based on various literature covering different contexts, the main benefits of mobile use at work include increases in efficiency, contact speed, flexible working opportunities, and the level of cooperation with colleagues and collaborators (Kossek & Lautsch, 2012; Kreiner, Hollensbe, & Sheep, 2009; Lanaj et al., 2014, as cited in Li & Lin, 2019). For instance, Middleton (2007) discovered that smartphones would help workers complete their assigned tasks more effectively by encouraging them to carry out their duties regardless of time or place. Frost and Sullivan (2016) found smartphones bring considerable value to staff because they allow them to remain up to date with continuing change and keep the company moving forward by improving time management (as cited in Li & Lin, 2019).

Furthermore, dependency on smartphones can promote and facilitate knowledge sharing in organizations. Any business must rely on the flow of information and expertise to grow its workforce and make them more profitable. People can quickly share their information and expertise through the integration of smartphone and social network apps. "Internal social networks have now seen an increase in popularity, giving staff and administrators a knowledge-share opportunity and a virtual networking forum that prevents email inboxes from being overwhelmed" (Miller-Merrell, 2012, as cited in Pitichat, 2013). One of the most powerful and standard platforms for knowledge sharing is "Cloud computing" (Anderson, 2010, p.1), which is a sharing platform hosted by other organizations, such as a social-sharing site like Facebook, a video-sharing site like Youtube, a document-sharing site like GoogleDocs, and so on (Anderson, 2010). For example, General Electric (GE) has used an internal social network as a tool for information sharing. The system employs over 100,000 internal consultants who respond to requests from their internal audiences around the world. This internal structure links GE employees; their employees can exchange records, documentation, and questions and answers that help them with their jobs (Naslund, 2010, as cited in Pitichat, 2013). Another example of an organization that prioritizes information and knowledge sharing is the Ford Motor Company. Rather than spending much money on help-desk service, Ford Motor Co. prefers to create a platform for their employees to exchange knowledge and help each other with their problems, especially with technology issues (Torode, 2011).

Concurring to the Pew Research Center's internet & American life project, 71% of respondents agreed with the following statement: "By 2020, most people would not do their job with apps running on a general-purpose PC." Instead, they can be found in Internet-based apps such as Google Docs and smartphone applications. Aspiring technology developers will work with phone manufacturers and businesses who offer Internet-based services, so the majority of creative work will be performed in that domain, rather than developing applications for PC operating systems" (Anderson, 2010, as cited in Pitichat, 2013). Therefore, the integration of smartphone and Cloud computing can accelerate and enhance knowledge growth as smartphone users can obtain information needed at any time and from any place, opening up more possibilities for them to learn more which will eventually lead to better job performance and the potential growth of organizations (Pitichat, 2013).

Another beneficial aspect of smartphone dependency is that it can provide autonomy for employees. Hackman and Oldham (1974) defined autonomy as the independence granted to employees in performing their tasks and deciding which tool best to use. They explained that autonomy is a vital psychological state in which employees are aware and accountable for the outcome of their work (as cited in Mohammad, Quoquab, Halimah, & Thurasamy, 2019). Employees may increase their sense of happiness because they have more control in their workplace by allowing them to access their smartphones. Employees would be happier and more likely to do their best for their employer if they feel their company values their smartphones and encourages them to use them for job purposes (Pitichat, 2013). Thus, giving employees the freedom and control over their smartphones provides them autonomy, and in return, it can increase their job performance.

Lastly, Pitichat (2013) suggested that smartphones aid in the improvement of relationships between subordinates as well as supervisors. As previously mentioned, mobile users tend to withdraw from people in their daily lives (Bozeman, 2011, as cited in Pitichat, 2013). Similarly, in the office, smartphone use distracts workers from meeting details and annoys others (Ebelhar, 2009, as cited in Pitichat, 2013). However, the smartphone is a high-potential interface that connects users via the internet network. CEOs and managers should seize the opportunity to turn their workers' smartphones into engagement tools. Instead of communicating with their friends outside of work, they could create an internal program or platform that connects people inside businesses (Pitichat, 2013). By connecting with one another through their smartphones, employees can improve their social relationships within the organization and thus, it can help improve their job performance.

DISCUSSION

In this section of the paper, the positive and negative impact of COVID-19 smartphone dependency on employees' job performance will be demonstrated using Ishikawa diagram, also known as the fishbone diagram. The fishbone analysis is a method for assessing the success of a business operation. It is also known as the "Ishikawa Diagram," after Mr. Kaoru Ishikawa, a Japanese quality control statistician who invented and incorporated it. Because of its structural outlook and shape, it is referred to as a fishbone. In its natural size, it resembles a fish skeleton. The fishbone diagram and study usually analyze the causes and sub-causes of a single crisis, assisting in the discovery of all the symptoms of a business problem (American Society for Quality, 2005, as cited in Bose, 2012). As a result, it is also known as 'Cause-Effect analysis' (Bose, 2012).

Figure 1. Ishikawa model of analysis in increase in job performance

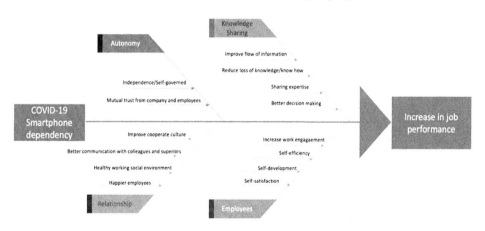

As a result of COVID-19 smartphone dependency, it can be expected that there will be an increase of smartphone usage at the workplace. With an increase of smartphone usage, it can increase the level of autonomy, relationships and knowledge sharing of employees. Pitichat (2013) stated that there are studies (Carayannis & Clark, 2011; Gagne & Deci, 2005; Miller-Merrell, 2012) which indicate that three key variables: autonomy, relationships, and knowledge-sharing, can foster a higher degree of job satisfaction, which can contribute to increased job performance. People's motivation and job satisfaction will improve if they have choice in their jobs; even those working in a mundane job will be inspired by the autonomy that they have (Gagne & Deci, 2005). Furthermore, when employees have stronger connections at work, as well as better internal collaboration or knowledge sharing, they are more comfortable with their jobs and prefer to be more productive (Miller-Merrell, 2012). During the stay at home period, organizations and employees employed different strategies, methods and technological platforms to do their work and employees were able to learn the benefits and downside of each strategies, platforms and methods. By doing so, they increased their tacit and explicit knowledge. When they return to work, it can be suggested that they will be more work efficient as they were exposed to new knowledge, have more useful tools in their smartphones that can help them perform better. Therefore, it can be implied that with the increase of smartphone dependency at work, the benefits attached to the dependency will increase thus, improving employees' job performance.

Figure 2. Ishikawa model of analysis for decrease in job performance

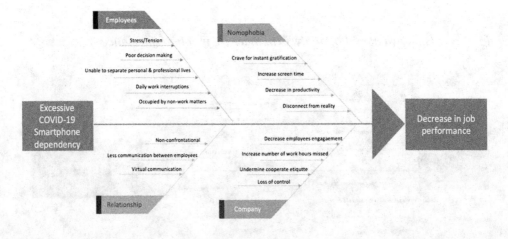

By considering the positive impact of COVID-19 on smartphone dependency for employees, it is just to consider the negative impact at the same time. As mentioned above, people are using their smartphones or electronic devices more directly due to the pandemic. The increase in smartphone usage can be seen as people need to satisfy their need to connect and communicate with others during the pandemic as human beings are social beings. Families that are apart can use Facetime, Zoom or WhatsApp to keep updated with one another. Another reason could be the boredom people feel during the lockdown or quarantine period; thus, they engage more in the virtual world to fill their time. By doing so, online platforms such as social media or online gaming capture and retain people's attention. In return, people will spend more time on their phones and eventually hack the brain's reward system by providing individuals with constant instant gratification. With the majority o' employees performing work from home, they communicate with their colleagues and superiors through their devices. Although this can be seen as efficient, it erases the line between professional work and personal lives. With boundaries crossed and people getting accustomed to communicating digitally, they may feel more pressured than before to instantly respond to work matter as they are more on their phones. Thus, it can be assumed there will be an increase in employees' smartphone usage when returning to physical work.

Individuals are used to checking their smartphones, indulging in contents, and this habit can be expected to be brought to the workplace. Employees may be accustomed to checking their smartphones often, and it can be argued they will indulge in non-work activities such as browsing through their social media, playing online games, discussing personal matters and even, making content for views. The latter is evident where one is able to search 'workplace' on TikTok and see employees making content at the workplace. Also, the blurred lines between professional and personal may cause some employees to bring personal matters to work without thinking of the consequences, such as stress and emotional burden. Although the employees may view it as harmless, from a management's perspective, employees indulging in non-work activities can cause more work interruptions, delaying their tasks and decreasing their job performance. Also, with employees getting accustomed to digitally communicating with their peers or superiors, it may impact employees' relationships. Employees may prefer to communicate digitally rather than face to face conversations. Although the message will be delivered promptly, the intended message may get lost in translation as different people interpret and give meaning subjectively. Thus, it may create tension between employees, and they may prefer to avoid physical confrontation. Therefore, the stress from the tension can negatively impact their working environment and excessive use can cause them to be addicted to their phones and, thus, develop nomophobia. Undeniably, nomophobia can and will have negative consequences on employees' job performance.

Based on the discussion, it should be noted that a general approach to the issue of smartphone dependency was taken. The results cannot be generalized to every organization as some companies may require their employees to use their smartphones as part of their job such as in an IT company and some may not require the need for a smartphone. Also, some information presented were based of this author's subjective point of view thus, one should be careful when extracting information from this review. Nevertheless, the information presented can be used as a benchmark for employers or managers when considering or making policies on smartphone usage at the workplace.

CONCLUSION

A smartphone is a gadget with a variety of features that reside in the capacity of a machine. It can be beneficial to the users, or can be distraction especially in the workplace. There are mixed opinions regarding how the use of smartphones can impact employees during working period. Therefore this paper aimed to discuss the positive and negative impact of smartphones at work especially when COVID-19 increased people's dependency towards smartphones. On the positive side, the use of smartphones actually offer several benefits towards the employee and organisations. Employees can improve their job performance when there is autonomy, relationships and knowledge-sharing from the use of smartphones. Also, smartphones enable the ease of tacit and explicit knowledge sharing and are very helpful during the COVID-19 pandemic because people have to distant or even quarantine themselves.

However, this smartphone dependency also poses as a threat where it can hinder the job performance level of employees. Due to COVID-19, people participate more in non-work related activities such as indulging in social media, which can be addictive causing them to be distracted at work. They can also develop nomophobia if one were to be heavily reliant on their smartphones, and as the majority of communication are through smart phones, they do not act professional by bringing their personal matters to work. This can affect their job performance as there are too many distractions caused by dependency towards smart phones.

REFERENCES

Ahad, A. D., Anshari, M., & Razzaq, A. (2017). Domestication of Smartphones among Adolescents in Darussalam, Journal of Cyber Behavior. *Psychology and Learning*, *7*(4), 26–39. doi:10.4018/IJCBPL.2017100103

Ali, A., Muda, M., Ridzuan, A.R., Nuji, M.N.N., Izzamuddin, M.H.M., Latiff, D.I.A. (2017) The relationship between phone usage factors and nomophobia. *International Journal of Research in Education and Sciences, 23*, 7610–7613.

Almunawar, M. N., Anshari, M., & Lim, S. A. (2020). Customer acceptance of ride-hailing in Indonesia. *Journal of Science and Technology Policy Management.*

Almunawar, M. N., Anshari, M., Susanto, H., & Chen, C. K. (2015). Revealing customer behavior on smartphones. *International Journal of Asian Business and Information Management, 6*(2), 33–49. doi:10.4018/IJABIM.2015040103

Almunawar, M. N., Anshari, M., Susanto, H., & Chen, C. K. (2018). How people choose and use their Smartphones. In *Management Strategies and Technology Fluidity in the Asian Business Sector* (pp. 235–252). IGI Global. doi:10.4018/978-1-5225-4056-4.ch014

Alsalameh, A. M., Harisi, M. J., Alduayji, M. A., Almutham, A. A., & Mahmood, F. M. (2019). Evaluating the relationship between smartphone addiction/overuse and musculoskeletal pain among medical students at Qassim University. *Journal of Family Medicine and Primary Care, 8*(9), 2953. doi:10.4103/jfmpc.jfmpc_665_19 PMID:31681674

Anshari, M., & Alas, Y. (2015). Smartphones habits, necessities, and big data challenges. *The Journal of High Technology Management Research, 26*(2), 177–185. doi:10.1016/j.hitech.2015.09.005

Anshari, M., Alas, Y., & Sulaiman, E. (2019b). Smartphone addictions and nomophobia among youth. *Vulnerable Children and Youth Studies, 14*(3), 242–247. doi:10.1080/17450128.2019.1614709

Anshari, M., & Almunawar, M. N. (2021). Adopting open innovation for SMEs and industrial revolution 4.0. *Journal of Science and Technology Policy Management.*

Anshari, M., Almunawar, M. N., Lim, S. A., & Al-Mudimigh, A. (2019a). Customer relationship management and big data enabled: Personalization & customization of services. *Applied Computing and Informatics, 15*(2), 94–101. doi:10.1016/j.aci.2018.05.004

Anshari, M., Almunawar, M. N., & Masri, M. (2022). Digital Twin: Financial Technology's Next Frontier of Robo-Advisor. *Journal of Risk and Financial Management, 15*(4), 163. doi:10.3390/jrfm15040163

Anshari, M., Almunawar, M. N., Masri, M., & Hamdan, M. (2019c). Digital marketplace and FinTech to support agriculture sustainability. *Energy Procedia*, *156*, 234–238. doi:10.1016/j.egypro.2018.11.134

Anshari, M., Almunawar, M. N., Younis, M. Z., & Kisa, A. (2021). Modeling Users' Empowerment in E-Health Systems. *Sustainability*, *13*(23), 12993. doi:10.3390u132312993

Anshari, M., Arine, M. A., Nurhidayah, N., Aziyah, H., & Salleh, M. H. A. (2021). Factors influencing individual in adopting eWallet. *Journal of Financial Services Marketing*, *26*(1), 10–23. doi:10.105741264-020-00079-5

Anshari, M., Hasmawati, F., Razzaq, A., & Samiha, Y. T. (2020). Understanding Nomophobia Among Digital Natives: Characteristics And Challenges. *Journal of Critical Reviews*, *7*(13), 122–131.

Anshari, M., & Lim, S. A. (2017). E-government with big data enabled through smartphone for public services: Possibilities and challenges. *International Journal of Public Administration*, *40*(13), 1143–1158. doi:10.1080/01900692.2016.1242619

Bartwal, J., & Nath, B. (2019). Evaluation of nomophobia among medical students using smartphone in north India. *Medical Journal, Armed Forces India*. PMID:33162655

Bose, T. K. (2012). Application of fishbone analysis for evaluating supply chain and business process-a case study on the St James Hospital. *International Journal of Managing Value and Supply Chains*, *3*(2), 17–24. doi:10.5121/ijmvsc.2012.3202

Cheever, N. A., Rosen, L. D., Carrier, L. M., & Chavez, A. (2014). Out of sight is not out of mind: The impact of restricting wireless mobile device use on anxiety levels among low, moderate and high users. *Computers in Human Behavior*, *37*, 290–297. doi:10.1016/j.chb.2014.05.002

Chen, B. X. (2012). Get Ready for 1 Billion Smartphones by 2016, Forrester Says. *New York Times*. https://bits.blogs.nytimes.com/2012/02/13/get-ready-for-1-billion-smartphones-by-2016-forrester-says/

David, M. E., & Roberts, J. A. (2021). Smartphone Use during the COVID-19 Pandemic: Social Versus Physical Distancing. *International Journal of Environmental Research and Public Health*, *18*(3), 1034. doi:10.3390/ijerph18031034 PMID:33503907

Hasmawati, F., Samiha, Y. T., Razzaq, A., & Anshari, M. (2020). Understanding nomophobia among digital natives: Characteristics and challenges. *Journal of Critical Reviews*, *7*(13), 122–131.

Haynes, T. (2018). Dopamine, Smartphones & You: A battle for your time. *Harvard Publications*. https://sitn.hms.harvard.edu/flash/2018/dopamine-smartphones-battle-time/

Kon, J. (2020). BruHealth QR code a must at all premises: MoH. *Borneo Bulletin* https://borneobulletin.com.bn/bruhealth-qr-code-a-must-at-all-premises-moh/

Li, L., & Lin, T. T. C. (2019). Smartphones at Work: A Qualitative Exploration of Psychological Antecedents and Impacts of Work-Related Smartphone Dependency. *International Journal of Qualitative Methods*, *18*. doi:10.1177/1609406918822240

Li, Y., Guan, M., Hammond, P., & Berrey, L. E. (2021). Communicating COVID-19 information on TikTok: A content analysis of TikTok videos from official accounts featured in the COVID-19 information hub. *Health Education Research*, *36*(3), 261–271. doi:10.1093/her/cyab010 PMID:33667311

Miller, G. (2012). The smartphone psychology manifesto. *Perspectives on Psychological Science*, *7*(3), 221–237. doi:10.1177/1745691612441215 PMID:26168460

Mohammad, J., Quoquab, F., Halimah, S., & Thurasamy, R. (2019). Workplace internet leisure and employees' productivity. *Internet Research*, *29*(4), 725–748. doi:10.1108/IntR-05-2017-0191

Motowidlo, S. J., & Kell, H. J. (2012). Job Performance. *Handbook of Psychology,* *12*(2), 82-103. https://www.researchgate.net/publication/236624589_Job_Performance

Muench, R., & Muench, C. (2020). Me Without My Smartphone? Never! Predictors of Willingness for Smartphone Separation and Nomophobia. *Communications in Computer and Information Science*, *1226*, 217–223. doi:10.1007/978-3-030-50732-9_29

Mulyani, M. A., Razzaq, A., Sumardi, W. H., & Anshari, M. (2019, August). Smartphone adoption in mobile learning scenario. In *International Conference on Information Management and Technology (ICIMTech)* (Vol. 1, pp. 208-211). IEEE. 10.1109/ICIMTech.2019.8843755

Pitichat, T. (2013). Smartphones in the workplace: Changing organizational behavior, transforming the future. *LUX: A Journal of Transdisciplinary Writing and Research*, *3*(1).

Ratan, Z. A., Zaman, S. B., Islam, S. M. S., & Hosseinzadeh, H. (2021). Smartphone overuse: A hidden crisis in COVID-19. *Health policy and technology*.

Razzaq, A., Samiha, Y. T., & Anshari, M. (2018). Smartphone habits and behaviors in supporting students self-efficacy. *International Journal of Emerging Technologies in Learning*, *13*(2), 94. doi:10.3991/ijet.v13i02.7685

Rodríguez-García, A. M., Moreno-Guerrero, A. J., & Lopez Belmonte, J. (2020). Nomophobia: An individual's growing fear of being without a smartphone—a systematic literature review. *International Journal of Environmental Research and Public Health*, *17*(2), 580. doi:10.3390/ijerph17020580 PMID:31963208

Rosli, S. N., Anshari, M., Almunawar, M. N., & Masri, M. (2022). Digital Wallet Ecosystem in Promoting Financial Inclusion. In *FinTech Development for Financial Inclusiveness* (pp. 31–49). IGI Global. doi:10.4018/978-1-7998-8447-7.ch003

Smith, A. (2012). Nearly half of American adults are smartphone owners. *Pew Research Center*. https://www.pewresearch.org/internet/2012/03/01/nearly-half-of-american-adults-are-smartphone-owners/

Sohn, S., Rees, P., Wildridge, B., Kalk, N. J., & Carter, B. (2019). Prevalence of problematic smartphone usage and associated mental health outcomes amongst children and young people: A systematic review, meta-analysis and GRADE of the evidence. *BMC Psychiatry*, *19*(1), 1–10. PMID:30606141

Statista. (2022). Time spent with nonvoice activities on mobile phones every day in the United States from 2019-2023. *Statista*. https://www.statista.com/statistics/1045353/mobile-device-daily-usage-time-in-the- us/

Torode, C. (2011). The realities of consumerization: Christina Torode takes a shop-floor look at Ford's bring-your-own-device programme. *Computer Weekly*, 1.

World Health Organization. (2020). Coronavirus disease (COVID-2019) situation report, (154). WHO. https://wwwwhoint/emergencies/diseases/novel-coronavirus-2019/ situation-reports/

Yildirim, C., & Correia, A. P. (2015). Exploring the dimensions of nomophobia: Development and validation of a self-reported questionnaire. *Computers in Human Behavior*, *49*, 130–137. doi:10.1016/j.chb.2015.02.059

Chapter 6
Delivery Workers, COVID–19, and Job Burnout

Nur Hazirah Mohd Sufian
Universiti Brunei Darussalam, Brunei

ABSTRACT

In the age of COVID-19, couriers are one of the jobs that have been categorised as essential; while other jobs have changed to working from home if they can, couriers and other essential workers still need to carry out their tasks as usual in order to maintain a semblance of normalcy for others. Yet, problems previously experienced by couriers have instead been made worse by COVID-19, such as the prevalence of overwork becoming more common as the demand of online shopping increases. As a result, job burnout has become more pronounced in this new norm. In view of this, exploratory research was conducted by reviewing various literature surrounding job burnout and courier work in the context of the COVID-19 pandemic. The findings are then analysed using Ishikawa's fishbone diagram, which are then categorised into four interlinked themes of environmental, psychological, physical, and financial factors. Afterwards, a discussion was made to further detail the extent of these factors towards job burnout, with recommendations being made to potentially remedy these factors.

1. INTRODUCTION

It can be said that COVID-19 has ushered in a new era within human history. In the span of a few months only, COVID-19 was able to rapidly spread throughout the world, surpassing 238 million infections on 13 October 2021 (CGTN, 2021). Despite our vast experience in handling previous pandemics (i.e., SARS and Ebola)

DOI: 10.4018/978-1-6684-6108-2.ch006

and repeated warnings from the World Health Organisation that another pandemic was imminent, governments and global health authorities were still unprepared for COVID-19 (WHO, 2017).

According to Ciotti et al. (2020), a COVID-19 positive patient can unknowingly transmit the virus via respiratory, saliva and ocular routes of the body, with an incubation period of about 6 to 14 days. Due to this reason, health authorities recommend restrictions to movements in order to avoid such incidents. Following this advice, global governments have been issuing nation-wide lockdowns to limit human-to-human interactions as one of the attempts to curb the spread of the virus (Vieira, 2020). By limiting movement, economic and social activities effectively paused, thereby affecting economies, supply chains and businesses as both workers and consumers are forced to stay indoors. As a result, Bhatti et al. (2020) observed that an increasing number of brick-and-mortar establishments - including food retailers and supermarkets – have been transitioning into e-commerce to adapt to this "new norm". This trend also coincides with the increasing usage of technology, such as using food delivery apps to continue serving food amidst a lockdown (Zanetta et al., 2021; Almunawar et al., 2018; Anshari et al., 2021c; Anshari & Hamdan, 2022a). Although, even before the current COVID-19 pandemic, online retailing has already been seeing an upward trend due to the accessibility of digital e-payments (Roggeveen & Sethuraman, 2020). Regardless, the COVID-19 pandemic is said to have changed the typical processes of the retail industry, with many firms rethinking their operations in order to survive in the current environment (Roggeveen and Sethuraman, 2020).

In order to lower the infected cases and safeguard the majority of the population, most countries have urged businesses to apply a work-from-home strategy, but this strategy is not applicable to every industry as workers that are deemed essential are still required to work such as health care, law enforcement, education, supermarket and even delivery workers (Reid et al., 2020; Almunawar et al., 2012; Anshari 2021). They are the employees whose efforts are critical to the preservation of societies' fabric (Reid et al., 2020; Rosli et al., 2022). However, many of these essential workers are negatively affected by the change in work environment due to COVID-19 because not only are they risking their lives, but they are physically and emotionally burdened due to added responsibilities (Rosa et al., 2020; Anshari et al., 2021a; Fithriyah, 2022).

Hence, this research will be focused on COVID-19 and essential workers specifically the courier workers since these workers not only are risking their lives by travelling to a lot of places including health hazard zones (zones that are known to have high cases of positive patients) but they are known to be underpaid and overworked (Olszewski, 2021; Mulyani et al., 2021; Almunawar & Anshari, 2022). These bad working conditions will consequently have negative effects on the workers such as in South Korea where Choon (2021) reported that South Korea's couriers went on strike, demanding employers to commit to an agreement that prevents overwork and improves working conditions following the death of 16 couriers. Moreover, there is not much literature on the effect and challenges of COVID-19 on courier workers so this research will attempt to fill in the research gap while also answering the research question *"does COVID-19 cause courier workers to experience job burnout?"* by using Ishikawa's Fishbone Diagram to investigate the root causes.

2. METHODOLOGY

This research will be a review paper based on previous research on COVID-19, delivery employees especially courier service workers, and job satisfaction. The papers were chosen from databases such as Google Scholar, Emerald, Springer, and ScienceDirect using a basic random selection and snowballing approach.

The abstracts and titles of articles were first reviewed to ensure the relevance of the topic. Afterwards, these articles were then filtered based on four criterias, the first being, articles must be published between 2015 and 2021. This is to avoid the human mistake of including research that is no longer valid at this time, guaranteeing that the knowledge from this study may be used in future studies. Secondly, the literature must also address the challenges faced by courier service workers amidst of COVID-19 and the relationship between COVID-19 and the feeling of burnout. Third, the majority of the articles gathered will focus on the delivery service sector in order to contextualize in the correct perspective while also providing relevant examples. Finally, to assure authenticity, the chosen publications must be peer-reviewed journal articles or books that have been published. However, internet articles from the specified time period were also gathered to serve as generic examples.

As a result, only 40 of the 58 literatures was chosen based on all four criteria. The material gathered from the chosen literature will be evaluated and organized into themes or features for use in the literature review, findings and discussion. In the finding section, the consolidated literature will then be further analysed using the fishbone diagram, otherwise known as the Ishikawa diagram. This analysis utilises a cause-and-effect methodology to identify how COVID-19 affects courier workers and what are the root causes of the courier workers feeling burnout.

3. FINDINGS & ANALYSIS

In this section, the consolidated literature will be utilised to synthesise a backdrop of information that will help provide the necessary contexts for the research findings.

This section will also explain the underlying factors contributing to a courier's burnout rate with the aid of the Ishikawa Diagram.

As previously mentioned, the COVID-19 pandemic has caused a ripple effect towards digitalisation. Schniederjans et al. (2020) observed that COVID-19 has also driven the digitalisation of the supply chain, which can be integrated with knowledge management tools. They elaborated by stating how digitalisation has enabled firms to process large amounts of data efficiently and instantaneously, among others by turning tacit knowledge of customers (in the form of their experiences using the service) into knowledge for workers to use as guidance. For courier workers, Schniederjans et al. (2020) supported the notion that digitalisation may enable easier accessibility for customer feedback through the apps or websites, which may help further improve their services by considering customer comments. In terms of convenience, digitalisation enables courier workers to plan out their delivery routes more efficiently, as addresses and GPS locations (the raw data) are consolidated for the workers (Anshari et al., 2022; Anshari et al., 2021b). In addition, courier workers can use these digital infrastructures to cross-reference orders, should there be a mistake in deliveries due to human error. However, with the growth of the digital economy, courier service workers face more physical and psychological demands where the workload has increased resulting in workers experiencing burnout from the exhausted and diminished work efficacy (Izzah et al., 2016, Yan & Xie, 2016).

By definition, burnout is an occupational phenomenon that is more than just stress or tiredness; it is a sense of overwhelming exhaustion, cynicism, and poor self-efficacy brought on by long-term job pressures (Rosa et al., 2021). From the gathered literature, the root causes fall under four emerging factors that can be observed to affect a courier's burnout rate: (i) environmental, (ii) physical, (iii) psychological and (iv) financial factors. Below is an illustration of Ishikawa's fishbone diagram (*Figure 1*) as a visual aid that summarises the root causes:

Figure 1. Ishikawa's Fishbone diagram on the root causes of Courier workers experiencing job burnout

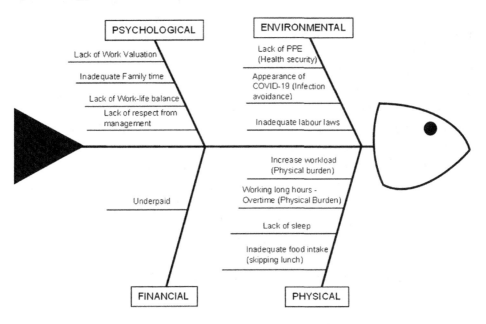

3.1 Environmental

The current COVID-19 pandemic creates a constant environment where fear of infection is constantly on the minds of the courier, especially if their own companies do not provide them with adequate personal protective equipment (PPE) (Polkowska, 2020; The Lancet, 2020; Anshari & Hamdan, 2022b). Normally, PPEs are used by medical frontliners to protect against infection, and these PPEs include equipment such as N95 masks, gloves and face shields. However, even with adequate PPEs, there is always a risk of a breakthrough. For every essential worker (including couriers), there is a perpetual worry of getting infected and bringing the virus home to their loved ones. Mui et al. (2021) illustrated this by explaining how couriers of Pos Laju Malaysia are always at risk of infections during deliveries, as they would be entering both red and green zones for delivery orders. Mui et al. (2021) also detailed how couriers are fearful when they are handling parcels at the mail processing centers prior to delivery; there are concerns that the COVID-19 virus is able to survive on the surface of the parcels, so each of the parcels received from overseas need to be sanitised before delivery to adhere to the latest standard of procedure (SOP) set by the Malaysian government, thereby increasing the workload of the couriers.

This constant fear of infection is also made worse when the labour laws of the country do not protect the welfare of couriers. Naturally, if companies' policies fail to protect the right to health for couriers, couriers would then look to the government for solutions, but not all governments are as benevolent. When the COVID-19 pandemic started to appear in Brazil, an emergency economic payout known as the "coronavoucher" was approved. Its aim was to support businesses and workers who will be affected by the government's reduction of labour hours and temporary suspension of labour contracts, the latter being the category that most couriers fall under. Under this scheme, couriers were supposed to receive full coverage of unemployment insurance (Greer et al.1, 2021). However, Nogueira et al. (2020) reported that the federal government would then suddenly exclude certain categories of workers (including gig economy workers, i.e., couriers) from being eligible to receive the "coronavoucher". They further theorised that this was the work of corrupt officials who were advancing the agenda of discrimination against workers of the gig economy. Due to this, couriers felt betrayed and frustrated, as they were looking to use the aid to cover their rent and utilities (Teixeira et al., 2020).

Eventually, these couriers will feel devoid of motivation and burnout as their problems only keep increasing without any solutions since not only they are to work in a dangerous situation, fearing for their lives and their families but they also do not have the financial stability they hoped to receive.

3.2 Physical

Anderson et al. (2020) reported that during this pandemic, executives often struggle to connect to their customers, but they are doing far worse in connecting to their employees. In the changing COVID-19 business environment, the perception gap between employees and employers has widened. Executives would place their employees under intense pressure to maintain pre-pandemic levels of profit which could cause the employees to be stressed.

For the courier service industry, since the pandemic, internet shopping has become a welcomed modern standard, with consumers being encouraged by the government to use such facilities to buy their necessities amidst lockdowns or movement restriction orders where even supermarkets are temporarily shut down (Mui et al., n.d.). As a result, the number of parcels to be delivered have understandably increased, leading to an increase in work intensification. According to Holst (2012), to measure the quality of work of courier workers, it is by seeing the number of parcels they deliver in a day. In the interview, drivers shared that depending on the geographic area, 200 parcels are delivered in a day and another 200 are picked up in the afternoon which sometimes caused them to work exceeding 12 hours in a day. In a study conducted by the Austrian transport and service workers' union, *Vida*, half of the drivers polled indicated that their cars are overcrowded on a regular basis and often, single "parcels" might weigh more than a courier can transport alone. As a result, many of the drivers interviewed lamented the physically demanding task and the effects on their physical health such as the occurrence of a locomotive issue at the back.

A similar occurrence is seen in a study by Mui et al. (2021) on the challenges faced by the workers at Pos Laju Malaysia. The increase of workload during COVID-19 has caused the workers to be fatigued from working. For delivery workers, they are even required to work during holiday seasons and their off-days in order to prevent a backlog of deliveries and maintain a seamless delivery schedule. Yoon et al. (2020) illustrated this by explaining that the number of couriers does not match the surge of delivery demand brought forth during the pandemic. Thus, couriers would often feel pressured to work overtime in order to achieve the same-day delivery of orders, causing them to work well beyond their supposed off-time such as working till midnight. As a consequence, the workers lack sleep, worsened by the fact that their next working session begins in the early morning. Besides that, Akamatsu et al. (2017) also detailed how couriers sometimes would skip their lunch breaks to finish their daily delivery orders, adding more physical burden onto their body as not only do they lack enough sleep, but they also do not have enough energy.

Therefore, the excessive workloads and lack of resources would result in high levels of stress and poor physical health for courier workers, leading the employees to suffer burnout easily (de Simone et al., 2016).

3.3 Psychological

Besides physical health, COVID-19 is also known to affect the mental health of individuals. Research done by Arslan et al. (2020) states that, due to the constant news of death and new cases of COVID-19, many individuals are diagnosed with psychological problems that include stress, anxiety, depression, and burnout.

A parcel courier's task is often underestimated and undervalued due to the lack of qualifications (validity of a driver's license) needed to perform the task. However, contrary to popular beliefs, couriers are under continuous stress and are constantly multi-tasking where they have to balance the demands from their management, state authorities (police, customs and tax) and as well customers within a very tight time schedule. According to Mat Desa et al. (2020), many courier workers complained that they did not receive the valuations (in monetary and societal terms) they deserved. In this situation, the employees would feel undervalued and not appreciated for the hard work they have done, affecting their morale and life satisfaction. Moreover, employees would lose the sense of worth within the job itself, resulting in burnout (Best, 2021).

The work-life balance of couriers has severely become unbalanced, especially during the COVID-19 pandemic where couriers have to work overtime (often unpaid) to prevent a backlog of orders. Riyanto et al. (2019) defined work-life balance as the management of responsibilities held at work and the obligations held at home. By not having a clear balance between work and life, couriers are often forced to be away from their families for long periods of time, as they are locked in an exhausting loop of tasks that does not end by their supposed clock-out time. By being away from their family, they are deprived of family time that is reported to be essential for the maintenance of mental health during this pandemic (Voo et al., 2020). Family time (and similarly, personal time) helps in breaking the perception that work is constant, warding away the sense of dread derived from never-ending work which would be felt otherwise. When a sense of balance is reached, employees would be more willing to carry out their jobs with renewed conviction and reduce the likelihood of burnout (Riyanto et al., 2019)

The relationship between the management and the management is also linked with the burnout rate of couriers. Liang and Chen (2020) discovered that burnout in couriers is exacerbated when the management lacks respect and harmony with their employees (and vice-versa), creating a non-welcoming atmosphere at work. Liang and Chen (2020) elaborated that this typically happens when the management places excessive expectations and workload on employees (whether it was done so out of spite or a lack of empathy). This is especially true for companies that prioritise maintaining profit over the welfare of their workers, especially during the COVID-19 pandemic (Camila et al., 2021).

3.4 Financial

The prolonged COVID-19 pandemic has escalated the fear of financial insecurity as working hours are cut down, companies are downsizing and salaries are being reduced (Lippens et al., 2020). Financial security is regarded as the most important element by employees, and they are likely to feel a complex variety of unpleasant emotions and work stress when their employers are unable to provide job security and income replacement.

It is no secret that courier workers are underpaid despite the heavy and straining work they do on a daily basis. One interviewee in Austria, for example, said that the number of stops he was required to make increased from 25 to 40 overnight during the start of COVID-19, but that his daily wages stayed the same (about 230 Euro per day) (Holst, 2012). For a company, this meant increased productivity per driver, while for the driver, it meant delivering nearly twice as many parcels in the same period without receiving a pay raise. From this, it can be insinuated that courier workers are not paid for overtime as well, a common problem seen almost everywhere such as in South Korea. The delivery workers are seen as temporary workers or self-employed because they are under a subcontract hence preventing them from receiving minimum wage or payment for overtime (Park, 2020).

Moreover, in some countries as mentioned before, government laws and company policies do not protect the rights of couriers, so drivers sometimes face fines if they fail to deliver express packages on schedule or skip a collection. Besides that, couriers also would intentionally breach traffic regulations to meet the demands of parcel delivery - a risky move as they might also be charged for breaking the law, hence constricting even more of their financial situation. Rasdi et al. (2021) explained the lack of resources, in this case, financial resources, experienced by employees can cause the aggravation of health impairment conditions such as stress. According to Price et al. (2002), as cited by Rasdi et al. (2021), employees who are under economic stress confront a slew of difficult consequences that go beyond physical and mental health issues which in turn, reduce life satisfaction, and increase the risk of emotional tiredness and burnout.

4. DISCUSSION

In reference to the research question *"does COVID-19 cause courier workers to experience job burnout?"*, it can be observed that there is a positive relationship between COVID-19 and the negative emotion of burning out. Courier workers do, in fact, feel more burned out because of the situations they are in that are aggravated further by COVID-19. These situations are identified as the root causes under the four main categories mentioned in the findings, which are acting as mediators between COVID-19 and experiences of burnout. Zadros (2021) and Singh et al. (2015) supported this notion where the current pandemic has caused changes to the work environment of couriers and emphasised pre-existing problems.

Maslow's Hierarchy of Needs theory is one of the theories that can explain the relationship between the root causes, job satisfaction, and job burnout. This theory explains that human needs are categorized (in ascending order) into five distinct levels which are physiological, safety, social, esteem and self-actualization (Hale et al., 2018). Hence, if the root causes were to be arranged according to the five levels of needs in the theory it will be as followed:

1. **Esteem**: Work Valuation (Psychological factor);
2. **Love and belonging**: Family time (Psychological factor); Work-Life Balance (Psychological factor) and Respect from management (Psychological factor)

3. **Safety Needs**: Infection Avoidance (Environmental factor); Health Security (Environmental factor); Financial Security (Financial factor); Adequate Labour Laws (Environmental Factor)
4. **Physiological Needs**: Physical Burden (Physical factor); Adequate Sleep (Physical factor), Food (Physical factor).

The theory further explains that employees will be motivated as long as these requirements are met, but the first requirement on the bottom stratum must be satisfied first before a subsequent need or strata can be considered. In addition, from the Root Cause Analysis in the form of the Ishikawa Diagram, it is observed that these four main categories are intertwined with each other where if one category is negatively affected by COVID-19, a domino effect will happen.

For example, the physical factor where the increase in workload and working overtime causes the body of couriers to slowly deteriorate. The stress is further added with their fear of getting infected by the virus (environmental factor) and their only motivation is through financial factors. If the financial aspect is taken away (such as when they are underpaid), they would feel undervalued and not respected (psychological factor). In addition, if anything were to happen to the couriers during the job, they would not have the money to solve it, consequently adding more pressure on their already heavy shoulders. The courier workers would feel dissatisfied with the situation they are in, causing the appearance of negative emotions such as demotivation, anger, depression and eventually leading to them feeling burned out. This coincides with the principles of Maslow's Hierarchy of Needs as clarified by McLeod (2020), the basic human requirements of survival (in this case psychological and safety needs) will always take precedence before work value-related needs (self-esteem and self-actualization). In addition, in some cases where courier workers have reached their limit in their level of burnout and realized they need to fulfil their self-actualization needs, their turnover intention will increase. This is proven by Kim (2018), where the study linked burnout and turnover to a high degree of role stress, a poor amount of job autonomy, and a low level of social support. As a result, when employment conditions include high levels of stress and task overload, workers' intention to leave is linked to their burnout. Moreover, Yoon et al. (2020) supported this theory with their own research where delivery workers that experienced burnout as a result of exhaustion and decreased work efficacy, leads to high levels of turnover intention.

When workers start to express their intentions to resign, a rippling effect will occur as other workers who may not be happy would consider the idea as well, thereby affecting the overall performance and morale of the company. To prevent this, Hale et al. (2018) suggested that addressing the five needs of Maslow's Hierarchy of Needs is the key to preventing burnout. As the findings touch upon financial, psychological, physical and environmental factors, Hale et al (2018) gave a number of suggestions based on the different layers of Maslow's Hierarchy of Needs. At the strata of base needs, companies may want to start providing their couriers with food packs to ensure they do not go hungry throughout the day, especially during busy periods. Moving up to safety needs, companies can organise financial talks such as debt management for couriers who may be interested. Courier companies may also simply consider setting aside a budget to provide PPEs for couriers, including the right training on how to use them. On the next strata of Love and Belonging, companies should invest in proper human resource management that will fairly assign shifts for courier workers to ensure they have days off to spend time with their families. In the same strata, companies should instill a collaborative working environment instead of a competitive one. Afterwards in the next strata of esteem, companies can also consider giving out rewards to show recognition of good behaviour and performance.

While suggestions have been given above, Abubakar et al. (2019) stated that effective knowledge management aids in making decisions, as the knowledge in the management's disposal will provide more context, understanding and hindsight. This means the top management needs to practice proper knowledge management to ensure informed decisions are fulfilling the needs of the employees as good leadership is vital for the success of the company since the performance of the company relies on the satisfaction of employees to lower the rate of turnover intention. This is supported in a study by Rožman et al. (2019) where it was stated that knowledge management strategies such as acquisition, creation, sharing, and application have a positive impact on employee engagement. These engaged individuals have a plethora of resources to invest in their job and their enthusiastic involvement will increase their job satisfaction and reduce job burnout, effectively lowering the rate of turnover.

5. CONCLUSION

In conclusion, courier burnout is closely linked to the nonfulfillment of the needs of the courier, which were made worse during the COVID-19. While other businesses have shifted to working from home, couriers experienced an increase in demand as their services are more used in this new norm. However, by venturing out of their homes, they will be constantly at the risk of exposure to COVID-19, as they would do deliveries in both red and green zones. This understandably weighs on the minds of couriers, who are often also overworked to complete the growing number of delivery orders, thereby increasing burnout rates. In connection to this, all of the factors and problems experienced by the couriers that were mentioned before were then divided into four "themes" - environmental factors, physical factors, psychological factors and financial factors. However, this paper argues that with proper knowledge management practices, courier companies can circumvent these issues by making informed decisions with the goal of protecting the welfare of couriers amidst the pandemic. Among these solutions that knowledge management brings, is the decision to have packed meals for couriers so they will always have something to eat, or the decision to implement proper scheduling for shifts that ensure couriers have adequate rest days to spend time with their families and have personal time off. Therefore, proper implementation of knowledge management is required to ensure fulfilment of the needs and mitigate the burnout rate if there's any.

As with the majority of research, this paper has also experienced limitations. At the outset, the data reviewed in this paper is derived from secondary sources, so there is a possibility for inaccuracies or limitations to be carried forward into this research. Secondly, the time frame given to carry out this research is very limited, therefore a more stringent criterion for literature is chosen to save time, so potential data may not be taken into account. Thirdly, the findings in this research may not always be applicable to certain contexts, as examples were mostly derived from western literature where it is more readily available. Lastly, contexts surrounding COVID-19 and delivery workers are still very much new, so there may still be unknown variables that may not be considered until more research is done.

REFERENCES

Abubakar, A. M., Elrehail, H., Alatailat, M. A., & Elci, A. (2019). Knowledge Management, Decision-making Style, and Organizational Performance. *Journal of Innovation & Knowledge.*, *4*(2), 104–114. doi:10.1016/j.jik.2017.07.003

Akamatsu, R., Mochida, K., Shimpo, M., & Sakurazawa, H. (2017). Drivers' Lunch Break, Health, and Work Performance: A Study on Japanese Drivers at a Courier Company Who Skip Lunch. *Journal of Nutrition Education and Behavior*, *49*(7), S42. doi:10.1016/j.jneb.2017.05.335

Almunawar, M. N., & Anshari, M. (2022). Customer acceptance of online delivery platform during the COVID-19 pandemic: the case of Brunei Darussalam. *Journal of Science and Technology Policy Management*. doi:10.1108/JSTPM-04-2022-0073

Almunawar, M. N., Anshari, M., Susanto, H., & Chen, C. K. (2018). How people choose and use their Smartphones. In *Management Strategies and Technology Fluidity in the Asian Business Sector* (pp. 235–252). IGI Global. doi:10.4018/978-1-5225-4056-4.ch014

Almunawar, M. N., Wint, Z., Low, K. C., & Anshari, M. (2012). Customer expectation of e-health systems in Brunei Darussalam. *Journal of Health Care Finance*, *38*(4), 36–49. PMID:22894020

Anderson, C., Bieck, C., & Marshall, A. (2020). How business is adapting to COVID-19: Executive insights reveal post-pandemic opportunities. *Strategy and Leadership*, *49*(1), 38–47. doi:10.1108/SL-11-2020-0140

Anshari, M. (2021). *E-Health Management Services in Supporting Empowerment*. Cornell University.

Anshari, M., Almunawar, M., & Masri, M. (2021a). Financial Technology Promoting Healthy Lifestyle and Community Development. In *Proceedings of the 1st International Conference on Law, Social Science, Economics, and Education, ICLSSEE 2021, Jakarta, Indonesia*. 10.4108/eai.6-3-2021.2306396

Anshari, M., Almunawar, M. N., & Masri, M. (2022). Digital Twin: Financial Technology's Next Frontier of Robo-Advisor. *Journal of Risk and Financial Management*, *15*(4), 163. doi:10.3390/jrfm15040163

Anshari, M., Almunawar, M. N., & Razzaq, A. (2021b). Developing talents vis-à-vis fourth industrial revolution. *International Journal of Asian Business and Information Management*, *12*(4), 20–32. doi:10.4018/IJABIM.20211001.oa2

Anshari, M., Almunawar, M. N., Younis, M. Z., & Kisa, A. (2021c). Modeling Users' Empowerment in E-Health Systems. *Sustainability*, *13*(23), 12993. doi:10.3390u132312993

Anshari, M., & Hamdan, M. (2022a). Enhancing e-government with a digital twin for innovation management. *Journal of Science and Technology Policy Management*. doi:10.1108/JSTPM-11-2021-0176

Anshari, M., & Hamdan, M. (2022b). Understanding knowledge management and upskilling in Fourth Industrial Revolution: Transformational shift and SECI model. *VINE Journal of Information and Knowledge Management Systems*. doi:10.1108/VJIKMS-09-2021-0203

Anshari, M., Hamdan, M., Ahmad, N., Ali, E., & Haidi, H. (2022). COVID-19, artificial intelligence, ethical challenges and policy implications. *AI & Society*, 1–14. doi:10.100700146-022-01471-6 PMID:35607368

Arslan, G., Yıldırım, M., Tanhan, A., Buluş, M., & Allen, K. A. (2020). Coronavirus Stress, Optimism-Pessimism, Psychological Inflexibility, and Psychological Health: Psychometric Properties of the Coronavirus Stress Measure. International Journal of Mental Health and Addiction. doi:10.100711469-020-00337-6

Best, J. (2021). Undermined and undervalued: how the pandemic exacerbated moral injury and burnout in the NHS. *BMJ,* n1858. doi:10.1136/bmj.n1858

Bhatti, A., Akram, H., Basit, H. M., Khan, A. U., Naqvi, S. M. R., & Bilal, M. (2020). E-Commerce during COVID-19 Pandemic. *International Journal of Future Generation Communication and Networking., 13*(2), 1449–1452.

Camila, S., Pereira, P., & Pereira-pereira, P. A. (2021). Capitalist Greed, Pandemic, and the Future of Social Policy. *Argumentum, 13*(1), 53–65.

CGTN. (2021, October 12). *COVID-19 Live Updates: Global cases surpass 238 million.* CGTN. https://www.cgtn.com/special/Latest-updates-on-COVID-19-pandemic.html

Choon, C. M. (2021, June 14). South Korea's delivery workers go on strike against overwork amid Covid-19. *The Straits Times.* https://www.straitstimes.com/asia/east-asia/south-koreas-delivery-workers-go-on-strike-against-overwork-amid-covid-19

Ciotti, M., Ciccozzi, M., Terrinoni, A., Jiang, W. C., Wang, C. B., & Bernardini, S. (2020). The COVID-19 pandemic. *Critical Reviews in Clinical Laboratory Sciences, 57*(6), 365–388. doi:10.1080/10408363.2020.1783198 PMID:32645276

De Simone, S., Cicotto, G., & Lampis, J. (2016). Occupational stress, job satisfaction and physical health in teachers. *European Review of Applied Psychology, 66*(2), 65–77. doi:10.1016/j.erap.2016.03.002

Desa, N. M., Asaari, M. H. A. H., & Yim, L. C. (2020). Human Resource Management Practices and Job Satisfaction among Courier Service Provider Employees. *International Journal of Asian Social Science, 10*(6), 327–338. doi:10.18488/journal.1.2020.106.327.338

Fithriyah, M., Masri, M., Almunawar, M. N., & Anshari, M. (2022). Financial Inclusion and Mobile Payment to Empower Small and Medium-Sized Enterprises: Post-COVID-19 Business Strategy. In FinTech Development for Financial Inclusiveness (pp. 50-59). IGI Global.

Greer, S. L., Jarman, H., Falkenbach, M., Massard Da Fonseca, E., Raj, M., & King, E. J. (2021). Social policy as an integral component of pandemic response: Learning from COVID-19 in Brazil, Germany, India and the United States. *Global Public Health: An International Journal for Research, Policy and Practice, 16*(8–9), 1209–1222. doi:10.1080/17441692.2021.1916831 PMID:33876715

Hale, A. J., Ricotta, D. N., Freed, J., Smith, C. C., & Huang, G. C. (2018). Adapting Maslow's Hierarchy of Needs as a Framework for Resident Wellness. *Teaching and Learning in Medicine, 31*(1), 109–118. doi:10.1080/10401334.2018.145692 8 PMID:29708437

Holst, H. (2012). On the move in Global Delivery Chains : Labour Relations and Working Conditions in the Parcel Delivery Industries of Austria, Germany, the Czech Republic and Hungary. *SODIPER Synthesis Report Work Package, 6.*

Izzah, N., Rifai, D., & Yao, L. (2016). Relationshipcourier partner logistics and e-commerce enterprises in Malaysia: A review. *Indian Journal of Science and Technology, 9*(9), 1–10. doi:10.17485/ijst/2016/v9i9/88721

Kim, J. (2018). The contrary effects of intrinsic and extrinsic motivations on burnout and turnover intention in the public sector. *International Journal of Manpower, 39*(3), 486–500. doi:10.1108/IJM-03-2017-0053

Liang, C., & Chen, J. (2020). *Analysis on Job Burnout Level and Influencing Factors of Young Employees in Guangdong Express Delivery Industry. 150* (Icoeme), 239–248. doi:10.2991/aebmr.k.200908.039

Lippens, L., Moens, E., Sterkens, P., Weytjens, J., & Baert, S. (2021). How do employees think the COVID-19 crisis will affect their careers? *PLoS One, 16*(5), e0246899. doi:10.1371/journal.pone.0246899 PMID:33956808

McLeod, S. A. (2020). Maslow's hierarchy of needs. *Simply Psychology.* https://www.simplypsychology.org/maslow.html

Mui, D., Kee, H., Nurul, S., Nasser, A., Syafiqah, N., & Sany, M. (n.d.). The Strategy, Impact, and Challenges Faced by Pos Malaysia Berhad during the COVID-19 Crisis. *Journal of the Community Development in Asia, 4*(2), 13–25.

Mulyani, M. A., Yusuf, S., Siregar, P., Nurihsan, J., Razzaq, A., & Anshari, M. (2021, August). Fourth Industrial Revolution and Educational Challenges. In *2021 International Conference on Information Management and Technology (ICIMTech)* (Vol. 1, pp. 245-249). IEEE. 10.1109/ICIMTech53080.2021.9535057

Nogueira, M., Amaral, A., & Jones, G. (2020). The impact of COVID-19 on Brazil's precarious labour market calls for far-reaching policies like universal basic income. *LSE,* 1–6. https://blogs.lse.ac.uk/latamcaribbean/

Olszewski, S. (2021, September 13). NYC food delivery workers face a 'harrowing world.' *Cornell Chronicle.* https://news.cornell.edu/stories/2021/09/nyc-food-delivery-workers-face-harrowing-world

Park, J. (2020, November 24). South Korean delivery workers say coronavirus boom means relentless toil. *Reuters.* https://www.reuters.com/article/health-coronavirus-southkorea-jobs-idINKBN2841PM

Polkowska, D. (2020). Platform work during the COVID-19 pandemic: a case study of Glovo couriers in Poland. *European Societies, 23*(sup1), S321–S331. doi:10.10 80/14616696.2020.1826554

Rasdi, R. M., Zaremohzzabieh, Z., & Ahrari, S. (2021). Financial Insecurity During the COVID-19 Pandemic: Spillover Effects on Burnout–Disengagement Relationships and Performance of Employees Who Moonlight. *Frontiers in Psychology, 12,* 610138. doi:10.3389/fpsyg.2021.610138 PMID:33679526

Reid, A., Ronda-Perez, E., & Schenker, M. B. (2020). Migrant workers, essential work, and COVID-19. *American Journal of Industrial Medicine, 64*(2), 73–77. doi:10.1002/ajim.23209 PMID:33355943

Riyanto, S., Ariyanto, E., & Lukertina, L. (2019). WORK LIFE BALANCE AND ITS INFLUENCE ON EMPLOYEE ENGAGEMENT "Y" GENERATION IN COURIER SERVICE INDUSTRY. *International Review of Management and Marketing, 9*(6), 25–31. doi:10.32479/irmm.8499

Roggeveen, A. L., & Sethuraman, R. (2020). How the COVID-19 Pandemic May Change the World of Retailing. *Journal of Retailing, 96*(2), 169–171. doi:10.1016/j.jretai.2020.04.002

Rosa, W. E., Schlak, A. E., & Rushton, C. H. (2020). A blueprint for leadership during COVID-19. *Nursing Management, 51*(8), 28–34. doi:10.1097/01.NUMA.0000688940.29231.6f PMID:32665503

Rosli, S. N., Anshari, M., Almunawar, M. N., & Masri, M. (2022). Digital Wallet Ecosystem in Promoting Financial Inclusion. In *FinTech Development for Financial Inclusiveness* (pp. 31–49). IGI Global. doi:10.4018/978-1-7998-8447-7.ch003

Rožman, M., Shmeleva, Z., & Tominc, P. (2019). Knowledge Management Components and Their Impact on Work Engagement of Employees. *Naše Gospodarstvo/Our Economy, 65*(1), 40–56. doi:10.2478/ngoe-2019-0004

Schniederjans, D. G., Curado, C., & Khalajhedayati, M. (2020). Supply chain digitisation trends: An integration of knowledge management. *International Journal of Production Economics, 220*, 107439. doi:10.1016/j.ijpe.2019.07.012

Singh, P., Aulak, D. S., Mangat, S. S., & Aulak, M. S. (2015). Systematic review: Factors contributing to burnout in dentistry. *Occupational Medicine, 66*(1), 27–31. doi:10.1093/occmed/kqv119 PMID:26443193

(1587). The Lancet. (2020). The plight of essential workers during the COVID-19 pandemic. *Lancet, 395*(10237). doi:10.10160140-6736(20)31200-9

Vieira, T. (2020). The lose-lose dilemmas of Barcelona's platform delivery workers in the age of COVID-19. *Social Sciences & Humanities Open, 2*(1), 100059. doi:10.1016/j.ssaho.2020.100059 PMID:34173497

Voo, T. C., Senguttuvan, M., & Tam, C. C. (2020). Family Presence for Patients and Separated Relatives During COVID-19: Physical, Virtual, and Surrogate. *Journal of Bioethical Inquiry, 17*(4), 767–772. doi:10.100711673-020-10009-8 PMID:32840835

World Health Organization. (2017). Pandemic influenza risk management: a WHO guide to inform and harmonize national and international pandemic preparedness and response. *World Health Organization.* https://apps.who.int/iris/handle/10665/259893

Yan, H., & Xie, S. (2016). How does auditors' work stress affect audit quality? Empirical evidence from the Chinese stock market. *China Journal of Accounting Research, 9*(4), 305–319. doi:10.1016/j.cjar.2016.09.001

Yoon, K. H., Lee, C. Y., & Peng, N. L. (2021). Burnout and work engagement among dispatch workers in courier service organizations. *Asia-Pacific Social Science Review, 21*(1), 1–19.

Zadros, K. (2021). Employee Satisfaction with the Employer's Health Safety Activities During the SARS-COV-2 Pandemic. *Sciendo. 3(*1), 228 - 238. https://sciendo.com/pdf/10.2478/czoto-2021-0023

Zanetta, L. D., Hakim, M. P., Gastaldi, G. B., Seabra, L. M. J., Rolim, P. M., Nascimento, L. G. P., Medeiros, C. O., & da Cunha, D. T. (2021). The use of food delivery apps during the COVID-19 pandemic in Brazil: The role of solidarity, perceived risk, and regional aspects. *Food Research International, 149*, 110671. doi:10.1016/j.foodres.2021.110671 PMID:34600673

Chapter 7
A Digital Ethnographic Account of a Digital Islamic Society During COVID–19:
An Islamic Governance Perspective

Hamizah Haidi

https://orcid.org/0000-0002-3252-2052
Universiti Brunei Darussalam, Brunei

ABSTRACT

Every aspect of one's life, from educating oneself through YouTube to finding a suitor on dating apps, shows how intertwined one's life is with digitalisation. COVID-19 has only allowed it to proliferate further. This chapter examines how different digitalisation policy initiatives in Brunei during COVID-19 have enabled the creation of a digital Islamic society through an Islamic governance perspective. A digital ethnographic approach was employed, and data were drawn from three sources: 1) document analysis, 2) social media, and 3) observation. Analysis was carried out using the Maqāṣid collaborative framework. Results from the study show that a digital Islamic society is currently being shaped in Brunei in all aspect of the Maqāṣid of the Sharia.

DOI: 10.4018/978-1-6684-6108-2.ch007

INTRODUCTION

The digitalisation process have changed the way people live their lives. From educating oneself through YouTube and various other online learning platforms to tracking one's step counts on exercise apps, from finding a suitor on dating apps to online shopping, many modern conveniences would not have taken place if not for the digital revolution. The Covid-19 pandemic only proliferated the digitalisation process even further, and such intertwining of one's daily life with digitalisation have led to the notion of a Digital Society. A digital society is a society that adopts and integrates information and communication technologies in every aspect of life (Foundation, 2021) and this includes religion.

The inclusion of religion in a digital society takes place when "technology has moved to the heard of religious teachings, mobilization and networking" (Bunt, 2018, p.18). In the context of the Islamic religion, religious inclusion in a digital society can be seen in many Muslim-majority countries around the world. In Brunei, Islam have gone beyond faith and rituals, but has been institutionalised to be part and parcel of the country's population (Sharbawi & Mabud, 2021). It is "an institution that covers all aspects of life and governance and serves as a significant form of socio-cultural identity that binds the society together" (Sharbawi & Mabud, 2021, p. 56). For this reason, the notion of Cyber Islamic Environment (CIE) defined by Bunt (2018), as an umbrella concept "utilised to cover a range of online activities, whether an online thesis from an Islamic scholar or a tweet from a social media activist" (p.26); do not hold true for the Bruneian society. Hence, in the case of Bruneian Muslims, it is more prudent to refer to digital society as a Digital Islamic Society.

Brunei is a small country with a population of 429, 999 in 2021 (Department of economic planning and statistics, n.d.) upon which 66% of the population are Muslim (Ministry of Foreign Affairs website, n.d.).

Brunei is a unique case to study the development of a Digital Islamic Society because of two reasons:

A) it is a Muslim-majority country that have successfully institutionalised Islam through a national ideology of "Melayu Islam Beraja" / Malay Islamic Monarchy. In addition, Brunei have also enacted Islamic law, under the Sharia Penal Code Order 2013 and strives to become a zikir nation (Mahmud, 2021) that is considered a "Baldatun Tayyibatun Warabbun Ghafur" - a country that is under the protection of Allah (Tema Hari Kebangsaan, 2021).

B) It has the highest internet penetration within Southeast Asia, with 95% in 2020 (CIA, n.d.)

This chapter has two objectives:

A) To give examples of different digitalisation policy initiatives that fall under the five *Maqāṣid* in Brunei's effort to preserve and promote life during the Pandemic

B) To document the various ways Bruneian Millennial Muslims interact with all five *Maqāṣid* through digital society during Covid-19

The study starts with a review of a digital society and the Islamic System of Governance. This is followed by the methodology, results, discussion and conclusion.

LITERATURE REVIEW

Digital Society

The term "digital" originated from its Latin form, "digitalis" - numbers. It refers to a system that became standard for digital computers from the mid-20th century (Ceruzzi, 2003; Steiner, 2012) - the binary system. The binary system and the logical framework that was built on top of it enables machines to be reprogrammed and updated without physically changing it, which is one of the most significant breakthroughs and characteristics of digital machines (Ceruzzi, 2003). Such breakthrough has allowed for digital technology being a necessary component of modern life.

The process of converting previously analogue or physical actions into digital data systems is referred to as digitalisation. Digitalisation advancement has sparked extensive and diverse speculation about culture and society in the future. Future reshapement of culture and society through digitalisation is one of the many megatrends, despite its ambiguous definition (Dufva & Dufva, 2019).

A digital society is a society where there is a widespread of digitalization processes, resulting in a networked population via online social networks and rapid information spread (Sá et al., 2021). Rapid information spread and a networked population have increasingly shape the acquisition of knowledge, especially during the Covid-19 pandemic. The Covid-19 pandemic has had far-reaching global consequences (Anshari et al., 2022), and can be regarded as first global epidemic of the digital age. Digital transformation acceleration is one of the effects of Covid-19, given its potential to harm emotional and spiritual well-being. Thus, it is critical for a digital society to be established within a religious framework.

Islamic System of Governance and the Maqasid Collaborative Framework

The notion of Islamic Governance is first explored by Maszlee Malik (2016) and Khan (2019). Both authors proposed Islamic Governance as an alternative to the notions of good governance put forward by the West. Abdul Aziz (2019) extended the ideas of Maszlee Malik (2016) and Khan (2019), by proposing that an Islamic system of Governance also comprises how one can self-govern one's self through building a society conducive for the worship of Allah. The concept of Islamic Governance is founded upon the Qur'ān and exemplified in the Prophetic Sunnah via the Rasūl ﷺ on the individual level, societal level, and governance level (Abdul Aziz, 2019)

An Islamic system of governance makes sure that policies put forward fulfil Al-Ghazali's Maqasid of the Sharia (Abdul Aziz, 2019), which comprises of:

A) Preservation and Promotion of Faith

Preservation and promotion of faith involve policies that help preserve the Islamic faith and promote its growth. Examples of policy initiatives within the preservation and promotion of the Islamic faith include dakwah initiatives.

In Brunei, preservation and promotion of the Islamic faith is within the jurisdiction of the Ministry of Religious Affairs (hereby MORA), whose main policy is to preserve and promote Islam and protect the peace and serenity of Negara Brunei Darussalam (Bahagian Dasar, 2017). To do so, MORA has set up several departments that enables society to preserve and promote faith.

These departments include Islamic Religious Department (*Jabatan Pengajian Islam*, hereby JPI), responsible for the management of Islamic religious primary and secondary government schools in the country; Islamic Dakwah Centre (Pusat Dakwah Islami'ah, hereby PDI), responsible for propagating Islam to the Society (Pusat Dakwah Islamiah, 2010); Counselling and Religious Understanding Unit, (*Unit Kaunseling dan Kefahaman Agama*, hereby KAFA), responsible for making sure that faith preservation and promotion in Brunei are free from all forms of extremism, radicalism, and liberal thought (Laman Utama - KAFA, n.d.); and Mosque Affairs Department (*Jabatan Hal Ehwal Masjid*), responsible for overseeing all local mosques and the activities within the mosque, including the activities of Government Non-Governmental Organisations, such as Youth Groups (*Belia Masjid*) and Women's Groups (*Muslimah Masjid*).

B) Preservation and Promotion of Life

Preservation and promotion of life involve policies that help preserve and promote all forms of life. It can be further subdivided into two sections: a) preserving and promoting health of human beings, b) preserving and promoting the environment: plants, animals the atmosphere and the earth and c) preserving and promoting the security.

In Brunei, various departments and Ministries are responsible for preservation and promotion of life. These include, the Ministry of Health (for preserving and promoting health), the Ministry of Primary Resources (for preserving and promoting the environment), and the Ministry of Defence, the Royal Brunei Armed Forces, the Royal Brunei Police Force and the Fire Department (for preserving and promoting security).

Policy initiatives that help preserve and promote the health of human beings include setting up hospitals, clinics and health promotion events. As for policy initiatives that help preserve and promote the environment, these include the Climate Action Policy (Brunei Climate Change Secretariat, 2020) and the Forest Act (Forest Act, 2013).

C) Preservation and Promotion of the Intellect

Preserving and promotion of the intellect involve policies that have to do with education. In Brunei, the preservation and promotion of intellect falls under the jurisdiction of the Ministry of Education (hereby MOE) and the Islamic Religious Department, MORA.

D) Preservation and Promotion of Progeny

Preservation and promotion of progeny involve policies that safeguard the family, women and children. In Brunei, preservation and promotion of progeny is under the jurisdiction of the Social Services (Perkhidmatan Sosial) and Societal Development Department (Jabatan Pembangunan Masyarat), both under the Ministry of Culture, Youth and Sports (KKBS Website, n.d.) . Policies that aim to foster kinship, such as the "Keluargaku Harapanku" campaign (Abdul Latif, 2019), is one such example.

E) Preservation and Promotion of Wealth

Preservation and promotion of wealth involve policies that involve monetary transactions, such as business and economics. In Brunei, preservation and promotion of wealth is under the jurisdiction of Ministry of Finance and Economy (hereby

MOFE). Examples of such policies include assimilation of micro, small and medium enterprises of Brunei to the international market (Anshari, Hamdan & Haidi, in press).

The interconnection of the five *Maqāṣid* with theologically motivating factors, the sets of expectations (juristic parameters), Quranic values, and cultural context is outlined in the Islamic Governance Conceptual Matrix or IGC Matrix (Figure 1).

Figure 1. The Islamic Governance Conceptual Matrix (source: Abdul Aziz, A. (2019). Special Forward: Islamic Governance and the Articulation of Maqāṣid al-Sharī'ah in Brunei Darussalam)

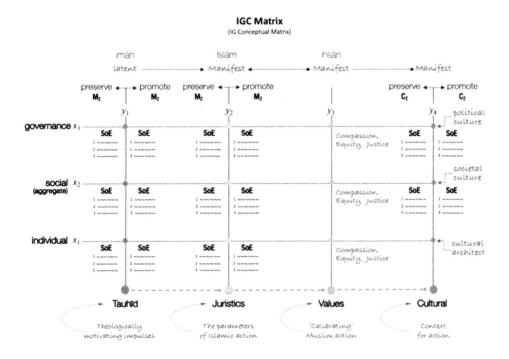

In the IGC Matrix, all Muslim actions start with embodying the Quranic verse from Chapter 6, Verse 162: "Surely my prayer, my worship, my life and my death are all for Allah - Lord of all worlds" (Quran.com, n.d.), a theologically motivating impulse in preserving and promoting the *Maqāṣid*.

This theologically motivating impulse affects the juristics, explaining the Sets of Expectations (SoE) that becomes the parameters of Muslim actions. Such parameters are used to operationalise the strategic objectives of an Islamic System of Governance. Such parameters involve all three forms of worship; from the individual forms of worship such as fasting, prayers, halal food consumptions; to the social forms of worship such as congregational Friday prayers; to the governance forms of worship, such as zakat distribution and collection. These juristic parameters, in turn, need to be calibrated using Quranic values; compassion, equity and justice; and will in turn, be contextualised according to different societal and political culture (Abdul Aziz, pers.comm.). Hence, a shift in cultural practices may happen as a result of

However, to build a society conducive for the worship of Allah, all five maqsad listed above need to work together and complement each other. For this purpose, Abdul Aziz (2019) proposed the *Maqāṣid* collaborative framework, as *Maqṣad* cannot be realized without factoring in all the other *Maqāṣid*.

Figure 2. The Maqāṣid Collaborative Framework (Source: Abdul Aziz, A. (2019). Special Forward: Islamic Governance and the Articulation of Maqāṣid al-Sharī'ah in Brunei Darussalam)

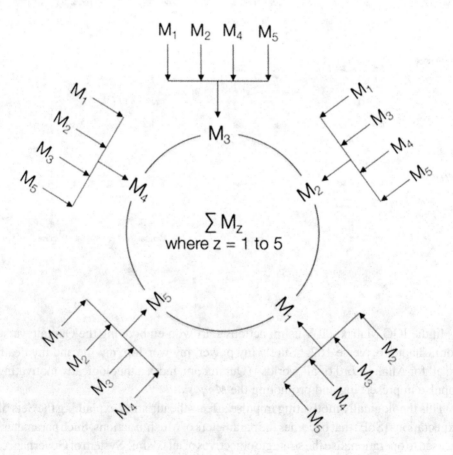

During the pandemic, the need to preserve and promote life is supported by the other *Maqāṣid* means physical distancing and restrictions. Thus, to preserve and promote one's faith, one turns to online dakwah; to preserve and promote one's intellect, one goes for online learning, to preserve and promote wealth, one uses online payments and to preserve and promote progeny, one can make use of online courtship services.

This study asks the following question:

1)   What are some examples of digitalisation policy initiatives that can help in preserving and promoting life through preserving and promoting the other maqsad?

2)   How do Bruneian Millennials fulfil the five Maqasid of Sharia through a digital society?

METHODOLOGY

The chapter makes use of ethnography, more specifically, digital ethnography and documentary analysis. Ethnography is the study of social interactions, behaviours and beliefs of small societies, through prolonged participation and observation, and data interpretation (Denzin and Lincoln, 2011; Reeves, Kuper and Hodges, 2008; Berry, 1991) while digital ethnography refers to ethnography carried out on the internet (Kaur-Gill & Dutta, 2017) because it represents "real-life cultures through combining the characteristic features of digital media with the elements of story" (Underberg & Zorn, 2013, p. 10). Documentary analysis was carried out to "provide access and facilitate insights into three related areas of knowledge about human activity" (McCulloch, 2011, p.248).

Data Sources

Data was gathered from three sources: a) documents - newspapers, government websites, b) Instagram and c) observation.

Data Analysis

All data sources mentioned above were analysed according to the five maqsad: a) preservation and promotion of faith, b) preservation and promotion of life, c) preservation and promotion of intellect, d) preservation and promotion of progeny and e) preservation and promotion of wealth.

LIMITATIONS

The study has three limitations. First; social media data was only gathered through Instagram. Instagram was chosen as the social media of choice because Brunei is its highest user per capita in the world (Othman, 2022). Second; this study is limited to Bruneian Millennials. Milennials are chosen because they grew into adulthood in time for internet explosion (Dimock, 2019) and thus is an appropriate group to study on the development of a digital Islamic Society. Third, the study only looked at some examples of digitalisation policy, as looking at the entire digitalisation policy examples was beyond the scale of the study.

FINDINGS

Examples Of Digitalisation Policy Initiatives According to the Five MAQSAD

Preservation and Promotion of Faith: Digital Faith Rituals by Ministry of Religious Affairs

MORA initiated digital communal prayers (*Majlis Malam Munajat*) to seek Allah's help in mitigating Covid-19 (Junaidi, 2020). In addition to Majlis Malam Munajat, MORA also hosted "majlis dikir syarafil anam" for twelve nights in a row, starting from the 1st Rabiulawal and ending on the night of 12th Rabiulawal (Junaidi, 2021), to commemorate Prophet Muhammadﷺ's birth month.

In addition to digital communal prayers, MORA has also conducted digital dakwah through reminders on their Instagram page (Kementerian Hal Ehwal Ugama on Instagram, 2021). Livestreaming of digital dakwah was also offered by MORA through various channels, such as on RTB Go and Instagram.

MORA also conducted digital tilawah (quran reading) through broadcasting live reading of surah Yassin on the government-run radio, television and online channels (Ahmad, 2021).

Preservation and Promotion of Life: BruHealth App by Ministry of Health

MOH introduced a health app (BruHealth) to work as a contact tracing app. The app provides data on the number of individuals at a specific location (Han, 2020). As a contact tracing app, the app generates a five-color classification system for its users (Han, 2020). Users with green or yellow health codes are granted access to premises while those with red (indicating that the user is a Covid-19 close contact), blue (indicating the user is a recovered Covid-19 patient) and purple (indicating that the user is a Covid-19 patient) health codes (Ministry of Health - BruHealth, n.d.) will not be allowed to enter public areas. To enable business premises into identifying user codes, a Quick Response (QR) code was issued to businesses and placed at the entrance of the premises so that customers can scan them prior to entrance.

With easing of restrictions, the BruHealth app now functions as more than just contact tracing. The app now provides the following services; a) public health; health code, home isolation, Covid-19 vaccination appointment, Covid-19 vaccination certificate, Vaccine Adverse Reaction (ADR) Reporting, Antigen Rapid Test (ART) reporting, and Covid-19 recovery certificate b) health services; such as booking appointments to see a medical personel, video consultations and accessing user's medical records, and c) articles concerning public health in the country, official press statements and infographics (see Figure 3)

Figure 3. BruHealth app screenshot showing public health options and Diabetes study

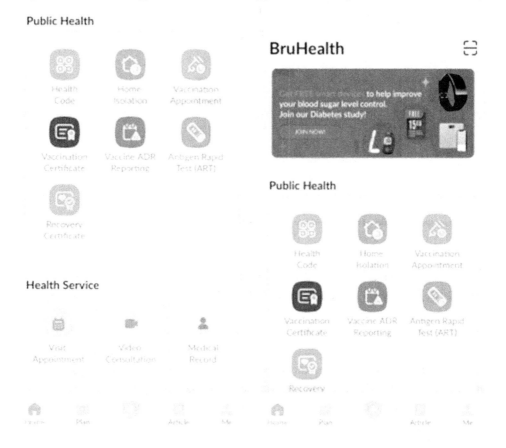

In addition, MOH also run surveys on the BruHealth app, as can be seen in Figure 3 where an advert asking users to join their Diabetes study in exchange for getting free smart devices to help improve blood sugar level control. As of 12 August 2022, the BruHealth app now have a steps plan called BN On The Move (Figure 4).

Figure 4. BruHealth app screenshot on BN On The Move

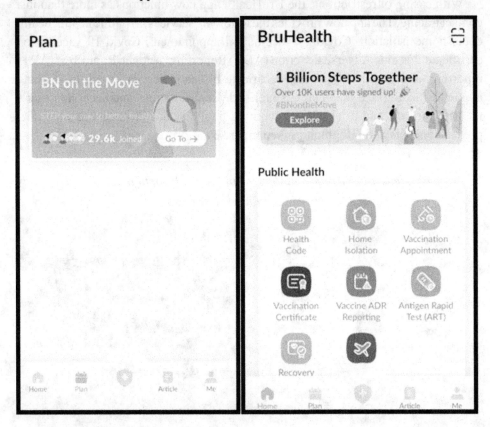

Preservation and Promotion of the Intellect: Online Learning Policy by Ministry of Education

Online learning policy was immediately adopted by the Ministry of Education during the Pandemic as a retreat for school closures during lockdown periods. Shahrill et al. (2021) described the steps taken by the MOE to ensure that teaching and learning activities continued during the COVID-19 First Wave. Government media was used to convey content to primary school children and online classes were conducted through various communication platforms (Kon & Roslan, 2020).

Online learning policy during the Covid-19 Second Wave were similar to those adopted during the First Wave.

Haidi and Hamdan (2022) analysed the home-based online teaching and learning policy during the Covid-19 Second Wave in Brunei and identified the online learning policies that existed prior to the pandemic, as well as the challenges faced by stakeholders that comes with conducting online teaching and learning outside the confines of a school campus.

Preservation and Promotion of Progeny: National Family Day online forum by Ministry of Youth, Culture and Sport and Digital Tahlil by NGOs

National Family Day Online Forum

While there were many policy examples that preserve and protect progeny during Covid-19, such as the temporary closure of daycares (Mahmud, 2022), none of them were digital in nature. However, the Ministry of Youth, Culture and Sport (hereby MCYS) did conduct an online forum on 31st May 2022 to commemorate National Family Day (Mahmud, 2022).

Digital Tahlil

After funerals, there is a custom known as tahlil where extended family and friends gather to pray for the departed, cheer up the bereaved, and reunite extended family branches (Warisno, 2017). Mass-gathering bans imposed during the pandemic permitted tahlil to be moved online, giving rise to a new tradition known as "online tahlil." Families in Brunei (Online Tahlil, 2020) have conducted online tahlil during the pandemic, alongside NGOs such as the Persatuan Siswazah Wanita (Mohamad, 2021) and GONGOs such as the National Football Association Brunei Darussalam (Kasharan, 2021) have also conducted online tahlil.

Preservation and Promotion of Wealth: E-commerce policy initiatives and digital donation

E-Commerce Policy Initiatives

Ministry of Transport and Infocommunications (MTIC), Ministry of Home Affairs (MOHA), Authority for Info-communications Technology Industry of Brunei Darussalam (AITI), and Darussalam Enterprise (DARe) launched eKadaiBrunei. com, an E-commerce directory for online marketplaces. eKadaiBrunei.com was launched prior to easing COVID-19 restrictions to allow businesses to connect with its customers without suffering a huge loss. In addition to eKadaiBrunei.com, delivery service providers such as Domo (mobile-based marketplace), Gomamam (mobile food delivery app), KadaiRuncit (online grocery store), (Wong, 2020) were also launched to ease e-commerce amongst MSMEs (Micro, Small and Medium Enterprises) (Othman, 2020).

Digital Donation

MORA launched FinTech policy initiatives prior to the pandemic to ease voluntary (sadaqah) donation processes via collaborating with Bank Islam Brunei Darussalam (BIBD) and its QuickPay technology; and the SMS Sadaqah (MORA, 2022). Until recently, the only options for doing this were to text a friend or deposit money into the MORA Tabung Dana Pembinaan Masjid Negara Brunei Darussalam account using a traditional cash deposit machine (MORA, n.d.). The ministry collected approximately B\$15 million between 2018 and March 2021 (Idris, 2021).

During the pandemic, these FinTech policy initiatives were extended to obligatory donations (zakat). The eZakat platform was launched to enable individuals pay zakat online (Abu Bakar, 2021).

Digital Islamic Society According to Bruneian Millennials

Preservation and Promotion of Faith: attending digital dakwah sessions and sharing Islamic reminders on Instagram

The author and many of her Instagram contacts attended digital dakwah sessions online, via Instagram's livestreaming (Instagram Live). One of the Instagram Live sessions that the author and her Instragram contacts attended was a sharing on mental health given by Yussof Majid, a MORA officer in collaboration with BIBD (BIBD On Instagram, 2021).

In addition to tuning in to livestreaming of Islamic reminders, many of her Instagram contacts regularly consume Islamic content from prominent individuals from Brunei and overseas, such as Ustaz Mizi Wahid (Mizi Wahid, n.d.) from Singapore and Ustadha Yasmin Mogahed (Yasmin Mogahed, n.d.) from USA.

Preservation and Promotion of Life: the use of health and fitness apps

The use of digital technology to monitor one's health is not new as Garmin, a popular smartwatch brand, launched its multi-sport smartwatches in 2003 (Ivanova, 2020). However, health and fitness apps only took root once Apple released its first smartwatch in 2014 (n.a., 2014) and launched the Apple Health app (Capritto, 2019). The Apple Health app stores data on steps, walking/running Distance, floors climbed, walking steadiness, respiratory rates, cardio fitness, heart rate, nutrition, sleep analysis and weight (Apple Health Guide, 2022).

The author and many of her contacts have been tracking their fitness using the Pacer app (Pacer, n.d.). Pacer is a fitness app that has been named the best running app in 2022 (The Pacer Blog, 2022), and are used to track steps and record any fitness activities such as running, walking or cycling. In addition to Pacer, health apps like Flo, a period and menstrual cycle tracking app is also a popular health app (Flo, n.d.) used by the author and her contacts. Flo was founded in 2015 and have since been awarded the ISO 27001 certification, the internationally recognised standard for information security (Flo, 2022).

Preservation and Promotion of Intellect: Online learning via Skillshare, YouTube and e-Readers

While the online learning policy have only started during the pandemic, self-taught online learning have been around for quite some time. Skillshare, a popular online teaching and learning community was launched in 2011 (Hernandez, 2012), nine years before the Pandemic. In addition, many content creators have uploaded documentaries or original videos on YouTube. An example is Oversimplified, who uploads explanatory videos explaining historical events in a simplified manner (Oversimplified, n.d.) and Legal Eagle, a creator (legaleagleprep.com, n.d) who started a YouTube channel for Law students but now explains legal perspectives on popular cases, such as the overturning of Roe v. Wade (Legal Eagle, 2022).

The author herself have used the YouTube channel, Ted Ed (Ted Ed, n.d.) for self-taught online learning and her teacher friends have also used Ted Ed as resources for their teaching. In addition to videos, e-Readers apps such as Apple Book and Amazon Kindle have now made it easier for the author and her community to read books on their iPads and smartphones. While e-Readers have not completely diminished the novelty of a physical book, the affordability of e-books means the author and her contacts can opt for e-book versions, if the physical book is too expensive or unavailable in Brunei.

Preservation and Promotion of Progeny: dating apps, Zoom parties and digital tahlil

The fast-paced modern yet connected world means it is now far easier to start a cross-border relationship or maintain a cross-border friendship. Maintaining relationships through social media and the internet have been especially useful as the pandemic have exacerbated the loneliness epidemic in the US (Goldstein, 2021; Leland, 2022) and the UK (Francis, 2022). The loneliness epidemic have started in the developed world prior to the pandemic (Howe, 2017) and loneliness is the number one fear of UK Millenials (Ewens, 2016). While there is no study on the loneliness epidemic in Brunei, Alam (2022) did report that Brunei university students felt lonely due to being isolated in their rooms. Hence, to combat or prevent the loneliness epidemic to take root in Brunei, it is important to maintain family relations, friendships and romantic relationships - preserving and promoting progeny.

The author reports on the apps that she and her contacts use to start relationships, maintain friendships and family relations during the Pandemic. These three apps are; a) dating apps such as Tinder and Muzz (formerly MuzMatch), b) Zoom and Google Meets to hold parties and online tahlil.

A)   Dating apps: Tinder and Muzz

Dating apps are apps created for the purpose of meeting a romantic partner, and is used frequently by millennials (Sumter, Vandenbosch, and Ligtenberg, 2017).

Tinder is a dating app where users can "swap like" with each other before the users can chat with each other (Goodall, 2016; Karniel & Lavie-Dinur, 2015), and it has since evolved into an app where people make friends (Tinder.com, n.d.). The author did use Tinder to make new friends, when she met a keen hiking enthusiast through the app.

Minder and Muzz (formerly MuzMatch) are two other dating apps where users can "swap like" with each other before making a match and chat on the app, but unlike Tinder, they are geared towards Muslims with matrimony in mind (Al-Heeti, 2019; Davies, 2016). Muzz even allow "chaperones" to monitor the chats (Al-Heeti, 2019).

The author and her Instagram contacts sporadically used MuzMatch (prior to its legal rebranding to Muzz) before the pandemic started. One of her contacts (unnamed for privacy reasons), met their cross-border spouse through the app prior to the Pandemic.

B)   Zoom Parties and digital tahlil

Zoom parties (Osborn, 2021) took place worldwide when lockdown restricted mass gatherings (Tenbarge, 2020). In the author's case, Zoom and Google Meets parties are the only way for her to meet her friends outside Brunei without having to physically be in places like Austria, Bangladesh, Germany, Malaysia, Turkey, UK, US and Canada simultaneously. The author and her Instagram contacts have also used Google Meets to catch up and play virtual games (Foster & Johnston, 2020) with friends when the curfew was still in place (Han, 2021), thus making virtual parties fun (McCulloch, 2020; Pennell, 2021).

Zoom and Google Meets were not just used for fun and games. During the pandemic, the author and her Instagram contacts uses Google Meets and Zoom to conduct digital tahlil to pray for family and friends who have passed away.

Preservation and Promotion of Wealth: online shopping, learning financial literacy through Instagram and YouTube, and digital donation

Online shopping has been around prior to the pandemic, where an e-Commerce survey by AITI revealed that 76% of their respondents use e-commerce to shop, bank, and pay bills; 57% of online shoppers prefers to use online shopping websites, while 24% prefers to use Facebook and Instagram for online shopping (Brunei e-Commerce, 2021). The author and her Instagram contacts frequently make use of online shopping to compare prices and buy products like Korean skincare (Koreacosmeticbn website, n.d.).

Closed-off borders have led to the proliferation of overseas personal shoppers who can shop at far-flung places like London and ship the items to Brunei. Many of these personal shoppers are active on Instagram, such as KL2BSB (KL2BSB on Instagram, n.d.), a personal shopper based in Kuala Lumpur who can shop in Kuala Lumpur and its surrounding areas for their Bruneian customers and London High Street (London High Street on Instagram, n.d.) who offer a similar service for luxury items from London. The author herself have never used the services of these personal shoppers, however, one of her Instagram contacts once used a personal shopper to order perfumes that otherwise cannot be delivered to Brunei from the UK.

The author and her Instagram contacts also uses social media to learn basic personal finance literacy. Financial literacy content from YouTube channels such as The Financial Diet (The Financial Diet, n.d.) and Instagram accounts such as MakeCents.bn (makecents.bn on Instagram, n.d.), finace.bn (finace.bn on Instagram, n.d.) and The Woke Salaryman (thewokesalarayman on Instagram, n.d.) were frequently consumed and shared by the author and her Instagram contacts.

As for digital donations, the author and her Instagram contacts have long used online charity platforms such as GoFundMe (gofundme.com, n.d.), JustGiving (justgiving.com, nd.) and LaunchGood (launchgood.com, n.d.) to fulfil their voluntary and obligatory donations digitally. The Pandemic have only allowed for these initiatives to go beyond Western charity organisations.

DISCUSSION

The policy and societal examples given in the Findings section showed that digitalising the preservation and promotion of all five Maqasid have already occurred and have been accelerated by the pandemic, thus paving the way to the evolution of a digital islamic society.

In this section, the author will discuss two issues that may arise with a digital Islamic society; a) privacy and b) security. Both issues are vital in a digital Islamic society, and indeed, BruCert have already started a public awareness campaign called "Secure Verify Connect" in 2013 to educate Bruneians by raising awareness on the responsibility to practice safe online behaviour, cyber-threats and privacy risks (Secure Verify Connect, n.d.).

Privacy

Facebook founder, Mark Zuckerberg was once quoted as to have said, "People have really gotten comfortable not only sharing more information and different kinds, but more openly and with more people," (Johnson, 2010), hence implying that privacy is no longer a social norm. However, privacy is a fundamental right in Islam, three aspects of which are pertinent to the discussion on a digital islamic society; 1) the right to protect one's privacy, 2) control over private information and 3) prohibition from spying (Hayat, 2007).

The two aspects of privacy mentioned in the paragraph above falls under the notion of privacy and data protection; both of which are protected in one hundred twenty countries, spearheaded by the European Union through their General Data Protection Regulation (hereby GDPR) Framework launched in May 2016 (Bottarelli, 2017).

In Brunei, a new law to protect people's personal data is being developed by Brunei's Authority for Info-communications Technology Industry (AITI). This law will be applicable to the sultanate's private sector, which includes both for-profit and nonprofit organisations (Xinhua, 2021).

Personal data protection is a fundamental human right which is also covered under the preservation and promotion of life. Hence, it is necessary that policies and regulations are put in place for privacy protection. It is also necessary for individuals to know how to access their privacy settings on Instagram and for Instagram contacts to respect each other's privacy by not taking screenshots of private accounts as it is akin to spying.

Security

The move towards digitalising all aspect of one's life means that one needs to be aware of their own security as their private information are vulnerable to scammers. Scammers come in different types, but the two most prominent scam that can jeopardise the security of an individual in a digital Islamic society are: a) scams that jeopardise mainly financial security, such as investment scams (common types of scams, n.d.), online shopping scams, banking scams, and charity scams (Consumer Finance website, 2022); and b) scams that jeopardise emotional security, such as dating and romance scams (FBI, n.d.; CNA insider, 2022).

Banks in Brunei such as BIBD and Standard Chartered have taken the initiative to educate their customers on financial scams (BIBD website, n.d.; Standard Chartered Brunei, n.d.), and BIBD have even alerted their customers on phone scams (The Star, 2020).

As for romance scams, there were cases from 2012 where Bruneian ladies were duped into sending money to their foreign lovers (Borneo Post, 2012) and in 2019

(Borneo Post, 2019). The Scoop in collaboration with Baiduri Bank, have written an article on how to recognise romance scammers' red flags and how to protect one's self from romance scammers, such as doing a reverse image search of the person's profile photo (The Scoop, 2022).

CONCLUSION

By examining a Digital Islamic Society through the IGC Matrix (Figure 1), it can be seen that the presence of all five *Maqāṣid* in the Bruneian digital society on both the governance level and societal level (at least amongst the Millennial generation) showed an ongoing evolution of a digital Islamic society in the country. The ongoing evolution coincided with Bruneian Millennials' ready adoption of digitalisation through their process of growing up with technology.

The shifting of cultural practices from a physical space to a digital space by Society, such as digital tahlil, to reunite extended family members and catch up with friends, demonstrates how culture evolves using technology. These cultural practices are of value and remain intact thanks to the Millennial generation's willingness to make it work remotely through digital means. On a governance level, digitalisation have allowed for cultural practices that was never before seen prior to the Pandemic, such as the *Majlis Malam Munajat*. This example yet again demonstrate that there is value in the digitalisation process, otherwise efforts and policy initiatives would not be made to migrate these practices to the digital space.

Hence, digitalisation from both the governance level and societal level amplifies both the M (Malay culture) and I (Islam) components of MIB and affirms the cultural and religious practices that Bruneians value.

This research is limited to the Millennial generation of Brunei. Further research is thus needed to look at the Bruneian Gen Z (those born between 1997 and 2012) and Alpha (those born after 2012). Gen Z and Alpha are born with tech (rather than growing up with tech), and whether the Gen Z also play a role in preserving and promoting all five Maqasid and thus help create a digital Islamic Society that is conducive for the worship of Allah.

REFERENCES

A timeline: A brief history of Apple Watch. (n.d.). Retrieved 12 August 2022, from https://www.verizon.com/articles/brief-history-of-apple-watch/

Abdul Aziz, A. (2019). Special Forward: Islamic Governance and the Articulation of Maqāṣid al-Sharī'ah in Brunei Darussalam. In R. Yunos (Ed.), *Maqāṣid Al-Sharī'ah in the Brunei Civil Service: Civil Servant's Perspectives*. Qasrun Nafis Publishing House.

About. (n.d.). Legaleagle. Retrieved 12 August 2022, from https://www.legaleagleprep.com/about

Abu Bakar, R. (2021, April 5). *Muslims can start paying zakat online this Ramadhan*. The Scoop. https://thescoop.co/2021/04/05/muslims-can-start-paying-zakat-online-this-ramadan/

Ahmad, A. (2021, August 18). Siaran Brunei serentak siar bacaan surah Yasin bagi kekang Covid-19. *Utusan Digital*. https://www.utusan.com.my/luar-negara/2021/08/siaran-brunei-serentak-siar-bacaan-surah-yasin-bagi-kekang-covid-19/

Al-Heeti, A. (n.d.). *Beyond Tinder: How Muslim millennials are looking for love*. CNET. Retrieved 12 August 2022, from https://www.cnet.com/culture/tinder-minder-muzmatch-eshq-how-muslim-millennials-are-looking-for-love/

Alam, M. (2022). Mental health impact of online learning: A look into university students in Brunei Darussalam. *Asian Journal of Psychiatry*, *67*, 102933. doi:10.1016/j.ajp.2021.102933 PMID:34837832

Anshari, M., Hamdan, M., Ahmad, N., Ali, E., & Haidi, H. (2022). COVID-19, artificial intelligence, ethical challenges and policy implications. *AI & Society*. Advance online publication. doi:10.100700146-022-01471-6 PMID:35607368

Apple Health guide: The powerful fitness app explained. (2022, April 14). Wareable. https://www.wareable.com/health-and-wellbeing/apple-health-guide-apps-wearables-8016

Apple Watch | History, Features, Specs, Deals. (n.d.). AppleInsider. Retrieved 12 August 2022, from https://appleinsider.com/inside/apple-watch

Berry, K. (2011). The Ethnographic Choice: Why Ethnographers Do Ethnography. *Cultural Studies. Critical Methodologies*, *11*(2), 165–177. doi:10.1177/1532708611401335

BIBD on Instagram. (2021). *'During these challenging times, it's important more than ever to take care of our mental health. BIBD is pleased to invite members to tune in to the 2nd session of motivational talks about mental health titled - Hold That Thought! The session will be covering mental health awareness from an islamic perspective with Ustaz Awang Muhammad Yussof bin Hj Abdul Majid, Special Duties Officer from the Religious Counselling and Understanding Department, MORA. Join us on this Friday, 22nd October 2021 on our BIBD IG Live or via this Zoom link* https://us02web.zoom.us/j/89072949006 *(Link allso available via our IG profile and Telegram group) #bibdbrunei #bibdmotivational #MentalHealthMatters'*. Instagram. https://www.instagram.com/p/CVSDHDyhgUk/

BIBD on Instagram: *'During these challenging times, it's important more than ever to take care of our mental health. This session covered mental health...'*. (n.d.). Retrieved 5 November 2021, from https://www.instagram.com/p/CVrpbEJBPH0/

Bilton, N. (2014, October 29). Tinder, the Fast-Growing Dating App, Taps an Age-Old Truth. *The New York Times.* https://www.nytimes.com/2014/10/30/fashion/tinder-the-fast-growing-dating-app-taps-an-age-old-truth.html

Brunei Climate Change Secretariat. (2020). Brunei National Climate Change Policy.

Brunei to launch new law to protect personal data—Xinhua. (n.d.). Retrieved 13 August 2022, from http://www.xinhuanet.com/english/2021-05/22/c_139963856.htm

Brunei woman loses RM153,000 to yet another 'love scam'. (n.d.). Retrieved 13 August 2022, from https://www.theborneopost.com/2019/08/27/brunei-woman-loses-rm153000-to-yet-another-love-scam/

Bruneians lose big money on romance scams online. (n.d.). *Borneo Post Online.* Retrieved 13 August 2022, from https://www.theborneopost.com/2012/07/13/bruneians-lose-big-money-on-romance-scams-online/

Brunei—ECommerce. (n.d.). Retrieved 12 August 2022, from https://www.trade.gov/country-commercial-guides/brunei-ecommerce

Bunt, G. R. (2009). *IMuslims: Rewiring the House of Islam.* Univ of North Carolina Press.

Bunt, G. R. (2018). *Hashtag Islam: How Cyber-Islamic Environmenonts Are Transforming Religious Authority.* University of North Carolina Press. doi:10.5149/northcarolina/9781469643168.001.0001

Buttarelli, G. (2017). Privacy matters: Updating human rights for the digital society. *Health and Technology, 7*(4), 325–328. doi:10.100712553-017-0198-y

Capritto, A. (n.d.). *The complete guide to Apple's Health app*. CNET. Retrieved 12 August 2022, from https://www.cnet.com/health/the-complete-guide-to-apples-health-app/

Ceruzzi, P. E. (2003). *A history of modern computing*. MIT press.

CIA. (2022). Brunei. In *The World Factbook*. Central Intelligence Agency. https://www.cia.gov/the-world-factbook/countries/brunei

Crowdfunding Incredible Muslims | LaunchGood. (n.d.). Retrieved 19 August 2022, from https://www.launchgood.com/

Dasar, B. (2017). *Perancangan dan Penyelidikan, K. H. E. U* (1st ed.). Dasar-Dasar Kementerian Hal Ehwal Ugama.

Davies, R. (n.d.). *The young Muslims finding love via an app*. Retrieved 12 August 2022, from https://www.aljazeera.com/features/2016/11/27/the-young-muslims-finding-love-via-an-app

Denzin, N. K., & Lincoln, Y. S. (Eds.). (2011). *The Sage handbook of qualitative research* (4th ed.). Sage.

Department of Economic Planning and Statistics—Population. (n.d.). Retrieved 18 August 2022, from https://deps.mofe.gov.bn/SitePages/Population.aspx

Department of Statistics. (2021). *Brunei Darussalam Key Indicators 2020*. Department of Economic Planning and Statistics Ministry of Finance and Economy Brunei Darussalam. http://www.deps.gov.bn/DEPD%20Documents%20Library/DOS/BDKI/BDKI_2020.pdf

Dimock, M. (n.d.). *Defining generations: Where Millennials end and Generation Z begins*. Pew Research Center. Retrieved 6 August 2022, from https://www.pewresearch.org/fact-tank/2019/01/17/where-millennials-end-and-generation-z-begins/

Dufva, T., & Dufva, M. (2019). Grasping the future of the digital society. *Futures*, *107*, 17–28. doi:10.1016/j.futures.2018.11.001

Ewens, H. (2016, September 21). What Young People Fear the Most. *Vice*. https://www.vice.com/en/article/nnyk37/what-vice-readers-fear-the-most-hannah-ewens-love-loneliness

Fin.Ace 🔟 Finances & Money (@finace.bn) • Instagram photos and videos. (n.d.). Retrieved 12 August 2022, from https://www.instagram.com/finace.bn/

Flo—Ovulation calendar, period tracker, and pregnancy app. (n.d.). Flo.Health - #1 Mobile Product for Women's Health. Retrieved 12 August 2022, from https:// flo.health

Forest Act. (2013). Forest Act Chapter 46. retrieved from http://www.forestry.gov. bn/SitePages/Forest%20Act%20and%20Forest%20Rules.aspx

Foster, M., & Johnston, R. (n.d.). *How to turn your next video call into an interactive game night.* TODAY.Com. Retrieved 13 August 2022, from https://www.today.com/ shop/11-best-games-play-zoom-t179862

Foundation, L. (n.d.). *Digital Society.* LIBRe Foundation. Retrieved 29 November 2021, from https://libreresearchgroup.org/en/a/digital-society

Francis, S. (2022, May 3). *Can councils end London's loneliness epidemic?* BBC News. https://www.bbc.com/news/uk-england-london-61191228

GoFundMe: No.1 Fundraising Platform for Crowdfunding. (n.d.). Retrieved 19 August 2022, from https://www.gofundme.com/en-gb

Goldstein, A. (2021, August 2). *The Pandemic of Loneliness.* California Health Care Foundation. https://www.chcf.org/blog/pandemic-loneliness/

Haidi, H., & Hamdan, M. (2022). Analysis of the home-based online teaching and learning policy during the Covid-19 second wave in Brunei: A joint parent/ teacher perception. *Asia Pacific Education Review.* Advance online publication. doi:10.100712564-022-09798-x

Han, S. (2021, October 4). *Brunei begins two-week COVID night restrictions.* The Scoop. https://thescoop.co/2021/10/04/brunei-begins-two-week-covid-night-restrictions/

Han, S. (n.d.). *Gov't rolls out BruHealth contact tracing app as restrictions loosened— The Scoop.* Retrieved 18 August 2022, from https://thescoop.co/2020/05/14/govt-launches-bruhealth-contact-tracing-app/

Hayat, M. A. (2007). Privacy and Islam: From the Quran to data protection in Pakistan. *Information & Communications Technology Law,* *16*(2), 137–148. doi:10.1080/13600830701532043

Hernandez, B. A. (2012, April 23). *How Skillshare Is Transforming Education as We Know It.* Mashable. https://mashable.com/archive/skillshare-teaching-learning

Home | Secure Verify Connect. (n.d.). Retrieved 13 August 2022, from https://www. secureverifyconnect.info/

Home. (n.d.). Retrieved 18 August 2022, from https://www.mfa.gov.bn/oman-muscat/SitePages/bruneiintroduction.aspx

Home—Utama. (n.d.). Retrieved 12 August 2022, from https://www.kkbs.gov.bn/Theme/Home.aspx

Howe, N. (n.d.). *Millennials And The Loneliness Epidemic*. Forbes. Retrieved 12 August 2022, from https://www.forbes.com/sites/neilhowe/2019/05/03/millennials-and-the-loneliness-epidemic/

Idris, H. (n.d.). Kutipan Tabung Dana Pembinaan Masjid menggalakkan. *Pelita Brunei*. https://www.pelitabrunei.gov.bn/Lists/Berita%202009/NewDisplayForm.aspx?ID=32553&ContentTypeId=0x01003909FAFC2C52C240BD1CCEDF92AC1BAE

Insider, C. N. A. (Director). (2022, June 2). *Asia's Tinder Swindlers: Exposing Love Scam Rings In Cambodia | Talking Point | Full Episode*. https://www.youtube.com/watch?v=ZacChEz3Am8

IOS - Health. (n.d.). Apple. Retrieved 12 August 2022, from https://www.apple.com/ios/health/

Ivanova, G. (2020, June 22). The History of Garmin Watches. *First Class Watches Blog*. https://www.firstclasswatches.co.uk/blog/2020/06/the-history-of-garmin-watches/

Johnson, B. (2010). *Privacy no longer a social norm, says Facebook founder | Facebook | The Guardian*. https://www.theguardian.com/technology/2010/jan/11/facebook-privacy

Join JustGiving and show you care. (n.d.). JustGiving. Retrieved 19 August 2022, from https://www.justgiving.com

Junaidi, Y. (2021a, October 11). Lebih 1,500 sertai Majlis Malam Munajat» Media Permata Online. *Lebih 1,500 Sertai Majlis Malam Munajat*. https://mediapermata.com.bn/lebih-1500-sertai-majlis-malam-munajat/

Junaidi, Y. (2021b, October 19). Laungan dikir 12 malam berakhir » Media Permata Online. *Laungan Dikir 12 Malam Berakhir*. https://mediapermata.com.bn/laungan-dikir-12-malam-berakhir-3/

✨*KL2BSB*✨ *(@kl2bsb)* • *Instagram photos and videos*. (n.d.). Retrieved 12 August 2022, from https://www.instagram.com/kl2bsb/?hl=en

Kasharan, A. Z. (2021, September 18). Majlis tahlil bagi tokoh bola sepak tempatan» Media Permata Online. *Majlis Tahlil Bagi Tokoh Bola Sepak Tempatan*. https://mediapermata.com.bn/majlis-tahlil-bagi-tokoh-bola-sepak-tempatan/

Kaur-Gill, S., & Dutta, M. J. (2017). Digital Ethnography. In J. Matthes, C. S. Davis, & R. F. Potter (Eds.), *The International Encyclopedia of Communication Research Methods* (1st ed., pp. 1–10). Wiley. doi:10.1002/9781118901731.iecrm0271

Kementerian Hal Ehwal Ugama on Instagram: 'Bersempena Sambutan Maulud Nabi Muhammad Shallallahu 'Alaihi Wasallam Peringkat Negara bagi Tahun 1443 Hijrah, orang ramai dialu-alukan...' (n.d.a). Retrieved 4 November 2021, from https://www.instagram.com/p/CVMKnqfhTpe/

Kementerian Hal Ehwal Ugama on Instagram: 'Bersempena Sambutan Maulud Nabi Muhammad Shallallahu 'Alaihi Wasallam Peringkat Negara bagi Tahun 1443 Hijrah, orang ramai dialu-alukan...' (n.d.b). Retrieved 4 November 2021, from https://www.instagram.com/p/CVFQlh-BuRt/

Kementerian Hal Ehwal Ugama on Instagram: 'Bersempena Sambutan Maulud Nabi Muhammad Shallallahu 'Alaihi Wasallam Peringkat Negara bagi Tahun 1443 Hijrah, orang ramai dialu-alukan...' (n.d.c). Retrieved 4 November 2021, from https://www.instagram.com/p/CVHihN9Bu2P/

Kementerian Hal Ehwal Ugama on Instagram: 'Bersempena Sambutan Maulud Nabi Muhammad Shallallahu 'Alaihi Wasallam Peringkat Negara bagi Tahun 1443 Hijrah, orang ramai dialu-alukan...' (n.d.d). Retrieved 4 November 2021, from https://www.instagram.com/p/CVJxCRSBPWI/

Kementerian Hal Ehwal Ugama on Instagram: 'Jabatan Hal Ehwal Masjid, Kementerian Hal Ehwal Ugama dengan kerjasama Radio Televisyen Brunei mengambil inisiatif untuk mengadakan Majlis...' (n.d.). Retrieved 4 November 2021, from https://www.instagram.com/p/CVMPkzThgau/

Kementerian Hal Ehwal Ugama on Instagram: 'Kementerian Hal Ehwal Ugama dengan kerjasama daripada Kementerian Pendidikan, Kementerian Kebudayaan, Belia dan Sukan...' (n.d.). Retrieved 14 December 2021, from https://www.instagram.com/p/CViMw5bh3tz/

Kementerian Hal Ehwal Ugama on Instagram: 'Repost @rampaipagi.rtb Disiarkan secara langsung di saluran RTB Perdana dan awda juga boleh mengikuti kami melalui penstriman langsung di...' (n.d.). Retrieved 4 November 2021, from https://www.instagram.com/p/CVtqnQdhKVa/

Kementerian Hal Ehwal Ugama on Instagram: 'Terapi Kejiwaan: Jangan Mudah Berputus Asa Disediakan oleh Unit Kaunseling dan Kefahaman Agama (KAFA), KHEU'. (n.d.). Retrieved 4 November 2021, from https://www.instagram.com/p/CVmQ3nVBZEJ/

Khan, M. A. M. (2019). *Islam and Good Governance: A Political Philosophy of Ihsan*. doi:10.1057/978-1-137-54832-0

Kon, J., & Roslan, W. (2020, September 23). Rising to the COVID-19 challenge » Borneo Bulletin Online. *Rising to the COVID-19 Challenge*. https://borneobulletin.com.bn/rising-to-the-covid-19-challenge/

Korea Cosmetics BN. (n.d.). Retrieved 12 August 2022, from https://koreacosmeticsbn.com/

Latif, A. (n.d.). *Berita KKBS - Ubah 'Mindset' Lebih Positif*. Retrieved 6 August 2022, from https://www.kkbs.gov.bn/Lists/News/NDispForm.aspx?ID=414&ContentTypeId=0x0100ECC89185A7F5E74A8CA7B999A4454ABE

LegalEagle (Director). (2022a, June 30). *How The Supreme Court Killed Roe v. Wade*. https://www.youtube.com/watch?v=wOvvBWSBwU0

LegalEagle (Director). (2022b, August 10). *Huge Verdict Against Alex Jones*. https://www.youtube.com/watch?v=SpVSiuQ_ILY

Leland, J. (2022, April 20). How Loneliness Is Damaging Our Health. *The New York Times*. https://www.nytimes.com/2022/04/20/nyregion/loneliness-epidemic.html

London High Street (@londonhighstr8) • Instagram photos and videos. (n.d.). Retrieved 12 August 2022, from https://www.instagram.com/londonhighstr8/?hl=en

Mahmud, R. (2021, May 12). Blessed as a Zikir Nation» Borneo Bulletin Online. *Blessed as a Zikir Nation*. https://borneobulletin.com.bn/blessed-zikir-nation/

Mahmud, R. (2022, May 31). Spotlight on importance of family ties » Borneo Bulletin Online. *Spotlight on Importance of Family Ties*. https://borneobulletin.com.bn/spotlight-on-importance-of-family-ties/

Majid, Y. (n.d.). *Yussof Majid (@yussof_majid) • Instagram photos and videos*. Retrieved 5 November 2021, from https://www.instagram.com/yussof_majid/

Makecents (@makecents.bn) • Instagram photos and videos. (n.d.). Retrieved 12 August 2022, from https://www.instagram.com/makecents.bn/?hl=en

Malik, M. (2018). Foundations of Islamic governance: A Southeast Asian perspective. Routledge.

Marvi, A., Shahraini, S. M., Yazdi, N., & Maleki, A. (2021). Iran and COVID-19: A Bottom-up, Faith-Driven, Citizen-Supported Response. *Public Organization Review*, *21*(4), 723–740. doi:10.100711115-021-00567-9

McCulloch, G. (2013). Historical and documentary research in education. In L. Cohen, L. Manion, & K. Morrison (Eds.), *Research Methods in Education* (0 ed.). Routledge., doi:10.4324/9780203720967

McCulloch, G. (n.d.). A Mission to Make Virtual Parties Actually Fun. *Wired*. Retrieved 13 August 2022, from https://www.wired.com/story/zoom-parties-proximity-chat/

Menelusuri Peranan Pusat Da"wah Islamiah dalam Pengurusan Program Pembangunan Saudara Baru. (n.d.). Retrieved 13 August 2022, from http://www.jised.com/PDF/JISED-2019-19-03-19.pdf

Ministry of Health—Bruhealth. (n.d.). Retrieved 12 August 2022, from https://www.moh.gov.bn/SitePages/bruhealth.aspx

Mizi Wahid (@miziwahid) • Instagram photos and videos. (n.d.). Retrieved 6 August 2022, from https://www.instagram.com/miziwahid/?hl=en

Mohamad, L. (2021, October 28). Virtual tahlil for late prince » Borneo Bulletin Online. *Virtual Tahlil for Late Prince.* https://borneobulletin.com.bn/virtual-tahlil-for-late-prince/

Nurdiyanah, R. (2021, September 18). Warga emas mantapkan bacaan Quran menerusi Tilawah Wal Istima» Media Permata Online. *Warga Emas Mantapkan Bacaan Quran Menerusi Tilawah Wal Istima.* https://mediapermata.com.bn/warga-emas-mantapkan-bacaan-quran-menerusi-tilawah-wal-istima/

Online Learning: Creative Classes on Skillshare | Start for Free. (n.d.). Retrieved 12 August 2022, from https://www.skillshare.com/

Online Tahlil | Brunei's No.1 News Website. (n.d.). Retrieved 4 November 2021, from https://www.brudirect.com/news.php?id=91894

Osborn, C. (2021, June 4). *How to Host a Zoom Party and Connect With Your Loved Ones.* MUO. https://www.makeuseof.com/how-to-host-a-zoom-party/

Othman, A. (2020). *MSMEs drive Brunei's economy» Borneo Bulletin Online.* https://borneobulletin.com.bn/their-majesties-meet-thai-defence-chief-and-spouse-2/

OverSimplified—YouTube. (n.d.). Retrieved 12 August 2022, from https://www.youtube.com/

Pacer Named Best Running App of 2022 by BestApp.com - The Pacer Blog: Walking, Health and Fitness. (2022, March 17). https://blog.mypacer.com/2022/03/17/pacer-named-best-running-app-of-2022-by-bestapp-com/

Pacer: Pedometer & Fitness App—Simple Fitness and Weight Loss. (n.d.). Retrieved 12 August 2022, from https://www.mypacer.com/

Pennell. (n.d.). *5 ways to make your Zoom parties feel fresh and exciting again.* TODAY.Com. Retrieved 13 August 2022, from https://www.today.com/tmrw/zoom-party-ideas-make-virtual-parties-feel-fresh-again-t207999

Pg Abd Hamid, A. A. A. A. (n.d.). *News 2021—Zakat Payments Online.* Retrieved 4 November 2021, from http://www.rtbnews.rtb.gov.bn/Lists/News%202018/DispForm.aspx?ID=26031&ContentTypeId=0x010009BBE23B3840184D80AE8D8DEA617660

Quran.com. (n.d.) *Chapter 6 Surah Al-Anam, Verse 162.* Retrieved 3 November 2022, from https://quran.com/6/162

Reeves, S., Kuper, A., & Hodges, B. D. (2008). Qualitative research methodologies: Ethnography. *BMJ, 337*(3), a1020–a1020. 1 doi:0.1136/bmj.a1020

Religions show faith in power of technology. (2019, December 4). *Financial Times.*

Romance Scams. (n.d.). Federal Bureau of Investigation. Retrieved 13 August 2022, from https://www.fbi.gov/scams-and-safety/common-scams-and-crimes/romance-scams

Roslan, B. (2021, August 17). Online learning resume for the third term amid pandemic. *The Brunei Post.* https://www.thebruneipost.co/health/covid-19/2021/08/18/online-learning-resume-for-the-third-term-amid-pandemic/

Roundup: Brunei introduces curfew to contain COVID-19 local transmission. (n.d.). Retrieved 12 August 2022, from http://www.news.cn/english/2021-10/01/c_1310222246.htm

Sá, M. J., Santos, A. I., Serpa, S., & Miguel Ferreira, C. (2021). Digitainability—Digital competences post-COVID-19 for a sustainable society. *Sustainability, 13*(17), 9564. doi:10.3390u13179564

Saim, H. S. H. (2013). Brunei Darussalam in 2012: Towards a Zikir Nation. *Southeast Asian Affairs, SEAA13*(1), 63–72. doi:10.1355/aa13-1e

Scoop, T. (2022, April 4). *Online romance scams: How to spot the red flags*. The Scoop. https://thescoop.co/2022/04/04/online-romance-scams-how-to-spot-the-red-flags/

Shahrill, M., Noorashid, N., & Keasberry, C. (2021). COVID-19: Educational Practices and Responses in Brunei Darussalam. In P. Le Ha, A. Kumpoh, K. Wood, R. Jawawi, & H. Said (Eds.), *Globalisation, Education, and Reform in Brunei Darussalam* (pp. 325–354). Springer International Publishing. doi:10.1007/978-3-030-77119-5_16

Sharbawi, S., & Mabud, S. A. (2021). Malay, Muslim and Monarchy: An Introduction to Brunei Darussalam and Its National Identity. In P. Le Ha, A. Kumpoh, K. Wood, R. Jawawi, & H. Said (Eds.), *Globalisation, Education, and Reform in Brunei Darussalam* (pp. 45–66). Springer International Publishing. doi:10.1007/978-3-030-77119-5_3

Skillshare. (n.d.). Retrieved 12 August 2022, from https://www.skillshare.com/about

Standard Chartered Brunei. (n.d.). Retrieved 13 August 2022, from https://ne-np.facebook.com/StandardCharteredBrunei/posts/pfbid0uguxqZkb3gbSYPUD3tzNTjgpXNztEnHpJnQzEVAWxkAor5d7mH8Yq2dtfC1YyqCU1

Staying Alert Online | Bank Islam Brunei Darussalam. (n.d.). Retrieved 13 August 2022, from http://www.bibd.com.bn/resource-centre/online-safety/

Steiner, C. (2012). *Automate this: How algorithms took over our markets, our jobs, and the world*. Penguin.

TED-Ed—YouTube. (n.d.). Retrieved 12 August 2022, from https://www.youtube.com/

Tema Hari Kebangsaan. (n.d.). Retrieved 20 November 2021, from http://www.kkbs.gov.bn/Hari%20Kebangsaan/Tema%20Hari%20Kebangsaan.aspx

Temporary closure of child care centre extended | Borneo Bulletin Online. (n.d.). Retrieved 6 August 2022, from https://borneobulletin.com.bn/temporary-closure-of-child-care-centre-extended/

Tenbarge, K. (n.d.). *How to throw a perfect Zoom party with your friends and family*. Business Insider. Retrieved 12 August 2022, from https://www.businessinsider.com/how-to-throw-zoom-party-custom-background-friends-family-2020-3

The Financial Diet—YouTube. (n.d.). Retrieved 12 August 2022, from https://www.youtube.com/c/thefinancialdiet/videos

@thewokesalaryman • *Instagram photos and videos*. (n.d.). Retrieved 12 August 2022, from https://www.instagram.com/thewokesalaryman/?hl=en

Tinder | Dating, make friends & meet new people. (n.d.). Retrieved 12 August 2022, from https://tinder.com/

Types of scams | Cyber.gov.au. (n.d.). Retrieved 13 August 2022, from https://www.cyber.gov.au/learn/threats/types-of-scams

Underberg, N. M., & Zorn, E. (2013). *Digital Ethnography: Anthropology, Narrative, and New Media*. University of Texas Press., doi:10.7560/744332

Warisno, A. (2017). Tradisi Tahlilan Upaya Menyambung Silaturahmi. *Riayah : Jurnal Sosial Dan Keagamaan*, 2(02), 69–97.

Watch out for phone scams, Bruneians reminded. (n.d.). The Star. Retrieved 13 August 2022, from https://www.thestar.com.my/aseanplus/aseanplus-news/2020/06/12/watch-out-for-phone-scams-bruneians-reminded

We Are Social. (2022, January 26). *Digital 2022: Another year of bumper growth*. We Are Social UK. https://wearesocial.com/uk/blog/2022/01/digital-2022-another-year-of-bumper-growth-2/

What are some common types of scams? (n.d.). Consumer Financial Protection Bureau. Retrieved 13 August 2022, from https://www.consumerfinance.gov/ask-cfpb/what-are-some-common-types-of-scams-en-2092/

Wong, A. (n.d.). *eKadaiBrunei: Brunei's first online E-commerce directory launched*. https://www.bizbrunei.com/2020/04/ekadaibrunei-bruneis-first-online-E-commerce-direc tory-launched/

Yasmin Mogahed (@yasminmogahed) • *Instagram photos and videos*. (n.d.). Retrieved 19 August 2022, from https://www.instagram.com/yasminmogahed/

Chapter 8
Maslow's Hierarchy of Needs and Digital Wallet Usage Among Youth

Iffah Haziyah Rumaizi
Universiti Brunei Darussalam, Brunei

Muhammad Anshari
🆔 https://orcid.org/0000-0002-8160-6682
Universiti Brunei Darussalam, Brunei

Mohammad Nabil Almunawar
🆔 https://orcid.org/0000-0001-5296-2576
Universiti Brunei Darussalam, Brunei

Masairol Masri
Universiti Brunei Darussalam, Brunei

ABSTRACT

Financial technology (FinTech) has become more ubiquitous in an era of accelerating internet technology and rising e-commerce. With the increasing digitisation of the marketplace, smartphones are now used not only for communication but also as a means of payment in a number of countries. Several initiatives have been undertaken to accelerate the digital transformation of the business, including the use of digital wallets by young adults. Given the scarcity of research examining FinTech adoption from a human behaviour perspective, this study will examine the elements that motivate people to use digital wallets. Three major themes were theoretically derived using a qualitative technique and Maslow's hierarchy of needs as the research instrument. The main reasons why young adults use digital wallets were found to be "youth digitalization," "technological anxiety," and a "positive attitude toward technology use."

DOI: 10.4018/978-1-6684-6108-2.ch008

INTRODUCTION

The existence of Internet Technology (IT) has created a pathway that could be taken advantage of by many users around the world. Hence, there is a growth of new technologies, mainly in the service sectors, which has led to the development of e-commerce (Kabango and Asa, 2015). E-commerce has been growing rapidly and it plays a significant role in commercial transactions (Samadi et al., 2011). With the increasing digitalisation of trading goods and services, payment methods are also evolving to keep up with the advancement of technology.

In the current era, smartphones have become an essential device to use in the daily lives of individuals of every age group. Besides using smartphones as a tool for communication and entertainment, they can also be used as a tool for payment. Thus, this device can also function as a digital wallet (Sharma, 2018). The use of digital wallets as an alternative payment method has increased the convenience for customers and business merchants, which has led to some changes in the payment infrastructure to adapt to technological advancement. Many individuals in countries such as South Korea and the United States of America use their smartphones on a daily basis to carry out various essential transactions such as paying for groceries and self-identification at airline ticket counters (Rathore, 2016). Additionally, Thailand takes the lead as one of the top countries across the Asia-Pacific regions that has high usage of mobile wallets among its population (GlobalData, 2021).

On the other hand, Brunei Darussalam is becoming increasingly aware of these global trends of digitization (Ahmad, 2022; Anshari et al., 2022a). In order to achieve one of the country's main agendas of transforming the country into a "Smart Nation", various strategies are being implemented in an effort to improve the country's e-commerce platforms and financial technology. The Authority for Info-communication Technology (AITI) revealed their five-year master plan to further revolutionise the nation's digital ecosystem (The Scoop, 2018). Within the master plan, it was recently announced that one of their targets is to have 1,200 MSMEs adopt the use of digital technology by the year 2025 (The Scoop, 2021). This target is significant in the nation's attempt to enhance its digital ecosystem for the facilitation of the advancing data industry, broadcast content industry, and a cashless society (Anshari et al., 2021a; Mulyani et al., 2019).

However, a survey by AITI revealed that only 24% of Bruneians utilize digital wallets (The Scoop, 2018). This is further supported by a recent study that shows that there is hesitation among Bruneians to embrace the adoption of digital wallets due to anxiety about the perceived risks when using digital wallets (Anshari et al., 2020;). Moreover, this research also found the inclination to use digital wallets would depend on the individuals' general attitude towards technology usage and may differ across different age groups. Based on this information, it indicates that

Brunei Darussalam is quite behind in fully embracing the use of digital wallets as the main mode of payment (Anshari et al., 2019).

In an attempt to investigate the issue of hesitation in embracing mobile wallets, this research aims to assess the motivation for its usage among Bruneian young adults. To achieve this main objective of the research, Maslow's Needs Hierarchy theory is used to understand the factors that may act as the drive and constraint for these individuals to use digital wallets.

LITERATURE REVIEW

Financial Technology

Financial technology, or "FinTech," is one of the fastest growing issues in the e-business world. The definition of FinTech is not rigid to one meaning, as there are many authors who explain this term based on their own understanding. Wilson (2017) defined financial technology as the use of technology by a company to gain more profit via the provision of financial services to its customers. Meanwhile, Kominfo (2017), as cited in Prawirasasra (2018), described financial technology as a merging occurrence between technology and monetary attributes that could revolutionise business ventures and reduce barriers to entry. In general, FinTech is the utilization of software and the latest technology to provide financial services to consumers (Anshari et al., 2021a).

FinTech is not a new phenomenon as it can be traced back to the late 19th century when there was an emergence of financial globalisation (Prawirasasra, 2018; Anshari et al., 2021b). During this time, technology plays a major role in passing on information globally, which includes financial processes such as commercial dealings and settlements. As the level of technology has further escalated, so has the area of information technology and communication, which is proven by the establishment of tech-based companies like International Business Machine in 1967 (Prawirasasra, 2018; Buckley et al., 2016; Anshari et al., 2022b). Eventually, the public is introduced to Automated Teller Machines (ATMs) that revolutionize financial services from analogue to digital. Thus, various companies in the financial industry began to increasingly utilise the technology in order to interlink local financial transactions overseas (Anshari et al., 2021b; Ahad et al., 2017). This has led to the computerisation of their business operations, which has come with the increased possibility of threats in the internal and external environment of the firms (Hasmawati et al., 2020).

From the 1970s to the 1980s, the rapid innovation of technology has made stock brokerage more convenient for investors, as the stocks can be digitally stored and the invention of the latest software guarantees that the data can be protected securely. With the increased consumption of the internet from the 1990s and onwards, companies in the financial industry became more involved in e-commercial activities (Prawirasasra, 2018; Hamdan & Anshari, 2020). This technological innovation occurs mostly in banks, where the majority of them have embraced the Core Banking System and transformed their operations in a way that allows them to stay virtually connected with their customers (Razzaq et al., 2018). In 2008, the Global Financial Crisis took a major toll on the banking and financial industry, which led to several issues (Wilson, 2017). The first is the downturn in the consumers' perception of the financial industry as they become aware of the main cause of the crisis. The next issue is the rising lack of customers' trust in the conventional banking system. As a result, there is a change in consumer behaviour as they demand more transparency in their transactions and easier accessibility to their financial accounts. Hence, these changes in behavior have encouraged companies to improve their business operations through the creation of applications for easier access and amplifying their cyber security. In the current era, the younger generation has become the target market for fintech startups as they are the majority of the population with heavy usage of the internet.

FinTech in Brunei Darussalam

Currently, there are several efforts to improve the state of FinTech in Brunei Darussalam. One of them is the establishment of a FinTech unit in 2017 by the Authority Monetary Brunei Darussalam (AMBD) which was recently renamed as Brunei Darussalam Central Bank (The Scoop, 2021). To counter this slow progression of Fintech, this unit has initiated a Regulatory Sandbox in order to encourage and promote local start-ups to test out applications and programmes with Brunei Darussalam Central Bank as the regulator. The participants of the Regulatory Sandbox have provided various FinTech solutions to transform the nation into a digital economy. One of the members is BruPay which is a digital payment company that aims to provide and equip businesses into allowing their operations to have an e-wallet functionality. However, this company has officially announced their closure on their facebook page in March 2021. Other members of the Regulatory sandbox are Beep Digital Solutions; a company that provides AliPay payments, MoneyMatch; a company which specialises in digital overseas money transfer and remittance and finally Jana Kapital, a company that provides a website as a Syariah compliant crowdfunding platform for qualified start-ups companies that seek funding to finance their business assets, search for investors and so on.

Another initiative that was made by the Brunei government is the establishment of the Digital Economy Council (DEC) in March 2019 (Borneo Bulletin, 2019). Their role is to direct the formulation of policy and systemize the efforts of the public sector to drive Brunei Darussalam to transform into a "Smart Nation powered by a digital economy." According to the DEC, their top priorities include: *"1) A cashless society fueled by digital payments 2) Digitalisation of government services 3) Export-driven initiatives supported by growing talent. "*

Another action of the Brunei Government is the 'Electric-Know Your Customer' (E-KYC) which is a type of FinTech service which allows the citizens to access various government online services using their e-darussalam account (BDCB, 2020). The government has also encouraged more data accessibility for individuals and private companies by appointing the Authority for Info-communications Technology Industry (AITI) and Ministry of Transport and Infocommunications ((MTIC) as the main facilitators for the enhancement of the nation's digital ecosystem.

On the other hand, corporations are also accelerating their level of innovation in adjusting to the growing digital era. For example, Bank Islam Brunei Darussalam (BIBD) is one of the top Islamic banks in Brunei that provides digital banking system called BIBD NEXGEN (BIBD, 2020). This system increases accessibility and convenience for the public to do online banking and payments via the BIBD Mobile application that can be downloaded using smartphones. This application provides several digital proficiencies such as biometric logins, scan to pay via BIBD Quickpay, purchase of eVouchers, transfer of funds via BIBD vCard and so on. Progresif, a telecommunication company has also made a collaboration with BIBD in the creation of a mobile wallet called Progresif Pay.

Digital Ecosystem in Brunei Darussalam

Briscoe and Wilde (2006) gave an architectural perspective of the digital ecosystem as a self-organised numerical equivalent of the biological ecosystem that has the proficiency to solve complex problems. Meanwhile, Karhu et al. (2011) view the digital ecosystem as the technical layer of the digital business ecosystem (DBE), which is a hi-tech framework to merge services and information via the internet in order to enable systematic transactions. Information and communication technologies (ICT) have a significant role as the enabler of these transactions and co-creators between various parties. Karhu et al. (2011) further illustrated the digital ecosystem as a "marketplace" where the main actors are the consumers and producers who are interlinked by the digital actors such as computers and servers.

To move forward in order to progress as a smart nation, Brunei Darussalam has to take initiatives towards improving their network infrastructure; the foundations are 4G, fiber, and Internet of Things (IoT) (The Scoop, 2019). Furthermore, it emphasizes the importance of prioritizing the strengthening of current foundations in order to be ready for future 5G developments. Thus, the following are new initiatives to adapt to the COVID-19 pandemic made by the Digital Economy Council (DEC) to improve digital activity within the country (APEC, 2020).

Firstly is by improving Brunei Darussalam's telecommunication infrastructure. An initiative to modernise the country's telecommunication infrastructure enables the Unified National Networks (UNN) to improve the quality and speed of the fixed mobile data and increase their fixed broadband data volume to support students' online learning during the COVID-19 pandemic and support the digitalisation of MSMEs. Next is the provision of e-commerce platforms, which are eKadaiBrunei and Community for Brunei. The former is to accommodate e-sellers by encouraging offline sellers to digitalise their business operations and providing logistics services to assist in delivering their products. Meanwhile, the latter is focused on aiding small-sized businesses, especially home-based and single mothers. Another initiative is the capacity-building programs such as "Go Digital Asean" and "Teens in AI". Other initiatives are efforts to transform the nation into a cashless society and the creation of the BruHealth Application as a tool to track close contacts of those who are infected with COVID-19, as well as providing online healthcare services such as booking appointments in clinics.

Accessibility of Digital Wallets Among the Younger Generation

The key constituents in influencing the ownership of a smartphone are the younger generation and their access to the internet via a smartphone (Silver, 2019). Additionally, the author highlighted that this varies across countries that have different levels of economies. According to her research, in Italy, the majority of the younger generations below the age of 35 own a smartphone (91–98%), while fewer than half of the older generation above the age of 50 do (48%). Hence, there is a major gap in smartphone ownership between the younger and older age groups. Many other advanced-economy countries, such as Japan and Hungary, exhibited similar characteristics to Italy. However, the percentage gap in smartphone usage between the younger and older age groups in advanced economies has been decreasing, and the opposite occurs in emerging economies. As there has been increasing ownership of a smartphone, it also allows people to access internet-enabled services such as various social media platforms, websites, and applications, which has also led to the increased access of digital wallets as a mode of payment, replacing physical cash (Cole et al., 2009).

A digital wallet is "an engine of mobile commerce" and, although it is an emerging concept, it is not a new phenomenon as it can be traced back to when online commerce started to grow (Aite, 2016). Furthermore, a digital wallet is a software application with some of these basic foundations: secure matriculation of the user (identity check) and safe provision of the user's credentials; the ability to store and protect customer identification data, such as their identity information, payment details, shipping address, and options for customers to choose their payment methods (such as online payment to merchants "in-app" or "in-store"); and finally, the ability to finance the wallet payment via debit or credit card, customer's bank account, and any other store of value.

According to a survey conducted by the Authority for Info-communications Technology Industry of Brunei Darussalam (AITI), 80% of the e-commercial activity is dominated by millennials (The Scoop, 2018). Moreover, the survey also indicated that they have increasingly shopped online, mainly for the sake of convenience. Additionally, the majority of the respondents have a high preference for using debit or credit cards as the main mode of payment. Therefore, although there is high traffic in the e-commercial activities conducted by the younger population of Brunei, not many have used mobile wallets as a means of payment.

Maslow's Needs Hierarchy theory

Maslow's needs hierarchy theory is a motivation theory that illustrates human needs as a five-tier pyramid where the needs at the bottom tier have to be satisfied first before moving on to the upper tier of the pyramid (McLeod, 2018). From the bottom to the top of the pyramid, the human needs are physiological safety, belongingness, esteem, and self-actualisation. Maslow further classified these human needs into two groupings: deficiency needs and growth needs (Mcleod, 2018; Huitt, 2007). The deficiency needs are the first four stages from the bottom of the model, whereas the growth or being needs are at the top of the model. Thus, the deficiency needs to be fulfilled first before moving upwards towards the person's needs. When the individuals' lower level needs are satisfied, the deficiency in that criteria is then eliminated and the focus will be on their self-actualization needs.

Figure 1. Maslow's Hierarchy of needs

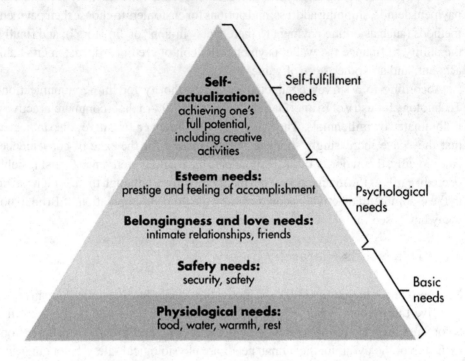

2.1.1 Physiological Needs

This refers to the most basic biological needs of humans; which includes food, water, clothing, shelter and procreation (Urwiler and Frolick, 2008). These are the essential components that are needed to fulfill the basic functions of human beings to survive.

2.1.2 Safety Needs

When the basic biological needs are fulfilled, the need for personal security and safety will become more evident. This depends on the environmental conditions that the individual faces, and the need to feel safer will become more apparent when their security is threatened.

Thus, when both the physiological and safety needs are satisfied, the individual will achieve personal stability before being able to move to the next hierarchy (Urwiler and Frolick, 2008).

2.1.3 Belongingness Needs

As the individual achieves comfort and safety, they will have the desire to look for a social group to belong into. They will need to search for one or more groups to join in order to have a sense of validation through the establishment of satisfying connections where they are able to exchange feelings, opinions and emotions. Hence, this will make the individual feel socially included (McLeod, 2018 ; Urwiler and Frolick, 2008).

2.1.4 Self-Esteem Needs

When the first three stages of the hierarchy are satisfied, the individual will be motivated to achieve a certain level of self-confidence within themselves. This refers to how pleased they are with their status, achievements and respect which could be the major components that influence their self-esteem (McLeod, 2018 ; Urwiler and Frolick, 2008).

2.5.5. Self Actualisation Needs

At this stage of the hierarchy, the individual questions themselves whether or not they have successfully achieved their full potential as a person, and taking the steps to discover what they are capable of becoming. Therefore, Maslow's hierarchy of needs provides a useful foundation to understand the motivation of humans through the satisfaction of successive needs (McLeod, 2018 ; Urwiler and Frolick, 2008).

METHODOLOGY

The main aim of this research is to assess the motivation of Bruneian young adults towards the use of digital wallets with the use of Maslow's hierarchy of needs as the research instrument. Thus, the study will be using a qualitative method to gather primary data using a semi-structured interview with participants. The use of qualitative data is more suitable for this research than quantitative data as this study attempts to discover the psychological aspects of motivation in using a digital wallet. Hence, detailed responses from the participants are highly useful and may produce the desired results to better understand the participants' motivation.

Participants

The participants were selected through purposive sampling. Purposive sampling is a nonrandom technique to obtain data which involves the selection of the respondents based on the researcher's own judgement whether these respondents are willing to share their information and knowledge (Ilker et al., 2015). Some of the criterias for these participants to fulfill are; they are young adults (around 22-38 years old) and they have some basic knowledge about digital wallets. So far, the study is limited to seven participants as not many are willing to be interviewed for this research. The sample that agreed to this research comprises 4 males and 3 females ranging in the ages of 23-25, in which all of them have substantial knowledge about digital wallets, although not many have experienced using it. In order to ensure anonymity, these participants will be denoted as P1, P2, P3, P4, P5, P6 and P7 when mentioning them.

Data Collection Method

The primary data collection methods are conducted as a face-to-face and online interview session using semi-structured interview questions, which are then transcribed into written data. The interview questions were built on similar studies and journal articles that utilizes Maslow's hierarchy of needs. Moreover, the semi-structured interview allows flexibility for the author to add on more questions to have a better understanding of the responses made by the participants. The transcribed data are then thematically coded into several key themes in accordance to the five hierarchy of needs. The secondary data are driven from any relevant materials available with the use of keywords "digital wallets", "Brunei Darussalam + eWallet", "Maslow's needs hierarchy theory + technology", "Youth + digital wallet", and "Maslow's needs hierarchy theory + digitisation".

Data Analysis

After the data has been collected, the audio recordings are then transcribed into written data. These data are then thematically organised according to the five hierarchy of needs. As a part of the thematic analysis process, these data are then coded into several keywords, which are then grouped into themes. The coding process involves re-reading the written data and highlighting the frequency of the ideas that were mentioned in the participants' responses. As the keywords are extracted, these provide the significant foundation to be grouped under several themes.

Ethics

Information sheet and consent form were provided to the respondents before the interview sessions started. Additionally, they were aware of their rights to continue to participate or withdraw from this research. The identities of these respondents are completely anonymised and the data obtained are solely used for research purposes and made only accessible to the author.

Thematic Analysis

Thematic analysis is the systematic process of recognising, organising and analyzing the patterns of meaning within the dataset (Braun & Clarke, 2012). This method mainly involves identifying the commonalities of the way the subject or issues are talked or written about and thus, drawing out further meaning from them. Thematic analysis is chosen mainly because of its flexibility for the author to talk and self-interpret on the identified themes, which is suitable to get insight into the psychological aspects of the participants' motivation. This type of analysis is considered to be suitable for the research as there is still limited literature that looks into Maslow's Hierarchy of Needs with technology use.

For this study, data collection started from 27th July until 15th August as the interview session was conducted based on the availability of the participants. These data are then transcribed into written data before analyzing. The author then proceeds to follow the six steps of thematic analysis, firstly by being familiar with the data, followed by coming up with initial codes, identifying themes, reviewing the potential themes, defining and naming themes and finally, producing the final report (Braun & Clarke, 2012).

DATA ANALYSIS

Table 2 summarises the data gathered from the interview session. The interview questions are orderly divided into five categories according to Maslow's Hierarchy of needs; physiological needs, safety needs, belongingness needs, self-esteem needs and self-actualisation needs.

With the main objective in mind, the context of all interview questions are within the subject matter of the participants' general technology and internet utilisation which also includes their digital wallet usage.

The first row is the physiological needs, which is the basic requirement to allow the participants to use a digital wallet. As depicted in the table, all of the participants have smartphones and consider this gadget significant in going through their daily life activities.

The next row is the participants' safety needs in their general online presence over the internet. The majority of the participants prefer to use cash over other modes of payment, mainly due to their high preference for doing their general shopping activity in physical stores, rather than shopping online. Moreover, some of the participants showed similar responses in having concerns for personal data vulnerability as depicted in P1 and P2. Hence, their personal data safety becomes one of the setbacks that prevents them from doing online transactions as often. Therefore, because of this reason, it can be assumed that there is a perceived lack of trust in using digital wallets, especially for P1. However, there is also a contradiction to this issue. Simultaneous with their concern for safety, they also view digital wallets as a convenient and fast mode of payment. Most notable was with P2 and P7, both are active in online shopping, hence they only proceed with online financial transactions with confidence when they are using BIBD virtual cards and when the online shopping platform is reliable.

Next is the social needs, which addresses the participants' needs to establish communication with other people, businesses and organisations over the internet. All of the participants have social media accounts and heavily depend on them to stay connected to the world. Through this connectivity to the online community, the participants are exposed to various issues.

Hence, there is seemingly a lack of correlation between their social needs and digital wallet usage.

The fourth row is the self esteem needs which is how the participants are using their online presence in their social media to boost their personal positive traits, such as confidence and good morals. There is a division of opinion that was given by the participants in this issue. P1, P3, P6 and P7 view the internet as a poor platform to boost their self esteem. They all gave similar responses in which self esteem comes from within, not from the validation of people in social media.

Finally is the self actualization needs which focuses on how their perception of themselves in terms of their online presence and whether they are ready to embrace being totally cashless in the future. The principal investigator analyzes that the majority of the participants are privileged to have their basic needs fulfilled and have divided opinions on the general use of technology. Moreover, not all the responses are relevant in investigating the factors that influenced the participants' digital wallet usage tendency.

Table 1. Summary of findings

Maslow's Hierarchy of needs	Notable participants quotes	Points
Physiological needs Whether participants: **Have their own smartphones and consider them essential. Can easily access the internet and their usage.**	"Smartphones are an essential device especially in this era where most things can be accessed through the use of smartphones especially during this time (COVID-19 Pandemic)" -P4	Smartphone ownership is important for all participants. All of them have the privilege to have wifi at home.
	".. I do own a smartphone, and it is important to me .. " All partcipants	
	"...I have wifi connection at home and consider myself as a heavy internet user.." -All participants	
Safety needs **Their safety when doing general online/physical financial transactions**	"I prefer physical shopping especially for groceries and daily necessities.." - P2, P3, P4 "Because of the digitized features, there is concern of hacking.." -P1 "I feel confident to use a digital wallet when using a v-card.." P2 "I prefer carrying physical cash as it is more convenient.." -P3, P5.	All of them prefer physical shopping for various purposes. Physical cash is preferable to digital wallet due to trust issues with online payment.
Social needs **Connectivity and communication with people/ businesses/organisations**	"It is important to use social media as physical interaction can be difficult.." -P6 "I prefer physical social interactions, it is easier to understand people better that way.." - All participants "When doing my shopping, it is unnecessary for me to interact with the retail employee to make my payments.." -P1,P2,P4,P6	Physical Social interaction is important for all participants. Using a digital wallet is a convenient choice of payment.
Esteem needs **The need to boost self-confidence fulfill personal desire to be a better version of oneself**	"Using the internet (social media) is not really an effective way to increase your self esteem" -P1, P3, P6 " I used the internet mainly for information and news updates." -P1 & P3 "Digital wallet is a useful tool nowadays especially to make donations to fund various community drives.." -P1, P4,P5,P6	The internet is useful to benefit others.

Continued on following page

Table 1. Continued

Maslow's Hierarchy of needs	Notable participants quotes	Points
Self-actualisation needs	"I have utilised online banking (BIBD) to donate a portion of the profit from my business to several charity drives.."-P1, P6 "Being totally cashless is not very convenient in certain situations, not all people have the privilege to have a smartphone and bank account .." -P4, P5	Participants are aware that making digital payments has its own benefits and also drawbacks. Allows them to not only utilize digital wallet as personal use, but also for the benefit of others donation.

Thematic Analysis Process

The data collected from the participants are transcribed into written data by the principal investigator, and this is done to ease noting down some initial thoughts and ideas before beginning the thematic analysis process which comprises six phases.

The first phase is to familiarize oneself with the data which is done through repeat reading of the textual data in order to be immersed with the content of the dataset and to identify which ones are relevant for the research objective (Braun and Clarke, 2012). This stage is illustrated in the first column in table 3 in which relevant dataset from each of the five sections are identified. The second phase is initiating a systematic analysis which is done through coding. Coding helps with providing structure from the dataset by identifying and labeling the attribute of the data (Braun and Clarke, 2012). Moreover, it can provide the summary or description of the data content which is depicted in the second column of the table below.

The next phase is generating the theme which emerges from the data. This involves the author's active process of crafting and reviewing the coded data to recognise the similarities and overlap that may occur between the codes. Hence, this cluster of code is then related to several broader topics or issues. The fourth stage is reviewing the potential themes which is a time consuming process of quality checking of the themes by re-reading the dataset and codes again ensuring they are coherent enough for the research.

The fifth phase is placing a name and definition to the themes, and being able to clearly sum up the essence of each of them. (Braun and Clarke, 2012) has recommended keeping the themes to have a singular focus, overlap but not repetitive and able to address the research question directly. Finally, the sixth phase of thematic analysis is producing the final report which involves further discussing the themes and arguing how it is relevant to the main objective of the research.

Table 2. Thematic analysis process

Dataset	Code	Theme
Physiological needs - Smartphone ownership To allow: - Communication - Connectivity - Accessibility - Source of entertainment	Fulfilled basic digital needs.	Digitalization of youth
Safety needs -Data protection -Vulnerability -Online Security concerns -Technical issue anxiety -Monetary Security	Cyber Safety Concerns	Technological anxiety
-Convenience -Faster and efficient -minimise physical interaction due to COVID-19	Benefit of digital wallet	
Social Needs -Staying updated -Accessibility -Technological utilization -Communication -interaction	Personal social needs fulfilled	Positive attitude towards technology use
-Efficiency of online shopping -minimal social interaction -Ease of payment	Online shopping convenience	
Esteem needs -General life updates -awareness of community issues -High exposure to information	Benefits of being active on the internet	
Self-Actualization needs Ease of donation Community contribution Convenience Increased importance	Benefits of digital payment	

DISCUSSION

The thematic analysis process that was applied to the transcripts have resulted in several key issues that were apparent in the data. These issues were categorised into themes that can be considered as essential in understanding the participants' motivation. These themes are labelled as "Digitization of youth", "Technological anxiety", and "positive attitude towards technology use". Additionally, these are interpretations of the participants' attitude towards their general technological utilisation and digital wallet usage.

Digitization of Youth

This theme is defined as the fulfillment of the participants' basic needs in order to utilise technology and have access to the internet. In this study, all of the participants have their own smartphones which automatically means they are able to connect to the internet. Additionally, these participants consider the gadget significant in making their lives easier. When asked the reason why this gadget is important to them, they have given similar responses such as communication, connectivity, accessibility and source of entertainment.

I: " Do you own a smartphone? If so, would you consider it an essential device for your daily life activities?"

P1: "Yes I do have one. It is important to stay connected with family and friends through messaging apps, browse on social media and the internet and use important apps such as Bruhealth and online banking."

P2: "I need my phone to communicate to others."

For these participants, having a smartphone is considered not as a want, but a necessity to carry out their daily life activities. One of the reasons is due to the perceived high importance for them to stay connected to their community and enable them to use smartphones as a communication tool. Considering the context of the current ongoing case of COVID-19, smartphones are especially needed not only for communication but also to access important applications to adapt to the new norm. P1 has expressed the need to access BruHealth applications and online banking.

P5: " it can be considered as an essential device in this era where most things can be accessed through the use of smartphones especially during this time (COVID-19 Pandemic), for example, we can check bank balance through an app without physically going out to an ATM machine."

P6: "I do own a smartphone and yes, it is an essential device for my daily activities (esp now since bruhealth scanning and whatnot)"

P5 and P6 have expressed the same necessary purpose to have a smartphone and this is mainly motivated by the COVID-19 pandemic. The BruHealth application plays a huge role for the whole nation to access any premises and book their vaccination slots. Moreover, the importance of online banking rises not only for convenience, but also for hygienic purposes in order to minimise physical contact with ATMs and handling cash. Moreover, online banking in general has become more appealing for these participants. Therefore, a significant event like a pandemic becomes one of the main factors that motivates them to use online banking in general. However, this does not seem to interest them in using mobile wallets despite their need to always have access to their online banking applications.

Technological Anxiety

This theme is defined as the factors that are viewed as the perceived risks and disadvantages when using technology which affects their behaviour towards its usage. All of the participants have expressed some issues that hold them back from using digital wallets which are mainly the general risks of making online payments over the internet. Some participants have conveyed their preference for cash rather than digital wallet as a mode of payment due to the perceived view of cash being a more secure choice.

It can be seen that P2 and P3 have a lack of trust in technology due to the risks they might encounter when doing their transactions such as technical issues and scams.

Moreover, the participants had also expressed discomfort when using digital mode of payment mainly due to their concerns for their personal data safety.

Based on P1 and P7's responses, these participants have made the assumption that due to the digitized feature of their finances, their personal information is vulnerable on the internet.

There is a fear of data exploitation and losing money to hackers and scammers. Despite growing up in an era of rapid growth of internet technology, these participants have shown a slight lack of trust in FinTech, specifically in terms of extent the financial institutions are able to protect them from the risk of cyber crime.

However, when asked for their final verdict for their preferred mode of payment either physical or digital, the majority of them have chosen the latter . A follow up question for this is how do they make sure they are keeping their personal data safe despite having trust issues. The majority of the participants gave similar responses, to carefully choose online retailers that can be trusted. Interestingly, only P2 and P6 acknowledged how digital wallets (BIBD virtual card and Paypal respectively) can be useful for their online shopping.

From here, the principal investigator realised that the majority of these participants seemed to be confused on what a digital wallet really is. It can be assumed that for these participants, there is a thin line between the usual digitised route of payments (transfers, debit and credit card) and eWallet (such as DSTpay, Progresif pay). Due to the digitised features of these, most of the participants are equalising mobile wallets with the usual online payments.

In addressing their issues with the risks of using technology, all of them have their own precautions and preference of mode of payments when doing their financial transactions digitally. Therefore, the issues that they are afraid of (stolen personal data, scams and hack) triggers a form of mistrust towards digital finance. However this does not totally hinder them from making use of the financial technology that is readily available to them. Hence, the majority of these participants have a misunderstanding of what a mobile wallet is due to their generalisation of any online payments features to be the same.

Positive Attitude Towards Technology Use

So far it is evident that there is an increased necessity for individuals to have access to the internet and having a smartphone is considered essential. Technology utilisation has drastically improved the way people live. Hence, a positive attitude towards technology use is defined as the extent of which any form of automation has benefited the participants. The participants have shared their various reasons to use the internet such as communication purposes, connectivity and staying updated with the general global issues.

One of the key issues that was mentioned was COVID-19 and how this has accelerated the need to do everything digital. When asked how digital wallets can possibly have an active role during such a situation, some of the participants have expressed how important digital finance in general was.

P1 and P7 have expressed that donating using a digital wallet can be useful during the pandemic because of its anonymity feature. It is assumed that in order to convey sincerity better is through making anonymous donations rather than making public ones.

Besides anonymity, other features that prompted the participants to have confidence in using digital payments is reduced risk of monetary thefts.

P1: "Being cashless reduce the risk of pickpockets, loss of wallets with all the cash at hand"

P7: "Digital cash is safer right because if let's say, I was robbed, then I can just call my bank to block any transactions made and my money would still be safe."

P1 and P7 addresses the benefits of utilising digital cash in general as it could reduce the concerns that are usually faced when carrying physical cash.

P3 have shared their thought benefit that is related to the pandemic was the need to stay hygienic by doing online payment rather than cash. Her response was partly influenced by the re-emergence of new local COVID-19 cases in August 2021.

P3: "Being totally cashless can be very convenient as all bills can be paid online, there's no need to queue physically to make payments. In the light of the Covid-19 situation, cashless payment can be very convenient to reduce physical contact and social interaction as much as possible."

Although cash was the preferred choice by the majority of the participants, in the end the necessity of minimising physical contact during the pandemic have made all of the participants to further realise the advantages of FinTech. Making payments online have become a necessity at a time of risks and uncertainty.

LIMITATIONS

This study is not without limitations. Although all of the participants have met the criteria for this research (young adults and have basic knowledge about digital wallet), it was clear that most of them are not able to clearly distinguish between digital wallet and online banking. Some of the participants' responses have to be excluded as not all of them are relevant for the research objective. On the other hand, combining the research method with a quantitative analysis may help to give better results as this research was conducted solely by relying on a qualitative method via interview sessions. Thus, there is a possibility that the collection of findings may not be able to deliver a more conclusive analysis.

CONCLUSION

In the efforts of improving the technological infrastructure, digital ecosystem and FinTech, this research has revealed that the young adults have considered digitisation in general as an integral part of their life. However, the role and utilisation of digital wallet has yet to become the main choice of payment. In the context of Maslow's hierarchy of needs for this research, there are three main themes that can be derived as a result of the thematic analysis; 'digitisation of youth', 'technological anxiety' and 'positive attitude towards technology use'. These themes can be considered as the main factors that drive and hinder these young adults to use mobile wallets. The section 'Digitisation of youth' has highlighted the essential role of smartphone usage and digital literacy for their daily use of BruHealth and online banking applications. With the fulfillment of their basic technology needs, there is also an emergence of uncertainty in terms of using digital wallets for their general payments. There is a perception of increased vulnerability of personal data due to the digitised feature of their finance which leads to the formation of the second theme; 'technological anxiety'. One of the key issues that hinders these participants to use digital wallets is their lack of ability to clearly distinguish between the general modes of payments (online transfers, debit and credit card) and digital wallets. Thus, their basic knowledge of digital wallet has led to a generalisation of the mobile wallet

concept. Lastly, the key issue that can be extracted from 'positive attitude towards technology' is the increased importance of online payments. This is mainly driven by COVID-19 where a few of the participants have prioritised their personal safety while being able to make donations and pay their bills. Hence, at a time of crisis, it can be seen that they are willing to put aside their previous fear of technology out of necessity of the current situation.

Based on the information so far, it can be assumed that young adults are ready to embrace the nation's efforts to further flourish their digital ecosystem. However, it is discovered that the possible reason why digital wallet does not become the number one choice of payment is simply due to lack of awareness of its benefits. As a result, these individuals prefer to still choose the traditional mode of payments (cash, online transfers, debit and credit cards). The COVID-19 only accelerates the concept of digitisation in general but it does not have a major impact in the use of mobile wallets. Hence, to encourage them to use digital wallets more, intervention may be required by policymakers. With AITI's plans to transform businesses to adapt digital technology by the year 2025, perhaps new policies will emerge and become the main drive to make digital wallet the top choice of payment for Bruneian consumers.

REFERENCES

Ahad, A. D., Anshari, M., & Razzaq, A. (2017). Domestication of smartphones among adolescents in Brunei Darussalam. *International Journal of Cyber Behavior, Psychology and Learning*, 7(4), 26–39. doi:10.4018/IJCBPL.2017100103

Ahmad, N. (2022). Demography of Brunei. In *Routledge Handbook of Contemporary Brunei* (pp. 61–78). Routledge. doi:10.4324/9781003020431-5

Aite. (2016). *The Evolution of Digital and Mobile Wallets*. Retrieved from: https://www.paymentscardsandmobile.com/wp-content/uploads/2016/10/The-Evoluti on-of-Digital-and-Mobile-Wallets.pdf

Anshari, M., Almunawar, M. N., & Masri, M. (2020). Financial Technology and Disruptive Innovation in Business: Concept and Application. *International Journal of Asian Business and Information Management*, 11(4), 29–43. doi:10.4018/IJABIM.2020100103

Anshari, M., Almunawar, M. N., & Masri, M. (2022b). Digital Twin: Financial Technology's Next Frontier of Robo-Advisor. *Journal of Risk and Financial Management*, *15*(4), 163. doi:10.3390/jrfm15040163

Anshari, M., Almunawar, M. N., Masri, M., & Hamdan, M. (2019). Digital marketplace and FinTech to support agriculture sustainability. *Energy Procedia*, *156*, 234–238. doi:10.1016/j.egypro.2018.11.134

Anshari, M., Almunawar, M. N., Masri, M., Hamdan, M., Fithriyah, M., & Fitri, A. (2021a). Digital Wallet in Supporting Green FinTech Sustainability. In *2021 Third International Sustainability and Resilience Conference: Climate Change* (pp. 352-357). IEEE. 10.1109/IEEECONF53624.2021.9667957

Anshari, M., Almunawar, M. N., Masri, M., & Hrdy, M. (2021). Financial technology with ai-enabled and ethical challenges. *Society*, *58*(3), 189–195. doi:10.100712115-021-00592-w

Anshari, M., Arine, M. A., Nurhidayah, N., Aziyah, H., & Salleh, M. H. A. (2021b). Factors influencing individual in adopting eWallet. *Journal of Financial Services Marketing*, *26*(1), 10–23. doi:10.105741264-020-00079-5

Anshari, M., Fithriyah, M., Polak, P., & Razzaq, A. (2021). Islamic FinTech and artificial intelligence (AI) for assessing creditworthiness. In *Artificial Intelligence and Islamic Finance* (pp. 48–60). Routledge. doi:10.4324/9781003171638-4

Anshari, M., Hamdan, M., Ahmad, N., Ali, E., & Haidi, H. (2022a). COVID-19, artificial intelligence, ethical challenges and policy implications. *AI & Society*, 1–14. doi:10.100700146-022-01471-6 PMID:35607368

APEC. (2020). *Brunei Darussalam and COVID-19: Shifting Towards Digital Transformation*. Retrieved from: http://mddb.apec.org/Documents/2020/MM/ SMEMM/20_smemm_016.pdf

Aruma, E. O., & Hanachor, M. E. (2017, December). *Abraham Maslow's Hierarchy of Needs and Assessment of Needs In Community Development*. https://www. eajournals.org/wp-content/uploads/Abraham-Maslow%E2%80%99s-Hierarchy-of-Needs-and-Assessment-of-Needs-in-Community-Development.pdf

BDCB. (2020). *The State of FinTech in Brunei Darussalam*. Retrieved from: https:// www.bdcb.gov.bn/SiteAssets/Lists/Publications/White-Paper-State-of-FinTec h-Brunei-Darussalam-2020.pdf

BIBD. (2020). *The State of FinTech in Brunei Darussalam*. Retrieved from: http://www.bibd.com.bn/assets/pdf/media-centre/annual-report/BIBD_Annual_Report_2020_ENG_online.pdf

Borneo Bulletin. (2019, March 13). *Digital Economy Council established to facilitate 'Smart Nation' drive*. https://borneobulletin.com.bn/digital-economic-council-established-to-facilitate-sma rt-nation-drive/

Braun, V., & Clarke, V. (2012). Thematic Analysis. *APA handbook of research methods in psychology*, 2, 57-71. https://www.researchgate.net/publication/269930410_Thematic_analysis

Briscoe, G., & Wilde, P. D. (2006). Digital ecosystems: evolving service-orientated architectures. In *Proceedings of the 1st International Conference on Bio Inspired Models of Network, Information and Computing Systems (BIONETICS '06)*. ACM.

Buckley, R., Arner, D., & Barberis, J. (2016). The Evolution of Fintech: A New Post-Crisis Paradigm? *Georgetown Journal of International Law*, 47, 1271–1319. doi:10.2139srn.2676553

Cole, A., McFaddin, S., Narayanawasmi, C., & Tiwari, A. (2009). *Toward a Mobile Digital Wallet. IBM research report*. Retrieved from: https://dominoweb.draco.res.ibm.com/reports/RC24965.pdf

GlobalData. (2021, September 21). *COVID-19 accelerates mobile wallet adoption across Asia-Pacific, finds GlobalData*. https://www.globaldata.com/covid-19-accelerates-mobile-wallet-adoption-across-asi a-pacific-finds-globaldata/

Hamdan, M., & Anshari, M. (2020). Paving the Way for the Development of FinTech Initiatives in ASEAN. In *Financial technology and disruptive innovation in ASEAN* (pp. 80–107). IGI Global. doi:10.4018/978-1-5225-9183-2.ch004

Hasmawati, F., Samiha, Y. T., Razzaq, A., & Anshari, M. (2020). Understanding nomophobia among digital natives: Characteristics and challenges. *Journal of Critical Reviews*, 7(13), 122–131.

Ilker, E., Alkassim, R. S., & Musa, S. A. B. (2015, December 22). *Comparison of Convenience Sampling and Purposive Sampling*. doi:10.11648/j.ajtas.20160501.11

Kabango, C. M., & Asa, A. R. (2015). Factors influencing e-commerce development: Implications for the developing countries. *International Journal of Innovation and Economic Development*, 1(1), 64–72. doi:10.18775/ijied.1849-7551-7020.2015.11.2006

Karhu, K. Botero, A., Vihavainen, S., Tang, T. & Hämäläinen, M. (2011). A Digital Ecosystem for Co-Creating Business with People. *Journal of Emerging Technologies in Web Intelligence, 3.* doi:10.4304/jetwi.3.3.197-205

McLeod, S. (2018, May 21). *Maslow's Hierarchy of Needs.* Retrieved from: https://canadacollege.edu/dreamers/docs/Maslows-Hierarchy-of-Needs.pdf

Mulyani, M. A., Razzaq, A., Sumardi, W. H., & Anshari, M. (2019, August). Smartphone adoption in mobile learning scenario. In *2019 International Conference on Information Management and Technology (ICIMTech)* (Vol. 1, pp. 208-211). IEEE. 10.1109/ICIMTech.2019.8843755

Prawirasasra, K. P. (2018). Financial Technology in Indonesia: Disruptive or Collaborative? *Reports on Economics and Finance, 4*(2), 83 – 90. www.m-hikari.com

Rathore, H. S. (2016, April). Adoption of Digital Wallet by Consumers. *BVIMSR's Journal of Management Research, 8*(1), 69–76.

Razzaq, A., Samiha, Y. T., & Anshari, M. (2018). Smartphone habits and behaviors in supporting students self-efficacy. *International Journal of Emerging Technologies in Learning, 13*(2), 94. doi:10.3991/ijet.v13i02.7685

Samadi, B., Nogoev, A., & Yazdanifard, A. (2011). *The Evolution and Development of E-Commerce Market and E-Cash.* doi:10.1115/1.859858

Sharma, J. (2018, Oct 7). *Importance of E-Wallets in Cashless Economy* (A Post Demonetisation Study with Special Reference to Ahmedabad City). Retrieved from: https://globalbizresearch.org/Dubai_Conference_2018_oct2/docs/doc/D818.pdf

Silver, L. (2019, Feb 5). *In emerging economies, smartphone adoption has grown more quickly among younger generations.* Retrieved from: https://www.pewresearch.org/global/2019/02/05/in-emerging-economies-smartphone-adoption-has-grown-more-quickly-among-younger-generations/

The Scoop. (2018). *Millennials driving e-commerce, says a new report from AITI.* Retrieved from: https://thescoop.co/2018/07/15/millennials-driving-ecommerce-report-aiti/

The Scoop. (2019). *Smart nation initiatives: The foundation of Brunei's digital economy.* Retrieved from: https://thescoop.co/2019/02/27/smart-nation-initiatives-the-foundation-of-bruneis-di gital-economy/

The Scoop. (2021a, June 18). *AITI eyes digitalisation of 1,200 MSMEs by 2025.* https://thescoop.co/2021/06/18/aiti-eyes-digitalisation-of-1200-msmes-by-2025/

The Scoop. (2021b, June 26). *AMBD renamed Brunei Darussalam Central Bank*. https://thescoop.co/2021/06/26/ambd-renamed-brunei-darussalam-central-bank/#:~:text=AMBD%20renamed%20Brunei%20Darussalam%20Central%20Bank%20%2D %20The%20Scoop

Urwiler, R., & Frolick, M. (2008). The IT Value Hierarchy: Using Maslow's Hierarchy of Needs as a Metaphor for Gauging the Maturity Level of Information Technology Use within Competitive Organizations. *Information Systems Management*, 25(1), 83–88. doi:10.1080/10580530701777206

Wilson, J. D. (2017). *Creating Strategic Value Through Financial Technology*. Wiley Finance. doi:10.1002/9781119318682

Chapter 9
The Digitization in Legal Education:
Picturing and Projecting Indonesia's Experience

Zuhda Mila Fitriana
UPN Veteran Jawa Timur, Indonesia

Eka Nanda Ravizki
UPN Veteran Jawa Timur, Indonesia

ABSTRACT

Digital psychology has affected human behavior, including in the educational sector. The advancement in digital exposure opens the possibility of learning in online-based systems. For years, this new shift has been considered to bring more advantages for people. Recently, this way of learning has been adopted by law schools as an impact of the pandemic in Indonesia. Forecasting the benefits of this digitalized education mechanism, this change is expected to last after the COVID-19 pandemic. Not only does offering help, but the change also raises some challenges and opportunities, including the potential markets for the higher education business, particularly law schools. This chapter analyzes challenges and opportunities to show how the digital world impacts legal education, its current development, and its future projection in Indonesia. This analysis applies qualitative methods supported by secondary data and information.

DOI: 10.4018/978-1-6684-6108-2.ch009

INTRODUCTION

The world's future is changing due to the advancement in technology which has affected almost every area of people's life. The advances impact people's communication and collaboration, taking into account the changes in the learning and teaching system. This world is undeniably becoming more digital, including the education sector. The increased access to internet connection is lessening the barrier of distance and location for higher education seekers (Oriji & Torunarigha, 2020). Online education has increased the rate of the previously disadvantaged populations to take part in higher education, such as students from rural areas and communities, as well as members of professional workers, including military staff (Kohnt, 2020).

Since we adapt to the growth of technology, the lines between education and work capacity are somewhat blurred. Digital psychology and mindset provide chances for education and training to be readjusted to an individual's career. Not limited to the learning materials and education approaches, the market for digitized education is at the next level. By 2018, more than a million students were enrolled in online graduate programs, and nearly one-third of students in higher education institutions had taken online courses (Seaman et al., 2018). This shows a chance for a transformative mindset in institutions of higher education, including Law School.

Legal education has traditionally relied on teaching the evolution of case law. Historically, legal education was broad and unspecified, creating lawyers licensed to practice in a more significant number of areas. However, following the change in the digital mindset, legal practice has rapidly changed, particularly in specific areas such as intellectual property and technology matters. Thus, it shows a chance for a transformative mindset in higher education institutions, including Law School. In the US alone, thirty-nine out of its fifty states required their lawyers to understand the advantages and disadvantages in the technology use (the American Bar Association, 2020). It now requires lawyers to adapt to the needs of changing markets, with well-trained lawyers in technology. That is the result of the digitization of law. Previously, a lawyer used to spend two months reviewing thousands of pages of documents, calculating six days per week and ten hours per day. The digitized literatures and systems help lawyers to shorten the time required (McGinnis & Pearce, 2014).

It is such a digital psychology influence on legal data and information. It changes the pictures of legal knowledge from normative sources to quantitative models represented from the existence of the histograms, tree diagrams and other types of charts in the legal studies and writings (De Oliveira Fornasier, 2021). The issue of how to use technology to teach law has been a minor preoccupation of the legal academia for many years (Lewin, 2012). Given the numerous obstacles law schools face, this situation is genuinely worrying. On the other hand, many law schools neglect context and continue to teach law conventionally, resulting in a widening gap between legal education and legal practice. The immediate impact is declining job prospects for graduates. In this context, technology presents a compelling opportunity to improve the efficiency and effectiveness of legal education—the content of legal education and the system in providing education and its business procedures. Like the pocketed MBA courses, the current legal education considers the "pocketed" legal education program run on a digital platform that helps lawyers -lawyers or non-lawyers- obtain specified skills in the legal field. It is such a digital psychology influence on legal data and information. This is due to the fact that the today education needs to reform its focuses, to become more visionary and based on skills, not on content alone (Mark Fenwick, Wulf A. Kaal, 2018). It depicts the democratization of legal education for a modern market and the effective functioning of society.

The pandemic has had notable effects on the use of digitized education, reforming nearly the whole system of education globally. In Indonesia, the shift is forcefully adopted due to the social distancing (Gumelar & Dinnur, 2020). It also affects the legal education at the national level to help knowledge exchanges still run. The virtual platforms are applied to deliver legal education. Not only the content of knowledge is digitized, but also the practical experiences are now placed on digital and tech-based platforms. For example, the litigation processes are done through an e-court mechanism, forcing the lawyers to adjust their skills in tech-based operations. The business system of legal education also attracts new markets, which results in the change of several law schools' schooling systems. The changes are represented by the born of online courses for specific skills as experienced in the US and some other countries. Not limited to non-degree courses, some distance learning system in law school offers the degree courses, such as Indonesia Open University. Although factually speaking, it established its online-based law degree before the pandemic and is still relevant to be pictured as a leading institution.

As of 2020, according to the Ministry of Higher Education Research and Technology report, the market cap for law students occupied nearly a hundred thousand students in Indonesia (PDDikti, 2020). It nearly represents ten percent of total registered undergraduate students in Indonesia. The prospective markets for practical legal education remain in the top-ten listed undergraduate degree in Indonesia. It shows that researching law school transformation is impactful. This writing aims to provide a clear picture of the digitized legal education systems for the forecasted future. This writing mainly discusses the impact of digital technology on learning systems, particularly legal education. Moreover, the discussion is divided into several points; the trajectory business system in legal education in Indonesia, the emerging trend of legal education, and the challenges-opportunities offered by the digital psychology influence in this sphere.

RESULT AND DISCUSSION

The Upward Trajectory Trends of Digitalization Towards Legal Education

Since 1980s, distance education was again looked at as teleconferencing technologies became more widespread (Michael G. Moore, 2013). This new technology would enable a more effective type of distant learning by allowing real-time group interaction between students and lecturers. It is recognized as the earlier form of digital education, which covers the method of delivering knowledge and value. This digitalization concept is relevant to this writing.

In the legal field, the concept of digitized learning also covers the urge to put digitization into the process of legal structure. It includes the adaptation of the pedagogy and curricula, which include today's digitized law system. Studies predict this change is partly due to digital technology (Epifanova et al., 2020; Galloway, 2017; Susskind, 2017). Indeed, the development of technology influences the practice of law, including case discoveries, legal searching machine, document and brief generation, and prediction of one case outcome. Moreover, digitization amplification will change the direction of movement of tools, resources, and market desires. Thus, legal education must also metamorphose from a 'place' of learning to a 'process' of learning. Susskind postulated that the digital platforms such as online lectures, internet-based tutorials, and virtual supervision takes part of the legal education in the future (Susskind, 2017). Not only do the platforms change, but the pedagogy also requires adjustment by specifically designing competencies and the ability to meet the market's needs. For example, the future law schools may adapt MBA's program logic in terms of forming the "pocket" education and encouraging the learning process to be more applicable and support the professionals graduate (Carpenter, 2021; Compagnucci et al., 2020; Fenwick et al., 2017). On the other hand, the more professional approach in legal education, which contains more specified skills in law, is also growing in number. This is modeled in such "pocketed" legal courses.

In the US alone, in 2020, five law schools[1] adapt the form of online-to-hybrid JD programs and some other design the similar program to follow (Kohnt, 2020). This number is continuously developed, particularly following the pandemic of Covid-19. Most law school activities are shifted during the pandemic to online platforms. For example, the JD programs in most American Law schools run their education online. The majority of the students enrolled in the fall 2020 and spring 2021 took half of their classes online. The research conducted by Gallup and AccessLex finds that most of the first-year students tested that the online program was good or excellent compared to the second or third-year students (Hrynowski & Carlson, 2021), as seen from the graph below.

Figure 1. Law student's perceptions of the quality of their programs, by year
Source: *https://news.gallup.com/poll/350351/law-schools-forced-shift-online-offers-insights-future.aspx*

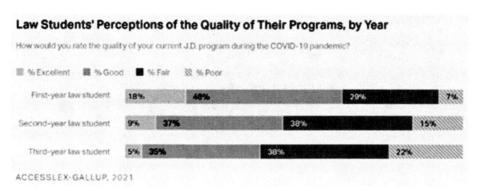

Law Students' Perceptions of the Quality of Their Programs, by Year

How would you rate the quality of your current J.D. program during the COVID-19 pandemic?

■ % Excellent　■ % Good　■ % Fair　▨ % Poor

First-year law student	18%	46%	29% 7%
Second-year law student	9% 37%	38%	15%
Third-year law student	5% 35%	38%	22%

ACCESSLEX-GALLUP, 2021

As of the pandemic era, this shift is also experienced in some of UK's best law schools (Gazette, 2020). For example, King's College London offers LL.M. program and support students to enroll this program (Murray, 2022). Moreover, University of Essex also offers online course for its LL.B. degree (University of Essex, 2022) and collaborate with Kaplan Open Learning for delivering the course. The change is part of student's protections during the pandemic which was taken by more than half of the law school surveyed by the CABS (CABS, 2021). The Y-o-Y satisfaction level decreased, from 84% to 73% which remains remarkable considering the limitation due to Covid-19. Moreover, nearly 50% of the participants feel contented by the course delivery during the pandemic. It served prominent foundation for the future change in the UK legal education.

Figure 2. CABS data, 2021
Retrieved by the authors

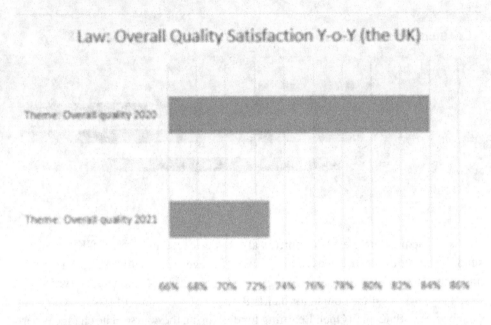

Figure 3. CABS Data, 2021. NSS Covid questions.
Retrieved by the authors

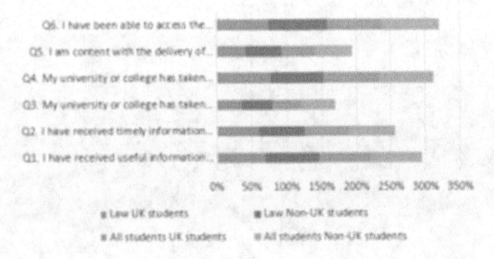

Indeed, the pandemic significantly affected the clinical activities of law students, yet it accelerated the use of LegalTech and online platforms. Following the closure of university campuses in March 2020, significant survey respondents moved to remote or online pro bono services. It shows that law schools are embracing LegalTech and integrating it as the result of physical limitation (LawWorks, 2020; Sandbach & Grimes, 2020).

Figure 4. LawWorks and CLEO, 2020

Law Schools are increasingly embracing LegalTech and integrating it into legal education and practice, has this impacted on your pro bono work?

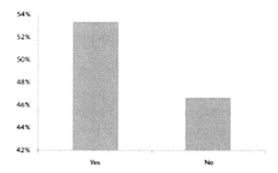

In Australia, the transformed of legal education delivery has been occurred for the last two decades. The lecturers run the classes either hybrid or totally online as the supplementary for the traditional face-to-face classes (Black & Black, 2018). As the students expect flexibility, some of the law schools in Australia offer fully online law degree. The trend firstly set by the Central Queensland University in 2011 (Black & Black, 2018; Kirby, 2011). By 2022, 31 law schools offer distance learning both for degree or non-degree programs. This number is still growing as seen from the page of Open Universities Australia[2].

Meanwhile, in Asia by 2022, more than twenty law schools[3] offer online LLB degree (Studies, 2022a). For JD program, there are seven law schools in Asia offer distance learning, including Korea National Open University and The University of Hong Kong by 2022 (Studies, 2022b). This is the result of the "new normal" concept shaped by the pandemic for education sectors (ADB, 2021). Before the pandemic, for example, Indonesia had no law school offering online courses. By 2022, the President University law school starts offer LL.B. degree in online platform.

As the legal practice rapidly change, the legal education needs to adapt by changing its focus on producing more well-trained and specialized lawyers. Instead of offering four-year law degree, the law schools can establish "pocketed" program providing more professional skills for both lawyers and other fields' practitioners (Carpenter, 2021). The innovation of digitized learning platforms is now experiencing growth. Some open learning providers offer short legal courses that last for weeks. Kaplan Open Learning, Open Universities Australia, ET-Asia, Hukumonline, and Coursera exemplify the current digitized platforms providing short law courses. To conclude, digital psychology has impacted not only the learning method but also the materials in teaching in global legal education. People demand more flexible learning experiences in a shorter time and condensed materials which influence the growth of online professional legal education.

The Emerging Digitized Legal Education: Indonesia Experiences (1219/1500)

Prior to tech-influenced distance learning, Indonesia had a conventional distance learning experience. Historically, in the 1950s, distance learning was done through correspondent courses for teachers, which grew to radio streams. As the demand rose, by 1984, Indonesia had its Open University, which became the guru of higher education's distance learning courses. In the earlier 2000s, the ministry circulated a decree regarding distance education for the first time. Continuously, the government has developed the model of distance learning in Indonesia.

Figure 5. The development of distance learning in Indonesia (Pannen, 2016)

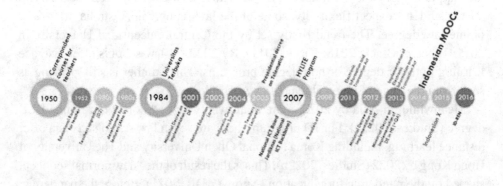

Pursuant to Article 31 Law No.12/2012 regarding the Higher Education (HE Law, hereinafter) jo. Ministry of Education Regulation No.109/2013, distance learning is defined as the teaching process done through various communication media by distance. It aims to provide inclusively, broadened, and accessible higher education services for all communities, particularly the group that faces limitations in attending face-to-face classes. This method is based on three principles; a. Open Learning, b. Distance Learning, and c. IT-based Learning (Pannen, 2016).

The mix of the Internet and education created a new method of education process and structure that is limited to the transfer of knowledge and does not cover the values (Purfitasari et al., 2019). It thus needs to be re-assessed because this development potentially shifts the orientation of the knowledge in general to create an atmosphere in which students, academicians, and professionals collaborate in the developing 4.0 ecosystem. Moreover, it also opens the global collaboration chances, which also holds spiritual, ethical, moral, national, and social values by transferring the cultures and values using the technology (Shahroom & Hussin, 2018). In Indonesia, at some levels of education, the institution prefers using technology to transfer knowledge to values. On the other hand, the digital psychology approach affects the pedagogy, creating the digital pedagogy. It is known as pedagogy which is grounded in the optimization of digital exposure for distance learning.

There are two instructional methods greatly applied in today's legal digital education: Synchronous and Asynchronous. Both of methods has emerged due to the needs of better quality method to hold in digitalized education (Mahoney & Hall, 2020). Mainly speaking, the need for rapid adjustment also occurred in Indonesia following the pandemic. For example, educational institutions, universities, colleges, and vocational schools must adjust their conventional pedagogy and method to the abovementioned ones.

The popular example of the use of technology in education is the Synchronous Model of Distance Learning (Pistone, 2015). The synchronous model of online education resembles traditional classroom instruction. Under a synchronous model, all the participants in the course, including all students and the teacher, participate simultaneously, albeit from different locations. Thus, the participants are together in time but not together in space. In addition, this model uses streaming videos in which all students participate simultaneously in online class meetings. Students virtually meet for class discussions, study groups and working assessments with a professor (Wash. U.l, 2015).

On the other hand, the practice of the asynchronous method occurred in Paris, France, which resembled a university that opens 24/7, providing free access to education. Free access means it has no lecturer, books, or tuition fees. Students enroll in this program and finish them by finishing given projects. At the end, students who will to pursue higher level need to earn points and collect them (Anderson, 2017; Shahroom & Hussin, 2018). This model is somewhat lessening the subjects and opening the objects contributed to this class.

Another example, in Indonesia, there is Universitas Terbuka (UT) or Indonesia Open University (IOU). It has been designed to be a flexible and inexpensive university focusing on serving people who lack the opportunity to attend face-to-face mode of the higher education system due to various constraints, including lack of funding, living in isolated and rural areas, and work as well as other commitments. In addition, IOU is also committed to developing a distance education system to support the implementation of distance learning in Indonesia. It implements a distance and opens the learning system. The term distance means that learning is not done face-to-face but uses media, both print media (modules) and non-prints (audio/video, computer/internet, radio broadcasts, and television). The open meaning is that there are no restrictions on age, year of diploma, study period, registration time, and frequency of taking exams.

The pandemic has brought this era to the next level, Circular Letter of Indonesia Ministry of Education No.4/2020 regarding Education Activity in the Covid-19 Emergency Stage regulates that all the teaching activities shall be run in distance-learning[4]. In 2021, the situation of Covid-19 has been controllable. Thus, the four ministries: Ministry of Education, Culture, Research and Technology, Ministry of Religious Affairs, Ministry of Health, and Ministry of Home Affairs regulate a joint decree: No.05/KB/2021, No. 137 the Year 2021, No. HK.01.08/ Menkes/6678/2021, and No.443-5847/the Year 2021 concerning the Handbook of Education Activity in the Covid-19 Emergency Stage. Briefly, this decree rules about the possibility of opening the conventional learning and run the hybrid model learning for certain areas (Joint Decree: Four Ministrials, 2021). Recently, the Circular Letter of Indonesia Ministry No.2 the Year 2022 regulates that the licensed study program possibly opens the distance-learning class, which automatically closes its old-styled off-site study program classes (Circular Letter of Indonesia Ministry of Education, Culture, Research and Technology No.2 Year 2022, 2022).

The learning method also occurs in legal education regardless of the current model run by the universities or study programs. Following the circular letter, distance learning runs through video teleconference, digital documents, and other media. The recommended platforms are Rumah Belajar, Google G Suites, Kelas Pintar, Microsoft Office 365, and other platforms managed by the universities. At this point, most of all, the universities run their educational purpose through distance learning. Ultimately, this enormous transformation of the learning system significantly impacted the world of education. This condition can be a reference on whether technology can effectively replace the role of teachers or lecturers as teaching staff or cannot replace the part of teachers or lecturers as teaching staff, no matter how sophisticated the technology is.

Challenges and Opportunities: Projecting the Shifts

The era of the industrial revolution 4.0 has brought rapid changes, including creating accelerated business activities, both at national and global levels. This acceleration of business activity is marked by productive digital business entities supported by quality digital services. This digital business entity has brought both positive and negative sides.

On the positive side, the activities of digital business entities can be carried out with very high speed, convenience, and accessibility. The positive impact is also felt in social changes that make it easier for people to meet their needs, for example, in the field of e-commerce business, payment systems through electronic media (financial technology/fintech), transportation and online distribution, health, distribution, transportation, and others. Meanwhile, the negative impact of using technology also makes it easier for people to violate social order in new forms such as cybercrime, hate speech news, bullying, controlling drug trafficking, trafficking, online prostitution, online gambling, and so on, all of which are related to the law and are challenges for legal professionals to handling. The use of technology is like 2 (two) sides of a knife for society.

The emergence of positive and negative phenomena from the activities of digital business entities has created a need in the legal field. Namely, legal readiness must be related to the actions of digital business entities. This readiness is not only limited to the availability of laws that support digital business entities, but these laws must be able to adapt to the characteristics of digital technology.

Thus, professional law graduates are needed to respond to the impact of the activities of digital business entities. The exciting thing about the need for law graduates who understand digital business is that they are not only able to do business law professional work, but they must also be able to do the work based on digital technology and respond to new cases due to the activities of digital business entities. Thus, after understanding the needs of business law human resources as a result of the activities of digital business entities, business law education becomes a fundamental part of this context.

Therefore, the orientation of the law study program must be able to prepare graduates to understand digital business law. As a result, the law graduate cannot only play a role as a business law professional in a judicial institution, but he is also a business law professional who acts as a reliable legal designer in digital business entities. If this can be realized, legal cases arising from digital business entities and entering the judiciary will be minimized because the law can already be adequately designed for the digital business entity.

Technological innovations are also influencing the practice of law (McGinnis & Pearce, 2014). Currently, several electronic systems have been developed whose purpose is to digitize law graduates' role/job desk, for example, e-court programs, e-litigation, e-notary, Etc. The existence of these programs indirectly shows that graduates of conventional law study programs or who lack technological insight will have difficulty competing and responding to the needs of the industrial world in the era of global technological disruption. As a result, to succeed professionally, lawyers and law students must master new skill sets.

Unfortunately, new graduates lack abilities in the increasingly advanced applications of technology for lawyering and law practice. Based on these conditions, in the future, a legal education curriculum is needed to produce law graduates with skills in the field of IT mastery related to law. For example, the number of startup companies growing in various areas of goods and services, such as Gojek in the transportation sector, online marketplace for goods, there is even a labor service marketplace, even now there is a legal tech startup that provides legal consulting services via the internet, starting from the establishment of a company (startup). Its licensing requires a notary or at least a legal consult. In its business dealing with consumers or producers, domestically and abroad, if someone experiences a dispute, he/she needs legal professionals, legal staff, and lawyers to judge. Suppose a criminal aspect uses technology, such as fraudulent investment, carding, online prostitution, pornography, and human trafficking. In that case, it will involve police investigators, prosecutors, lawyers, and judges to enforce the law. This condition opens up new job opportunities for legal professionals who do not previously exist and require knowledge of information technology.

This activity must be supported by information and communication technology, so it requires skills to use information technology tools that provide a lot of data and information about the law. During the COVID-19 pandemic, these skills are very much needed, for example, by judges, prosecutors, lawyers, and the public seeking justice. For instance, by summoning parties via e-mail, court hearings (especially civil ones) have been conducted via e-court, virtual hearings using various zoom applications or Google conferences, and others.

This condition shows that the results of the digitization of education should also affect the professionalism of law graduates in the world of work, where digital technology is applied and centered on humans (professional actors / legal professionals) to solve service problems for justice seekers by using a system that integrates cyberspace with physical space. Where they are, justice seekers can solve their problems with a virtual integrated technology system so that the time and costs incurred are relatively less compared to going to court. Challenges for legal professionals and the public to be skilled at using internet technology tools.

It must be initiated and trained early in legal higher education. In the future, legal professionals must respond to changes in society due to the rapid progress of science and technology. Legal questions and issues are not sufficiently explained at this time based on basic knowledge of the law and legal dogma, but the legal reality develops in society. Moreover, various legal events that use digital technology are growing, as are increasingly diverse crimes that require the help of science and technology to prove it. Therefore, legal professionals must be able to elaborate skills, insights, knowledge, and moral ethics.

The update of legal knowledge is necessary because the law and legal events continue to develop along with the development of society. The story of a community in the digital era has a lot to do with the field of international law, both criminal and international civil, as well as other disciplines such as economics, politics, social and information systems, or information technology. Law. In addition, the impact of information technology is global, and legal relations will also be international without national borders. Therefore, the scope of work of legal professionals has the opportunity not only in the national environment but also in the multinational, regional and global environment. Therefore, graduates who can be competitive in the worldwide industry are needed.

The legal education industry should be changed to answer the demands of the industrial world. Therefore, the legal education industry must also change to answer the demands of the industrial world. The urgency to change is in line with the concept of Digital Psychology, where the market will tend to consider digital aspects in how we behave, learn, and interact with others. Interestingly, human psychology also influences the development and evolution of digital media and technology, impacting corporate performance, growth, and the economy. As a result, colleges must respond to these problems by reforming their learning curricula and techniques. The goal is simply the purpose of meeting market expectations.

FUTURE RESEARCH DIRECTIONS

Digital psychology influences legal education and its market condition. We propose that the current model of law curricula is outdated and requires innovation to adapt to IR 4.0 and society 5.0. The pandemic has forced all sectors to well-adapt to the new normal. It opens a massive change for the education ways of learning. However, the analysis needs further research and be examined in an actual legal education business scenario. The law schools, particularly in Indonesia, should accommodate the change and research that preceded this innovation.

CONCLUSION

Law schools in Indonesia have a potential market cap in the educational business. Thus, it needs to adjust to the market expectations under the circumstances of the digitized world. It will help the higher education institution to obtain better recognition and meet the market expectations. Although some law schools in Indonesia have offered digitized education systems, it remains the potential to grow and adjust following the forceful trend of digital change due to the pandemic. Despite the advantages the digital learning system offer, there are also several challenges to coping with law schools. To solve those challenges, today's digital exposures and information provide plenty of sources through training, for example, helping the educators and students to be familiar with the technology used in the learning systems. In the end, by achieving the training, students are expected to meet the tech-based skills required by the industries. In conclusion, digital psychology indeed has influenced the majority of people's life by bringing enlightenment and ease to human activities such as the education system. It is hoped that legal education will be more inclusive, open, and limitless in the future.

REFERENCES

ADB. (2021). *Covid-19 and Education in Asia and the Pacific*. ADB.

Anderson, B. J. (2017). *TALENT POOL A free, teacher-less university in France is schooling thousands of future-proof programmers*. Academic Press.

Black, A., & Black, P. (2018). Going Global: Australia Looks to Internationalise Legal Education. In Legal Education in Asia: From Imitation to Innovation (p. 54). Koninklijke Brill NV.

CABS. (2021). *National Student Survey 2021 : Results for Law*. National Student Survey 2021. https://charteredabs.org/national-student-survey-2021-results-for-law/

Carpenter, M. (2021). A Digital Mindset Will Revolutionize Education: Legal Education as a Global Model Article By. *National Law Review, 11*(266). https://www.natlawreview.com/article/digital-mindset-will-revolutionize-education-legal-education-global-model

Circular Letter of Indonesia Ministry of Education, Culture, Research and Technology No.2 Year 2022, Pub. L. No. No.2 Year 2022 (2022).

Compagnucci, M. C., Kono, T., Teramoto, S., & Vermeulen, E. P. M. (2020). *Legal Tech and the New Sharing Economy*. http://link.springer.com/10.1007/978-981-15-1350-3

De Oliveira Fornasier, M. (2021). Legal Education in the 21st Century and the Artificial Intelligence. *Revista Opiniao Juridica*, *19*(31), 1–32. doi:10.12662/2447-6641oj.v19i31.p1-32.2021

Epifanova, T. V., Vovchenko, N. G., Toporov, D. A., & Pozdnyshov, A. N. (2020). Development of Legal Education and Machine-Readable Law in the Conditions of Economy Digitization. *Lecture Notes in Networks and Systems*, *87*(January), 971–979. doi:10.1007/978-3-030-29586-8_110

Fenwick, & Kaal. (2018). Legal Education in a Digital Age: Why "Coding for Lawyers". *Matters*.

Fenwick, M., Kaal, W. A., & Vermeulen, E. P. M. (2017). Legal Education in the Blockchain Revolution. SSRN *Electronic Journal, 20*(2). doi:10.2139/ssrn.2939127

Galloway, K. (2017). A Rationale and Framework for Digital Literacies in Legal Education. *Legal Education Review*, *27*(1). Advance online publication. doi:10.53300/001c.6097

Gazette. (2020). *Coronavirus: Top law schools move teaching online*. https://www.lawgazette.co.uk/news/coronavirus-top-law-schools-move-teaching-online/5103496.article

Gumelar, D. R., & Dinnur, S. S. (2020, Sept.). Digitalisasi Pendidikan Hukum dan Prospeknya Pasca Pandemi Covid-19. *Al-Ahwal Al-Syakhsiyyah*.

Hrynowski, B. Y. Z. A. C. H., & Carlson, M. T. (2021). *Law Schools' Forced Shift Online Offers Insights for Future*. Gallup. https://news.gallup.com/poll/350351/law-schools-forced-shift-online-offers-insights-future.aspx

Joint Decree: Four Ministrials, Pengelola Web Kemdikbud 1. (2021). https://www.kemdikbud.go.id/main/blog/2021/12/keputusan-bersama-4-menteri-tentang-panduan-penyelenggaraan-pembelajaran-di-masa-pandemi-covid19

Kirby, M. (2011, May). *Online Legal Education: The New CQU Law*. https://www.michaelkirby.com.au/images/stories/speeches/2000s/2011/2542-SPEECH-CQU-NEW-LAW-DEGREE-LAUNCH-MAY-2011.pdf

Kohnt, N. A. (2020). Online Learning and The Future of Legal Education: Symposium Introduction. *Syracuse Law Review, 70*.

LawWorks. (2020). *Survey shows UK law students increasingly delivering pro bono advice to vulnerable people*. https://www.fenews.co.uk/skills/survey-shows-uk-law-students-increasingly-delivering-pro-bono-advice/

Lewin, T. (2012, May 8). Law School Plans to Offer Web Courses for Master's. *The New York Times*. https://www.nytimes.com/2012/05/09/education/law-school-plans-to-offer-web-courses-for-masters.html

Mahoney, J., & Hall, C. A. (2020). *Exploring Online Learning Through Synchronous and Asynchronous Instructional Methods*. doi:10.4018/978-1-7998-1622-5.ch003

McGinnis, J. O., & Pearce, R. G. (2014). The great disruption: How machine intelligence will transform the role of lawyers in the delivery of legal services. *Fordham Law Review*, 82(6), 3041–3066. doi:10.21202/1993-047X.13.2019.2.1230-1250

Murray, S. (2022). *Pandemic Accelerates Growth of Online and Hybrid LLMs*. https://llm-guide.com/articles/pandemic-accelerates-growth-of-online-and-hybrid-llms

Oriji, A., & Torunarigha, Y. D. (2020). Digitized education: Examining the challenges of digital immigrant educators in the face of net generation learners. *KIU Journal of Social Sciences*, 5(4), 337–347.

Pannen, P. (2016). Kebijakan Pendidikan Jarak Jauh dan E-Learning di Indonesia. Ministry of Research and Higher Education Indonesia. doi:10.35913/jk.v8i2.204

PDDikti. (2020). *Higher Education Statistics 2020*. https://pddikti.kemdikbud.go.id/publikasi

Pistone, M. (2015). *Law Schools and Technology: Where We Are and Where We Are Heading*. Public Law and Legal Theory Working Paper Series.

Purfitasari, S., Masrukhi, Prihatin, T., & Mulyono, S. E. (2019). Digital Pedagogy sebagai Pendekatan Pembelajaran di Era Industri 4.0. *Prosiding Seminar Nasional Pascasarjana (PROSNAMPAS), 2*(1), 806–811. https://proceeding.unnes.ac.id/index.php/snpasca/article/view/374/225

Sandbach, J., & Grimes, R. (2020). *Law School Pro Bono and Clinic Report 2020*. https://drive.google.com/file/d/1GaRpXy7WeID0eJM27VplY-e9ovjme1kd/view

Seaman, J. E., Allen, I. E., & Seaman, J. (2018). *Grade Increase : Tracking Distance Education in the United States*. https://files.eric.ed.gov/fulltext/ED580852.pdf

Shahroom, A. A., & Hussin, N. (2018). Industrial Revolution 4.0 and Education. *International Journal of Academic Research in Business & Social Sciences*, 8(9), 314–319. doi:10.6007/IJARBSS/v8-i9/4593

Studies, K. L. (2022a). *23 Online LLB Programs in Asia*. Academic Press.

StudiesK. L. (2022b). *9 Online JD Programs in Asia*. https://www.lawstudies.com/Juris-Doctor/Asia/Online/

Susskind, R. (2017). Tomorrow's Lawyers: An Introduction to Your Future (2nd ed.). Oxford University Press. doi:10.1177/1037969X1303800316

the American Bar Association. (2020). *Model Rules of Professional Conduct and Practice*. https://www.americanbar.org/groups/professional_responsibility/publications/model_rules_of_professional_conduct/rule_1_1_competence/comment_on_rule_1_1/

University of Essex. (2022). *LLB (Hons) Law*. https://online.essex.ac.uk/courses/llb-hons-law/

ENDNOTES

[1]   They are Mitchell Hamline School of Law, Syracuse University College of Law, University of Dayton School of Law, Southwestern Law School, and New Hampshire School of Law.

[2]   Some of Australia's best law schools offer from the Graduate Diploma to Juris Doctor Degree in distance learning platforms. For example, Macquarie University in Sydney adds the opportunity for students to obtain JD degree through online study.

[3]   Listed on the web page, there are twenty-three law school in the Asia offering online LLG degree. It is unclear whether all those twenty-three has been offering this program pre or post the pandemic.

[4]   See also Circular Letter of Ministry Education, Culture, Research and Technology of Indonesia No. 36962/MPK.A/HK/2020 regarding Learning and Working from Home to prevent the Covid-19 spread. This letter regulates distance-learning during the Pandemic.

Chapter 10
Digital Transformation in Higher Education Institutions

Siti Nurbarizah Haji Mohammad Azari
Universiti Brunei Darussalam, Brunei

ABSTRACT

This chapter aims to explore the digital transformation in higher education institutions, especially in regards to the increased use of e-learning in recent years by identifying the parties who are affected by the transformation and the challenges people may face in implementing the use of e-learning. By using the CATWOE analysis technique, it identified that the main parties that are affected by this transformation into e-learning are the students and teachers of higher education institutions and to an extent the institutions themselves. Furthermore, through the construction of the fishbone diagram, it identified the main issues of implementing e-learning: cost, internet connectivity, lack of interaction, suitability of e-learning, and lack of knowledge. As the parties affected and challenges have been identified, this study can be used to improve e-learning processes in the future.

INTRODUCTION

It was clear that the sudden outbreak of the COVID-19 pandemic posed a giant obstacle to education systems globally. This is particularly due to the restrictions that were imposed to limit face-to-face activities, including the conduction of physical classes in educational institutions causing the immediate shift to e-learning. Blended learning has always been inherent in education systems, which is when traditional learning methodologies incorporate some e-learning methodologies and tools into the system. For example, LMS platforms such as Canvas by Instructure

DOI: 10.4018/978-1-6684-6108-2.ch010

and Blackboard have been utilised in higher education institutions to let students access their course materials online as well as to receive announcements from their instructors even prior to the pandemic (Hamdan et al., 2020a). However, the outbreak of the virus did accelerate the progression of digital transformation of e-learning, and students and teachers were both forced to undergo a full transformation abruptly causing them to adapt to the "new normal" (Hasmawati et al., 2020). This led to more e-learning initiatives and tools being utilised in all institutions, especially the use of video conferencing platforms such as Zoom and Microsoft Teams and the use of e-assessments as a form of measuring the students' knowledge in place of traditional tests that they would normally sit for pre-pandemic. However, because of the abrupt transition from traditional and/or blended learning to a full e-learning system, it is significant to study the parties who are affected by this transformation and the challenges faced with the implementation of e-learning.

RESEARCH QUESTIONS

1. Who are affected by the digital transformation of e-learning in higher education institutions?
2. What are the challenges faced when implementing e-learning in higher education institutions?

LITERATURE REVIEW

Digital Transformation in Higher Education Institutions

Digital transformation dates back to the 1970s and is the use of the latest digital technology to enable improvements and changes in all aspects of society, including boosting customer experiences and implementing new business models (Stolterman et al, 2004; Fitzgerald et al, 2014). With the development of IT skills, digital transformation has become so relevant in the modern world where digitisation has been one of the top priorities in various sectors, to ensure relevance and success (Bond et al, 2018; Jackson, 2019; Anshari et al., 2021). Digital technology has always been a helping hand in higher education programming (Jackson, 2019). However, digital transformation in higher education institutions are apparent and the technology is disruptive in its purpose, thus allowing higher education institutions to prioritise and make use of the digital technologies that are made available to them to their full potential (Jackson, 2019; Benavides, 2020; Anshari et al., 2017).

Although, digital transformation has existed for decades and it has been inherent in higher education institutions even before the global outbreak of COVID-19, with the outbreak, it has further sped up the process which has led to the changes in traditional teaching and assessment methods to the "new normal" to fit COVID-19 guidelines and mitigate the risk of catching the virus (Garcia-Morales, 2021). Thus, anything that was once done in-person pre-COVID-19 became virtual, be it through emails or videoconferencing. However, because the COVID-19 pandemic came abruptly, most institutions had very minimal time to prepare themselves for a full digital transformation (Daniel, 2020; Anshari et al., 2016). This meant that the universities who hadn't implemented many online learning facilities prior to the pandemic had to quickly come up with strategies on how they will be able to conduct their classes, provide the resources to the instructors and students, and come up with plans on how to conduct their assessments.

E-Learning Tools Used for Digital Transformation

Online Learning or E-Learning

Online learning, or e-learning, involves learning which incorporates the use of computers, communications technology and any form of electronic resources (Dada et al, 2019; Maatuk et al, 2022). It has become a well-favoured tool for learners and instructors in the current century as information and communication technologies (ICT) is innovative and can provide distinctive learning and teaching experiences (Ayu, 2020; Ahad & Anshari, 2017). There is a large range of technologies that able to support the process of e-learning, including instant messaging applications (e.g. WhatsApp), video-conferencing platforms (e.g. Zoom, Microsoft Teams, BigBlueButton, Google Meet and Skype), cloud-based storage platforms that allow for the sharing of materials (e.g. Google Drive and iCloud Drive), applications that allow users to create and edit documents together simultaneously (e.g. Google Docs and Google Slides) and the institutions' learning management system platform (e.g. Canvas by Instructure and Blackboard) (Garcia-Morales, 2021; Alas & Anshari, 2014).

There are two modes wherein e-learning is conducted, namely synchronous and asynchronous e-learning.

i. Synchronous E-Learning

Synchronous e-learning, as the name suggests, is the occasion where the instructor and students would log on to an online video conferencing platform for their lessons at a specific given time (Amiti, 2020).

Video Conferencing in Higher Education Institutions

In this case, it is a learner-centred class and students would have their attention on the instructor who would be carrying out the lessons how they would normally do in physical classrooms, however it would be through the videoconference and it allows the instructor to share visual and audio facilities in real time (Amiti, 2020; Al-Samarraie, 2019; Alas et al., 2016). Further,

students are able to ask questions through their own microphone or use the chat-box function (Anshari, Alas, & Guan, 2016). Popular video conferencing platforms among universities include Zoom and Microsoft Teams.

ii. Asynchronous E-Learning

On the other hand, asynchronous e-learning is often done independently as self-induced learning and occurs according to the students' time and location (Dada et al, 2019; Hamdan et al., 2020b). This includes the use of emails as a form of communication between the student and the teacher and the use of learning management systems (LMS).

Learning Management Systems (LMS)

An example of one of the most useful technologies that many higher education institutions have implemented and that falls under the category of asynchronous e-learning is the LMS. LMS is a system on a platform that can deliver and manage content including videos and documents that have been uploaded by the teachers and the students who are registered on that platform can have access to that content (Ahad et al., 2017; Tran et al, 2019; Mulyani et al., 2019a). Other common features on LMS platforms include a section where students can take quizzes, submit assignments, participate in discussions, send messages to their teachers and classmates, and in turn, teachers are also able to grade their quizzes and assignments and respond to their messages through the inbox (Tran et al, 2019). Essentially, it is a system that encourages engagement and two-way involvement between the students and the teachers all through one platform (Handal et al, 2009; Anshari et al., 2015). A benefit of LMS is that it is easy to manage on the part of both instructors and students as they are able to access their course materials from wherever they are, provided that they have an internet connection to access the LMS platform (Gautam, 2020; Mulyani et al., 2019b). Examples of well-known LMS platforms are Blackboard, Canvas by Instructure and Google Classroom (Razzaq et al., 2018).

A popular trend among universities in implementing online learning is through the use of learning management systems (LMS) and the conduction of either synchronous or asynchronous online classes.

Blended Learning or Hybrid Learning

Blended learning or hybrid learning is a system that incorporates both elements of traditional learning, which includes face-to-face learning between a teacher and their students, as well as incorporating elements of e-learning (Castro, 2018; Sait & Anshari, 2021). There are many models of blended learning, and the most common ones include 1) face-to-face, where the teacher would conduct the lesson in a physical classroom but they would elevate the experience with digital tools; 2) rotations, where the lessons are divided between online classes and physical classes and; 3) flex, where most of the lessons are delivered online and students are still able to consult with their teachers face-to-face should they need to (Nebrosky, 2020). The system of blended learning has been used in universities even prior to the outbreak of COVID-19.

E-Assessment

E-assessment is the use of electronic media "to create, deliver, store and/or report students' assessment marks and feedback" (Elkund et al, 2013; Appiah & van Tonder, 2018).

There are two ways in which e-assessment can occur (Appiah & van Tonder, 2018; Samiha et al., 2022). Firstly, there is web-based delivery where students would have to access their assessment tasks online. The second method is download delivery and the students can download their assessment materials online when it has been released by their instructors and do them offline and submit them onto an online portal before a set deadline. These two forms of e-assessment are often done through the respective institutions' LMS platform where they are able to do quizzes and have access to the assessment materials (Samiha et al., 2021).

User Perceptions and Challenges Towards the Use of E-Learning Tools

This section shows the users' points of views on the different tools of e-learning found in several studies. It shows the areas in which digital transformation in e-learning is thriving and the areas in which digital transformation takes a step back from being progressive, thus showing where institutions are still lacking the capability to utilise the technology to its full potential (Benavides, 2020).

Internet Connection

One of the main concerns of utilising e-learning is that it requires good internet connection and oftentimes low quality internet becomes a barrier for users to fully utilise the e-learning facilities (Subedi et al, 2020; Araka et al, 2021). In fact, instructors have also raised that learning requires good and secure internet connection (Windiarti, 2019). Having low quality internet connection would only allow for poor quality of visual outputs and slow

downloading speed for the materials both students and instructors would need access to online (Gismalla et al, 2021). In the study by Araka et al (2021), 28 percent of the students (n=234) involved in the study raised internet connection as a barrier to engaging in online study. Additionally, in the study by Casillano (2019) conducted in the Philippines, many rural areas do not have good internet connection, causing students to travel to areas that do. In contrast, in the study by Bond et al (2018), where in the study conducted in Germany, 99 percent of higher education students are equipped with good internet connection at home and thus, would not have to face such quality problems. This shows the difference between the access to internet connection in developing and developed countries and how digital transformation can progress in respective countries.

Costs

The utilisation of e-learning requires investments if the facilities are not already available for users' use (Windiarti et al, 2019). This issue is especially evident in developing countries, as in the study conducted in Sudan by Gismalla et al (2021), a majority of the participants in the study agreed that having access to good internet connection that would allow them to utilise e-learning facilities efficiently is expensive. In the same study, less than half of the students have access to devices like computers and having access to such devices are crucial in order for e-learning to take place (Windiarti, 2019; Gismalla et al, 2021). Furthermore, in the study by Kundu and Bej (2021) which was conducted in India, 85 percent of the students did not have computers at home. This means that they would have to purchase new ones if the e-learning facilities require the use of computers, should the facilities not be compatible to be used on smartphones which most students would have (Gismalla et al, 2021). However, similar to what is mentioned in section 3.5.4 above, this issue is more prevalent among students in developing countries. For example, in Germany, 99 percent of students have access to such devices at home (Bond et al, 2018).

In the study by Maatuk et al (2022), the instructors involved in the study also raised the issue of high costs to implement its use. For instance, in the case of video conferencing platforms like Zoom, unless the university has a paid subscription that allows its users to fully utilise its features, they would only have limited access to the application's features (Azlan et al, 2020). In the case of Zoom, users are only allowed 40 minutes for a single video conference with a free account, which would not be efficient for instructors to carry out lectures with. Furthermore, internet data plans and high technological cost, including having to purchase devices in order to be able to use these e-learning platforms contribute to the instructors' and students' expenses (Azlan et al, 2020).

However, in contrast, the utilisation of e-learning can be cost-saving in other ways, as per Subedi et al (2020), it saves people travel costs from doing their work remotely.

Lack of Interaction

In traditional learning methodologies, the instructors are always physically approachable, and despite most of e-learning taking place remotely, it does not dissipate that teachers are meant to be approachable, but instead, they are approachable in different forms (Sandybayev, 2020). This means that students can make queries to their instructors online through personal messengers, email, the messaging function in their respective institutions' LMS platforms and so on. This was emphasised in the study by Araka et al (2021), 19 percent (n=154) and 15 percent (n=127) of the students emphasised the lack of interaction between the instructors and lack of individualised feedback on students' learning habits, respectively. For these two aforementioned issues, the main concerns were that the students were not given adequate support and involvement on the part of the teachers when students raised concerns in their academics, as teachers would respond late or not respond at all to queries posted on the LMS platform.

Similarly, instructors would also face the same issue from the lack of participation from the students. As classes have shifted online and video conferencing is used to carry out the lessons, students tend to talk less when being asked questions, and this may stem from their lack of confidence to answer online as compared to answering in person (Thorpe & Godwin, 2006). However, instructors can incorporate quizzes during the class time in order to maintain engagement with the students as suggested in Azlan et al (2020). This could be done with built in features on the video conferencing platform, for example, Zoom has a poll feature where instructors can use as a tool for quizzes, or by using independent quiz applications and websites such as Kahoot!.

Use of Videoconferencing

In the study by Al-Samarraie (2019), it can be seen that video conferencing would be able to take over traditional in-person teaching and learning models in the case of conducting constructivist activities, including activities that require collaborative teamwork between

peers and problem solving tasks, as it can let the students engage with one another. For example, students can be divided into groups in breakout rooms, which is a feature available on most video conferencing platforms like Zoom and BigBlueButton. Instructors will then be able to go in and out of breakout rooms to assess the groups' teamwork and interaction in order to complete the tasks (Al-Samarraie, 2019).

There are also concerns that were raised with the use of video conferencing, including delays, technological glitches and background noises (Gillies, 2008 as cited in Al-Samarraie, 2019). This can also be linked back to the issue of having a good internet connection, as without strong internet connection, there are high chances that the speakers' voices will lag and the speakers' video may not appear properly. Additionally, this issue can also be linked to the issue of the cost of implementing e-learning, as the use of video conferencing platforms can use up a large amount of internet data which can be expensive (Sakkir et al, 2021).

Suitability of E-Learning Tools

It is worth noting that different subjects may require different needs in terms of how the lessons are being carried out. E-learning may not be suitable where students are required to conduct technical practicals which require techniques that can only be shown clearly to them face-to-face (Nebrosky, 2020). This was seen in the study conducted by Zalat et al (2021) where about 71.6 percent (n=248) of the teaching staff in the medical field agreed that carrying out practicals in an online setting is difficult. This raises the importance of matching the correct e-learning tools to the field of study in order for the e-learning experience to be effective (Wright, 2017).

E-Assessment

In the study by Alruwais et al (2018), it was found that students do prefer undergoing e-assessments because it often provides instant feedback in contrast to traditional tests, and this is often seen in the case of multiple choice quizzes where students can get their scores almost instantly.

However, because of the sudden shift from traditional assessment methods to e-assessments, many were unprepared for it (Kundu & Bej, 2021). In the study by Kundu and Bej (2021), it was found that 81 percent of the students who participated in the study had very low awareness of e-assessment and that their universities had not provided them sufficient knowledge on e-assessment upon implementing it.

Student Preferences

In the studies by Wright (2017), Abassi et al (2020) and Kabir et al (2022), the majority of the students in the studies had a preference for in-person lessons as the environment contributes to their motivation to learn and piques their interests more. Students also raised that e-learning has little impact on their studies and this stems from their lack of acceptance of e-learning, their lack of knowledge and their lack of self-confidence to undergo e-learning (Abassi et al, 2020; Kabir et al 2022).

METHODOLOGY

The research methodology in this study is a qualitative secondary analysis which utilises secondary data, whereby data from existing journal articles and publications in this field of study was compiled and studied to come to an overall conclusion for the research. These papers have been sourced from multiple databases, including Google Scholar, Emerald, Dimensions AI, Elsevier and Semantic Scholar. Furthermore, the CATWOE analysis technique is utilised in this study to understand the problem and the different perspectives of stakeholders who are affected by this problem and the Fishbone Diagram is used to see the factors that contribute to any difficulty in using e-learning in higher education institutions.

ANALYSIS AND DISCUSSION

In this section, one will be analysing the issues with two analysis techniques, namely the CATWOE analysis technique and the Fishbone diagram and a thorough discussion on the issues discussed have been incorporated. In both analysis methods, the impact of COVID-19 in accelerating the digital transformation process in e-learning may be considered as well.

CATWOE ANALYSIS

At this stage, one will be looking at a CATWOE analysis on digital transformation in higher education institutions. The CATWOE analysis is a problem solving technique to explore and study the problem source and anything that may be related to the problem. Furthermore, this analysis technique allows researchers to fully understand the stakeholders' perspectives by looking into the entire process of the subject matter in order to find appropriate solutions to combat the problem (Elmansy, 2015). Through this analysis and discussion, one can see who and what are being affected by the digital transformation of e-learning.

Customer or Clients

The customer refers to the people who are using the system and are affected by any changes or initiatives implemented by the system, and depending on the outcome they may either gain value or suffer a loss (Rachmayanti and Arumsari, 2021; Think Insights, 2022).

In the present case, the customers who are affected by the digital transformation through e-learning are those who are currently students in higher education institutions, especially those who are using the e-learning tools. These students are the ones who had to undergo the transition from conducting their studies traditionally or through blended learning before the outbreak of the virus, to adapting to the "new normal" once the pandemic started and they had to do things completely online remotely to prevent the spread of the virus. The students' entire learning experience is changed. Furthermore, in a literal sense as well, the students are actually paying customers of the institutions, and thus, any changes implemented by the institution will have an effect on them as the quality of the facilities brought by the change should be in line with the quality of the facilities they had initially paid for before the change.

Similarly, the instructors are also considered customers in this case because how they are carrying out their classes are being completely changed as well. Although students are just as greatly affected, the instructors would have to be the ones who initiate and implement the changes first and students would follow suit. The instructors are also the ones who would have to test the e-learning platforms, learn how to use them and see which ones would suit their classes better.

Actor

Actors are the parties who are involved with the implementation of the changes and they are the ones who ensure that these changes take place (Think Insights, 2022). This includes the employees and stakeholders within the organisation (Elmansy, 2015).

In the present case, the main actors are the instructors and lecturers in the higher education institutions. The instructors are the ones who would have waited for guidelines from institutions at the beginning of the pandemic on what they should do during the transition, such as how they are supposed to carry out their lessons, through what platforms they should be conducting their lectures and tutorials on and how they should be carrying out assessments and tests for the students. Furthermore, as mentioned in the section above, it is the instructors who would have to implement the changes first and test out the e-learning platforms for them to teach their students. It is their role to implement these changes for the students.

Additionally, the students here can be considered as actors as well because in order for the transformation to happen, the students have to actually act on and interact with the new systems – by adhering to the institutions' guidelines and using the e-learning facilities that are made available for their use.

Furthermore, the other stakeholders that could be considered actors are the universities' administrative help desks, as they would be the point of contact for both instructors and students while undergoing the transformation on any technical queries regarding their e-learning facilities.

Transformation

Transformation refers to the actual change that is taking place within the system and what part of the system is going to be affected (Think Insights, 2022). Rachmayanti and Arumsari (2021) mentioned that the initial conditions before the transformation and the conditions desired to be achieved are defined in this stage.

In the present scenario, the transformation would be the transition from traditional teaching and learning methodologies before the pandemic, to new modern teaching and learning methodologies that incorporate digital technology into the processes that are fit for remote learning. Although there are some elements of e-learning that institutions have adopted pre-pandemic through blended learning, in regards to the initial conditions before the change would refer to the students and instructors having to attend physical classes within the institution's grounds, having the students' coursework and assessments be submitted physically to the instructor and having to access their resources in the library. Meanwhile, the achieved conditions would be for the students and instructors to be able to conduct classes virtually rather than in-person, being able to submit their assignments online through the university's LMS platforms, as well as providing a space where students can get the materials they would normally get physically online. Table 1 below shows examples of the initial and desired conditions for digital transformation in e-learning.

Table 1. Initial and desired conditions for digital transformation in e-learning

Initial Conditions	Desired Conditions
Use of institutions' LMS platforms.	No transformation – LMS platforms are still being used.

Lessons and tutorials being carried out face-to-face.

Lessons and tutorials being carried out through video conferencing platforms, such as Zoom and Microsoft Teams or through online recorded video lectures.

Physical copies of assignments to be submitted to the instructors.

Assignments submitted through online portals prepared by the instructors, mostly through LMS platforms.

Assessments, including tests and quizzes done in a classroom setting.

Tests and quizzes done remotely online, normally done through the institutions' LMS platforms – for example, on Canvas by Instructure it can be done through the "Quizzes" feature.

Searching for resources in libraries.

Searching for resources in online databases provided by the institutions.

Worldview

Worldview refers to the bigger picture – the perspectives of the individuals who are being affected by the transformation or change and the wider impact it may have towards the stakeholders (Think Insights, 2022). It has also been described as the viewpoints that make the transformation meaningful to the stakeholders (Checkland and Scholes, 1990 as cited in O'Loughlin, 2013). At this stage, one will be able to see the differing point of views it has on different stakeholders.

In this case, the various differing opinions from individual students and instructors can be distinguished from each other, and therefore be considered differing worldviews. This is because different students would have different needs, and some students may not be able to adapt to e-learning as well as other students. This can consequently impact the students' motivation and participation in class.

Owner

Owner refers to the owner of the organisation, particularly the people who possess the decision-making power for whether the changes in the system are to be implemented or not (Elmansy, 2015; Pestle Analysis, 2015). Essentially, they would hold the highest authority in the organisation and who have the power to stop the transformation from happening (Rachmayanti and Arumsari, 2021; Think Insight, 2022).

In this case, the owner would be the respective institutions' governing bodies who have the right to make the decisions on what kind of transformation the institutions should be undergoing. Furthermore, they are also the authority that can provide the students and instructors with support throughout the transformation process which can be in the form of providing them with the relevant training to go through with the transition (Turnbull et al, 2021).

Environmental Constraints

Environmental constraints are the environmental components that can act as barriers which can prevent or limit the transformation from being carried out (Think Insights, 2022).

In this case, the environmental constraints could include the institutions' budget to undergo digital transformation. Digital transformation can be expensive for institutions as they have to provide the relevant facilities for not only the entire student body but for their staff as well. Some institutions may put off subscription to certain e-learning facilities as there are other free alternatives that can be used. For example, some universities may not pay for video conferencing platforms such as Zoom, because there are other platforms that are free to use such as Google Meet. Thus, instead of paying for platforms that have free alternatives, institutions might pay for other facilities that may be useful for students' e-learning experience, such as subscription to online resource databases such as LexisNexis.

Another environmental constraint could be the students' and instructors' accessibility to electricity and good internet connection as in certain regions, these two factors may be unstable and inconsistent which can cause disruption in their e-learning experience.

Summary of CATWOE Analysis

Table 2. Summary of CATWOE Analysis for digital transformation in e-learning in HEIs

CATWOE	Question	Analysis
Customer	Who are being affected by the changes?	Students and instructors of higher education institutions.
Actors	Who are the ones implementing the change?	Students, instructors and administrators of higher education institutions.
Transformation	What are the initial conditions and the conditions desired to be achieved?	Initial conditions: the use of traditional learning and teaching methods.
		Achieved conditions: incorporating modern digital technologies into the learning and teaching methods.
Worldview	What are the worldviews that make the transformation meaningful?	Individual perceptions from users of e-learning facilities (students and instructors).
Owner	Who has the power to stop the transformation from happening?	Institutions' governing body.
Environmental	What are the environmental	Budget; availability of electricity;
Constraints	components that can impact the transformation from being carried out?	and internet connectivity.

5.0 Fishbone Diagram

The Fishbone Diagram, which is also known as the Ishikawa Diagram, is an analysis tool which identifies the causes and effects of issues which are sorted into their own categories (Gartlehner, 2017). Through this analysis and discussion, one can see the challenges faced by users in implementing e-learning.

The problem in this case is the difficulty in adapting to digital transformation of e-learning in higher education institutions, and the factors that contribute to this problem include: costs, internet connectivity, lack of interaction, suitability for technical courses and expertise. The Figure 1 below shows the fishbone diagram that corresponds to the problem and factors mentioned above.

Figure 1. Fishbone diagram

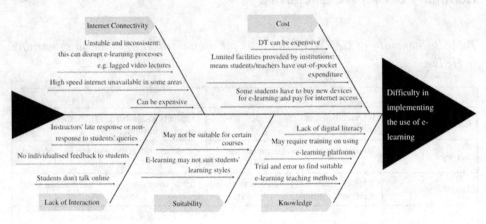

Cost

Implementing digital transformation in e-learning in higher education institutions is expensive, and achieving a viable digital transformation can happen if the institutions have a set budget for its implementation. Some students have relied on the institutions' facilities that are available for their use on campus, such as the computers and wireless connection. However, with e-learning, especially in the context of the COVID-19 pandemic with everything done remotely, some students are forced to make out-of-pocket purchases on

devices such as laptops and pay for their own WiFi. Furthermore, some e-learning facilities use up a lot of internet quota and depending on the internet provider company, the cost can get quite high. This is especially evident in using video conferencing platforms such as Zoom, where an hour session can use up 800MB to 2.4GB of data (Sakkir et al, 2021; Abbott, 2022). There are also some e-learning facilities that are not provided by the institutions that the instructors would have to pay for on their own.

Internet Connection

With e-learning, having a good internet connection is crucial as everything is online. Although students might still be able to work with low internet quality, it may disrupt their e-learning experiences as e-learning platforms will take longer to load and if they are watching online video lectures or are joining a synchronous online class, the video and audio quality would not be par (Gismalla et al, 2021). This issue is evident in developing countries where access to good internet connection is limited. This issues is evident in developing countries such as the Philippines and Nepal where people face difficulties in getting access to internet connection and often have to travel to get access and even if it is easily accessible, not everyone can afford to subscribe to those internet plans (Casillano, 2019; Azlan et al, 2020; Subedi et al, 2020). On the other hand, it can be seen that in developed countries it is easier to have access to high quality internet connection and thus, e-learning would not be difficult to implement (Bond et al, 2018).

Lack of Interaction

In terms of the interaction between the student and the instructor, there can be issues in regards to the students' participation in online classes. For example, the instructor may ask a question through video conferencing, but students may not answer. This may be due to a lack of preference to e-learning, which can impact their motivation and confidence to participate in classes (Thorpe & Godwin, 2006; Kabir et al, 2022). Furthermore, because it is through video conferencing and students may have the option to not turn on their cameras or microphone, it is easier to get distracted and will participate less. There may be instances where instructors show a lack of communication towards the students, where the students' emails and messages are ignored or overlooked as they might have many messages coming from multiple students (Araka et al, 2021). Interaction between the students and instructors is important as students can raise their concerns and instructors can give their feedback to ensure the students are on the right track and actually understand the material that is being taught.

Suitability

E-learning may not be suitable for all subjects and may not be suitable for all students. Some subjects are difficult to conduct via e-learning, for example, it is difficult to conduct practicals that are normally done in-person and in laboratory or classroom settings online (Nebrosky, 2020; Zalat et al, 2021). Furthermore, different students have different learning styles, and e-learning may not suit their learning style if they work better in physical classroom environments. This can lead to students feeling like e-learning is not beneficial to their learning experience as it does not suit them, fostering a non-preference towards e-learning (Abassi et al, 2020). This suggests that coordination between e-learning teaching methods and students' learning needs is important to ensure that the students' learning experience through e-learning is effective.

Knowledge

Although e-learning has been around for a long time, many are still unfamiliar with some of its components. For example, Kundu and Bej (2021) showed that the students were not very knowledgeable on the use of e-assessments and they were not given much training or guidance by experts. Furthermore, students' non-preference to e-learning may be linked with the fact that students may not have sufficient knowledge, competencies and confidence to navigate themselves through e-learning (Kabir et al, 2021; Kundu & Bej, 2021; Turnbull et al, 2021). This suggests that digital readiness may not be inherent in some students as per in the study by Kim et al (2019), those who have digital readiness are those who are confident in their digital skills in their academic work. This issue is also inherent among instructors, and training can help with building their digital literacy to improve the e-learning experiences.

6. LIMITATIONS

There are several limitations of the study. Firstly, this study is a secondary research study which only utilises secondary data and no primary data was collected through this study. Through primary research, relevant information that fits the scope of the research from a specific demographic may be collected. Secondly, this research was conducted over a shorter time frame. With a longer time frame, primary research would have been possible and the study would have been able to produce quality data.

7. CONCLUSION

In conclusion, although e-learning has been around for a long time and components of it have been embedded in education systems for years, with the outbreak of the COVID-19 pandemic, it is now clearer who is being affected by the transformation and how it affects them. Through this study, it was found that the two main parties that have been greatly affected by digital transformation in e-learning are the two main groups of users who have to undergo it on an almost daily basis, the students and the instructors themselves. Furthermore, this study also found the various challenges faced by users include the the costs they have to bear in order to implement it effectively, the limited accessibility to good internet connection, the lack of interaction between the users, how e-learning methodologies are unsuitable for certain subject areas and learning styles and lastly, the lack of knowledge on the use of e-learning. Overall, this study provides an insight on the digital transformation in e-learning, particularly in the higher education institution setting, and how it has impacted the education system as well as those who are involved in the system.

REFERENCES

Abassi, S., Ayoob, T., Malik, A. & Memon, S. I. (2020). Perceptions of students regarding E-learning during Covid-19 at a private medical college. *Pak J Med Sci, 36*(S4). doi: 1 doi:0.12669/pjms.36.COVID19-S4.2766

Abbott, T. (2022). *How Much Data Does a Zoom Meeting Use?* Reviews Org. https://www.reviews.org/internet-service/how-much-data-does-zoom-use/

Ahad, A. D., & Anshari, M. (2017). Smartphone habits among youth: Uses and gratification theory. *International Journal of Cyber Behavior, Psychology and Learning, 7*(1), 65–75. doi:10.4018/IJCBPL.2017010105

Ahad, A. D., Anshari, M., & Razzaq, A. (2017). Domestication of smartphones among adolescents in Brunei darussalam. *International Journal of Cyber Behavior, Psychology and Learning, 7*(4), 26–39. doi:10.4018/IJCBPL.2017100103

Al-Samarraie, H. (2019). A Scoping Review of Videoconferencing Systems in Higher Education Learning Paradigms, Opportunities, and Challenges. *International Review of Research in Open and Distributed Learning, 20*(3). Advance online publication. doi:10.19173/irrodl.v20i4.4037

Alas, Y., & Anshari, M. (2014). *Constructing strategy of online learning in higher education: Transaction cost economy.* arXiv preprint arXiv:1411.4345.

Alas, Y., Anshari, M., Sabtu, N. I., & Yunus, N. (2016). Second-chance university admission, the theory of planned behaviour and student achievement. *International Review of Education, 62*(3), 299–316. doi:10.100711159-016-9558-5

Alruwais, N., Wills, G., & Wald, M. (2018). Advantages and Challenges of Using e-Assessment. *International Journal of Information and Education Technology (IJIET), 8*(1), 34–37. doi:10.18178/ijiet.2018.8.1.1008

Amiti, F. (2020). Synchronous and Asynchronous E-Learning. *European Journal of Open Education and E-learning Studies, 5*(2). Advance online publication. doi:10.46827/ejoe.v5i2.3313

Anshari, M., Alas, Y., & Guan, L. S. (2016). Developing online learning resources: Big data, social networks, and cloud computing to support pervasive knowledge. *Education and Information Technologies*, *21*(6), 1663–1677. doi:10.100710639-015-9407-3

Anshari, M., Alas, Y., & Guan, L. S. (2017). Pervasive knowledge, social networks, and cloud computing: E-learning 2.0. *Eurasia Journal of Mathematics, Science and Technology Education*, *11*(5), 909–921. doi:10.12973/eurasia.2015.1360a

Anshari, M., Alas, Y., Hamid, M. H. S. A., & Smith, M. (2016). Learning management system 2.0: Higher education. In *Handbook of research on engaging digital natives in higher education settings* (pp. 265–279). IGI Global. doi:10.4018/978-1-5225-0039-1.ch012

Anshari, M., Alas, Y., Sabtu, N. P. H., & Hamid, M. S. A. (2016). Online Learning: Trends, issues and challenges in the Big Data Era. *Journal of E-learning and Knowledge Society*, *12*(1).

Anshari, M., Alas, Y., Yunus, N., Sabtu, N. I., & Hamid, M. H. (2015). Social customer relationship management and student empowerment in online learning systems. *International Journal of Electronic Customer Relationship Management*, *9*(2-3), 104–121. doi:10.1504/IJECRM.2015.071711

Anshari, M., Almunawar, M. N., & Razzaq, A. (2021). Developing talents vis-à-vis fourth industrial revolution. *International Journal of Asian Business and Information Management*, *12*(4), 20–32. doi:10.4018/IJABIM.20211001.oa2

Anshari, M., Almunawar, M. N., Shahrill, M., Wicaksono, D. K., & Huda, M. (2017). Smartphones usage in the classrooms: Learning aid or interference? *Education and Information Technologies*, *22*(6), 3063–3079. doi:10.100710639-017-9572-7

Appiah, M., & van Tonder, F. (2018). E-Assessment in Higher Education: A Review. *International Journal of Business Management and Economic Research*, *9*(6), 1454–1460.

Araka, E., Maina, E., Gitonga, R., Oboko, R., & Kihoro, J. (2021). University Students' Perception on the Usefulness of Learning Management System Features in Promoting Self-Regulated Learning in Online Learning. *IJEDICT*, *17*, 45–64.

Ayu, M. (2020). Online Learning: Leading E-Learning at Higher Education. *The Journal of English Literacy Education*, *7*(1), 47–54. doi:10.36706/jele.v7i1.11515

Azlan, C. A., Wong, J. S. D., Tan, L. K., & Tan, A. D., Huri, M. S., Ung, N. M., Pallath, V., C. P. L., Yeong, C. H., & Ng, K. H. (2020). Teaching and learning of postgraduate medical physics using Internet-based e-learning during the COVID-19 pandemic - A case study from *Malaysia. Physica Medica, 80*, 10–16. doi:10.1016/j.ejmp.2020.10.002 PMID:33070007

Benavides, L. M. C., Arias, J. A. T., Serna, M. D. A., Bedoya, J. W. B., & Burgos, D. (2020). Digital Transformation in Higher Education Institutions: A Systematic Literature Review. *Sensors (Basel), 20*(3291), 3291. doi:10.339020113291 PMID:32526998

Bond, M., Marin, V. I., Dolch, C., Bedenlier, S., & Zawacki-Richter, O. (2018). Article. *International Journal of Educational Technology in Higher Education, 15*(48). Advance online publication. doi:10.118641239-018-0130-1

Casillano, N. F. B. (2019). Challenges of Implementing an E-learning Platform in an Internet Struggling Province in the Philippines. *Indian Journal of Science and Technology, 12*(10), 12. doi:10.17485/ijst/2019/v12i10/137594

Castro, R. (2019). Blended learning in higher education: Trends and capabilities. *Education and Information Technologies, 24*(4), 2523–2546. Advance online publication. doi:10.100710639-019-09886-3

Dada, E. G., Alkali, A. H., & Oyewola, D. O. (2019). An Investigation into the Effectiveness of Asynchronous and Synchronous E-learning Mode on Students' Academic Performance in National Open University (NOUN). *Maiduguri Centre. I. J. Modern Education and Computer Science, 5*, 54–64.

Daniel, J. (2020). Education and the COVID-19 pandemic. *Prospects, 49*(1-2), 91–96. doi:10.100711125-020-09464-3 PMID:32313309

Elkund, J., Kay, M., & Lynch, H. M. (2003). E-learning: Emerging issues and key trends: A discussion paper. Australian National Training Authority, 25.

Elmansy, R. (2015). *CATWOE: Building a Problem-Solving Checklist.* Designorate. https://www.designorate.com/catwoe-problem-solving/

Fitzgerald, M., Kruschwitz, N., Bonnet, D., & Welch, M. (2014). Embracing digital technology: A new strategic imperative. *MIT Sloan Management Review, 55*(2), 1.

Garcia-Morales, V. J., Garrido-Moreno, A., & Martin-Rojas, R. (2021). The Transformation of Higher Education After the COVID Disruption: Emerging Challenges in an Online Learning Scenario. *Frontiers in Psychology, 12*, 616059. Advance online publication. doi:10.3389/fpsyg.2021.616059 PMID:33643144

Gartlehner, G., Schultes, M. T., Titscher, V., Morgan, L. C., Bobashev, G. V., Williams, P., & West, S. L. (2017). User testing of an adaptation of fishbone diagrams to depict results of systematic reviews. *BMC Medical Research Methodology*, *17*(169), 169. doi:10.118612874-017-0452-z PMID:29233133

Gautam, P. (2020). *Advantages and Disadvantages of Online Learning*. eLearning Industry. https://elearningindustry.com/advantages-and-disadvantages-online-learning

Gismalla, M. D., Mohamed, M. S., Ibrahim, O. S. O., Elhassan, M. M. A., & Mohamed, M. E. (2021). Medical students' perception towards E-learning during COVID-19 pandemic in high burden developing country. *BMC Medical Education*, *21*(1), 377. Advance online publication. doi:10.118612909-021-02811-8 PMID:34246254

Hamdan, M., Ahmad, N., Jaidin, J. H., & Anshari, M. (2020). Internationalisation in Brunei's higher education and its policy implications: Case study of Universiti Brunei Darussalam. *TEST Engineering and Management*, *83*, 764–779.

Hamdan, M., Jaidin, J. H., Fithriyah, M., & Anshari, M. (2020, December). E-learning in time of COVID-19 pandemic: Challenges & experiences. In *2020 Sixth International Conference on e-Learning (econf)* (pp. 12-16). IEEE. 10.1109/econf51404.2020.9385507

Handal, B., Groenlund, C., & Gerzina, T. (2009). Dentistry students' perceptions of learning management systems. *European Journal of Dental Education*, *1*(14), 50–54. doi:10.1111/j.1600-0579.2009.00591.x PMID:20070799

Hasmawati, F., Samiha, Y. T., Razzaq, A., & Anshari, M. (2020). Understanding nomophobia among digital natives: Characteristics and challenges. *Journal of Critical Reviews*, *7*(13), 122–131.

Jackson, N. C. (2019). Managing for competency with innovation change in higher education: Examining the pitfalls and pivots of digital transformation. *Business Horizons*, *62*(6), 761–772. doi:10.1016/j.bushor.2019.08.002

Kabir, J., Tonmon, T. T., Hasan, M. K., Biswas, L., Chowdhury, M. A. H., Islam, M. D., Rahman, M., & Mitra, D. K. (2022). Association between preference and e-learning readiness among the Bangladeshi female nursing students in the COVID-19 pandemic: A cross-sectional study. *Bulletin of the National Research Center*, *48*(8), 8. doi:10.118642269-022-00697-0 PMID:35039742

Kim, H. J., Hong, A. J., & Song, H. D. (2019). The roles of academic engagement and digital readiness in students' achievements in university e-learning environments. International. *Journal of Educational Technology in Higher Education*, *16*(21). Advance online publication. doi:10.118641239-019-0152-3

Kundu, A., & Bej, T. (2021). *Experiencing e-assessment during COVID-19: an analysis of Indian students' perception*. Higher Education Evaluation and Development Emerald Publishing Limited. doi:10.1108/HEED-03-2021-0032

Maatuk, A. M., Elberkawi, E., Aljawarneh, S., Rashaideh, H., & Alharbi, H. (2022). The COVID-19 pandemic and E-learning: Challenges and opportunities from the perspective of students and instructors. *Journal of Computing in Higher Education*, *34*(1), 21–38. doi:10.100712528-021-09274-2 PMID:33967563

Mulyani, M. A., Razzaq, A., Ridho, S. L. Z., & Anshari, M. (2019, October). Smartphone and Mobile Learning to Support Experiential Learning. In *2019 International Conference on Electrical Engineering and Computer Science (ICECOS)* (pp. 6-9). IEEE. 10.1109/ICECOS47637.2019.8984501

Mulyani, M. A., Razzaq, A., Sumardi, W. H., & Anshari, M. (2019, August). Smartphone adoption in mobile learning scenario. In *2019 International Conference on Information Management and Technology (ICIMTech)* (Vol. 1, pp. 208-211). IEEE. 10.1109/ICIMTech.2019.8843755

Mulyani, M. A., Yusuf, S., Siregar, P., Nurihsan, J., Razzaq, A., & Anshari, M. (2021, August). Fourth Industrial Revolution and Educational Challenges. In *2021 International Conference on Information Management and Technology (ICIMTech)* (Vol. 1, pp. 245-249). IEEE. 10.1109/ICIMTech53080.2021.9535057

Nebrosky, E. V., Boguslavsky, M. V., Ladyzhets, N. S., & Naumova T. A. (2020). Digital Transformation of Higher Education: International Trends. *Advances in Social Science, Education and Humanities Research, 437.*

O'Loughlin, R. (2013). Teacher perceptions of a language curriculum: A CATWOE Analysis. *Studies in Linguistics and Language Teaching*, *24*, 93–106.

Pestle Analysis. (2015). *How CATWOE Helps in Business Analysis and Decision Making*. https://pestleanalysis.com/catwoe/

Rachmayanti, W., & Arumsari, P. (2021). Risk factors analysis affecting project time delay in construction projects using CATWOE analysis. *IOP Conf. Ser.: Earth Environ Sci., 794.* https://iopscience.iop.org/article/10.1088/1755-1315/794/1/012010/pdf

Razzaq, A., Samiha, Y. T., & Anshari, M. (2018). Smartphone habits and behaviors in supporting students self-efficacy. *International Journal of Emerging Technologies in Learning, 13*(2), 94. doi:10.3991/ijet.v13i02.7685

Sait, M. A., & Anshari, M. (2021). Industrial Revolution 4.0: A New Challenge to Brunei Darussalam's Unemployment Issue. *International Journal of Asian Business and Information Management, 12*(4), 33–44. doi:10.4018/IJABIM.20211001.oa3

Sakkir, G., Dollah, S., & Ahmad, J. (2021). E-Learning in COVID-19 Situation: Students' Perception. *EduLine: Journal of Education and Learning Innovation, 1*(1). Advance online publication. doi:10.35877/454RI.eduline378

Samiha, Y. T., Handayani, T., Razaq, A., Fithriyah, M., Fitri, A., & Anshari, M. (2022, March). Implementation of Education 4.0 as Sustainable Decisions for a Sustainable Development. In *2022 International Conference on Decision Aid Sciences and Applications (DASA)* (pp. 846-850). IEEE. 10.1109/DASA54658.2022.9765080

Samiha, Y. T., Handayani, T., Razzaq, A., Fitri, A., Fithriyah, M., & Anshari, M. (2021, November). Sustainability of Excellence in Education 4.0. In *2021 Sustainable Leadership and Academic Excellence International Conference (SLAE)* (pp. 1-5). IEEE. 10.1109/SLAE54202.2021.9788095

Sandybayev, A. (2020). The Impact of E-Learning Technologies on Students' Motivation: Student Centred Interaction in Business Education. *International Journal of Research in Tourism and Hospitality, 6,* 16–24. doi:10.20431/2455-0043.0601002

Stolterman, E., Fors, A. C., Truex, D. P., & Wastell, D. (2004). Information technology and the good life. In *Information systems research: Relevant theory and informed practice* (Vol. 143, pp. 687–693). Kluwer Academic Publishers. doi:10.1007/1-4020-8095-6_45

Subedi, S., Nayaju, S., Subedi, S., Shah, S. K., & Shah, J. M. (2020). Article. *International Journal of Science and Healthcare Research, 5*(3).

Think Insights. (2022). *CATWOE - How to assess the influence of stakeholders' viewpoints?* https://thinkinsights.net/consulting/catwoe-technique/

Thorpe, M., & Godwin, S. (2006). Interaction and e-learning: The student experience. *Studies in Continuing Education, 28*(3), 203–221. doi:10.1080/01580370600947330

Tran, V. A., Nguyen, H. T. T., & Nguyen, T. M. L. (2019). Digital Transformation: A Digital Learning Case Study. *Proceedings of the 2019 The World Symposium on Software Engineering - WSSE 2019,* 119-124. 10.1145/3362125.3362135

Turnbull, D., Chugh, R., & Luck, J. (2021). Transitioning to E-Learning during the COVID-19 pandemic: How have Higher Education Institutions responded to the challenge? *Education and Information Technologies*, 26(5), 4601–4619. doi:10.100710639-021-10633-w PMID:34177349

Windiarti, S., Fadilah, N., Dhermawati, E., & Pratolo, B. W. (2019). Teachers' perception towards the Obstacles of E-Learning Classes. *Journal of Language Teaching and Literature*, 6(2), 117–128. doi:10.30605/25409190.v6.117-128

Wright, B. M. (2017). Blended Learning, Student Perception of Face-to-Face and Online EFL Lessons. *Indonesian Journal of Applied Linguistics*, 7(1), 64–71. doi:10.17509/ijal.v7i1.6859

Zalat, M. M., Hamed, M. S., & Bolbol, S. A. (2021). The experiences, challenges, and acceptance of e-learning as a tool for teaching during the COVID-19 pandemic among university medical staff. *PLoS One*, 16(3), e0248758. doi:10.1371/journal.pone.0248758 PMID:33770079

Chapter 11
Heartfulness Meditation:
A Technique to Reduce the Health Impacts of Digital Psychology

Anjum Nazir Qureshi Sheikh
Rajiv Gandhi College of Engineering Research and Technology, Chandrapur, India

Manisha Urkude
Rajiv Gandhi College of Engineering Research and Technology, Chandrapur, India

ABSTRACT

The advancement of technology has increased the usage of the internet and social media platforms like Facebook, Twitter, WhatsApp, and Instagram. Many people face health and psychological issues due to overuse of social media. So, there is a need to promote techniques of a healthy lifestyle for the people, especially the youth. After studying the ill effects of social media and excessive phone usage by the youth, the authors have tried to use heartfulness to reduce the impact of the digital world on their physical and mental health. If we can train our minds properly, we can avoid unwanted thoughts and focus inward. But we have to know the correct techniques to train our minds. The heart plays a very important role so by meditating on the heart one can control their thoughts. It happens only through heartfulness meditation practice. Meditation helps us to improve sleep quality and sound sleep gives us a healthy lifestyle. By regular practice of heartfulness meditation, one can have better awareness and self-control by which the health of an individual remains good.

DOI: 10.4018/978-1-6684-6108-2.ch011

INTRODUCTION

Digital technology and media have influenced our life to a great extent. The world had come to our fingertips and we handle most of our tasks online through our smart phones and laptops. Whether it is studying, doing research or shopping, everything is being performed online by a number of people worldwide. But a very few of them are aware about the impacts of digital technologies on our mental and physical health.

According to the social media statistics of India in 2022, there are 467 million social media users that is equivalent to nearly 33.4 percent of the total population (Simon Kemp, 2022). Disturbed sleep due to social media use (DSSM) is defined as reduced or disturbed sleep caused due to specific behaviors like checking notifications, incoming messages and updates on the social media. Such behavior leads to poor academic performance among the students. (Katerina et al., 2020). Most of the youth in India use social media on their phones. Though many of them believe that social media helps them in education and can be entertaining at times but at the same time the youth agree that due to more time on social media they are not able to interact with their family and friends. Along with this some more disadvantages of social media are increasing cases of depression and loosing concentration on daily tasks (Abhani, 2019). Too much involvement with the social media leads to bad habits. The youth are more susceptible to cyber bullying which in some cases may lead to suicides or physical and mental disturbance (B.E. George & Noblelyne, 2017). A lot of time on social media leads to social isolation which has become one of the prominent reasons for mental, psychological, physical and emotional problems like depression and anxiety (Danielle Reed, 2017). The over usage of social media is kills time and has negative impact on their studies (Yogesh & Avinash, 2021).

A study published in the Indian Journal of Community Medicine and Public Health 2020 discloses that about 3.5 percent of the Indian adolescents suffer from Internet Gaming Disroder (IGD). Nearly 8% boys and 3% girls suffer from IGD according to this study. The extended screen time is the major reason for this disorder (Vamsi et. al., 2020). The people addicted to computer games spend more time playing games. Some of the games may include violence and completion of targets. The addicts are so obsessed with the game that they give least importance to studies and other daily routines. Addiction to online computer games is another factor that has disturbed lives of many youngsters. With excessive usage of online games, the people get addicted to it that causes many health issues like headache, neck pain, vision problems and mental problems (Avasthy et. al, 2019). There exists a direct relationship between IGD and anxiety, depression and stress among the male students (Sandhiya & Ayesha, 2019).

Besides games and social media online shopping is another reason that compels the youth to use their phones and internet. The people prefer online shopping due to availability of wide variety of products and saving time required to visit the nearby shops and malls. Many people have developed the habit of compulsive shopping called as buying shopping disorder (BSD). People with BSD use shopping as a means of coping up with their emotions and feel relaxed after shopping. BSD is often liked with depression, anxiety and other mood disorders that may cause financial instability, los of self control and conflicts with family and friends (Ginni Correa, 2020). Following online news is another craze among the people in this digital age. Fear of missing out on updates, high future anxiety and low interpersonal trust are some of the affects of online news addiction (Shabahang et.al. 2021). Some common effects of online usage are depression, anxiety, fear, stress, sleeplessness. One of the solutions to these problems is to reduce the usage of internet. But it is difficult to convince people to change their habits suddenly. A lot of research is going on in this field to deviate the effects of internet usage on the physical and mental health of the people. In this paper we have tried to study the affect of heartfulness meditation on a group of students. Heartfulness is a simple and practical method to relax and concentrate on heart. There are many studies that have shown positive impact of heartfulness on in controlling stress, heart beat rate etc. (Arya et.al. 2018). The rest of the paper is organized in the following way: section 2 covers literature review to study the importance of heartfulness, section 3 will discuss about the methods used for study, section 4 will discuss the results of study and section 5 will conclude the paper.

Background Study

Heartfulness is an effective heart based practice to achieve balanced mind. A study on the effect of heartfulness meditation, on a group of nurses and physicians indicate that practicing heartfulness meditation over a period of 12 weeks helped in enhancing wellness (Thimmapuram, J, et al 2017). Another study has investigated the effectiveness of heartfulness meditation on chronic insomnia. The study was conducted on 32 adult patients with chronic primary insomnia who were involved in heartfulness meditation along with sleep hygiene techniques. Before practicing meditation most of them relied on sedative hypnotics. Statistical improvements were observed among the patients, resulting into cessation of sedative hypnotics in nearly 87.5% of them (Jayaram Thimmapuram, et.al 2020). There are a few more studies that reveal that heartfulness meditation can have positive effects on the people with health complications like anxiety, depression and physical ailments. Similarly as study conducted on hypertensive patients found reduction in perceived stress and serum cortisol levels (Soumya Mishra et.al, 2017). Heartfulness has also been found effective in improving the overall life and sleep quality of patients with type 2 diabetes (Sai et.al, 2020) .The analysis of half an hour session of heartfulness meditation on a group of experienced as well as new meditators of different age groups shows that meditation plays a significant role in controlling heart rate, blood pressure and respiratory rate. Practice of heatfulness meditation on regular basis helps in reducing the effects of changes that are induced in body due to stress and also develop positive feelings (Raja Amarnath G, et.al, 2017) .

Mental health issues and depression are increasing rapidly among the teenagers. Depression hampers the development of young brains. The teenagers under this mental tension avoid social interaction, tend to discontinue their studies thereby increasing the rate of academic dropouts and increase the chances of suicides among them (Copeland W. E, et.al 2014). Heartfulness can be considered to be a mental support tool as is t reduces workload, worries, tension, harassment scores and at the same time increases joyscores (Amaranth et.al,2018). A thirty minutes heartfulness session and 15 minutes brainwave entertainment sessions were used to help the teenagers with mental health issues. The effectiveness of heartfulness has been demonstrated in this study which helps in regulating the overall mood, stress levels, anger and state depression (Yadav G.S. et.al, 2021). Increased work pressure and social isolations increased loneliness and sleep problems among the health professionals during the covid-19 pandemic periods. A study was conducted on a group of physicians and advanced service providers during which they participated in the heartfulness meditation program for a period of four weeks. After practicing heartfulness meditation, over the four weeks period an improvement in sleep quality and loneliness was observed (Thimmapuram J. et. al, 2021). A study conducted for a period of two years on a group of retired older adults of four South Asian Cities shows that meditation was effective in reducing loneliness and improving life satisfaction, contentment and well being (Samta Pandya, 2021). The effects of heartfulness cleaning and meditation under the guidance of a heartfulness trainer were studied on a group of 30 participants. The study was done to know the effects of cleaning and meditation on heart rate and blood pressure. The two parameters were recorded before as well as after meditation. The comparison shows better values of heart rate and blood pressure after practicing heartfulness and meditation (Narendra K.A, et. al. 2018).

METHOD OF STUDY

This survey was conducted on a group of 30 students in the age group of 19-21 years that included both the genders. The group of students received training on heartfuless meditation for 10 days under the guidance of experienced trainers called as Preceptors. The participants learned the different constituents of heartfulness that includes relaxation, cleaning, prayer and meditation. Along with the meditations techniques the students were informed about importance of humanity skills like compassion, gratitude, empathy and emotional balance that help the people in making life more meaningful. These qualities help people to handle all the kind of situations in life and survive in all the adverse conditions. The participants were given questionnaire before and after the training and the response of the participants were compared. The questionnaire was prepared after studying the negative impacts of digital psychology on health. It is a common picture that the youngsters spend most of their time on the smart phones. Though the smartphone users are from every age group but the young people are more addicted towards the phones compared to the middle aged or elderly people. The majority of the phone users are in the age group of 15 to 25 years. The phone addiction is one of the major causes of mental and physical ailments among the young generation (Alpana Vaidya, et.al. 2016). Therefore we tried to conduct a survey to know affect of heartfulness meditation on the young students. The questionnaire was prepared after studying some of the basic problems observed in the youth due to over usage of internet. The study will be helpful in observing the effectiveness of heartfulness meditation on the internet users.

The questionnaire included the following questions: (i) How do you feel after meditation (ii) Why do you practice meditation (iii) Are you able to solve daily problems after you started heartfulness meditation. (iv) I lead a meaningful life (v) I am able to control my emotions (vi) I am focused on life goals (vii) I am confident for face to face interaction (viii) I am able to share my feelings and discuss problems with my family and friends (ix) I am able to sleep properly everyday (x) I am engaged and interested in daily activities.

Table 1. Questionnaire for the participants

Question	Answers (in Percentage)					
	Before workshop	After workshop	Before workshop	After workshop	Before workshop	After workshop
How do you feel after meditation	Relax: 60.6	Relax: 80.6	Focus: 24.1	Focus: 14.4	Cannot define: 15.3	Cannot define: 5
Why do you practice meditation?	Improve engagement and presentence: 41.87	Improve engagement and presentence:61.97	Improve physical wellness: 28.9	Improve physical wellness:23.8	be more aware of thoughts and feelings:19.33	be more aware of thoughts and feelings:8
Are you able to solve daily problem very easily after Heartfulness Meditation	Yes: 67.5	Yes: 90.5	May be: 17.2	May be: 9.5	No: 25.3	No: 0
I lead a purposeful and meaningful life after starting meditation	Yes: 52.4	Yes: 100	May be: 25.4	May be: 0	No: 22.2	No: 0
My social relationships are supporting and rewarding	Yes : 53.6	Yes : 85.7	May Be:28.82	May Be: 14.3	No:18.2	No: 0
I am able to control my emotions.	Yes: 72.6	Yes: 85.7	Maybe: 21.8	Maybe: 9.16	No: 5.6	No: 4.8
I am focused on my life goals	Yes: 78.9	Yes: 91.8	May be: 17.9	May be: 8.2	No: 3.2	No: 0
I am confident for face to face interaction	Yes: 84.6	Yes: 95.2	May be:10.1	May be: 4.8	No: 5.3	No: 0
I am able to share my feelings and discuss my problems with my parents and friends	Yes: 76.8	Yes: 88.5	May be: 13. 8	May be: 8.4	No: 9.4	No: 3.1
I am able to sleep properly every day	Yes: 83.4	Yes: 95.2	May be: 11.8	May be: 4.8	No:4.8	No: 0
I am engaged and interested in my daily activities	Yes: 76.8	yes: 97.3	May be: 17.4	May be:2.7	No:5.8	No: 0

RESULTS AND DISCUSSIONS

The study was conducted after identifying the behavioral changes in the youth as a result of the usage of digital devices and social media. Some of the problems identified were lack of sleep, social isolation, less interaction and sharing of emotions with family and friends, lack of confidence, stress and anxiety that led to poor academic performance among the students. On the other hand when we tried to study the impact of heatfulness meditation we found that according to the surveys done earlier for heartfulness, the meditation technique seemed to be helpful in solving the issues like sleep disorder, reducing loneliness, improving life satisfaction and developing positive attitude. The questionnaire had some questions that tried to study if the hearfulness meditation is able to address these problems among the students. The group of students was identified as they complained about problems related to addiction to phone and social media that was affecting their academic performance.

The questionnaire was given to the students before and after the workshop and the results were compared. In the questionnaire one of the questions asked was if the participants were able to solve their daily problems. According to the comparison, an increase of 23% was observed in the number of individuals who agreed to it that their problem solving capacity has improved after practicing meditation. Nearly all of them agreed that they are leading a meaningful life after starting heartfulness meditation while only 52% of them agreed to it before the workshop. 85.7% of the participants agreed to it that they feel that their social relationships seem to be rewarding as compared to the period before practicing meditation while only 53.6% of participants have agreed for it before the workshop. Another question asked during the survey was if they are able to control their emotions. The percentage of participants who agreed for it was 72.6% before the workshop that increased to 85.7 at the end of the workshop. Similarly for the question regarding focus on life goals the percentage of participants agreeing to the question increased from 78.9% to 91.8% after the workshop. 84.6% of the people expressed that they are confident for face to face interaction before the workshop and the percentage of participants agreeing to it increased to 95.2% after the workshop. Another question was regarding sharing their problems with their parents and friends. The comparative results indicate that the number of people who were more confident to discuss their issues with the parents increased from 76.8% to 88.5%. The question regarding sound sleep every day indicates an increase of 83.4% to 95.2% and the results of engagement in daily activities increased from 76.2% to 97.3%.

All the questions that were included in the study indicated favorable results. The results indicate that heartfulness meditation was helpful in improving sleep, improved the decision making ability of the students, increased their confidence and they were able to interact and share their feelings with their family and friends.

Their concentration levels increased and due to which they were able to complete their daily activities on time and were more focused on their life goals. Most of them felt that they feel relaxed after heartfulness meditation and regular practice has increased their engagement, presentence and physical wellness.

Figure 1. Comparative results for question 1

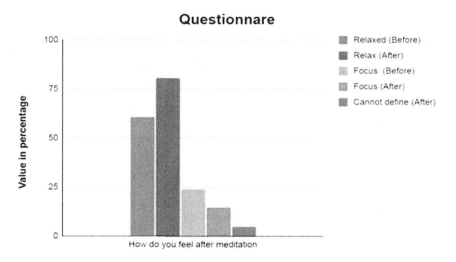

Figure 2. Comparative results for question 2

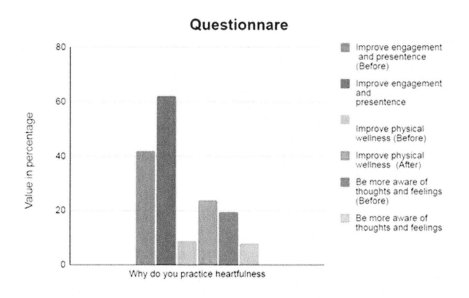

Figure 3. Comparative results for question 3-7

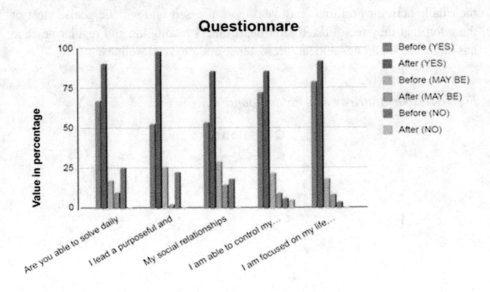

Figure 4. Comparative results for question 8-11

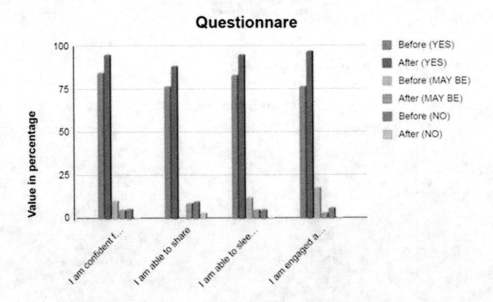

CONCLUSION

In this survey we tried to identify the changes in the behavior of the youngsters as a result of the usage of digital devices and social networking sites. The we studied how heartfulness meditation is able to control some of the problems like sleep disorder, lack of confidence, lack of concentration and social isolations. As heartfulness is able to solve these problems we tried using heartfulness for students who spend most of their time on phones. The behavorial changes observed in the students after a period of 10 days indicate that practicing heartfulness helped in boosting the confidence of the students in interacting with their family members and friends which reduced social isolation and feeling of loneliness among them. the students felt more confident and focused. Therefore it can be said that regular practice of heartfulness can reduce the negative impacts of digital psychology on health of youngsters. The study can be elaborated further by increasing the number of participants, increasing the period of practicing the meditation and by studying if meditation helps in reducing the phone addiction. We would also try to use some advanced statistical techniques to obtain better results.

REFERENCES

Abhani Dara, K. (2019). A Study on Impact of Social Media Over Youth of India. *International Journal of Engineering Development and Research*, *7*(2), 24–33.

Amarnath, R., Marimuthu, R., Jenitha, S., & Rajan, C. (2018). Impact of Heartfulness Meditation On Reducing Stress In Nursing Students: A Prospective Observational Study. *Int. J. Med. Res. Health Sci.*, *7*, 98–109.

Arya, N. K., Singh, K., Malik, A., & Mehrotra, R. (2018). Effect of Heartfulness Cleaning And Meditation On Heart Rate Variability. *Indian Heart Journal*, *70*, S50–S55. doi:10.1016/j.ihj.2018.05.004 PMID:30595318

Aswathy, V., Devika, E., & Girish, S. (2019, June). A Study on Impact of Online Gaming and Its Addiction among Youth with Special Reference to Kerala. *International Journal of Management, IT & Engineering*, *9*(6), 308–316.

Copeland, W. E., Angold, A., Shanahan, L., & Costello, E. J. (2014). Longitudinal Patterns Of Anxiety From Childhood To Adulthood: The Great Smoky Mountains Study. *Journal of the American Academy of Child and Adolescent Psychiatry*, *53*(1), 21–33. doi:10.1016/j.jaac.2013.09.017 PMID:24342383

Correa, G. (2022). *Shopping Addiction Fueled by Online Shopping.* https://www.addictioncenter.com/news/2020/01/shopping-addiction-online-shopping/

Dimitrov, B. E. G., & Nongkynrih, N. (2017). A Study On Social Media And Its Impact On Youth, International Journal of Creative Research Thoughts. *International Conference People Connect: Networking For Sustainable Development*, 149-158.

Evers, K., Chen, S., Rothmann, S., Dhir, A., & Pallesen, S. (2020). Investigating the relation among disturbed sleep due to social media use, school burnout, and academic performance. *Journal of Adolescence*, *84*(1), 156–164. doi:10.1016/j.adolescence.2020.08.011 PMID:32920331

Mishra, Sailesh, & Bashetti, Archana, Reddy, Jayashree, & Mukaddam. (2017). Effect of Heartfulness Meditation on Perceived Stress and Cognition in Hypertensive Patients. *International Journal of Research in Pharmaceutical Sciences*, *8*(4), 690–692.

Pandya, S. P. (2021). Meditation Program Mitigates Loneliness and Promotes Well Being Life Satisfaction and Contentment Among Retired Older Adults: A Two Year Follow-up Study in four South Asian Cities. *Aging & Mental Health*, *25*(2), 286–298. doi:10.1080/13607863.2019.1691143 PMID:31755300

Priyadarshini & Zinna. (n.d.). Exploring The Relationship Between Gaming Addiction, Depression, Anxiety And Stress In Young Males. *International Journal of Research and Analytical Reviews, 6*(1), 40-46.

Puri, Y., & Shukla, A. (2021). How Social Media Is Affecting The Youth. *Journal of Emerging Technologies and Innovative Research*, *8*(9), 192–201.

Raja, A. G., Sharma, N., Jenitha, S., & Ranjan, C. (2017). Efficacy of Heartfulness Meditation in Moderating Vital Parameters –A Comparison Study of Experienced and New Meditators. *International Journal of Medical Research and Health Sciences*, *6*(7), 70–78.

Reed, D. (2017). *Negative Impacts of Social Networking Sites.* https://socialnetworking.lovetoknow.com/Negative_Impact_of_Social_Networking_Sites

Sai, S. K. G., Padmanabha, B. V., Srilatha, B., & Mukkadan, J. K. (2020). Effectiveness of Heartfulness Meditation On Sleep Quality And Quality Of Life In Patients With Type 2 Diabetes. *MOJ Anat. Physiol.*, *7*(1), 19–21. doi:10.15406/mojap.2020.07.00283

Shabahang, R., Aruguete, M. S., & Shim, H. (2021). Online News Addiction: Future Anxiety, Fear of Missing Out on News, and Interpersonal Trust Contribute to Excessive Online News Consumption. *Online Journal of Communication and Media Technologies, 11*(2), e202105. doi:10.30935/ojcmt/10822

Simon Kemp. (2022). *Digital 2022, India.* https://datareportal.com/reports/digital-2022-india#:~:text=Social%20media%20statistics%20for%20India,in%20India%20in%20January%202022

Thimmapuram, J., Pargament, R., Sibliss, K., Grim, R., Risques, R., & Toorens, E. (2017). Effect of heartfulness meditation on burnout, emotional wellness, and telomere length in health care professionals. *Journal of Community Hospital Internal Medicine Perspectives, 7*(1), 21–27. doi:10.1080/20009666.2016.12708 06 PMID:28634520

Thimmapuram, J., Yommer, D., Tudor, L., Bell, T., Dumitrescu, C., & Davis, R. (2020). Heartfulness meditation improves sleep in chronic insomnia. *Journal of Community Hospital Internal Medicine Perspectives, 10*(1), 1, 10–15. doi:10.1080 /20009666.2019.1710948 PMID:32128052

Thimmapuram, Pargament, Bell, Shurck, & Madhusudan. (2021). Heartfulness Meditation Improves Loneliness and Sleep in Physicians and Advance Practice Providers During Covid 19 Pandemic. *Hospital Practice, 49*(3). 1 doi:0.1080/215 48331.2021.1896858

Undavalli, V. K., Rani, G. S., & Kumar, J. R. (2020). Prevalence Of Internet Gaming Disorder In India: A Technological Hazard Among Adolescents. *International Journal of Community Medicine and Public Health, 7*(2), 688–693. doi:10.18203/2394-6040. ijcmph20200450

Vaidya, A., Pathak, V., & Vaidya, A. (2016). Mobile Phone Usage Among Youth. *International Journal of Applied Research and Studies, 5*(13). DOI: doi:10.20908/ ijars.v5i3.9483

Yadav, G. S., Cidral-Filho, F. J., & Iyer, R. B. (2021). Using Heartfulness Meditation and Brainwave Entrainment to Improve Teenage Mental Wellbeing. *Frontiers in Psychology, 12*, 742892. doi:10.3389/fpsyg.2021.742892 PMID:34721219

Chapter 12
Digital Footprint and Human Behavior:
Potential and Challenges

Awangku Adi Putra Pengiran Rosman
Universiti Brunei Darussalam, Brunei

ABSTRACT

This chapter addresses digital footprints and how they can affect today's modern world, whether it be on the behaviour of humans, effects on society and governments, or even a person's ability to maintain their security or privacy. There is a possibility that leaving a digital footprint, regardless of the information that individuals post online, can have both positive and negative effects. The greater a person's digital footprint is, the more active they are in their interactions on the internet. It is necessary to bring attention to the matter at hand, which is the concept behind digital footprint being put into practise. It discusses digital footprints in a variety of contexts, such as real-life examples that illustrate how a digital footprint can have an impact in the actual world.

INTRODUCTION

Many will think that they only have a digital footprint if they are well known on social media, websites and the internet. However, this is not really the case. Even if you are not active on the internet, you still have a digital footprint. Do not think that a person could disappear completely if they wanted to, in reality in today's era that is not possible anymore without any higher intervention. No matter what, everyone will leave some kind of digital footprint anywhere on the internet. The Internet is

DOI: 10.4018/978-1-6684-6108-2.ch012

a vast cyber space which can hold unlimited amount of information available on everyone, even those who have never used the internet. This information can be found through a variety of sources, including public records, social media, and even personal interactions.

It is not all about collecting data from a single person's online activity; it is about understanding how that data can be used to provide insights into that person's behavior. To get a comprehensive understanding of someone's online behavior, you would need to collect data from a variety of sources. This would include, for example, their social media activity, their browsing history, and any other online activity they may engage in. The person's actions are the main concern. If someone is heading down a dark path, their online activity will be the first sign. The issue at hand is serious, and having a digital footprint will provide the most information on it. The digital footprint is a record of a person's online activity that can reveal their likes, preferences, and thoughts. If someone we know is posting something obnoxious or disgraceful on a regular basis, you can stop them from continuing down that path by asking them to stop or by unfriending or unfollowing them.

Digital footprints, as the name suggests, have much to do with developing digital technologies. Internet development also falls under this area and is closely interwoven with the concept of digital footprints. The following literature reviews from other researches summarize the current discourse on digital footprints, describe the theoretical concept, and present an overview of recent research.

LITERATURE REVIEW

Digital information that tracks our online activity can say a lot about who we are as people, including our likes, dislikes, and even our psychological makeup. This is made possible by advances in hardware and software, as well as the emergence of computational social science. The study provides insights that can help target persuasive appeals to the specific psychological needs of different audiences. This allows for the manipulation of large groups of people for their own benefit. The methods used have their own benefits to help individuals make better decisions and lead healthier, happier lives. There are several potential problems with data manipulation, protection and privacy breaches. Even the most well-thought-out data protection plans may not be enough to stop the misuse of online information for psychological targeting. The importance of the government taking further action to protect its citizens cannot easily be understated.

Persuasion is a process by which one person can encourage other people to believe in and act on their viewpoint. This can be done through many number of methods, such as providing evidence, reasoning, or appealing to emotion. Mass communication is a type of persuasive activity designed to encourage large groups of people to accept a certain viewpoint or take a particular action. The advertising industry uses advertising to motivate people to adopt healthy behaviours, such as eating a balanced diet and exercising regularly. Consumer marketing also uses advertising to promote healthy behaviours, such as choosing healthy foods and products. Political campaigns also use advertising to encourage people to adopt healthy behaviours, such as voting and registering to vote. Persuasive communication is more effective when it is tailored to an individual's specific psychological traits and motivations. To obtain accurate psychological profiles of millions of users, psychologists or other communicators can use online surveys, questionnaires, and other research methods. Given the limitations imposed by data protection regulations, how can they better navigate the landscape of collective psychological persuasion? There are considerable amount of risks and potential problems associated with using highly personalized methods to persuade large numbers of people. Some risks associated with persuasion include the potential for people to be convinced to do something they don't want to do, or to do something that isn't in their best interests. Additionally, hyper-personalised mass persuasion can lead to false assumptions and inaccurate assumptions about others, which can lead to harmful actions.

Digital footprints are remarkably predictive of human behaviour. More and more of our daily activities – such as social interactions, entertainment, shopping, and searching for information – take place in the digital space. The presence of human activity can provide clues about the preferences, habits, and personality of the person or people who were responsible for it. This is thanks to better hardware and software and the growth of computational social science. Digital records of human behaviour can be used to accurately estimate a wide range of personal attributes, such as political ideology, sexual orientation, and personality. Most people would typically assume these attributes to be private. It can provide more accurate assessments than traditional, scale-based personality assessments, and they can also be used to track changes over time. In a series of studies, many have found that digital footprints can be very accurate in the assessment of personality characteristics of large groups of people and that these footprints can also be used to create more effective communication tools.

Students need to shape their profound and unmistakable digital footprints. The future professions outlined in this document provide a reference point for students as they build their individual educational routes. The authors describe various approaches to defining the digital footprint of a person, including moderating an online educational platform. Projects and technologies are important tools that can help shape a positive digital footprint for students. Maps are a great way to track students' progress and achievement. The research methods use various approaches to studying the phenomenon, as well as using expert appraisal to get a good understanding of what products have been created as a result. The materials of this paper are of practical importance to students, higher education teachers, and teachers of educational institutions.

In light of these factors, the digital footprints of students must be designed with reference to developing critical thinking and self-development systems. Many scholars emphasise that the implementation of digital technologies, the creation of a digital educational environment, a digital toolkit, and digital prints lead to the digitisation of education (Robert, 2020; Kondakov, 2019; Polichka et al., 2020; Soltovets et al., 2019; Dmitrova et al., 2019).

One of the ways that we're digitising education is by implementing online platforms into the learning process. As moderators of educational platforms, students use the available services and resources on the Internet to create virtual educational startups. They develop a high level of information competency, shape individual educational routes, and have profound and unmistakable digital footprints. These factors help to focus attention on training specialists in new fields. In education, there are many professions that match the description above. This aligns with my statements. There are studies that show the importance of the digital footprints of students when it comes to moderating online educational platforms.

Your digital footprint is a valuable source of information that can be used to understand your online behaviour. The process of creating a "digital footprint" depends on a structured approach that combines input (collection) and output (value) with a feedback loop that controls the whole process. The feedback loop will gradually increase the value of the outcome and adjust the outcome value to ensure a positive result. Our data analysis techniques help us generate valuable insights that help us improve our operations. Behavioural DNA provides a detailed description of the person.

As the use of sensors in mobile phones and the Internet continues to grow, so does the number of people who leave a digital footprint in the cyber world. When the current university students join the campus, they will leave a unique digital footprint in the university's IT system. A student's digital footprint includes important demographic data, academic records, assignments and test results, library access and borrows and return history and access to WiFi or other networks.

One way to create innovation in student services is to change the way we think about why the services exist and how they are provided. Students are now the focus of all interactions. A boarding school is an excellent educational option for students. It provides them with an intensive learning environment and provides them with the stability and support they need to succeed. The school provides a variety of extra-curricular activities that help students learn, as well as great facilities, including computer labs and gym and entertainment rooms, which help students relax and develop their brains.

One way to create innovation in student services is to change the way we think about why the services exist and how they are provided. Students are now the focus of all interactions. A boarding school is an excellent educational option for students. It provides them with an intensive learning environment and provides them with the stability and support they need to succeed. The school provides a variety of extra-curricular activities that help students learn, as well as great facilities, including computer labs and gym and entertainment rooms, which help students relax and develop their brains.

The development of innovation in educational institutions should be in line with key trends in the industry, such as image and branding, creating and changing sustainably, lifelong relationships, and supporting and improving student/customer experience.

Every time a user visits a webpage, information about their interaction is automatically logged. By analysing log files, we can understand user behaviour. Behaviour varies depending on the event and time and can be observed from phone usage data stored in phone log files. The integration of social networks into IoT infrastructure, as well as the popularity of mobile devices, helps to establish identification, which is the basis of the behaviour exhibited when using social networks. As a result, a new concept has been created. The prediction of user attributes and preferences can be used to improve products and services. Student behaviour analysis can provide evidence of the effectiveness of the university. The tool can be used to create an organisational culture and manage the lives of students.

The digital world has become a crucial mechanism as part of the lives of individuals. The 21st century has seen dramatic advances in many areas of knowledge. Digital electronics have undergone a dramatic transformation over the past few decades, from being a luxury item to one that is essential for the modern world. The radical transformation we have seen in electronics accessibility and services is due in large part to the improvement of these technologies. This discovery suggests that there may be an alternative to the natural world.

Among the many things people are bored of during the covid-19 pandemic, some people choose to play games, browsing the Internet, or check out entertainment platforms online. The real world is an important part of the sustainability of the digital world, but recent developments in the digital world have begun to have an impact on the infrastructure of our society (privacy, democracy, etc.). There are a number of important institutions in our society, both individual and state-level. The impact of this work can be classified as either positive or negative, depending on its effect on society. Digital footprints play an important role in developing a realistic understanding of threats, opportunities, and responsibilities in a digital environment.

The digital footprint is a trail of activity that is left behind when an individual uses digital technologies, such as television, mobile phones, the Internet, music players, and more. Your personal identity or bank account number is not included in the exhaustive data array that sketches out your identity (likes, hobbies, etc.) by looking at your frequently visited websites or opened files. There is a great degree of truth to what you say.

Lambiotte and Kosinsai (2014) definition of a digital footprint is spot-on. It includes everything an individual does online and offline, making it an accurate representation of their behaviour. As stated by Chen et al. (2017) are that your digital footprint is easily tracked between you and the cyber world. We, the authors, believe that this paper is a valuable contribution to the literature.

According to the literature on digital footprints, there are two main types: passive and active. Passive prints are left passively interacting with infrastructure that provides input to location records, such as GPS-enabled mobile devices. Active prints are made explicitly by the user when they reflect their location or other crucial data in photographs, messages, and sensory measures. These five renowned chefs have created incredible meals. (Girardin, Calabresa, Dalfoliore, Ratti and Blat, 2008).

Digital experience is a wide variety for individuals. Therefore, a digital footprint cannot be completely portrayed as a threat, and an individual cannot completely reduce their digital footprint. Its role in providing relevant searches and advertisements is critical. There's no guarantee that someone looking for a restaurant would see an advertisement for recruitment. Such conditions would be a loss for both seller and buyer, increasing the cost of internet access and accompanying services. Digital footprints can help people learn about people with similar interests or habits through various social networking platforms or by relying on Google for movie recommendations.

The digital footprint poses a big challenge to individual liberty and sovereignty of institutions, as it targets individuals based on their past online behavior. Individuals do encounter online advertisements for clothes after an online shopping or other instances of equivalent case.

The Internet revolutionises how everything can be accessed, creating a new era of possibilities. However, despite these advantages, the new era of new technology also has disadvantages. Through studies, it is showned that the youth category is one of the largest group that is synonymous with technology. Most of the young people nowadays enjoy using the features but lack the information regarding their internet browsing history footprint.

When individuals use the Internet, they leave behind a complex trail of digital footprints that can reveal their various presentations of self, based on social profiles and comments, traces of their activities, and anything they have uploaded into the Internet. However, it is unclear to what extent netizens are aware that they are making these traces and have ways to take control over it online. The purpose of this paper is to determine the level of awareness among youth about their digital footprint.

Today, digital technologies make it easy and frequent for consumers to access social media. This has increased the uptake of social media significantly. This is leading to people giving out more personal information about themselves online than ever before, such as sharing their locations, contact information, and credit card numbers on sites of media social networks (Czodli, 2016).

Digital footprints are important because they show what people do online and how often. The use of digitised footprints as a means of identity verification and the suitability of applicants for roles within an organisation is growing,especially among university applicants and employers. The digital footprints left behind when someone is using the Internet and social media can provide a wealth of information about an individual. By looking at someone's online activity, it is possible to learn about their interests, opinions, and relationships. This information can be used to paint a picture of who someone is and what they are like. This may have a significant impact on their future careers or opportunities for employment. Recent media reports suggest that more and more people are losing their jobs or having their social media accounts discounted from higher education programmes. (Thatcher, 2014)

As stated by Czodli, most people do not realise the hidden agenda behind their computers and the data they share. The addition of these features makes it a powerful tool that can help children learn and make decisions about what to buy, play computer games, and read or watch on the Internet. One of the ways that a digital footprint is left behind is through retailers who leave cookies on a user's system to track their activities.

This is because they can place advertisements on any devices browsers for products that have recently been looked-up or may be interested in based on a user's search history. The new media also plays an important role in promoting human rights and freedoms of life. They believe that using new media can have a positive impact on social, economic, and cultural life, as well as being easy to share. However, users unintentionally left footprints on the websites they visited by leaving behind digital traces. The digital footprint can be used to manipulate or direct the effects it generates to third parties for personal gain or exploitation. Due to the fact that all information has been shared online, it is difficult to delete this information.

The media usually portrays the Internet as a technology that gives bad influences for the younger generation since it is so accessible, such as addiction to the Internet, stalkers of kids online, cyberbullying, and the destruction of their lives. However, there have been so many positive aspects to the Internet which literally help a lot of people to satisfy their daily needs, such as product purchase frauds, depression in social networks, and sexual harassment. Besides, your digital footprint can also be seen as a passive participation by netizens in the content of production and sharing on social media (Buchanan et al., 2017).

With the advancement of global technology, social media can be categorised under the development of the Internet of Things (IoT). IoT is the latest trend in web-based architecture, revealing the next generation of data flow through the supply chain network. IoT acted as one of nine milestones for the challenges of the 4th industrial revolution. The Revolution 4.0 was started by most Asian countries in order to help with the yearly growth rate. Revolution 4.0 is used to describe the integration of machines and the Internet of things in order to create more efficient production systems. This is a network of real-world objects – devices, wearables, cars, etc. – that interact with each other to exchange data and carry out tasks. This rich description features sensors, software, and network connectivity that allow information to be collected and exchanged between objects through the web or wireless communication technologies. This allows for a great deal of information exchange and connectivity between devices. The Internet of Things will allow everyday objects to be connected to the Internet, leading to a range of new and advanced capabilities in the future. This channel provides opportunities and challenges for the new era. The Internet of Things has created an opportunity for citizens to access information in a new way (Almunawar & Anshari, 2022). This provides a significant advantage by allowing people to connect with each other and share data more easily.

Sharon found that people prefer alternative news websites because they believe the sources are more accurate and thus more trustworthy. The media is teaching its readers things that are not true and appropriate, contrary to what Bambang (2019) says. Every advantage has a corresponding disadvantage.

Bughin et al. (2011) found that the McKinsey Global Institute released a study on how businesses use social media. The study found that businesses that use social media effectively can enhance their activities and take advantage of new market opportunities.

Social media has made a significant impact indefinitely on the way people interact with each other and the world around them. By harnessing the power of social networking, the Internet of Things has been able to optimize interactions between objects and people. The use of social media has resulted in the development of comprehensive apps that allow businesses to incorporate social media into their operations. Social networks provide a good platform for users to take simple actions that contribute to their digital footprint, such as liking, favoriting, following, or commenting (Büchi, Lutz & Micheli, 2017; Anshari & Lim, 2017). Although young people are often online, but they don't think about how their online activity affects their digital identity. Instead, they focus on the short-term benefits of being able to connect with friends (Oxley, 2010; Anshari, Alas, & Sulaiman, 2019).

According to Thatcher, one of the most popular uses of the Internet is communicating with others through social networking platforms. When someone goes online, they create a digital footprint that can be traced back to them. This footprint is made up of data and information that the user generates while they are online (Anshari et al., 2016).

Our digital footprints are used by companies to collect data about us which they can then use to target us with more personalized advertising (Anshari et al., 2020; Razzaq et al., 2018). Each user search and post reaction is recorded in databases. These databases help business psychologists understand how to target their advertising to consumers more effectively. By understanding what consumers want and need, businesses can create targeted advertising campaigns that are more likely to be successful. This information is not only used to determine how to best advertise to users, but also to understand when users are most receptive to advertisements. By understanding users' moods, businesses can better target their advertising campaigns for maximum impact.

Azucar et al. claim that the data that researchers can glean from people's online activity can help them reach larger, more diverse audiences, customize their marketing, and create more personalized computer-human interactions. This, in turn, can lead to more targeted and effective health campaigns.

Maureen McDermott's 2018 book Distance Learning discusses the importance of learning how to create and manage a positive online presence. Without this knowledge, people may accidentally create digital footprints with negative consequences, which can be difficult to fix. So this means as more and more people share aspects of their personal lives on social media, it becomes more important for people to learn how to manage their digital footprints. This includes understanding how to control the amount and types of information that are shared online.

Some students think they don't need to be concerned about their digital footprints because social media present an accurate portrayal of who they are, and therefore they're not doing any damage to their reputations. The study found by Mar Camacho, Janaina Minelli, and Gabriel Grosseck that most students are comfortable with social media and understand the concept of a digital footprint. The results of the study showed that students are content with the virtual selves they display on social media (Anshari et al., 2022; Hasmawati et al., 2020). They are also aware of their privacy settings and think they use them properly. The average student surveyed has over two hundred friends, but the settings they are comfortable with only allow for a fraction of those friends to be displayed. Can those students truthfully say that they have a close relationship with each of those friends and would feel comfortable sharing everything they post on social media? They find it hard to believe that most people only discuss their true feelings with a handful of people.

As stated by Oyeyemi, the rate of digital development and evolution of technologies has resulted in tremendous changes in communication and information seeking patterns. Because of this, librarians need to make sure they have a strong online presence. This paper discussed the prospects and steps of creating a digital footprint, with the goal of producing librarians who are resilient to innovative and destructive technologies. It covers the needs of both library users and non-users who need access to information and allied services.

From the article by Chin and Wang (2020) states that COVID-19 pandemic has caused widespread damage to global health and economies. However, the status of the spread of COVID-19 differed from country to country. The role that public perceptions play in combating the COVID-19 epidemic is vitally important, given the high infectivity and uncertainty of the disease. The study sets out to gauge public awareness of epidemics by monitoring the digital footprint of "face mask" searches on Google. It will compare the effectiveness of epidemic prevention in Taiwan, Singapore, the Philippines, Italy, Spain, and South Korea.

The data on Google search volume for face masks and confirmed cases of COVID-19 were collected between December 31, 2019 and March 17, 2020. They found that people's awareness of epidemics varies from country to country, based on their digital footprints. Making the public aware of an epidemic early on and keeping them informed is crucial for preventing the spread of the disease. The study found that public awareness of epidemics is high in Taiwan and that this awareness helps to prevent epidemics from occurring.

The study found that digital footprints can be used to establish an early warning system for the government by tracking the public's attitudes and response to emerging infectious diseases. The Google search volume index could be used by the government to manage health services based on timely information. In the era of big data, there is a huge amount of online data that can be gathered and analyzed to improve or create new services.

There are countless digital footprints that users leave behind every day, either consciously or unconsciously, on digital services such as websites, social media, and search engines. These footprints can take the form of IP addresses, browsing and search history, and posts or comments made online. The digital footprints we leave behind can provide valuable insights into our behaviours, preferences and characteristics (Arakerimath and Gupta, 2015; Anshari et al., 2019a).

Digital data are increasingly being used in health care research to improve health services in a variety of ways, including detecting disease outbreaks, providing clinical decision support, and enabling personalized care (Aiello, Renson, and Zivich, 2020; Saranya and Asha, 2019; Mulyani et al., 2019).

Google Trend is a reliable way to track the spread of infectious diseases and measure public reaction to them. A recent study found that people tend to search for information about diseases online more frequently during an outbreak of the disease. The study found that the number of people searching for information about Ebola was correlated with the number of weekly Ebola cases during the 2014 outbreak. The findings suggest that the Google search volume index data for disease information-seeking behavior can be used as an indicator for predicting influenza outbreaks. This means that by looking at how many people are searching for information on diseases, we can get an idea of how many people are likely to be affected by an outbreak (Zulkarnain et al., 2021; Anshari et al., 2021a). This method of measuring public perceptions of infectious disease through traditional cross-sectional telephone surveys provides valuable information, but is time-consuming and expensive, making it difficult to use for policymaking that requires immediate and continuous data. As data sets continue to grow exponentially, researchers are finding new ways to glean useful information from them. By analyzing digital footprints, they can extract valuable insights that can be used to improve our understanding of the world around us (Anshari et al., 2021b).

In the past three months, Taiwan has shown how well it can handle epidemics. This is thanks to the country's robust prevention measures. As of March 31, 2020, there were 322 confirmed cases of COVID-19 in Taiwan. This number includes both Taiwanese citizens and foreign nationals. Taiwan has been praised for its quick and effective response to the pandemic, with measures such as widespread testing and contact tracing. According to the TCDC, there have been 276 confirmed cases of imported infection and 46 indigenous cases, indicating that local transmission has been effectively contained. According to the Database of COVID-19 at Our World in Data website, Taiwan ranks 77th in the world on the total confirmed cases of COVID-19 (Roser et al., 2020). This study seeks to contribute to the existing body of literature by demonstrating how the digital footprint of the public's web search behaviors for "face mask" can be used as a valuable metric of public awareness of an epidemic, and how this relates to the effectiveness of epidemic prevention measures during the course of the COVID-19 pandemic in Taiwan. The cross-country comparison data were provided in addition to the data from the study. This allowed for a more comprehensive understanding of the results.

ANALYSIS AND DISCUSSION

In order to understand about digital footprint and its relevance to technology and its effects to the human society, it is believed that digital footprint will affect a person or a community in a way that it can have control over the entity itself. It is because digital footprint is considered a rigid data bank that can contain any information on anyone and can be access anywhere anytime, not considering any ethical or unethical actions being done of course.

In terms of security and privacy wise is quite on the grey area where it is considered somehow unethical where we can get a person information with a click of a button, but that is not the case since this information is already on the internet whether the person likes it or not. I strongly believe that this method is how online marketers and giant social media companies know what to show for their advertisements on certain regions (Anshari & Hamdan, 2022).

Digital footprint may also be the reason why a certain place or region can get better emergency response or quickest to get what they need, for example during Covid-19 we need supply of face masks. Digital footprint can help mitigate this problem and can be sent to the areas that are the most in need rather than blindly sending to everyone and becoming unused stockpiles.

It's important to stay focused and track all the details of your online activity (Ahad & Anshari, 2017). In today's world, where technology is everywhere and impacting all aspects of our lives, it's important to analyze your digital footprint. This will give you valuable insights into what you are doing and what you should avoid.

Digital footprints can help organizations ensure that nothing is being leaked, by providing a record of who has accessed what information (Almunawar et al., 2020). This is especially important in cases where people are working under a hidden network. This will provide detailed information on aspects that are vulnerable to being breached by anyone.

Digital footprints can be both beneficial and harmful. On the one hand, they can provide a person with a richer online experience (Ahad et al., 2017). On the other hand, they can also be used to exploit a person's personal information. People who regularly check their online activity tend to learn things about themselves that they would never have otherwise discovered.

The use of digital footprints to detect fraudulent activity is becoming increasingly popular and easy to do. Fraud cases are often detected by checking online for related activity (Anshari et al., 2019b). This can include looking for red flags such as unusual activity on financial accounts or accounts being created in someone's name. You take into consideration the products you use on a daily basis, as this reflects your sense of choice. You need to know what assets and resources you have at your disposal, and what you are willing to risk or sacrifice in order to achieve your goal. This is an advertisement that provides information about yourself that can be used to improve your life. Companies that use the internet as a its core and backbone can easily track what their employees are doing and reward them with incentives that motivate them to work better in the future. If you put more effort into your work, you will improve your performance and the company will benefit as a whole from the

decision to give you an award. If teachers regularly check their students' online activity, they will have a better idea of their progress. He can tell which activities are appropriate for a given course, and which are not, based on his own experience as a student.

CONCLUSION

In conclusion, digital footprint does come with advantages and its disadvantages but if it is being utilized correctly it can definitely benefit everyone. That is the main idea of having all information on the internet so that the world can function more efficiently. It is essential that young people who use the internet are taught how to exercise caution and practice good cyber discipline. This is because anything that is shared online becomes permanent and can be used to track people and commit cybercrimes. Your online activity can have a significant impact on your reputation, relationships and job prospects (both positive and negative). This is important to understand so that the impact is positive. Your digital footprint can have a positive or negative effect on your reputation, both online and offline. It is recommended to create a positive digital footprint if you want to protect your reputation both now and in the future. This means be aware and careful about what we want to post online and making sure that any digital interactions you have are respectful and professional.

REFERENCES

Abbott, J. (2019). Digital Footprints: Managing Our Irrevocable Traces. *Verbal Equinox*, 75.

Ahad, A. D., & Anshari, M. (2017). Smartphone habits among youth: Uses and gratification theory. *International Journal of Cyber Behavior, Psychology and Learning*, 7(1), 65–75. doi:10.4018/IJCBPL.2017010105

Ahad, A. D., Anshari, M., & Razzaq, A. (2017). Domestication of smartphones among adolescents in Brunei Darussalam. *International Journal of Cyber Behavior, Psychology and Learning*, 7(4), 26–39. doi:10.4018/IJCBPL.2017100103

Aiello, A. E., Renson, A., & Zivich, P. N. (2020). Social media– and Internet-based disease surveillance for public health. *Annual Review of Public Health*, 41(1), 1–18. doi:10.1146/annurev-publhealth-040119-094402 PMID:31905322

Almunawar, M. N., & Anshari, M. (2022). Customer acceptance of online delivery platform during the COVID-19 pandemic: the case of Brunei Darussalam. *Journal of Science and Technology Policy Management*, ahead-of-print.

Almunawar, M. N., Anshari, M., & Lim, S. A. (2020). Customer acceptance of ride-hailing in Indonesia. *Journal of Science and Technology Policy Management*.

Anshari, M., Alas, Y., Hardaker, G., Jaidin, J. H., Smith, M., & Ahad, A. D. (2016). Smartphone habit and behavior in Brunei: Personalization, gender, and generation gap. *Computers in Human Behavior, 64*, 719–727. doi:10.1016/j.chb.2016.07.063

Anshari, M., Alas, Y., Razzaq, A., Shahrill, M., & Lim, S. A. (2021). Millennials consumers' behaviors between trends and experiments. In Research Anthology on E-Commerce Adoption, Models, and Applications for Modern Business (pp. 1492-1508). IGI Global.

Anshari, M., Alas, Y., & Sulaiman, E. (2019). Smartphone addictions and nomophobia among youth. *Vulnerable Children and Youth Studies, 14*(3), 242–247. doi:10.108 0/17450128.2019.1614709

Anshari, M., Alas, Y., & Yunus, N. (2019). A survey study of smartphones behavior in Brunei: A proposal of Modelling big data strategies. In Multigenerational Online Behavior and Media Use: Concepts, Methodologies, Tools, and Applications (pp. 201-214). IGI Global.

Anshari, M., Almunawar, M. N., Lim, S. A., & Al-Mudimigh, A. (2019). Customer relationship management and big data enabled: Personalization & customization of services. *Applied Computing and Informatics, 15*(2), 94–101. doi:10.1016/j. aci.2018.05.004

Anshari, M., Almunawar, M. N., & Masri, M. (2020). An overview of financial technology in Indonesia. *Financial technology and disruptive innovation in ASEAN*, 216-224.

Anshari, M., Arine, M. A., Nurhidayah, N., Aziyah, H., & Salleh, M. H. A. (2021). Factors influencing individual in adopting eWallet. *Journal of Financial Services Marketing, 26*(1), 10–23. doi:10.105741264-020-00079-5

Anshari, M., & Hamdan, M. (2022). Enhancing e-government with a digital twin for innovation management. *Journal of Science and Technology Policy Management*, ahead-of-print.

Anshari, M., & Lim, S. A. (2017). E-government with big data enabled through smartphone for public services: Possibilities and challenges. *International Journal of Public Administration, 40*(13), 1143–1158. doi:10.1080/01900692.2016.1242619

Anshari, M., Syafrudin, M., & Fitriyani, N. L. (2022). Fourth Industrial Revolution between Knowledge Management and Digital Humanities. *Information (Basel), 13*(6), 292. doi:10.3390/info13060292

Arakerimath, P. A. R., & Gupta, P. K. (2015). Digital footprint: Pros, cons, and future. *International Journal of Latest Technology in Engineering*, *4*(10), 52–56.

Azucar, D., Marengo, D., & Settanni, M. (2018). Predicting the Big 5 personality traits from digital footprints on social media: A meta-analysis. *Personality and Individual Differences*, *124*, 150–159. doi:10.1016/j.paid.2017.12.018

Buchanan, R., Southgate, E., Smith, S. P., Murray, T., & Noble, B. (2017). Post no photos, leave no trace: Children's digital footprint management strategies. *E-Learning and Digital Media*, *14*(5), 275–290. doi:10.1177/2042753017751711

Büchi, M., Lutz, C., & Micheli, M. (2017, May). Life online: The digital footprint gap. *International Scientific Conference for the Partnership for Progress on the Digital Divide*.

Bughin, J., Byers, A. H., & Chui, M. (2011). How social technologies are extending the organization. *The McKinsey Quarterly*, *20*(11), 1–10.

Chen, C., Chen, X., Wang, L., Ma, X., Wang, Z., Liu, K., Guo, B., & Zhou, Z. (2016). MA-SSR: A memetic algorithm for skyline scenic routes planning leveraging heterogeneous user- generated digital footprints. *IEEE Transactions on Vehicular Technology*, *66*(7), 5723–5736. doi:10.1109/TVT.2016.2639550

Chin, C. Y., & Wang, C. L. (2020). Effectiveness of COVID-19 pandemic prevention: A cross- country comparison of digital footprint of google search data. *Advances in Management and Applied Economics*, *10*(4), 23–34.

Csavina, J., Field, J., Félix, O., Corral-Avitia, A. Y., Sáez, A. E., & Betterton, E. A. (2014). Effect of wind speed and relative humidity on atmospheric dust concentrations in semi-arid climates. *The Science of the Total Environment*, *487*, 82–90. doi:10.1016/j.scitotenv.2014.03.138 PMID:24769193

Czodli, B. (2016). *Privacy and security online: Protecting your digital footprint*. Retrieved from http://www.users.miamioh.edu/viscokj/IMS201/website/chapter-04.html

Dmitrova, A. V., Chigisheva, O. P., & Timoshenko, Y. S. (2019). Oxford's Apple Podcasts Multimedia Platform as an Online Digital Literacy Tool for Oxford University Students. International Journal of Economics and Education, 5(3), 5-22.

Girardin, F., Calabrese, F., Dal Fiore, F., Ratti, C., & Blat, J. (2008). Digital footprinting: Uncovering tourists with user-generated content. *IEEE Pervasive Computing*, *7*(4), 36–43. doi:10.1109/MPRV.2008.71

Hasmawati, F., Samiha, Y. T., Razzaq, A., & Anshari, M. (2020). Understanding nomophobia among digital natives: Characteristics and challenges. *Journal of Critical Reviews*, *7*(13), 122–131.

Hildebrand, C. (2019). The machine age of marketing: How artificial intelligence changes the way people think, act, and decide. *NIM Marketing Intelligence Review*, *11*(2), 11–10. doi:10.2478/nimmir-2019-0010

Hong, D. N. M. (2021). Trust and credibility of urban youth on online news media. *Ad Alta: Journal of Interdisciplinary Research*.

Kondakov, A. M. (2019). *Education in the Context of Digital Transformation of Russian Society*. Available from http://vcht.center/wp-content/uploads/2019/06/Kondakov-Peterburg25maya2019-2.pdf

Kumar, H., & Raj, P. (2020). An indagation on experiences and awareness of digital footprint among pupils of higher education. *Academic Research International*, *11*, 16–31.

Lambiotte, R., & Kosinski, M. (2014). Tracking the digital footprints of personality. *Proceedings of the IEEE*, *102*(12), 1934–1939. doi:10.1109/JPROC.2014.2359054

McDermott, M. (2018). Digital footprints. *Distance Learning*, *15*(1), 51–54.

Mulyani, M. A., Razzaq, A., Sumardi, W. H., & Anshari, M. (2019, August). Smartphone adoption in mobile learning scenario. In *2019 International Conference on Information Management and Technology (ICIMTech)* (Vol. 1, pp. 208-211). IEEE. 10.1109/ICIMTech.2019.8843755

Oxley, C. (2011). Digital citizenship: Developing an ethical and responsible online culture. *Access*, *25*(3), 5–9.

Oyeyemi, O. O. (n.d.). *Librarians' Building a digital footprint*. Academic Press.

Polichka, A. E., Malykhina, O. A., Karpova, I. V., & Tabachuk, N. P. (2020). *Modern Problems of Education in IT and Mathematics: Scientific and Methodological Bases of Improving the Professional Competence of Mathematics Teachers*. Publishing house of Pacific National University.

Razzaq, A., Samiha, Y. T., & Anshari, M. (2018). Smartphone habits and behaviors in supporting students self-efficacy. *International Journal of Emerging Technologies in Learning*, *13*(2), 94. doi:10.3991/ijet.v13i02.7685

Robert, I. V. (2020). Axiological Approach to the Development of Education in Conditions of the Digital Paradigm. *Pedagogical Informatics, 2*.

Soltovets, E., Chigisheva, O., & Dubover, D. (2019). Foreign Language E-Course as Informal Learning Tool for Digital Literacy Development. *Dilemas Contemporaneos-Educacion Politica y Valores, 6*(3), Art. 50.

Songsom, N., Nilsook, P., & Wannapiroon, P. (2019). The synthesis of the student relationship management system using the internet of things to collect the digital footprint for higher education institutions. *International Journal of Online & Biomedical Engineering, 15*(6), 99. doi:10.3991/ijoe.v15i06.10173

Thatcher, J. (2014). Big data, big questionsǀ Living on fumes: Digital footprints, data fumes, and the limitations of spatial big data. *International Journal of Communication, 8*, 19.

Wijaya, B. S. (2019). Dancing with the impropriety of media: How Indonesian consumers think and behave towards the unethical and illogical online news. *Malaysian Journal of Communication, 35*(1), 187–205. doi:10.17576/JKMJC-2019-3501-13

Wook, T. S. M., Mohamed, H., Noor, S. F. M., Muda, Z., & Zairon, I. Y. (2019). Awareness of digital footprint management in the new media amongst youth. *Jurnal Komunikasi: Malaysian Journal of Communication, 35*(3), 407–421.

Zulkarnain, N., Anshari, M., Hamdan, M., & Fithriyah, M. (2021, August). Big data in business and ethical challenges. In *2021 International Conference on Information Management and Technology (ICIMTech)* (Vol. 1, pp. 298-303). IEEE. 10.1109/ICIMTech53080.2021.9534963

Compilation of References

(1587). The Lancet. (2020). The plight of essential workers during the COVID-19 pandemic. *Lancet*, *395*(10237). doi:10.10160140-6736(20)31200-9

.Musek, J. (2017). The general factor of personality: Ten years after. *Psihologijske teme, 26*(1), 61-87.

@ thewokesalaryman • Instagram photos and videos. (n.d.). Retrieved 12 August 2022, from https://www.instagram.com/thewokesalaryman/?hl=en

❀*KL2BSB*❀ *(@kl2bsb) • Instagram photos and videos*. (n.d.). Retrieved 12 August 2022, from https://www.instagram.com/kl2bsb/?hl=en

A timeline: A brief history of Apple Watch. (n.d.). Retrieved 12 August 2022, from https://www.verizon.com/articles/brief-history-of-apple-watch/

Abassi, S., Ayoob, T., Malik, A. & Memon, S. I. (2020). Perceptions of students regarding E-learning during Covid-19 at a private medical college. *Pak J Med Sci, 36*(S4). doi: 1 doi:0.12669/pjms.36.COVID19-S4.2766

Abbott, T. (2022). *How Much Data Does a Zoom Meeting Use*? Reviews Org. https://www.reviews.org/internet-service/how-much-data-does-zoom-use/

Abbott, J. (2019). Digital Footprints: Managing Our Irrevocable Traces. *Verbal Equinox*, 75.

Abdollahi, H., Mahoor, M., Zandie, R., Sewierski, J., & Qualls, S. (2022). Artificial emotional intelligence in socially assistive robots for older adults: A pilot study. *IEEE Transactions on Affective Computing*, 1. doi:10.1109/TAFFC.2022.3143803

Abdul Aziz, A. (2019). Special Forward: Islamic Governance and the Articulation of Maqāṣid al-Sharī'ah in Brunei Darussalam. In R. Yunos (Ed.), *Maqāṣid Al-Sharī'ah in the Brunei Civil Service: Civil Servant's Perspectives*. Qasrun Nafis Publishing House.

Abele, A. E., & Spurk, D. (2009). How do objective and subjective career success interrelate over time? *Journal of Occupational and Organizational Psychology*, *82*(4), 803–824. doi:10.1348/096317909X470924

Abhani Dara, K. (2019). A Study on Impact of Social Media Over Youth of India. *International Journal of Engineering Development and Research*, 7(2), 24–33.

About. (n.d.). Legaleagle. Retrieved 12 August 2022, from https://www.legaleagleprep.com/about

Abu Bakar, R. (2021, April 5). *Muslims can start paying zakat online this Ramadhan*. The Scoop. https://thescoop.co/2021/04/05/muslims-can-start-paying-zakat-online-this-ramadan/

Abubakar, A. M., Elrehail, H., Alatailat, M. A., & Elci, A. (2019). Knowledge Management, Decision-making Style, and Organizational Performance. *Journal of Innovation & Knowledge.*, 4(2), 104–114. doi:10.1016/j.jik.2017.07.003

Acele, B. (2020). *Investigation of Digital Footprint Concepts of Information Technology Teachers and Teacher Candidates*. [Unpublished Master Thesis, Institute of Education Sciences, Hacettepe University].

ADB. (2021). *Covid-19 and Education in Asia and the Pacific*. ADB.

Advisory Gropup, A. R. C. 2020. *What is Digitization, Digitalization, and Digital Transformation?* ARCweb. https://www.arcweb.com/blog/what-digitization-digitalization-digital-transformation

Ahad, A. D., & Anshari, M. (2017). Smartphone habits among youth: Uses and gratification theory. *International Journal of Cyber Behavior, Psychology and Learning*, 7(1), 65–75. doi:10.4018/IJCBPL.2017010105

Ahad, A. D., Anshari, M., & Razzaq, A. (2017). Domestication of smartphones among adolescents in Brunei darussalam. [IJCBPL]. *International Journal of Cyber Behavior, Psychology and Learning*, 7(4), 26–39. doi:10.4018/IJCBPL.2017100103

Ahmad, A. (2021, August 18). Siaran Brunei serentak siar bacaan surah Yasin bagi kekang Covid-19. *Utusan Digital*. https://www.utusan.com.my/luar-negara/2021/08/siaran-brunei-serentak-siar-bacaan-surah-yasin-bagi-kekang-covid-19/

Ahmad, N. (2022). Demography of Brunei. In *Routledge Handbook of Contemporary Brunei* (pp. 61–78). Routledge. doi:10.4324/9781003020431-5

Ahmed, Imy & Ramzan, Muqadas & Qazi, Tehmina & Jabeen, Shaista. (2011). An investigation of mobile phone consumption patterns among students and professionals; is there any difference?. *European Journal of Economics, Finance and Administrative Sciences,* 136-143.

Aiello, A. E., Renson, A., & Zivich, P. N. (2020). Social media– and Internet-based disease surveillance for public health. *Annual Review of Public Health*, 41(1), 1–18. doi:10.1146/annurev-publhealth-040119-094402 PMID:31905322

Aite. (2016). *The Evolution of Digital and Mobile Wallets*. Retrieved from: https://www.paymentscardsandmobile.com/wp-content/uploads/2016/10/The-Evoluti on-of-Digital-and-Mobile-Wallets.pdf

Akamatsu, R., Mochida, K., Shimpo, M., & Sakurazawa, H. (2017). Drivers' Lunch Break, Health, and Work Performance: A Study on Japanese Drivers at a Courier Company Who Skip Lunch. *Journal of Nutrition Education and Behavior*, *49*(7), S42. doi:10.1016/j.jneb.2017.05.335

Akanni, A. A., & Oduaran, C. A. (2022). Person-job fit and work-life balance of female nurses with cultural competence as a mediator: Evidence from Nigeria. *Frontiers of Nursing*, *9*(1), 81–86. doi:10.2478/fon-2022-0010

Akkoyunlu, B. & ve Yılmaz S. M. (2010). A study on teachers' numerical competencies. *Turkish Librarianship*, *24*(4), 748–768.

Alam, M. (2022). Mental health impact of online learning: A look into university students in Brunei Darussalam. *Asian Journal of Psychiatry*, *67*, 102933. doi:10.1016/j.ajp.2021.102933 PMID:34837832

Alas, Y., & Anshari, M. (2014). *Constructing strategy of online learning in higher education: Transaction cost economy.* arXiv preprint arXiv:1411.4345.

Alas, Y., Anshari, M., Sabtu, N. I., & Yunus, N. (2016). Second-chance university admission, the theory of planned behaviour and student achievement. *International Review of Education*, *62*(3), 299–316. doi:10.100711159-016-9558-5

Al-Heeti, A. (n.d.). *Beyond Tinder: How Muslim millennials are looking for love.* CNET. Retrieved 12 August 2022, from https://www.cnet.com/culture/tinder-minder-muzmatch-eshq-how-muslim-millennials-are-looking-for-love/

Ali, A., Muda, M., Ridzuan, A.R., Nuji, M.N.N., Izzamuddin, M.H.M., Latiff, D.I.A. (2017) The relationship between phone usage factors and nomophobia. *International Journal of Research in Education and Sciences, 23*, 7610–7613.

Almunawar, M. N., & Anshari, M. (2022). Customer acceptance of online delivery platform during the COVID-19 pandemic: the case of Brunei Darussalam. *Journal of Science and Technology Policy Management*, ahead-of-print.

Almunawar, M. N., & Anshari, M. (2022). Customer acceptance of online delivery platform during the COVID-19 pandemic: the case of Brunei Darussalam. *Journal of Science and Technology Policy Management.* doi:10.1108/JSTPM-04-2022-0073

Almunawar, M. N., Anshari, M., & Lim, S. A. (2020). Customer acceptance of ride-hailing in Indonesia. *Journal of Science and Technology Policy Management.*

Almunawar, M. N., & Anshari, M. (2014). Empowering customers in electronic health (e–health) through social customer relationship management. *International Journal of Electronic Customer Relationship Management*, *8*(1-3), 87–100. doi:10.1504/IJECRM.2014.066887

Almunawar, M. N., Anshari, M., Susanto, H., & Chen, C. K. (2015). Revealing customer behavior on smartphones. *International Journal of Asian Business and Information Management*, *6*(2), 33–49. doi:10.4018/IJABIM.2015040103

Almunawar, M. N., Anshari, M., Susanto, H., & Chen, C. K. (2018). How people choose and use their Smartphones. In *Management Strategies and Technology Fluidity in the Asian Business Sector* (pp. 235–252). IGI Global. doi:10.4018/978-1-5225-4056-4.ch014

Almunawar, M. N., Anshari, M., & Younis, M. Z. (2015). Incorporating customer empowerment in mobile health. *Health Policy and Technology*, *4*(4), 312–319. doi:10.1016/j.hlpt.2015.08.008

Almunawar, M. N., Wint, Z., Low, K. C., & Anshari, M. (2012). Customer expectation of e-health systems in Brunei Darussalam. *Journal of Health Care Finance*, *38*(4), 36–49. PMID:22894020

Alruwais, N., Wills, G., & Wald, M. (2018). Advantages and Challenges of Using e-Assessment. *International Journal of Information and Education Technology (IJIET)*, *8*(1), 34–37. doi:10.18178/ijiet.2018.8.1.1008

Alsalameh, A. M., Harisi, M. J., Alduayji, M. A., Almutham, A. A., & Mahmood, F. M. (2019). Evaluating the relationship between smartphone addiction/overuse and musculoskeletal pain among medical students at Qassim University. *Journal of Family Medicine and Primary Care*, *8*(9), 2953. doi:10.4103/jfmpc.jfmpc_665_19 PMID:31681674

Al-Samarraie, H. (2019). A Scoping Review of Videoconferencing Systems in Higher Education Learning Paradigms, Opportunities, and Challenges. *International Review of Research in Open and Distributed Learning*, *20*(3). Advance online publication. doi:10.19173/irrodl.v20i4.4037

Althoff, T., White, R.W., & Horvitz, E., (2016), Influence of Pokemon Go on Physical Activity: Study and Implication. *Journal of Medical Internet Research, 18*(12).

Altman, Y., & Baruch, Y. (2012). Global self-initiated corporate expatriate careers: A new era in international assignments? *Personnel Review*, *41*(2), 233–255. doi:10.1108/00483481211200051

Amarnath, R., Marimuthu, R., Jenitha, S., & Rajan, C. (2018). Impact of Heartfulness Meditation On Reducing Stress In Nursing Students: A Prospective Observational Study. *Int. J. Med. Res. Health Sci.*, *7*, 98–109.

Amiti, F. (2020). Synchronous and Asynchronous E-Learning. *European Journal of Open Education and E-learning Studies*, *5*(2). Advance online publication. doi:10.46827/ejoe.v5i2.3313

Anderson, B. J. (2017). *TALENT POOL A free, teacher-less university in France is schooling thousands of future-proof programmers*. Academic Press.

Anderson, C., Bieck, C., & Marshall, A. (2020). How business is adapting to COVID-19: Executive insights reveal post-pandemic opportunities. *Strategy and Leadership*, *49*(1), 38–47. doi:10.1108/SL-11-2020-0140

Annanperä, E., Jurmu, M., Kaivo-oja, J., Kettunen, P., Knudsen, M., Lauraéus, T., & Porras, J. (2021). From Industry X to Industry 6.0: Antifragile Manufacturing for People, Planet, and Profit with Passion. *Business Finland AIF, White Paper 5,* 1-38.

Anshari, M. & Alas, Y., Hardaker, G., Jaidin, J., Smith, M., & Abdullah, A. D. (2016). Smartphone habit and behaviour in Brunei: Personalization, gender, and generation gap. *Computers in Human behaviour. 64*, 719- 727. doi:. doi:10.1016/j.chb.2016.07.063

Anshari, M. (2021). *E-Health Management Services in Supporting Empowerment.* Cornell University.

Anshari, M., & Almunawar, M. N. (2021). Adopting open innovation for SMEs and industrial revolution 4.0. *Journal of Science and Technology Policy Management.*

Anshari, M., & Hamdan, M. (2022). Enhancing e-government with a digital twin for innovation management. *Journal of Science and Technology Policy Management*, ahead-of-print.

Anshari, M., & Hamdan, M. (2022a). Enhancing e-government with a digital twin for innovation management. *Journal of Science and Technology Policy Management.* doi:10.1108/ JSTPM-11-2021-0176

Anshari, M., Alas, Y., & Yunus, N. (2019). A survey study of smartphones behavior in Brunei: A proposal of Modelling big data strategies. In Multigenerational Online Behavior and Media Use: Concepts, Methodologies, Tools, and Applications (pp. 201-214). IGI Global.

Anshari, M., Alas, Y., Razzaq, A., Shahrill, M., & Lim, S. A. (2021). Millennials consumers' behaviors between trends and experiments. In Research Anthology on E-Commerce Adoption, Models, and Applications for Modern Business (pp. 1492-1508). IGI Global.

Anshari, M., Almunawar, M. N., & Masri, M. (2020). An overview of financial technology in Indonesia. *Financial technology and disruptive innovation in ASEAN*, 216-224.

Anshari, M. (2020, March). Workforce mapping of fourth industrial revolution: Optimization to identity. *Journal of Physics: Conference Series, 1477*(7), 072023. doi:10.1088/1742-6596/1477/7/072023

Anshari, M., & Alas, Y. (2015). Smartphones habits, necessities, and big data challenges. *The Journal of High Technology Management Research, 26*(2), 177–185. doi:10.1016/j. hitech.2015.09.005

Anshari, M., Alas, Y., & Guan, L. S. (2016). Developing online learning resources: Big data, social networks, and cloud computing to support pervasive knowledge. *Education and Information Technologies, 21*(6), 1663–1677. doi:10.100710639-015-9407-3

Anshari, M., Alas, Y., & Guan, L. S. (2017). Pervasive knowledge, social networks, and cloud computing: E-learning 2.0. *Eurasia Journal of Mathematics, Science and Technology Education, 11*(5), 909–921. doi:10.12973/eurasia.2015.1360a

Anshari, M., Alas, Y., Hamid, M. H. S. A., & Smith, M. (2016). Learning management system 2.0: Higher education. In *Handbook of research on engaging digital natives in higher education settings* (pp. 265–279). IGI Global. doi:10.4018/978-1-5225-0039-1.ch012

Anshari, M., Alas, Y., Sabtu, N. P. H., & Hamid, M. S. A. (2016). Online Learning: Trends, issues and challenges in the Big Data Era. *Journal of E-learning and Knowledge Society*, *12*(1).

Anshari, M., Alas, Y., & Sulaiman, E. (2019b). Smartphone addictions and nomophobia among youth. *Vulnerable Children and Youth Studies*, *14*(3), 242–247. doi:10.1080/17450128.2019.1 614709

Anshari, M., Alas, Y., Yunus, N., Sabtu, N. I., & Hamid, M. H. (2015). Social customer relationship management and student empowerment in online learning systems. *International Journal of Electronic Customer Relationship Management*, *9*(2-3), 104–121. doi:10.1504/IJECRM.2015.071711

Anshari, M., Almunawar, M. N., Lim, S. A., & Al-Mudimigh, A. (2019a). Customer relationship management and big data enabled: Personalization & customization of services. *Applied Computing and Informatics*, *15*(2), 94–101. doi:10.1016/j.aci.2018.05.004

Anshari, M., Almunawar, M. N., Low, P. K. C., & Al-Mudimigh, A. S. (2013a). Empowering clients through e-health in healthcare services: Case Brunei. *International Quarterly of Community Health Education*, *33*(2), 189–219. doi:10.2190/IQ.33.2.g PMID:23661419

Anshari, M., Almunawar, M. N., Low, P. K. C., Wint, Z., & Younis, M. Z. (2013b). Adopting customers' empowerment and social networks to encourage participations in e-health services. *Journal of Health Care Finance*, *40*(2), 17–41. PMID:24551960

Anshari, M., Almunawar, M. N., & Masri, M. (2020). Financial Technology and Disruptive Innovation in Business: Concept and Application. *International Journal of Asian Business and Information Management*, *11*(4), 29–43. doi:10.4018/IJABIM.2020100103

Anshari, M., Almunawar, M. N., & Masri, M. (2022). Digital Twin: Financial Technology's Next Frontier of Robo-Advisor. *Journal of Risk and Financial Management*, *15*(4), 163. doi:10.3390/jrfm15040163

Anshari, M., Almunawar, M. N., Masri, M., & Hamdan, M. (2019c). Digital marketplace and FinTech to support agriculture sustainability. *Energy Procedia*, *156*, 234–238. doi:10.1016/j.egypro.2018.11.134

Anshari, M., Almunawar, M. N., Masri, M., Hamdan, M., Fithriyah, M., & Fitri, A. (2021a). Digital Wallet in Supporting Green FinTech Sustainability. In *2021 Third International Sustainability and Resilience Conference: Climate Change* (pp. 352-357). IEEE. 10.1109/IEEECONF53624.2021.9667957

Anshari, M., Almunawar, M. N., Masri, M., & Hrdy, M. (2021). Financial technology with ai-enabled and ethical challenges. *Society*, *58*(3), 189–195. doi:10.100712115-021-00592-w

Anshari, M., Almunawar, M. N., & Razzaq, A. (2021b). Developing talents vis-à-vis fourth industrial revolution. *International Journal of Asian Business and Information Management*, *12*(4), 20–32. doi:10.4018/IJABIM.20211001.oa2

Anshari, M., Almunawar, M. N., Shahrill, M., Wicaksono, D. K., & Huda, M. (2017). Smartphones usage in the classrooms: Learning aid or interference? *Education and Information Technologies*, *22*(6), 3063–3079. doi:10.100710639-017-9572-7

Anshari, M., Almunawar, M. N., Younis, M. Z., & Kisa, A. (2021). Modeling Users' Empowerment in E-Health Systems. *Sustainability*, *13*(23), 12993. doi:10.3390u132312993

Anshari, M., Almunawar, M., & Masri, M. (2021a). Financial Technology Promoting Healthy Lifestyle and Community Development. In *Proceedings of the 1st International Conference on Law, Social Science, Economics, and Education, ICLSSEE 2021, Jakarta, Indonesia.* 10.4108/eai.6-3-2021.2306396

Anshari, M., Arine, M. A., Nurhidayah, N., Aziyah, H., & Salleh, M. H. A. (2021). Factors influencing individual in adopting eWallet. *Journal of Financial Services Marketing*, *26*(1), 10–23. doi:10.105741264-020-00079-5

Anshari, M., Fithriyah, M., Polak, P., & Razzaq, A. (2021). Islamic FinTech and artificial intelligence (AI) for assessing creditworthiness. In *Artificial Intelligence and Islamic Finance* (pp. 48–60). Routledge. doi:10.4324/9781003171638-4

Anshari, M., & Hamdan, M. (2022b). Understanding knowledge management and upskilling in Fourth Industrial Revolution: Transformational shift and SECI model. *VINE Journal of Information and Knowledge Management Systems.* doi:10.1108/VJIKMS-09-2021-0203

Anshari, M., Hamdan, M., Ahmad, N., Ali, E., & Haidi, H. (2022). COVID-19, artificial intelligence, ethical challenges and policy implications. *AI & Society*, 1–14. doi:10.100700146-022-01471-6 PMID:35607368

Anshari, M., Hasmawati, F., Razzaq, A., & Samiha, Y. T. (2020). Understanding Nomophobia Among Digital Natives: Characteristics And Challenges. *Journal of Critical Reviews*, *7*(13), 122–131.

Anshari, M., & Lim, S. A. (2017). E-government with big data enabled through smartphone for public services: Possibilities and challenges. *International Journal of Public Administration*, *40*(13), 1143–1158. doi:10.1080/01900692.2016.1242619

Anshari, M., Syafrudin, M., & Fitriyani, N. L. (2022). Fourth Industrial Revolution between Knowledge Management and Digital Humanities. *Information (Basel)*, *13*(6), 292. doi:10.3390/info13060292

APEC. (2020). *Brunei Darussalam and COVID-19: Shifting Towards Digital Transformation.* Retrieved from: http://mddb.apec.org/Documents/2020/MM/SMEMM/20_smemm_016.pdf

Appiah, M., & van Tonder, F. (2018). E-Assessment in Higher Education: A Review. *International Journal of Business Management and Economic Research*, *9*(6), 1454–1460.

Apple Health guide: The powerful fitness app explained. (2022, April 14). Wareable. https://www.wareable.com/health-and-wellbeing/apple-health-guide-apps-wearables-8016

Apple Watch | History, Features, Specs, Deals. (n.d.). AppleInsider. Retrieved 12 August 2022, from https://appleinsider.com/inside/apple-watch

Apple, (2018), ios 12 introduces new features to reduce interruptions and manage Screen Time. *Apple Newsroom*. https://www.apple.com/newsroom/2018/06/ios-12-introduces-new- features-to-reduce-interruptions-and-manage-screen-time/

Araka, E., Maina, E., Gitonga, R., Oboko, R., & Kihoro, J. (2021). University Students' Perception on the Usefulness of Learning Management System Features in Promoting Self-Regulated Learning in Online Learning. *IJEDICT*, *17*, 45–64.

Arakerimath, P. A. R., & Gupta, P. K. (2015). Digital footprint: Pros, cons, and future. *International Journal of Latest Technology in Engineering*, *4*(10), 52–56.

Ardèvol, E. (2005, Aralık). Cyberculture: Anthropological perspectives of the internet. Using anthropological theory to understand media forms a practices workshop. *European Association of Social Anthropologists (EASA) Media Anthropology Network*. https:// eardevol.files.wordpress. com/2008/10/cyberculture.pdf

Arslan, G., Yıldırım, M., Tanhan, A., Buluş, M., & Allen, K. A. (2020). Coronavirus Stress, Optimism-Pessimism, Psychological Inflexibility, and Psychological Health: Psychometric Properties of the Coronavirus Stress Measure. International Journal of Mental Health and Addiction. doi:10.100711469-020-00337-6

Arthur, M. B., & Rousseau, D. M. (1996). The Boundaryless Career as a New Employment Principle. In M. B. Arthur amd D. M. Rousseau (eds.) The Boundaryless Career, pp. 3-20. Oxford University Press.

Aruma, E. O., & Hanachor, M. E. (2017, December). *Abraham Maslow's Hierarchy of Needs and Assessment of Needs In Community Development*. https://www.eajournals.org/wp-content/uploads/Abraham-Maslow%E2%80%99s-Hi erarchy-of-Needs-and-Assessment-of-Needs-in-Community-Development.pdf

Arya, N. K., Singh, K., Malik, A., & Mehrotra, R. (2018). Effect of Heartfulness Cleaning And Meditation On Heart Rate Variability. *Indian Heart Journal*, *70*, S50–S55. doi:10.1016/j.ihj.2018.05.004 PMID:30595318

Aswathy, V., Devika, E., & Girish, S. (2019, June). A Study on Impact of Online Gaming and Its Addiction among Youth with Special Reference to Kerala. *International Journal of Management, IT & Engineering*, *9*(6), 308–316.

Audrin, C., & Audrin, B. (2022). Key factors in digital literacy in learning and education: A systematic literature review using text mining. *Education and Information Technologies*, *27*(6), 1–25. doi:10.100710639-021-10832-5

Australian National University. (n.d), *Physical Wellbeing*, ANU. https://www.anu.edu.au/covid-19-advice/health-wellbeing/strategies-for-wellbeing-at- home-or-on-campus/physical-wellbeing

Ayu, M. (2020). Online Learning: Leading E-Learning at Higher Education. *The Journal of English Literacy Education*, *7*(1), 47–54. doi:10.36706/jele.v7i1.11515

Azlan, C. A., Wong, J. S. D., Tan, L. K., & Tan, A. D., Huri, M. S., Ung, N. M., Pallath, V., C. P. L., Yeong, C. H., & Ng, K. H. (2020). Teaching and learning of postgraduate medical physics using Internet-based e-learning during the COVID-19 pandemic - A case study from *Malaysia. Physica Medica*, *80*, 10–16. doi:10.1016/j.ejmp.2020.10.002 PMID:33070007

Azucar, D., Marengo, D., & Settanni, M. (2018). Predicting the Big 5 Personality Traits from Digital Footprints on Social Media: A Meta-Analysis. *Personality and Individual Differences*, *124*, 150–159. doi:10.1016/j.paid.2017.12.018

Bagheri, E., Esteban, P. G., Cao, H. L., Beir, A. D., Lefeber, D., & Vanderborght, B. (2020). An autonomous cognitive empathy model responsive to users' facial emotion expressions. *ACM Transactions on Interactive Intelligent Systems*, *10*(3), 1–23. doi:10.1145/3341198

Baiyere, A., Salmela, H., & Tapanainen, T. (2020). Digital transformation and the new logics of business process management. *European Journal of Information Systems*, *29*(3), 238–259. doi:10.1080/0960085X.2020.1718007

Barnes, S. A., Green, A., & De Hoyos, M. (2015). Crowdsourcing and work: Individual factors and circumstances influencing employability. *New Technology, Work and Employment*, *30*(1), 16–31. doi:10.1111/ntwe.12043

Bartwal, J., & Nath, B. (2019). Evaluation of nomophobia among medical students using smartphone in north India. *Medical Journal, Armed Forces India*. PMID:33162655

Baruch, Y. (2004). Transforming careers: from linear to multidirectional career paths: organizational and individual perspectives. *Career Development International*, *9*(1), 58–73. doi:10.1108/13620430410518147

Baruch, Y. (2006). Career development in organizations and beyond: Balancing traditional and contemporary viewpoints. *Human Resource Management Review*, *16*(2), 125–138. doi:10.1016/j.hrmr.2006.03.002

Baruch, Y., & Rosenstein, E. (1992). Human resource management in Israeli firms: Planning and managing careers in high technology organizations. *International Journal of Human Resource Management*, *3*(3), 477–495. doi:10.1080/09585199200000161

Baştürk Akca, E., Sayımer, İ., & Balaban Salı, J., & ve Ergün Başak, B. (2014). Causes and types of cyberbullying and the place of media literacy education in preventive studies. *Electronic Journal of Professional Development and Research*, *2*, 17–30.

BDCB. (2020). *The State of FinTech in Brunei Darussalam*. Retrieved from: https://www.bdcb.gov.bn/SiteAssets/Lists/Publications/White-Paper-State-of-FinTec h-Brunei-Darussalam-2020.pdf

Beattie, A., & Daubs, M. S. (2020). Framing'digital well-being'as a social good. *First Monday*. doi:10.5210/fm.v25i12.10430

Bell, D. (2001). *An introduction to cybercultures*. Routledge.

Belsey, B. (2007). Cyberbullying: A real and growing threat. *ATA Magazine*, *88*(1), 14–21.

Benavides, L. M. C., Arias, J. A. T., Serna, M. D. A., Bedoya, J. W. B., & Burgos, D. (2020). Digital Transformation in Higher Education Institutions: A Systematic Literature Review. *Sensors (Basel)*, *20*(3291), 3291. doi:10.339020113291 PMID:32526998

Bennett, S., Maton, K., & Kervin, L. (2008). The 'digital natives debate: A critical review of the evidence. *British Journal of Educational Technology*, *39*(5), 775–786. doi:10.1111/j.1467-8535.2007.00793.x

Benz, M., & Frey, B. S. (2008). The value of doing what you like: Evidence from the self-employed in 23 countries. *Journal of Economic Behavior & Organization*, *68*(3-4), 445–455. doi:10.1016/j.jebo.2006.10.014

Berry, K. (2011). The Ethnographic Choice: Why Ethnographers Do Ethnography. *Cultural Studies. Critical Methodologies*, *11*(2), 165–177. doi:10.1177/1532708611401335

Best, J. (2021). Undermined and undervalued: how the pandemic exacerbated moral injury and burnout in the NHS. *BMJ,* n1858. doi:10.1136/bmj.n1858

Bhatti, A., Akram, H., Basit, H. M., Khan, A. U., Naqvi, S. M. R., & Bilal, M. (2020). E-Commerce during COVID-19 Pandemic. *International Journal of Future Generation Communication and Networking.*, *13*(2), 1449–1452.

Bian, M., & Leung, L. (2015). Linking loneliness, shyness, smartphone addiction symptoms, and patterns of smartphone use to social capital. *Social Science Computer Review*, *33*(1), 61–79. doi:10.1177/0894439314528779

BIBD on Instagram. (2021). *'During these challenging times, it's important more than ever to take care of our mental health. BIBD is pleased to invite members to tune in to the 2nd session of motivational talks about mental health titled - Hold That Thought! The session will be covering mental health awareness from an islamic perspective with Ustaz Awang Muhammad Yussof bin Hj Abdul Majid, Special Duties Officer from the Religious Counselling and Understanding Department, MORA. Join us on this Friday, 22nd October 2021 on our BIBD IG Live or via this Zoom link* https://us02web.zoom.us/j/89072949006 *(Link allso available via our IG profile and Telegram group) #bibdbrunei #bibdmotivational #MentalHealthMatters'*. Instagram. https://www.instagram.com/p/CVSDHDyhgUk/

BIBD on Instagram: *'During these challenging times, it's important more than ever to take care of our mental health. This session covered mental health …'*. (n.d.). Retrieved 5 November 2021, from https://www.instagram.com/p/CVrpbEJBPH0/

BIBD. (2020). *The State of FinTech in Brunei Darussalam*. Retrieved from: http://www.bibd.com.bn/assets/pdf/media-centre/annual-report/BIBD_Annual_Repo rt_2020_ENG_online.pdf

Bilton, N. (2014, October 29). Tinder, the Fast-Growing Dating App, Taps an Age-Old Truth. *The New York Times*. https://www.nytimes.com/2014/10/30/fashion/tinder-the-fast-growing-dating-app-taps-an-age-old-truth.html

Binder, M. (2018). *The way to wellbeing. A multidimensional strategy for improving wellbeing of the self-employed.* Center for research on self-employment. http://crse.co.uk/sites/default/files/The%20Way%20to%20Wellbeing%20Full% 20Report_0.pdf

Binder, M., & Blankenberg, A. K. (2020). Self-employment and subjective well-being. Handbook of Labor, Human Resources and Population Economics, 1-25.

Black, A., & Black, P. (2018). Going Global: Australia Looks to Internationalise Legal Education. In Legal Education in Asia: From Imitation to Innovation (p. 54). Koninklijke Brill NV.

Blanchflower, D. G. (2000). Self-employment in OECD countries. *Labour Economics*, 7(5), 471–505. doi:10.1016/S0927-5371(00)00011-7

Block, J. H., & Wagner, M. (2010). Necessity and Opportunity Entrepreneurs in Germany: Characteristics and Earnings Differentials. *Schmalenbach Business Review*, 62(2), 154–174. doi:10.1007/BF03396803

Bodhani, A. (2012). Digital footprints step up. *Engineering & Technology*, 7(1), 82–83. doi:10.1049/et.2012.0125

Boguszewicz, C., Boguszewicz, M., Iqbal, Z., Khan, S., Gaba, G. S., Suresh, A., & Pervaiz, B. (2021). The fourth industrial revolution-cyberspace mental wellbeing: Harnessing science & technology for humanity. *White Paper.* Global foundation for cyber studies and research.

Bond, M., Marin, V. I., Dolch, C., Bedenlier, S., & Zawacki-Richter, O. (2018). Article. *International Journal of Educational Technology in Higher Education*, 15(48). Advance online publication. doi:10.118641239-018-0130-1

Borneo Bulletin. (2019, March 13). *Digital Economy Council established to facilitate 'Smart Nation' drive.* https://borneobulletin.com.bn/digital-economic-council-established-to-facilitate-sma rt-nation-drive/

Bose, T. K. (2012). Application of fishbone analysis for evaluating supply chain and business process-a case study on the St James Hospital. *International Journal of Managing Value and Supply Chains*, 3(2), 17–24. doi:10.5121/ijmvsc.2012.3202

Braña, F. J. (2019). A fourth industrial revolution? Digital transformation, labor and work organization: A view from Spain. *Economia e Politica Industriale*, 46(3), 415–430. doi:10.100740812-019-00122-0

Braun, V., & Clarke, V. (2012). Thematic Analysis. *APA handbook of research methods in psychology, 2*, 57-71. https://www.researchgate.net/publication/269930410_Thematic_analysis

Bray, J. H., & Howard, G. S. (1980). Methodological considerations in the evaluation of a teacher-training program. *Journal of Educational Psychology*, 72(1), 62–70. doi:10.1037/0022-0663.72.1.62

Brennen, J. S., & Kreiss, D. (2016a). Information society. *The international encyclopedia of communication theory and philosophy*, 1-8.

Brennen, J. S., & Kreiss, D. (2016b). Digitalization. *The international encyclopedia of communication theory and philosophy*, 1-11.

Briscoe, G., & Wilde, P. D. (2006). Digital ecosystems: evolving service-orientated architectures. In *Proceedings of the 1st International Conference on Bio Inspired Models of Network, Information and Computing Systems (BIONETICS '06)*. ACM.

Brunei Climate Change Secretariat. (2020). Brunei National Climate Change Policy.

Brunei to launch new law to protect personal data—Xinhua. (n.d.). Retrieved 13 August 2022, from http://www.xinhuanet.com/english/2021-05/22/c_139963856.htm

Brunei woman loses RM153,000 to yet another 'love scam'. (n.d.). Retrieved 13 August 2022, from https://www.theborneopost.com/2019/08/27/brunei-woman-loses-rm153000-to-yet-another-love-scam/

Bruneians lose big money on romance scams online. (n.d.). *Borneo Post Online*. Retrieved 13 August 2022, from https://www.theborneopost.com/2012/07/13/bruneians-lose-big-money-on-romance-scams-online/

Brunei—ECommerce. (n.d.). Retrieved 12 August 2022, from https://www.trade.gov/country-commercial-guides/brunei-ecommerce

Brynjolfsson, E., & Kahin, B. (Eds.). (2002). *Understanding the digital economy: data, tools, and research*. MIT press.

Buchanan, R., Southgate, E., Smith, S. P., Murray, T., & Noble, B. (2017). Post no photos, leave no trace: Children's digital footprint management strategies. *E-Learning and Digital Media*, 14(5), 275–290. doi:10.1177/2042753017751711

Büchi, M. (2020). *A proto-theory of digital well-being*. OSF. https://osf. io/k3e2j

Büchi, M., Lutz, C., & Micheli, M. (2017, May). Life online: The digital footprint gap. *International Scientific Conference for the Partnership for Progress on the Digital Divide*.

Büchi, M. (2021). Digital well-being theory and research. *New Media & Society*, 1–20. doi:10.1177/14614448211056851

Buckley, R., Arner, D., & Barberis, J. (2016). The Evolution of Fintech: A New Post-Crisis Paradigm? *Georgetown Journal of International Law*, 47, 1271–1319. doi:10.2139srn.2676553

Bughin, J., Byers, A. H., & Chui, M. (2011). How social technologies are extending the organization. *The McKinsey Quarterly*, 20(11), 1–10.

Bugiotti, F., Goasdoué, F., Kaoudi, Z., & Manolescu, I. (2012, March). RDF data management in the Amazon cloud. In *Proceedings of the 2012 Joint EDBT/ICDT Workshops* (pp. 61-72). 10.1145/2320765.2320790

Bunt, G. R. (2009). *IMuslims: Rewiring the House of Islam.* Univ of North Carolina Press.

Bunt, G. R. (2018). *Hashtag Islam: How Cyber-Islamic Environmenonts Are Transforming Religious Authority.* University of North Carolina Press. doi:10.5149/northcarolina/9781469643168.001.0001

Burnham, C. (2018). *Does the internet have an unconscious?: Slavoj Zizek and digital culture.* Bloomsbury.

Bush, V. (1945). As we may think. *Atlantic Monthly, 176*(1), 101–108.

Buttarelli, G. (2017). Privacy matters: Updating human rights for the digital society. *Health and Technology, 7*(4), 325–328. doi:10.100712553-017-0198-y

CABS. (2021). *National Student Survey 2021 : Results for Law.* National Student Survey 2021. https://charteredabs.org/national-student-survey-2021-results-for-law/

Cahuc, P., & Postel-Vinay, F. (2002). Temporary jobs, employment protection and labor market performance. *Labour Economics, 9*(1), 63–91. doi:10.1016/S0927-5371(01)00051-3

Calhoun, J. (2015). *Antacedents and Consequences of Lodging Employees' Career Success: An Application of Motivational Theories* [Doctoral dissertation, Auburn University, USA].

Calvani, A., Cartelli, A., Fini, A., & Ranieri, M. (2008). Models and instruments for assessing digital competence at school. *Journal of e-Learning and Knowledge Society, 4*(3), 183-193.

Camacho, M., Minelli, J., & Grosseck, G. (2012). Self and identity: Raising undergraduate students' awareness of their digital footprints. *Procedia: Social and Behavioral Sciences, 46,* 3176–3181. doi:10.1016/j.sbspro.2012.06.032

Camila, S., Pereira, P., & Pereira-pereira, P. A. (2021). Capitalist Greed, Pandemic, and the Future of Social Policy. *Argumentum, 13*(1), 53–65.

Capritto, A. (n.d.). *The complete guide to Apple's Health app.* CNET. Retrieved 12 August 2022, from https://www.cnet.com/health/the-complete-guide-to-apples-health-app/

Carey, R. N., Donaghue, N., & Broderick, P. (2014). Body image concern among Australian adolescent girls: The role of body comparisons with models and peers. *Body Image, 11*(1), 81–84. doi:10.1016/j.bodyim.2013.09.006 PMID:24148894

Carpenter, M. (2021). A Digital Mindset Will Revolutionize Education: Legal Education as a Global Model Article By. *National Law Review, 11*(266). https://www.natlawreview.com/article/digital-mindset-will-revolutionize-education-legal-education-global-model

Carter, N. M., Gartner, W. B., Shaver, K. G., & Gatewood, E. J. (2003). The Career Reasons of Nascent Entrepreneurs. *Journal of Business Venturing, 18*(1), 13–39. doi:10.1016/S0883-9026(02)00078-2

Casillano, N. F. B. (2019). Challenges of Implementing an E-learning Platform in an Internet Struggling Province in the Philippines. *Indian Journal of Science and Technology*, *12*(10), 12. doi:10.17485/ijst/2019/v12i10/137594

Castro, R. (2019). Blended learning in higher education: Trends and capabilities. *Education and Information Technologies*, *24*(4), 2523–2546. Advance online publication. doi:10.100710639-019-09886-3

Çelik, K. & ve Sökmen, A. (2018). The Effect of Perceived Performance on Satisfaction of E-Learning Users. *Electronic Turkish Studies*, *13*(21), 73–92.

Ceruzzi, P. E. (2003). *A history of modern computing*. MIT press.

CGTN. (2021, October 12). *COVID-19 Live Updates: Global cases surpass 238 million*. CGTN. https://www.cgtn.com/special/Latest-updates-on-COVID-19-pandemic.html

Chalmers, I., & Altman, D. G. (Eds.). (1995). *Systematic reviews* (pp. 86–95). BMJ Publishing.

Cheever, N. A., Rosen, L. D., Carrier, L. M., & Chavez, A. (2014). Out of sight is not out of mind: The impact of restricting wireless mobile device use on anxiety levels among low, moderate and high users. *Computers in Human Behavior*, *37*, 290–297. doi:10.1016/j.chb.2014.05.002

Chen, B. X. (2012). Get Ready for 1 Billion Smartphones by 2016, Forrester Says. *New York Times*. https://bits.blogs.nytimes.com/2012/02/13/get-ready-for-1-billion-smartphones-by-2016-forrester-says/

Chen, C. L. (2019). Value creation by SMEs participating in global value chains under industry 4.0 trend: Case study of textile industry in Taiwan. *Journal of Global Information Technology Management*, *22*(2), 120–145. doi:10.1080/1097198X.2019.1603512

Chen, C., Chen, X., Wang, L., Ma, X., Wang, Z., Liu, K., & Zhou, Z. (2017). MA-SSR: A memetic algorithm for skyline scenic routes planning leveraging heterogeneous user-generated digitalfootprints. *IEEE Transactions on Vehicular Technology*, *66*(7), 5723–5736. doi:10.1109/TVT.2016.2639550

Chin, C. Y., & Wang, C. L. (2020). Effectiveness of COVID-19 pandemic prevention: A cross-country comparison of digital footprint of google search data. *Advances in Management and Applied Economics*, *10*(4), 23–34.

Choon, C. M. (2021, June 14). South Korea's delivery workers go on strike against overwork amid Covid-19. *The Straits Times*. https://www.straitstimes.com/asia/east-asia/south-koreas-delivery-workers-go-on-strike-against-overwork-amid-covid-19

Christie, A., & Barling, J. (2006). Careers and health. Encyclopedia of career development, 1, 158-62.

CIA. (2022). Brunei. In *The World Factbook*. Central Intelligence Agency. https://www.cia.gov/the-world-factbook/countries/brunei

Ciotti, M., Ciccozzi, M., Terrinoni, A., Jiang, W. C., Wang, C. B., & Bernardini, S. (2020). The COVID-19 pandemic. *Critical Reviews in Clinical Laboratory Sciences, 57*(6), 365–388. doi:1 0.1080/10408363.2020.1783198 PMID:32645276

Circular Letter of Indonesia Ministry of Education, Culture, Research and Technology No.2 Year 2022, Pub. L. No. No.2 Year 2022 (2022).

Clayton, R. B., Leshner, G., & Almond, A. (2015). The Extended iSelf: The Impact of iPhone Separation on Cognition, Emotion, and Physiology. *Journal of Computer-Mediated Communication, 20*(2), 119–135. doi:10.1111/jcc4.12109

Cohen, G. L., & Sherman, D. K. (2014). The psychology of change: Self-affirmation and social psychological intervention. *Annual Review of Psychology, 65*(1), 333–371. doi:10.1146/annurev-psych-010213-115137 PMID:24405362

Cole, A., McFaddin, S., Narayanawasmi, C., & Tiwari, A. (2009). *Toward a Mobile Digital Wallet. IBM research report.* Retrieved from: https://dominoweb.draco.res.ibm.com/reports/RC24965.pdf

Coleman, S. & ve Ross, K. (2010). The media and the public "Them" and "Us" in media discourse. Wiley-Blackwell.

Compagnucci, M. C., Kono, T., Teramoto, S., & Vermeulen, E. P. M. (2020). *Legal Tech and the New Sharing Economy.* http://link.springer.com/10.1007/978-981-15-1350-3

Copeland, W. E., Angold, A., Shanahan, L., & Costello, E. J. (2014). Longitudinal Patterns Of Anxiety From Childhood To Adulthood: The Great Smoky Mountains Study. *Journal of the American Academy of Child and Adolescent Psychiatry, 53*(1), 21–33. doi:10.1016/j.jaac.2013.09.017 PMID:24342383

Correa, G. (2022). *Shopping Addiction Fueled by Online Shopping.* https://www.addictioncenter.com/news/2020/01/shopping-addiction-online-shopping/

Crowdfunding Incredible Muslims | LaunchGood. (n.d.). Retrieved 19 August 2022, from https://www.launchgood.com/

Csavina, J., Field, J., Félix, O., Corral-Avitia, A. Y., Sáez, A. E., & Betterton, E. A. (2014). Effect of wind speed and relative humidity on atmospheric dust concentrations in semi-arid climates. *The Science of the Total Environment, 487,* 82–90. doi:10.1016/j.scitotenv.2014.03.138 PMID:24769193

Çubukçu, A., ve Bayzan, Ş. (2013). Digital citizenship perception in Turkey and methods to increase this perception with conscious, safe and effective internet use. *Middle Eastern & African Journal of Educational Research, 5,* 148–174.

Czodli, B. (2016). *Privacy and security online: Protecting your digital footprint.* Retrieved from http://www.users.miamioh.edu/viscokj/IMS201/website/chapter-04.html

Dada, E. G., Alkali, A. H., & Oyewola, D. O. (2019). An Investigation into the Effectiveness of Asynchronous and Synchronous E-learning Mode on Students' Academic Performance in National Open University (NOUN). *Maiduguri Centre. I. J. Modern Education and Computer Science*, *5*, 54–64.

Daniel, J. (2020). Education and the COVID-19 pandemic. *Prospects*, *49*(1-2), 91–96. doi:10.100711125-020-09464-3 PMID:32313309

Darlington, N. (2014). Freelancer vs. Contractor vs. Employee: What Are You Being Hired As. *Freshbooks*. https://www.freshbooks.com/blog/are-you-being-hired-as-an-employee-or-freelancer

Dasar, B. (2017). *Perancangan dan Penyelidikan, K. H. E. U* (1st ed.). Dasar-Dasar Kementerian Hal Ehwal Ugama.

Davenport, T. H. (2005). *Thinking for a living: how to get better performances and results from knowledge workers*. Harvard Business Press.

David, M. E., & Roberts, J. A. (2021). Smartphone Use during the COVID-19 Pandemic: Social Versus Physical Distancing. *International Journal of Environmental Research and Public Health*, *18*(3), 1034. doi:10.3390/ijerph18031034 PMID:33503907

Davies, R. (n.d.). *The young Muslims finding love via an app*. Retrieved 12 August 2022, from https://www.aljazeera.com/features/2016/11/27/the-young-muslims-finding-love-via-an-app

Davis, S. N., Shevchuk, A., & Strebkov, D. (2014). Pathways to satisfaction with work-life balance: The case of Russian-language internet freelancers. *Journal of Family and Economic Issues*, *35*(4), 542–556. doi:10.100710834-013-9380-1

De Oliveira Fornasier, M. (2021). Legal Education in the 21st Century and the Artificial Intelligence. *Revista Opiniao Juridica*, *19*(31), 1–32. doi:10.12662/2447-6641oj.v19i31.p1-32.2021

De Simone, S., Cicotto, G., & Lampis, J. (2016). Occupational stress, job satisfaction and physical health in teachers. *European Review of Applied Psychology*, *66*(2), 65–77. doi:10.1016/j.erap.2016.03.002

De Vos, A., & Van der Heijden, B. I. (2017). Current thinking on contemporary careers: The key roles of sustainable HRM and sustainability of careers. *Current Opinion in Environmental Sustainability*, *28*, 41–50. doi:10.1016/j.cosust.2017.07.003

Deccax, R. A., & Campani, C. H. (2022). Segmentation of current and potential investors in retirement plans to retain and capture customers. Brazilian Business Review (Portuguese Edition), 19(1). doi:10.15728/bbr.2022.19.1.2

DeFillippi, R. J., & Arthur, M. B. (1994). The boundaryless career: A competency-based perspective. *Journal of Organizational Behavior*, *15*(4), 307–324. doi:10.1002/job.4030150403

Deli, F. (2011). Opportunity and Necessity Entrepreneurship: Local Unemployment and the Small Firm Effect. *Journal of Management Policy and Practice*, *12*(4), 38–57.

Demir, Y. P., & Sumer, M. M. (2019). Effects of smartphone overuse on headache, sleep and quality of life in migraine patients. *Neurosciences, 24*(2), 115–120. doi:10.17712/nsj.2019.2.20180037 PMID:31056543

Denzin, N. K., & Lincoln, Y. S. (Eds.). (2011). *The Sage handbook of qualitative research* (4th ed.). Sage.

Department of Economic Planning and Statistics—Population. (n.d.). Retrieved 18 August 2022, from https://deps.mofe.gov.bn/SitePages/Population.aspx

Department of Statistics. (2021). *Brunei Darussalam Key Indicators 2020.* Department of Economic Planning and Statistics Ministry of Finance and Economy Brunei Darussalam. http://www.deps.gov.bn/DEPD%20Documents%20Library/DOS/BDKI/BDKI_2020.pdf

Desa, N. M., Asaari, M. H. A. H., & Yim, L. C. (2020). Human Resource Management Practices and Job Satisfaction among Courier Service Provider Employees. *International Journal of Asian Social Science, 10*(6), 327–338. doi:10.18488/journal.1.2020.106.327.338

Deutschkron & Pearce. (2019). Sixth annual "Freelancing in America" study finds that more people than ever see freelancing as a long-term career path. *Buisnesswire.* https://www.businesswire.com/news/home/20191003005032/en/Sixth-annual-%E2%80%9CFreelancing-America%E2%80%9D-study-finds-people .

Diener, E. D., Emmons, R. A., Larsen, R. J., & Griffin, S. (1985). The satisfaction with life scale. *Journal of Personality Assessment, 49*(1), 71–75.

Diener, E., Oishi, S., & Lucas, R. E. (2003). Personality, culture, and subjective well–being. *Annual Review of Psychology, 54*(1), 403–425. doi:10.1146/annurev.psych.54.101601.145056 PMID:12172000

Digital Citizenship Adventures. (2017). Managing your digital footprint. *Google.* https://sites.google.com/site/digcitizenshipadventures/managing-your-digital-footprint

Dimitrov, B. E. G., & Nongkynrih, N. (2017). A Study On Social Media And Its Impact On Youth, International Journal of Creative Research Thoughts. *International Conference People Connect: Networking For Sustainable Development*, 149-158.

Dimock, M. (n.d.). *Defining generations: Where Millennials end and Generation Z begins.* Pew Research Center. Retrieved 6 August 2022, from https://www.pewresearch.org/fact-tank/2019/01/17/where-millennials-end-and-generation-z-begins/

Dmitrova, A. V., Chigisheva, O. P., & Timoshenko, Y. S. (2019). Oxford's Apple Podcasts Multimedia Platform as an Online Digital Literacy Tool for Oxford University Students. International Journal of Economics and Education, 5(3), 5-22.

Doğan, U., & Karakuş, Y. (2016). Lise Öğrencilerinin sosyal ağ siteleri kullanımının yordayıcısı olarak çok boyutlu yalnızlık. *Sakarya Üniversitesi Journal of Education, 6*(1), 57–71. doi:10.19126uje.40198

Dufva, T., & Dufva, M. (2019). Grasping the future of the digital society. *Futures*, *107*, 17–28. doi:10.1016/j.futures.2018.11.001

Elkund, J., Kay, M., & Lynch, H. M. (2003). E-learning: Emerging issues and key trends: A discussion paper. Australian National Training Authority, 25.

Elmansy, R. (2015). *CATWOE: Building a Problem-Solving Checklist.* Designorate. https://www.designorate.com/catwoe-problem-solving/

Emanuel, R., Bell, R., Cotton, C., Craig, J., Drummond, D., & Gibson, S. (2015). The truth about smartphone addiction. *College Student Journal*, *49*(2), 291–299.

Epifanova, T. V., Vovchenko, N. G., Toporov, D. A., & Pozdnyshov, A. N. (2020). Development of Legal Education and Machine-Readable Law in the Conditions of Economy Digitization. *Lecture Notes in Networks and Systems*, *87*(January), 971–979. doi:10.1007/978-3-030-29586-8_110

Erstad, O. (2007). Conceiving digital literacies in schools-Norwegian experiences. In *3rd International workshop on Digital Literacy*, Crete, Greece.

Eryılmaz, A. (2010). Ergenlerde öznel iyi oluşu artırma stratejilerini kullanma ile akademik motivasyon arasındaki ilişki. *Klinik Psikiyatri*, *13*, 77–84.

Eryılmaz, B. & ve Zengin, B. (2014). Consumer for Hospitality Businesses in Social Media A Study on Approaches. *Journal of Business Science*, *2*(1), 147–167.

Eshet-Alkalai, Y. (2004). Digital Literacy: A Conceptual Framework for Survival Skills in the Digital Era. *Journal of Educational Multimedia and Hypermedia*, *13*(1), 93.

European Commission. (2010b). *A Digital Agenda for Europe.* European Commission. https://eur-lex.europa.eu/LexUriServ/LexUriServ.do?uri=COM:2010:0245:FIN:EN:PDF

European Commission. (2015b). *A Digital Single Market Strategy for Europe.* EC.https://eur-lex.europa.eu/legal-content/EN/TXT/PDF/?uri=CELEX:52015DC0192&from=FI

European Commission. (2019). *Digital Economy and Society Index (DESI) 2019.* EC. https://data.consilium.europa.eu/doc/document/ST-10211-2019-INIT/en/pdf

European Commission. (2019). High-Level Expert Group on the Impact of the Digital Transformation on EU Labor Markets. EC. https://www.voced.edu.au/content/ngv:82994

European Commission. (2021). *Commission proposals to improve the working conditions of people working through digital labour platforms.* EC. https://ec.europa.eu/commission/presscorner/detail/en/ip_21_6605

European Commission. (2021d). *Commission proposals to improve the working conditions of people working through digital labor platforms.* EC. https://ec.europa.eu/social/main.jsp?langId=en&catId=89&newsId=10120&furtherNews=yes

Evers, K., Chen, S., Rothmann, S., Dhir, A., & Pallesen, S. (2020). Investigating the relation among disturbed sleep due to social media use, school burnout, and academic performance. *Journal of Adolescence, 84*(1), 156–164. doi:10.1016/j.adolescence.2020.08.011 PMID:32920331

Ewens, H. (2016, September 21). What Young People Fear the Most. *Vice.* https://www.vice.com/en/article/nnyk37/what-vice-readers-fear-the-most-hannah-ewens-love-loneliness

Falco, P., Maloney, W. F., Rijkers, B., & Sarrias, M. (2015). Heterogeneity in subjective wellbeing: An application to occupational allocation in Africa. *Journal of Economic Behavior & Organization, 111*, 137–153. doi:10.1016/j.jebo.2014.12.022

Fardouly, J., & Vartanian, L. (2016). Social Media and Body Image Concerns: Current Research and Future Directions. *Current Opinion in Psychology, 9*, 1–5. doi:10.1016/j.copsyc.2015.09.005

Fennel, C., Glickman, E. L., Lepp, A., Kingsley, J. D., & Barkley, J. E. (2018). The Relationship between Cell Phone Use, Physical Activity, and Sedentary behaviour in United States Adults above College-age. *International Journal of Human Movement and Sports Sciences, 6*(4), 63–70. doi:10.13189aj.2018.060401

Fenwick, M., Kaal, W. A., & Vermeulen, E. P. M. (2017). Legal Education in the Blockchain Revolution. SSRN *Electronic Journal, 20*(2). doi:10.2139/ssrn.2939127

Fenwick, & Kaal. (2018). Legal Education in a Digital Age: Why "Coding for Lawyers". *Matters.*

Ferrari, A. (2012) Digital Competence in Practice: An Analysis of Frameworks. A Technical Report. *The Joint Research Centre of the European Commission.*

Fin.Ace🔒 Finances & Money (@finace.bn) • *Instagram photos and videos.* (n.d.). Retrieved 12 August 2022, from https://www.instagram.com/finace.bn/

Fithriyah, M., Masri, M., Almunawar, M. N., & Anshari, M. (2022). Financial Inclusion and Mobile Payment to Empower Small and Medium-Sized Enterprises: Post-COVID-19 Business Strategy. In FinTech Development for Financial Inclusiveness (pp. 50-59). IGI Global.

Fitzgerald, M., Kruschwitz, N., Bonnet, D., & Welch, M. (2014). Embracing digital technology: A new strategic imperative. *MIT Sloan Management Review, 55*(2), 1.

Flo—Ovulation calendar, period tracker, and pregnancy app. (n.d.). Flo.Health - #1 Mobile Product for Women's Health. Retrieved 12 August 2022, from https://flo.health

Forest Act. (2013). Forest Act Chapter 46. retrieved from http://www.forestry.gov.bn/SitePages/Forest%20Act%20and%20Forest%20Rules.aspx

Forrier, A., Sels, L., & Stynen, D. (2009). Career mobility at the intersection between agent and structure: A conceptual model. *Journal of Occupational and Organizational Psychology, 82*(4), 739–759. doi:10.1348/096317909X470933

Foster, M., & Johnston, R. (n.d.). *How to turn your next video call into an interactive game night*. TODAY.Com. Retrieved 13 August 2022, from https://www.today.com/shop/11-best-games-play-zoom-t179862

Foundation, L. (n.d.). *Digital Society*. LIBRe Foundation. Retrieved 29 November 2021, from https://libreresearchgroup.org/en/a/digital-society

Francis, S. (2022, May 3). *Can councils end London's loneliness epidemic?* BBC News. https://www.bbc.com/news/uk-england-london-61191228

Fraser, J., & Gold, M. (2001). 'Portfolio workers': Autonomy and control amongst freelance translators. *Work, Employment and Society*, *15*(4), 679–697.

Futurelab. (2010) Digital Literacy. *National Foundation for Educational Research*. http://www2.futurelab.org.uk/resources/documents/handbooks/digital_ literacy.pdf

Galloway, K. (2017). A Rationale and Framework for Digital Literacies in Legal Education. *Legal Education Review*, *27*(1). Advance online publication. doi:10.53300/001c.6097

Galloway, M. T., & Jokl, P. (2000). Aging Successfully. *The Importance of Physical Activity in Maintaining Health and Function*, *8*(1), 37–38. PMID:10666651

Gallup (Firm). (2018). The gig economy and alternative work arrangements. *Gallup's Perspective*.

Garcia-Morales, V. J., Garrido-Moreno, A., & Martin-Rojas, R. (2021). The Transformation of Higher Education After the COVID Disruption: Emerging Challenges in an Online Learning Scenario. *Frontiers in Psychology*, *12*, 616059. Advance online publication. doi:10.3389/fpsyg.2021.616059 PMID:33643144

Garfinkel, S. L. (2010). Digital forensics research: The next 10 years. *Digital Investigation*, *7*, 64–73. doi:10.1016/j.diin.2010.05.009

Gartlehner, G., Schultes, M. T., Titscher, V., Morgan, L. C., Bobashev, G. V., Williams, P., & West, S. L. (2017). User testing of an adaptation of fishbone diagrams to depict results of systematic reviews. *BMC Medical Research Methodology*, *17*(169), 169. doi:10.118612874-017-0452-z PMID:29233133

Gattiker, U. E., & Larwood, L. (1986). Subjective career success: A study of managers and support personnel. *Journal of Business and Psychology*, *1*(2), 78–94. doi:10.1007/BF01018805

Gautam, P. (2020). *Advantages and Disadvantages of Online Learning*. eLearning Industry. https://elearningindustry.com/advantages-and-disadvantages-online-learning

Gazette. (2020). *Coronavirus: Top law schools move teaching online*. https://www.lawgazette.co.uk/news/coronavirus-top-law-schools-move-teaching-online/5103496.article

Gezgin, D. M., Cakir, O., & Yildirim, S. (2016). *The Relationship between Levels of Nomophobia Prevalence and Internet Addiction among Adolescents* [*Ergenler arasında Nomofobi Yaygınlık Düzeyinin İnternet Bağımlılığı ile İlişkisi*] [Paper presented]. The 3rd International Eurasian Educational Research Congress, Muğla, Turkey.

Gezgin, D. M., Sumuer, E., Arslan, O., & Yildirim, S. (2017). Nomophobia prevalenc among pre- service teachers: A case of Trakya university. *Trakya Üniversitesi Egitim Fakültesi Dergisi, 7*(1), 86–89. https://dergipark.org.tr/en/pub/trkefd/issue/27304/287423/.

Giacomin, O., Janssen, F., Pruett, M., Shinnar, R. S., Llopis, F., & Toney, B. (2011). Entrepreneurial Intentions, Motivations and Barriers: Differences Among American, Asian and European Students. *The International Entrepreneurship and Management Journal, 7*(2), 219–238. doi:10.100711365-010-0155-y

Gillen, J. (2009). Literacy Practices in Schome Park: A Virtual Literacy Ethnography. *Journal of Research in Reading, 32*(1), 57–74. doi:10.1111/j.1467-9817.2008.01381.x

Gilster, P. (1997). *Digital literacy*. John Wiley & Sons.

Girardin, F., Calabrese, F., Dal Fiore, F., Ratti, C., & Blat, J. (2008). Digital footprinting: Uncovering tourists with user-generated content. *IEEE Pervasive Computing, 7*(4), 36–43. doi:10.1109/MPRV.2008.71

Gismalla, M. D., Mohamed, M. S., Ibrahim, O. S. O., Elhassan, M. M. A., & Mohamed, M. E. (2021). Medical students' perception towards E-learning during COVID-19 pandemic in high burden developing country. *BMC Medical Education, 21*(1), 377. Advance online publication. doi:10.118612909-021-02811-8 PMID:34246254

GlobalData. (2021, September 21). *COVID-19 accelerates mobile wallet adoption across Asia-Pacific, finds GlobalData.* https://www.globaldata.com/covid-19-accelerates-mobile-wallet-adoption-across-asi a-pacific-finds-globaldata/

GoFundMe: No.1 Fundraising Platform for Crowdfunding. (n.d.). Retrieved 19 August 2022, from https://www.gofundme.com/en-gb

Golder, S. A., & Macy, M. W. (2014). Digital footprints: Opportunities and challenges for online social research. *Annual Review of Sociology, 40*(1), 40. doi:10.1146/annurev-soc-071913-043145

Goldstein, A. (2021, August 2). *The Pandemic of Loneliness.* California Health Care Foundation. https://www.chcf.org/blog/pandemic-loneliness/

Grant, J., & Schofield, M. (2007). Career-long supervision: Patterns and perspectives. *Counselling & Psychotherapy Research, 7*(1), 3–11. doi:10.1080/14733140601140899

Greenhaus, J. H., Callanan, G. A., & DiRenzo, M. (2008). A boundaryless perspective on careers. Handbook of organizational behavior, 1, 277-299.

Greenhaus, J. H., & Beutell, N. J. (1985). Sources of conflict between work and family roles. *Academy of Management Review, 10*(1), 76–88. doi:10.2307/258214

Greenhaus, J. H., & Kossek, E. E. (2014). The contemporary career: A work–home perspective. *Annual Review of Organizational Psychology and Organizational Behavior, 1*(1), 361–388. doi:10.1146/annurev-orgpsych-031413-091324

Greenhaus, J. H., Parasuraman, S., & Wormley, W. M. (1990). Effects of race on organizational experiences, job performance evaluations, and career outcomes. *Academy of Management Journal, 33*(1), 64–86. doi:10.2307/256352

Greer, S. L., Jarman, H., Falkenbach, M., Massard Da Fonseca, E., Raj, M., & King, E. J. (2021). Social policy as an integral component of pandemic response: Learning from COVID-19 in Brazil, Germany, India and the United States. *Global Public Health: An International Journal for Research, Policy and Practice, 16*(8–9), 1209–1222. doi:10.1080/17441692.2021.1916831 PMID:33876715

Gumelar, D. R., & Dinnur, S. S. (2020, Sept.). Digitalisasi Pendidikan Hukum dan Prospeknya Pasca Pandemi Covid-19. *Al-Ahwal Al-Syakhsiyyah*.

Gümüş, İ., Harries, T., Eslambolchilar, P., Stride, C., Rettie, R., & Walton, S. (2013). *Walking in the Wild – Using an Always-On Smartphone Application to Increase Physical Activity*. Springer.

Güzel, Ș. (2018). Fear of the age: Nomophobia (No-Mobile-Phone). *Journal of Academic Perspective on Social Studies, 1*(1), 20–24. http://dergipark.gov.tr/japss/issue/43202/519609/. doi:10.35344/japss.519609

Gvin Dun & Bradstreet. (2019). [Data set]. https://accounts.bisnode.si/Authenticate/?product=0&language=en-US&returnUrl=https%3a%2f%2faccounts.bisnode.si%2fHome%2f%3fproduct%3d0%26language%3den-US

Haidi, H., & Hamdan, M. (2022). Analysis of the home-based online teaching and learning policy during the Covid-19 second wave in Brunei: A joint parent/teacher perception. *Asia Pacific Education Review*. Advance online publication. doi:10.100712564-022-09798-x

Hale, A. J., Ricotta, D. N., Freed, J., Smith, C. C., & Huang, G. C. (2018). Adapting Maslow's Hierarchy of Needs as a Framework for Resident Wellness. *Teaching and Learning in Medicine, 31*(1), 109–118. doi:10.1080/10401334.2018.1456928 PMID:29708437

Hale, L. A. (2021). Courtship for business model innovation: Early-stage value negotiation for the sustainability of smart homes. *Journal of Cleaner Production, 297*, 126610. doi:10.1016/j.jclepro.2021.126610

Hamdan, M., Ahmad, N., Jaidin, J. H., & Anshari, M. (2020). Internationalisation in Brunei's higher education and its policy implications: Case study of Universiti Brunei Darussalam. *TEST Engineering and Management, 83*, 764–779.

Hamdan, M., & Anshari, M. (2020). Paving the Way for the Development of FinTech Initiatives in ASEAN. In *Financial technology and disruptive innovation in ASEAN* (pp. 80–107). IGI Global. doi:10.4018/978-1-5225-9183-2.ch004

Hamdan, M., Jaidin, J. H., Fithriyah, M., & Anshari, M. (2020, December). E-learning in time of COVID-19 pandemic: Challenges & experiences. In *2020 Sixth International Conference on e-Learning (econf)* (pp. 12-16). IEEE. 10.1109/econf51404.2020.9385507

Han, S. (2021, October 4). *Brunei begins two-week COVID night restrictions.* The Scoop. https://thescoop.co/2021/10/04/brunei-begins-two-week-covid-night-restrictions/

Han, S. (n.d.). *Gov't rolls out BruHealth contact tracing app as restrictions loosened—The Scoop.* Retrieved 18 August 2022, from https://thescoop.co/2020/05/14/govt-launches-bruhealth-contact-tracing-app/

Handal, B., Groenlund, C., & Gerzina, T. (2009). Dentistry students' perceptions of learning management systems. *European Journal of Dental Education*, *1*(14), 50–54. doi:10.1111/j.1600-0579.2009.00591.x PMID:20070799

Harteis, C., Goller, M., & Caruso, C. (2020, January). Conceptual change in the face of digitalization: Challenges for workplaces and workplace learning. In Frontiers in Education (Vol. 5, p. 1). Frontiers Media SA. doi:10.3389/feduc.2020.00001

Hasmawati, F., Samiha, Y. T., Razzaq, A., & Anshari, M. (2020). Understanding nomophobia among digital natives: Characteristics and challenges. *Journal of Critical Reviews*, *7*(13), 122–131.

Hayat, M. A. (2007). Privacy and Islam: From the Quran to data protection in Pakistan. *Information & Communications Technology Law*, *16*(2), 137–148. doi:10.1080/13600830701532043

Hayes, H. (2004). The role of libraries in the knowledge economy. *Serials*, *17*(3), 231–238. doi:10.1629/17231

Haynes, T. (2018). Dopamine, Smartphones & You: A battle for your time. *Harvard Publications.* https://sitn.hms.harvard.edu/flash/2018/dopamine-smartphones-battle-time/

Healthgrades. (2021). *Vision Loss.* Health Grades. https://www.healthgrades.com/right- care/eye-health/vision-loss

Hengstler, J. (2017). Managing your digital footprint: Ostriches v. eagles. *Education for a Digital World*, *2*(1), 89–139.

Hernandez, B. A. (2012, April 23). *How Skillshare Is Transforming Education as We Know It.* Mashable. https://mashable.com/archive/skillshare-teaching-learning

Hew, K. (2011). Students' and teachers' use of Facebook. *Computers In. Human Behavior*, *27*(2), 662–676. doi:10.1016/j.chb.2010.11.020

Hewson, K. (2013). What size is your digital footprint? *Phi Delta Kappan*, *94*(7), 14–22. doi:10.1177/003172171309400704

Hildebrand, C. (2019). The machine age of marketing: How artificial intelligence changes the way people think, act, and decide. *NIM Marketing Intelligence Review*, *11*(2), 11–10. doi:10.2478/nimmir-2019-0010

Hobbs, R. (2010) Digital and Media Literacy: A plan of Action, 2010. *The Aspen Institute.*

Hohmann, C. (2007). Emotional Digitalization as Technology of the Postmodern: A Reflexive Examination from the View of the Industry. *International Journal of Technology and Human Interaction, 3*(1), 17–29. doi:10.4018/jthi.2007010102

Holst, H. (2012). On the move in Global Delivery Chains : Labour Relations and Working Conditions in the Parcel Delivery Industries of Austria, Germany, the Czech Republic and Hungary. *SODIPER Synthesis Report Work Package, 6.*

Home | Secure Verify Connect. (n.d.). Retrieved 13 August 2022, from https://www.secureverifyconnect.info/

Home. (n.d.). Retrieved 18 August 2022, from https://www.mfa.gov.bn/oman-muscat/SitePages/bruneiintroduction.aspx

Home—Utama. (n.d.). Retrieved 12 August 2022, from https://www.kkbs.gov.bn/Theme/Home.aspx

Hong, D. N. M. (2021). Trust and credibility of urban youth on online news media. *Ad Alta: Journal of Interdisciplinary Research.*

Howe, N. (n.d.). *Millennials And The Loneliness Epidemic.* Forbes. Retrieved 12 August 2022, from https://www.forbes.com/sites/neilhowe/2019/05/03/millennials-and-the-loneliness-epidemic/

Hrynowski, B. Y. Z. A. C. H., & Carlson, M. T. (2021). *Law Schools' Forced Shift Online Offers Insights for Future.* Gallup. https://news.gallup.com/poll/350351/law-schools-forced-shift-online-offers-insights-future.aspx

Hutmacher, F. (2019), *Why Is There So Much More Research on Vision Than on Any Other Sensory Modality?* NCBI. https://www.ncbi.nlm.nih.gov/pmc/articles/PMC6787282/

Idris, H. (n.d.). Kutipan Tabung Dana Pembinaan Masjid menggalakkan. *Pelita Brunei.* https://www.pelitabrunei.gov.bn/Lists/Berita%202009/NewDisplayForm.aspx?ID=32553&ContentTypeId=0x01003909FAFC2C52C240BD1CCEDF92AC1BAE

Ilker, E., Alkassim, R. S., & Musa, S. A. B. (2015, December 22). *Comparison of Convenience Sampling and Purposive Sampling.* doi:10.11648/j.ajtas.20160501.11

Ince, F. (2021b). Creating Synergic Entrepreneurship as Support of Sustainability: Opportunities and Challenges. In R. Perez-Uribe, D. Ocampo-Guzman, N. Moreno-Monsalve, & W. Fajardo-Moreno (Eds.), Handbook of Research on Management Techniques and Sustainability Strategies for Handling Disruptive Situations in Corporate Settings (pp. 464-486). IGI Global. doi:10.4018/978-1-7998-8185-8.ch022

Ince, F. (2023a). Leadership Perspectives on Effective Intergenerational Communication and Management. IGI Global. doi:10.4018/978-1-6684-6140-2

Ince, F. (2023b). Transformational Leadership, In A Diverse and Inclusive Organizational Culture, In Perez-Uribe, R. I., Ocampo-Guzman, D., & Moreno-Monsalve, N. (Eds.). Promoting an Inclusive Organizational Culture for Entrepreneurial Sustainability. IGI Global. doi:10.4018/978-1-6684-5216-5

Ince, F. (2018a). International Businesses and Environmental Issues. In S. Idris (Ed.), *Promoting Global Environmental Sustainability and Cooperation* (pp. 86–111). IGI Global. doi:10.4018/978-1-5225-3990-2.ch004

Ince, F. (2018b). Perceptions of Environmental Sustainability Amongst Mineworkers. *Global Journal of Environmental Science and Management*, *4*(1), 1–8. doi:10.22034/GJESM.2018.04.01.001

Ince, F. (2018c). Green Environment and Management: Environmental Management System (EMS). In S. Tsai, B. Liu, & Y. Li (Eds.), *Green Production Strategies for Sustainability* (pp. 100–116). IGI Global., doi:10.4018/978-1-5225-3537-9.ch006

Ince, F. (2020a). The Effects of COVID-19 Pandemic on the Workforce in Turkey. *Smart Journal*, *6*(32), 1125–1134. doi:10.31576mryj.546

Ince, F. (2020b). Financial Literacy in Generation Z: Healthcare Management Students. *Smart Journal*, *6*(36), 1647–1658. doi:10.31576mryj.616

Ince, F. (2021a). COVID-19 Pandemic Made Me Use It: Attitude Of Generation Z Towards E-Learning. *Smart Journal*, *7*(54), 3489–3494. doi:10.31576mryj.1215

Ince, F. (2021c). A Revolutionary Business Model for Global Purpose-Driven Corporations: Mobility as a Service (MaaS). In R. Perez-Uribe, C. Largacha-Martinez, & D. Ocampo-Guzman (Eds.), *Handbook of Research on International Business and Models for Global Purpose-Driven Companies* (pp. 22–42). IGI Global. doi:10.4018/978-1-7998-4909-4.ch002

Ince, F. (2021d). Opportunities and Challenges of E-Learning in Turkey. In B. Khan, S. Affouneh, S. Hussein Salha, & Z. Najee Khlaif (Eds.), *Challenges and Opportunities for the Global Implementation of E-Learning Frameworks* (pp. 202–226). IGI Global. doi:10.4018/978-1-7998-7607-6.ch013

Ince, F. (2022a). Creative Leadership: A Multidisciplinary Approach to Creativity. In Z. Fields (Ed.), *Achieving Sustainability Using Creativity, Innovation, and Education: A Multidisciplinary Approach* (pp. 30–49). IGI Global. doi:10.4018/978-1-7998-7963-3.ch002

Ince, F. (2022b). The Human Resources Perspective on the Multigenerational Workforce. In F. Ince (Ed.), *International Perspectives and Strategies for Managing an Aging Workforce* (pp. 274–297). IGI Global. doi:10.4018/978-1-7998-2395-7.ch013

Ince, F. (2022c). Digital Literacy Training: Opportunities and Challenges. In M. Taher (Ed.), *Handbook of Research on the Role of Libraries, Archives, and Museums in Achieving Civic Engagement and Social Justice in Smart Cities* (pp. 185–199). IGI Global. doi:10.4018/978-1-7998-8363-0.ch009

Ince, F. (2023c). Socio-Ecological Sustainability (SES) within the scope of industry 5.0. In M. Sajid, S. Khan, & Z. Yu (Eds.), *Implications of Industry 5.0 on Environmental Sustainability*. IGI Global. doi:10.4018/978-1-6684-6113-6

Information Technologies and Communications Authority. (2016). The risks and harms of the internet. *BTK*. https://internet.btk.gov.tr/internetin-riskleri-ve-zararlari-detay-61.html

Insider, C. N. A. (Director). (2022, June 2). *Asia's Tinder Swindlers: Exposing Love Scam Rings In Cambodia | Talking Point | Full Episode*. https://www.youtube.com/watch?v=ZacChEz3Am8

International Data Corporation (IDC). (2021). *Second quarter report 2021*. IDC. https://www.idc.com/promo/smartphone-market-share

International Monetary Fund (IMF). (2000). Globalization: Treats or opportunity. *IMF Publications*. https://www.imf.org/external/np/exr/ib/2000/041200to.htm#II

IOS - Health. (n.d.). Apple. Retrieved 12 August 2022, from https://www.apple.com/ios/health/

IPSE. (2020). The Cost of COVID: How the Pandemic Is Affecting the Self-Employed. IPSE. https://www.ipse.co.uk/resource/the-cost-of-covid.html

Isaksson, A. J., Harjunkoski, I., & Sand, G. (2018). The impact of digitalization on the future of control and operations. *Computers & Chemical Engineering*, *114*, 122–129. doi:10.1016/j.compchemeng.2017.10.037

İspir, B., Birsen, H., Binark, F. M., Özata, F. Z., Bayraktutan, G., Öztürk, M. C., & Ayman, M. (2013). *Digital communication and new media*. Web-Ofset.

Ivanova, G. (2020, June 22). The History of Garmin Watches. *First Class Watches Blog*. https://www.firstclasswatches.co.uk/blog/2020/06/the-history-of-garmin-watches/

Izzah, N., Rifai, D., & Yao, L. (2016). Relationshipcourier partner logistics and e-commerce enterprises in Malaysia: A review. *Indian Journal of Science and Technology*, *9*(9), 1–10. doi:10.17485/ijst/2016/v9i9/88721

Jackson, N. C. (2019). Managing for competency with innovation change in higher education: Examining the pitfalls and pivots of digital transformation. *Business Horizons*, *62*(6), 761–772. doi:10.1016/j.bushor.2019.08.002

Jacobsson, K. (2003). European Politic for Employability: The Political Discourse on Employability of the EU and the OECD. In C. Garsten, & K. Jacobsson. (eds.). Learning to Be Employable. New Agendas on Work, Responsibility, and Learning in a Globalizing World. Palgrave Macmillan.

Jarvis, P. S. (2003). *Career Management Paradigm Shift: Prosperity for Citizens*. Windfalls for Governments.

Jarvis, P. S., & Keeley, E. S. (2003). From vocational decision making to career building: Blueprint, real games, and school counseling. *Professional School Counseling*, *6*(4), 244–250.

Jenkins, K. (2017). *Exploring the UK freelance workforce in 2016*. Small Business Research Centre.

Johannes, N., Vuorre, M., & Przybylski, A. K. (2021). Video game play is positively correlated with well-being. *Royal Society Open Science*, *8*(2), 202049. doi:10.1098/rsos.202049 PMID:33972879

Johnson, B. (2010). *Privacy no longer a social norm, says Facebook founder | Facebook | The Guardian.* https://www.theguardian.com/technology/2010/jan/11/facebook-privacy

Join JustGiving and show you care. (n.d.). JustGiving. Retrieved 19 August 2022, from https://www.justgiving.com

Joint Decree: Four Ministrials, Pengelola Web Kemdikbud 1. (2021). https://www.kemdikbud.go.id/main/blog/2021/12/keputusan-bersama-4-menteri-tentang-panduan-penyelenggaraan-pembelajaran-di-masa-pandemi-covid19

Jones, S. G. (Ed.). (1997) Virtual culture: Identity & communication in cybersociety. Sage.

Judge, T. A., & Bretz, R. D. Jr. (1994). Political influence behavior and career success. *Journal of Management*, *20*(1), 43–65. doi:10.1177/014920639402000103

Judge, T. A., Higgins, C. A., Thoresen, C. J., & Barrick, M. R. (1999). The big five personality traits, general mental ability, and career success across the life span. *Personnel Psychology*, *52*(3), 621–652. doi:10.1111/j.1744-6570.1999.tb00174.x

Junaidi, Y. (2021a, October 11). Lebih 1,500 sertai Majlis Malam Munajat » Media Permata Online. *Lebih 1,500 Sertai Majlis Malam Munajat.* https://mediapermata.com.bn/lebih-1500-sertai-majlis-malam-munajat/

Junaidi, Y. (2021b, October 19). Laungan dikir 12 malam berakhir » Media Permata Online. *Laungan Dikir 12 Malam Berakhir.* https://mediapermata.com.bn/laungan-dikir-12-malam-berakhir-3/

Just, N. (2018). Governing online platforms: Competition policy in times of platformization. *Telecommunications Policy*, *42*(5), 386–394. doi:10.1016/j.telpol.2018.02.006

Kabango, C. M., & Asa, A. R. (2015). Factors influencing e-commerce development: Implications for the developing countries. *International Journal of Innovation and Economic Development*, *1*(1), 64–72. doi:10.18775/ijied.1849-7551-7020.2015.11.2006

Kabir, J., Tonmon, T. T., Hasan, M. K., Biswas, L., Chowdhury, M. A. H., Islam, M. D., Rahman, M., & Mitra, D. K. (2022). Association between preference and e-learning readiness among the Bangladeshi female nursing students in the COVID-19 pandemic: A cross-sectional study. *Bulletin of the National Research Center*, *48*(8), 8. doi:10.118642269-022-00697-0 PMID:35039742

Karhu, K. Botero, A., Vihavainen, S., Tang, T. & Hämäläinen, M. (2011). A Digital Ecosystem for Co-Creating Business with People. *Journal of Emerging Technologies in Web Intelligence,* 3. doi:10.4304/jetwi.3.3.197-205

Karimi, J., & Walter, Z. (2021). The role of entrepreneurial agility in digital entrepreneurship and creating value in response to digital disruption in the newspaper industry. *Sustainability*, *13*(5), 2741. doi:10.3390u13052741

Kasharan, A. Z. (2021, September 18). Majlis tahlil bagi tokoh bola sepak tempatan » Media Permata Online. *Majlis Tahlil Bagi Tokoh Bola Sepak Tempatan.* https://mediapermata.com.bn/majlis-tahlil-bagi-tokoh-bola-sepak-tempatan/

Kaur-Gill, S., & Dutta, M. J. (2017). Digital Ethnography. In J. Matthes, C. S. Davis, & R. F. Potter (Eds.), *The International Encyclopedia of Communication Research Methods* (1st ed., pp. 1–10). Wiley. doi:10.1002/9781118901731.iecrm0271

Kementerian Hal Ehwal Ugama on Instagram: 'Bersempena Sambutan Maulud Nabi Muhammad Shallallahu 'Alaihi Wasallam Peringkat Negara bagi Tahun 1443 Hijrah, orang ramai dialu-alukan …' (n.d.a). Retrieved 4 November 2021, from https://www.instagram.com/p/CVMKnqfhTpe/

Kementerian Hal Ehwal Ugama on Instagram: 'Bersempena Sambutan Maulud Nabi Muhammad Shallallahu 'Alaihi Wasallam Peringkat Negara bagi Tahun 1443 Hijrah, orang ramai dialu-alukan …' (n.d.b). Retrieved 4 November 2021, from https://www.instagram.com/p/CVFQlh-BuRt/

Kementerian Hal Ehwal Ugama on Instagram: 'Bersempena Sambutan Maulud Nabi Muhammad Shallallahu 'Alaihi Wasallam Peringkat Negara bagi Tahun 1443 Hijrah, orang ramai dialu-alukan …' (n.d.c). Retrieved 4 November 2021, from https://www.instagram.com/p/CVHihN9Bu2P/

Kementerian Hal Ehwal Ugama on Instagram: 'Bersempena Sambutan Maulud Nabi Muhammad Shallallahu 'Alaihi Wasallam Peringkat Negara bagi Tahun 1443 Hijrah, orang ramai dialu-alukan …' (n.d.d). Retrieved 4 November 2021, from https://www.instagram.com/p/CVJxCRSBPWI/

Kementerian Hal Ehwal Ugama on Instagram: 'Jabatan Hal Ehwal Masjid, Kementerian Hal Ehwal Ugama dengan kerjasama Radio Televisyen Brunei mengambil inisiatif untuk mengadakan Majlis …' (n.d.). Retrieved 4 November 2021, from https://www.instagram.com/p/CVMPkzThgau/

Kementerian Hal Ehwal Ugama on Instagram: 'Kementerian Hal Ehwal Ugama dengan kerjasama daripada Kementerian Pendidikan, Kementerian Kebudayaan, Belia dan Sukan …' (n.d.). Retrieved 14 December 2021, from https://www.instagram.com/p/CViMw5bh3tz/

Kementerian Hal Ehwal Ugama on Instagram: 'Repost @rampaipagi.rtb Disiarkan secara langsung di saluran RTB Perdana dan awda juga boleh mengikuti kami melalui penstriman langsung di …' (n.d.). Retrieved 4 November 2021, from https://www.instagram.com/p/CVtqnQdhKVa/

Kementerian Hal Ehwal Ugama on Instagram: 'Terapi Kejiwaan: Jangan Mudah Berputus Asa Disediakan oleh Unit Kaunseling dan Kefahaman Agama (KAFA), KHEU '. (n.d.). Retrieved 4 November 2021, from https://www.instagram.com/p/CVmQ3nVBZEJ/

Kenton, W. (2020). 3-D Printing. *Investopedia.* https://www.investopedia.com/terms/1/3dprinting.asp

Keşf Conscious Internet Movement Project. (2017). Information Notes. *Kesfet Project.* http://www.kesfetprojesi.org/kesfet/iceriklist/kesfet-projesi/bilgi-notlari

Khan, M. A. M. (2019). *Islam and Good Governance: A Political Philosophy of Ihsan.* doi:10.1057/978-1-137-54832-0

Khapova, S. N., & Arthur, M. B. (2011). Interdisciplinary approaches to contemporary career studies. *Human Relations, 64*(1), 3–17. doi:10.1177/0018726710384294

Kim, H. J., Hong, A. J., & Song, H. D. (2019). The roles of academic engagement and digital readiness in students' achievements in university e-learning environments. International. *Journal of Educational Technology in Higher Education, 16*(21). Advance online publication. doi:10.118641239-019-0152-3

Kim, J. (2018). The contrary effects of intrinsic and extrinsic motivations on burnout and turnover intention in the public sector. *International Journal of Manpower, 39*(3), 486–500. doi:10.1108/IJM-03-2017-0053

Kim, Y., Park, J. Y., Kim, S. B., Jung, I. K., Lim, Y. S., & Kim, J. H. (2010). The effects of internet addiction on the lifestyle and dietary behaviour of Korean adolescents. *Nutrition Research and Practice, 4*(1), 51–57. doi:10.4162/nrp.2010.4.1.51 PMID:20198209

King, D. L., & Delfabbro, P. H. (2013). Issues for dsm-5: Video-gaming disorder? *The Australian and New Zealand Journal of Psychiatry, 47*(1), 20–22. doi:10.1177/0004867412464065 PMID:23293310

Kirby, M. (2011, May). *Online Legal Education: The New CQU Law.* https://www.michaelkirby.com.au/images/stories/speeches/2000s/2011/2542-SPEECH-CQU-NEW-LAW-DEGREE-LAUNCH-MAY-2011.pdf

Kitching, J., & Smallbone, D. (2012). Are freelancers a neglected form of small business? *Journal of Small Business and Enterprise Development, 19*(1), 74–91. doi:10.1108/14626001211196415

Kohnt, N. A. (2020). Online Learning and The Future of Legal Education: Symposium Introduction. *Syracuse Law Review, 70.*

Kon, J. (2020). BruHealth QR code a must at all premises: MoH. *Borneo Bulletin* https://borneobulletin.com.bn/bruhealth-qr-code-a-must-at-all-premises-moh/

Kon, J., & Roslan, W. (2020, September 23). Rising to the COVID-19 challenge » Borneo Bulletin Online. *Rising to the COVID-19 Challenge.* https://borneobulletin.com.bn/rising-to-the-covid-19-challenge/

Kondakov, A. M. (2019). *Education in the Context of Digital Transformation of Russian Society.* Available from http://vcht.center/wp-content/uploads/2019/06/Kondakov-Peterburg25maya2019-2.pdf

Korea Cosmetics BN. (n.d.). Retrieved 12 August 2022, from https://koreacosmeticsbn.com/

Korunovska, J., & Spiekermann, S. (2019). *The effects of digitalization on human energy and fatigue: A review.* Vienna University of Economics and Business. https://arxiv.org/vc/arxiv/papers/1910/1910.01970v1.pdf

Kosinski, M., Stillwell, D., & Graepel, T. (2013). Private traits and attributes are predictable from digital records of human behaviour. *Proceedings of the National Academy of Sciences of the United States of America, 110*(15), 5802–5805. doi:10.1073/pnas.1218772110 PMID:23479631

Krishna, K., Karumuri, N., Christopher, C., & Jayapandian, N. (2021, May). Research Challenges in Self-Driving Vehicle by Using Internet of Things (IoT). In *5th International Conference on Intelligent Computing and Control Systems (ICICCS)* (pp. 423-427). IEEE.

Kuehn, L. (2012). Manage your digital footprint. *Our Schools / Our Selves, 21*(2), 67-69.

Kumar, H., & Raj, P. (2020). An indagation on experiences and awareness of digital footprint among pupils of higher education. *Academic Research International, 11*, 16–31.

Kunda, G., Barley, S. R., & Evans, J. (2002). Why do Contractors Contract? The Experience of Highly Skilled Professionals in a Contingent Labor Market. *Industrial & Labor Relations Review, 55*(2), 234–261. doi:10.1177/001979390205500203

Kundu, A., & Bej, T. (2021). *Experiencing e-assessment during COVID-19: an analysis of Indian students' perception*. Higher Education Evaluation and Development Emerald Publishing Limited. doi:10.1108/HEED-03-2021-0032

Kuss, D. J., & Griffiths, M. D. (2011). Online social networking and addiction—A review of the psychological literature. *International Journal of Environmental Research and Public Health, 8*(9), 3528–3552. doi:10.3390/ijerph8093528 PMID:22016701

Kwon, J.-H., Chung, C.-S., & Lee, J. (2011). The effects of escape from self and interpersonal relationship on the pathological use of internet games. *Community Mental Health Journal, 47*(1), 113–121. doi:10.100710597-009-9236-1 PMID:19701792

Lambiotte, R., & Kosinski, M. (2014). Tracking the digital footprints of personality. *Proceedings of the IEEE, 102*(12), 1934–1939. doi:10.1109/JPROC.2014.2359054

Lam, L. T., & Peng, Z. W. (2010). Effect of pathological use of the internet on adolescent mental health: A prospective study. *Archives of Pediatrics & Adolescent Medicine, 164*(10), 901–906. doi:10.1001/archpediatrics.2010.159 PMID:20679157

Lankshear, C., & Knobel, M. (2008). *Digital literacies: concepts, policies and practices*. Peter Lang.

Larjovuori, R. L., Bordi, L., & Heikkilä-Tammi, K. (2018, October). Leadership in the digital business transformation. In *Proceedings of the 22nd international academic mindtrek conference* (pp. 212-221). MindTrek Conference. 10.1145/3275116.3275122

Latif, A. (n.d.). *Berita KKBS - Ubah 'Mindset' Lebih Positif*. Retrieved 6 August 2022, from https://www.kkbs.gov.bn/Lists/News/NDispForm.aspx?ID=414&ContentTypeId=0x0100ECC89185A7F5E74A8CA7B999A4454ABE

LawWorks. (2020). *Survey shows UK law students increasingly delivering pro bono advice to vulnerable people*. https://www.fenews.co.uk/skills/survey-shows-uk-law-students-increasingly-delivering-pro-bono-advice/

Lee, K. H., Slattery, O., Lu, R., Tang, X., & McCrary, V. (2002). The state of the art and practice in digital preservation. *Journal of Research of the National Institute of Standards and Technology*, *107*(1), 93. doi:10.6028/jres.107.010 PMID:27446721

LegalEagle (Director). (2022a, June 30). *How The Supreme Court Killed Roe v. Wade*. https://www.youtube.com/watch?v=wOvvBWSBwU0

LegalEagle (Director). (2022b, August 10). *Huge Verdict Against Alex Jones*. https://www.youtube.com/watch?v=SpVSiuQ_ILY

Leland, J. (2022, April 20). How Loneliness Is Damaging Our Health. *The New York Times*. https://www.nytimes.com/2022/04/20/nyregion/loneliness-epidemic.html

Lewin, T. (2012, May 8). Law School Plans to Offer Web Courses for Master's. *The New York Times*. https://www.nytimes.com/2012/05/09/education/law-school-plans-to-offer-web-courses-for-masters.html

Li, S.M., & Chung, T.M. (2006). Internet Function and Internet Addictive behaviour. *Computers in Human behaviour, 22*(6), pp. 1067–1071.

Liang, C., & Chen, J. (2020). *Analysis on Job Burnout Level and Influencing Factors of Young Employees in Guangdong Express Delivery Industry. 150* (Icoeme), 239–248. doi:10.2991/aebmr.k.200908.039

Li, L., & Lin, T. T. C. (2019). Smartphones at Work: A Qualitative Exploration of Psychological Antecedents and Impacts of Work-Related Smartphone Dependency. *International Journal of Qualitative Methods, 18*. doi:10.1177/1609406918822240

Line, T., Jain, J., & Lyons, G. (2011). The role of ICTs in everyday mobile lives. *Journal of Transport Geography*, *19*(6), 1490–1499. doi:10.1016/j.jtrangeo.2010.07.002

Lippens, L., Moens, E., Sterkens, P., Weytjens, J., & Baert, S. (2021). How do employees think the COVID-19 crisis will affect their careers? *PLoS One*, *16*(5), e0246899. doi:10.1371/journal.pone.0246899 PMID:33956808

Lister, M., Dovey, J., Giddings, S., & Grant, I., & ve Kelly, K. (2009). New media is a critical introduction. Routledge.

Li, X., & Santhanam, R. (2008). Will it be disclosure or fabrication of personal information? An examination of persuasion strategies on prospective employees. *International Journal of Information Security and Privacy*, *29*(4), 91–113. doi:10.4018/jisp.2008100105

Li, Y., Guan, M., Hammond, P., & Berrey, L. E. (2021). Communicating COVID-19 information on TikTok: A content analysis of TikTok videos from official accounts featured in the COVID-19 information hub. *Health Education Research*, *36*(3), 261–271. doi:10.1093/her/cyab010 PMID:33667311

Lo Presti, A., Pluviano, S., & Briscoe, J. P. (2018). Are freelancers a breed apart? The role of protean and boundaryless career attitudes in employability and career success. *Human Resource Management Journal, 28*(3), 427–442. doi:10.1111/1748-8583.12188

Locke, E. A., Sirota, D., & Wolfson, A. D. (1976). An experimental case study of the successes and failures of job enrichment in a government agency. *The Journal of Applied Psychology, 61*(6), 701–711. doi:10.1037/0021-9010.61.6.701

London High Street (@londonhighstr8) • *Instagram photos and videos*. (n.d.). Retrieved 12 August 2022, from https://www.instagram.com/londonhighstr8/?hl=en

Low, K. C. P., & Anshari, M. (2013). Incorporating social customer relationship management in negotiation. *International Journal of Electronic Customer Relationship Management, 7*(3-4), 239–252. doi:10.1504/IJECRM.2013.060700

Lu, X., Watanabe, J., Liu, Q., Uji, M., Shono, M., & Kitamura, T. (2011). Internet and mobile phone text-messaging dependency: Factor structure and correlation with dysphoric mood among Japanese adults. *Computers in Human behaviour, 27*(5), 1702- 1709

Lynn Thompson, T. (2012). I am deleting as fast as possible: Negotiating learning practices in cyberspace. *Pedagogy, Culture & Society, 20*(1), 93–112. doi:10.1080/14681366.2012.649417

Maatuk, A. M., Elberkawi, E., Aljawarneh, S., Rashaideh, H., & Alharbi, H. (2022). The COVID-19 pandemic and E-learning: Challenges and opportunities from the perspective of students and instructors. *Journal of Computing in Higher Education, 34*(1), 21–38. doi:10.100712528-021-09274-2 PMID:33967563

Madden, M., Fox, S., Smith, A., & Vitak, J. (2007). Digital footprints: Online identity management and search in the age of transparency. *Pew/Internet & American Life Project*.

Mahmud, R. (2021, May 12). Blessed as a Zikir Nation » Borneo Bulletin Online. *Blessed as a Zikir Nation*. https://borneobulletin.com.bn/blessed-zikir-nation/

Mahmud, R. (2022, May 31). Spotlight on importance of family ties » Borneo Bulletin Online. *Spotlight on Importance of Family Ties*. https://borneobulletin.com.bn/spotlight-on-importance-of-family-ties/

Mahoney, J., & Hall, C. A. (2020). *Exploring Online Learning Through Synchronous and Asynchronous Instructional Methods*. doi:10.4018/978-1-7998-1622-5.ch003

Majid, Y. (n.d.). *Yussof Majid (@yussof_majid)* • *Instagram photos and videos*. Retrieved 5 November 2021, from https://www.instagram.com/yussof_majid/

Makecents (@makecents.bn) • *Instagram photos and videos*. (n.d.). Retrieved 12 August 2022, from https://www.instagram.com/makecents.bn/?hl=en

Malhotra, A., Totti, L., Meira, W., Kumaraguru, P., & Almeida, V. (2012). Studying user footprints in different online social networks. *Proceedings of the 2012 International Conference on Advances in Social Networks Analysis and Mining (ASONAM 2012)*, (pp. 1065-1070). 10.1109/ASONAM.2012.184

Malik, M. (2018). Foundations of Islamic governance: A Southeast Asian perspective. Routledge.

Malt & EFIP. (2019). The state of European Freelancing in 2018 – results of the first European freelancers' survey. *Malt*. https://news.malt.com/en-gb/2019/02/12/the-state-of-european-freelancing-in-2018-results-of-the-first-european-freelancers-survey-2/

Malt and Boston Consulting Group. (2021). Freelancing in Europe. *Malt*. https://web-assets.bcg.com/77/62/07a1c84f4be6b671ca10ec16f6f1/malt-bcg-freelancing-in-europe-2021.pdf

Malt, Q. D. (2021). Overview of the European Freelance Industry. *Medium*. https://medium.com/@reshaping_work/overview-of-the-european-freelance-industry-c464b2497960

Manovich, L. (2001). *The language of new media*. The MIT Press.

Margaryan, A., Littlejohn, A., & Vojt, G. (2011). Are digital natives a myth or reality? University students' use of digital technologies. *Computers & Education*, *56*(2), 429–440. doi:10.1016/j.compedu.2010.09.004

Marketing Week. (2011), Smart ways to attract smartphone shoppers. Marketing Week. https://www.marketingweek.com/smart-ways-to-attract-smartphone-shoppers/

Martin, A. (2008). Digital Literacy and the "Digital Society". In C. Lankshear & M. Knobel (Eds.), *Digital Literacies: Concepts, Policies and Practices* (pp. 151–176). Peter Lang.

Martínez Lucio, M., & MacKenzie, R. (2017). The state and the regulation of work and employment: Theoretical contributions, forgotten lessons and new forms of engagement. *International Journal of Human Resource Management*, *28*(21), 2983–3002. doi:10.1080/09585192.2017.1363796

Marvi, A., Shahraini, S. M., Yazdi, N., & Maleki, A. (2021). Iran and COVID-19: A Bottom-up, Faith-Driven, Citizen-Supported Response. *Public Organization Review*, *21*(4), 723–740. doi:10.100711115-021-00567-9

Matt, C., Hess, T., & Benlian, A. (2015). Digital transformation strategies. *Business & Information Systems Engineering*, *57*(5), 339–343. doi:10.100712599-015-0401-5

Matusik, S. F., & Mickel, A. E. (2011). Embracing or embattled by converged mobile devices? Users' experiences with a contemporary connectivity technology. *Human Relations*, *64*(8), 1001–1030. doi:10.1177/0018726711405552

McCulloch, G. (n.d.). A Mission to Make Virtual Parties Actually Fun. *Wired*. Retrieved 13 August 2022, from https://www.wired.com/story/zoom-parties-proximity-chat/

McCulloch, G. (2013). Historical and documentary research in education. In L. Cohen, L. Manion, & K. Morrison (Eds.), *Research Methods in Education* (0 ed.). Routledge., doi:10.4324/9780203720967

McDermott, M. (2018). Digital footprints. *Distance Learning*, *15*(1), 51–54.

McGinnis, J. O., & Pearce, R. G. (2014). The great disruption: How machine intelligence will transform the role of lawyers in the delivery of legal services. *Fordham Law Review*, *82*(6), 3041–3066. doi:10.21202/1993-047X.13.2019.2.1230-1250

McKinsey Global Institute. (2016). Independent work: Choice, necessity, and the gig economy. *Mckinsey.* https://www.mckinsey.com/featured-insights/employment-and-growth/independent-work-choice-necessity-and-the-gig-economy

McLeod, S. (2018, May 21). *Maslow's Hierarchy of Needs*. Retrieved from: https://canadacollege.edu/dreamers/docs/Maslows-Hierarchy-of-Needs.pdf

McLeod, S. A. (2020). Maslow's hierarchy of needs. *Simply Psychology*. https://www.simplypsychology.org/maslow.html

Meier, E., & Gray, J. (2014). Facebook Photo Activity Associated with Body Image Disturbance in Adolescent Girls. *Cyberpsychology, Behavior, and Social Networking*, *17*(4), 199–206. doi:10.1089/cyber.2013.0305 PMID:24237288

Menelusuri Peranan Pusat Da"wah Islamiah dalam Pengurusan Program Pembangunan Saudara Baru. (n.d.). Retrieved 13 August 2022, from http://www.jised.com/PDF/JISED-2019-19-03-19.pdf

Miller, G. (2012). The smartphone psychology manifesto. *Perspectives on Psychological Science*, *7*(3), 221–237. doi:10.1177/1745691612441215 PMID:26168460

Milosevic, T. (2016). Social media companies' cyberbullying policies. *International Journal of Communication*, *10*, 5164–5185.

Minh-Nhat, H. O., Nguyen, H. L., & Mondal, S. R. (2022). Digital Transformation for New Sustainable Goals with Human Element for Digital Service Enterprises: An Exploration of Factors. In *Sustainable Development and Innovation of Digital Enterprises for Living with COVID-19* (pp. 85–103). Springer. doi:10.1007/978-981-19-2173-5_6

Ministry of Health—Bruhealth. (n.d.). Retrieved 12 August 2022, from https://www.moh.gov.bn/SitePages/bruhealth.aspx

Mishra, Sailesh, & Bashetti, Archana, Reddy, Jayashree, & Mukaddam. (2017). Effect of Heartfulness Meditation on Perceived Stress and Cognition in Hypertensive Patients. *International Journal of Research in Pharmaceutical Sciences*, *8*(4), 690–692.

Mizi Wahid (@miziwahid) • Instagram photos and videos. (n.d.). Retrieved 6 August 2022, from https://www.instagram.com/miziwahid/?hl=en

Mohamad, L. (2021, October 28). Virtual tahlil for late prince » Borneo Bulletin Online. *Virtual Tahlil for Late Prince.* https://borneobulletin.com.bn/virtual-tahlil-for-late-prince/

Mohammad, J., Quoquab, F., Halimah, S., & Thurasamy, R. (2019). Workplace internet leisure and employees' productivity. *Internet Research, 29*(4), 725–748. doi:10.1108/IntR-05-2017-0191

Moon, J.H., Kim, K.W., & Moon, N.J., (2016), Smartphone use is a risk factor for pediatric dry eye disease according to region and age: a case control study. *BMC ophthalmology, 16*(1), 1-7.

Motowidlo, S. J., & Kell, H. J. (2012). Job Performance. *Handbook of Psychology, 12*(2), 82-103. https://www.researchgate.net/publication/236624589_Job_Performance

Muench, R., & Muench, C. (2020). Me Without My Smartphone? Never! Predictors of Willingness for Smartphone Separation and Nomophobia. *Communications in Computer and Information Science, 1226,* 217–223. doi:10.1007/978-3-030-50732-9_29

Mui, D., Kee, H., Nurul, S., Nasser, A., Syafiqah, N., & Sany, M. (n.d.). The Strategy, Impact, and Challenges Faced by Pos Malaysia Berhad during the COVID-19 Crisis. *Journal of the Community Development in Asia, 4*(2), 13–25.

Mulyani, M. A., Razzaq, A., Ridho, S. L. Z., & Anshari, M. (2019, October). Smartphone and Mobile Learning to Support Experiential Learning. In *2019 International Conference on Electrical Engineering and Computer Science (ICECOS)* (pp. 6-9). IEEE. 10.1109/ICECOS47637.2019.8984501

Mulyani, M. A., Razzaq, A., Sumardi, W. H., & Anshari, M. (2019, August). Smartphone adoption in mobile learning scenario. In *2019 International Conference on Information Management and Technology (ICIMTech)* (Vol. 1, pp. 208-211). IEEE. 10.1109/ICIMTech.2019.8843755

Mulyani, M. A., Yusuf, S., Siregar, P., Nurihsan, J., Razzaq, A., & Anshari, M. (2021, August). Fourth Industrial Revolution and Educational Challenges. In *2021 International Conference on Information Management and Technology (ICIMTech)* (Vol. 1, pp. 245-249). IEEE. 10.1109/ICIMTech53080.2021.9535057

Murray, S. (2022). *Pandemic Accelerates Growth of Online and Hybrid LLMs.* https://llm-guide.com/articles/pandemic-accelerates-growth-of-online-and-hybrid-llms

Muszyński, K., Pulignano, V., & Domecka, M. (2022). *Self-employment in the platform economy and the quality of work. Problems and challenges during the COVID-19 pandemic. Draft for comment.* OECD.

Nahavandi, S. (2019). Industry 5.0-A human-centric solution. *Sustainability, 11*(16), 4371. doi:10.3390u11164371

Nebrosky, E. V., Boguslavsky, M. V., Ladyzhets, N. S., & Naumova T. A. (2020). Digital Transformation of Higher Education: International Trends. *Advances in Social Science, Education and Humanities Research, 437.*

Nelson, T. (1974). *Dream machines/Computer lib.* The Distributors.

Newman, K. L. (2011). Sustainable careers. *Organizational Dynamics*, *40*(2), 136–143. doi:10.1016/j.orgdyn.2011.01.008

Ng, T. W., & Feldman, D. C. (2014). Subjective career success: A meta-analytic review. *Journal of Vocational Behavior*, *85*(2), 169–179. doi:10.1016/j.jvb.2014.06.001

Ng, W. (2012). Can we teach digital natives digital literacy? *Computers & Education*, *59*(3), 1065–1078. doi:10.1016/j.compedu.2012.04.016

Nogueira, M., Amaral, A., & Jones, G. (2020). The impact of COVID-19 on Brazil's precarious labour market calls for far-reaching policies like universal basic income. *LSE*, 1–6. https://blogs.lse.ac.uk/latamcaribbean/

Nurdiyanah, R. (2021, September 18). Warga emas mantapkan bacaan Quran menerusi Tilawah Wal Istima » Media Permata Online. *Warga Emas Mantapkan Bacaan Quran Menerusi Tilawah Wal Istima*. https://mediapermata.com.bn/warga-emas-mantapkan-bacaan-quran-menerusi-tilawah-wal-istima/

O'Brien, D., & Scharber, C. (2008). Digital Literacies Go to School: Potholes and Possibilities. *Journal of Adolescent & Adult Literacy*, *52*(1), 66–68. doi:10.1598/JAAL.52.1.7

O'Keeffe, G. S., & Clarke-Pearson, K. (2011). The impact of social media on children, adolescents, and families. *Paediatrics*, *127*(4), 800–804. doi:10.1542/peds.2011-0054 PMID:21444588

O'Loughlin, R. (2013). Teacher perceptions of a language curriculum: A CATWOE Analysis. *Studies in Linguistics and Language Teaching*, *24*, 93–106.

Odabaşı, F., Varank, İ., Yıldırım, S., Koyuncu, F., Dönmez, O., & ve Şumuer, E. (2015). *Conscious internet use research*. http://www.kesfetprojesi.org/source/Bilincli_internet_Kullanim%20Arastirmasi.pdf

OECD. (2018). *Good Jobs for All in a Changing World of Work: The OECD Jobs Strategy*. OECD Publishing.

OECD. (2019). *The missing entrepreneurs 2019: policies for inclusive entrepreneurship*. OECD Publications Centre.

OECD. (2021a). Digital trade. *OECD*. https://www.oecd.org/trade/topics/digital-trade/

OECD. (2021b). *Model Reporting Rules for Digital Platforms: International Exchange Framework and Optional Module for Sale of Goods*. OECD.

OLI. (2020). The Online Labor Index. *OLI*. https://ilabor.oii.ox.ac.uk/how-many-online-workers/

Olszewski, S. (2021, September 13). NYC food delivery workers face a 'harrowing world.' *Cornell Chronicle*. https://news.cornell.edu/stories/2021/09/nyc-food-delivery-workers-face-harrowing-world

Online Learning: Creative Classes on Skillshare | Start for Free. (n.d.). Retrieved 12 August 2022, from https://www.skillshare.com/

Online Tahlil | Brunei's No.1 News Website. (n.d.). Retrieved 4 November 2021, from https://www.brudirect.com/news.php?id=91894

Örgev, C. (2015). Önlisans öğrencilerinin akıllı cep telefon kullanmalarının başarı ve harcama düzeylerine olası etkileri üzerine bir çalışma. *ISCAT/Akademik Platform*, 310-315. http://kritik-analitik.com/ISCAT2015_bildiriler/C1-ISCAT2015ID65.pdf

Oriji, A., & Torunarigha, Y. D. (2020). Digitized education: Examining the challenges of digital immigrant educators in the face of net generation learners. *KIU Journal of Social Sciences*, *5*(4), 337–347.

Osborn, C. (2021, June 4). *How to Host a Zoom Party and Connect With Your Loved Ones.* MUO. https://www.makeuseof.com/how-to-host-a-zoom-party/

Osmanoğlu, D. E., & Kaya, H. İ. (2013). Öğretmen adaylarının yükseköğretime dair memnuniyet durumları ile öznel iyi oluş durumlarının değerlendirilmesi: Kafkas Üniversitesi örneği. *Sosyal Bilimler Enstitüsü Dergisi*, *12*, 45–70.

Othman, A. (2020). *MSMEs drive Brunei's economy» Borneo Bulletin Online.* https://borneobulletin.com.bn/their-majesties-meet-thai-defence-chief-and-spouse-2/

Oulasvirta, A., Rattenbury, T., Ma, L., & Raita, E. (2012). Habits make smartphone use more pervasive. *Personal and Ubiquitous Computing*, *16*(1), 105–114. doi:10.100700779-011-0412-2

OverSimplified—YouTube. (n.d.). Retrieved 12 August 2022, from https://www.youtube.com/

Oxley, C. (2011). Digital citizenship: Developing an ethical and responsible online culture. *Access*, *25*(3), 5–9.

Oyeyemi, O. O. (n.d.). *Librarians' Building a digital footprint.* Academic Press.

Özgür Güler, E. Veysíkaraní, D. ve Keskín, D. (2019). A Study on Social Media Addiction of University Students. *Çağ University. Journal of Social Sciences*, *16*(1), 1–13.

Pacer Named Best Running App of 2022 by BestApp.com - The Pacer Blog: Walking, Health and Fitness. (2022, March 17). https://blog.mypacer.com/2022/03/17/pacer-named-best-running-app-of-2022-by-bestapp-com/

Pacer: Pedometer & Fitness App—Simple Fitness and Weight Loss. (n.d.). Retrieved 12 August 2022, from https://www.mypacer.com/

Pandya, S. P. (2021). Meditation Program Mitigates Loneliness and Promotes Well Being Life Satisfaction and Contentment Among Retired Older Adults: A Two Year Follow-up Study in four South Asian Cities. *Aging & Mental Health*, *25*(2), 286–298. doi:10.1080/13607863.2019.1691143 PMID:31755300

Pannen, P. (2016). Kebijakan Pendidikan Jarak Jauh dan E-Learning di Indonesia. Ministry of Research and Higher Education Indonesia. doi:10.35913/jk.v8i2.204

Parasuraman, S., Sam, A. T., Yee, S. W. K., Chuon, B. L. C., & Ren, L. Y. (2017). Smartphone usage and increased risk of mobile phone addiction: A concurrent study. *International Journal of Pharmaceutical Investigation, 7*(3), 125–131. https://doi.o rg/ doi:10.4103/jphi.jphi_56_17

Park, J. (2020, November 24). South Korean delivery workers say coronavirus boom means relentless toil. *Reuters.* https://www.reuters.com/article/health-coronavirus-southkorea-jobs-idINKBN2841PM

Partington, R. (2019). *Gig economy in Britain doubles, accounting for 4.7 million workers. The Guardian.* https://www.theguardian.com/business/2019/jun/28/gig-economy-in-britain-doubles-accounting-for-47-million-workers

Partners, M. B. O. (2021.) The great realization. *MBO Partners.* https://www.mbopartners.com/state-of-independence/ .

Patchin, J. W., & Hinduja, S. (2006). Bullies move beyond the schoolyard. A preliminary look at cyberbullying. *Youth Violence and Juvenile Justice, 4*(2), 148–169. doi:10.1177/1541204006286288

Patton, M. Q. (1997). *How to use qualitative methods in evaluation.* SAGE Publications.

Patton, W., & McMahon, M. (2006). The systems theory framework of career development and counseling: Connecting theory and practice. *International Journal for the Advancement of Counseling, 28*(2), 153–166. doi:10.100710447-005-9010-1

Pavot, W., & Diener, E. (1993). The affective and cognitive context of self-reported measures of subjective well-being. *Social Indicators Research, 28*(1), 1–20. doi:10.1007/BF01086714

PDDikti. (2020). *Higher Education Statistics 2020.* https://pddikti.kemdikbud.go.id/publikasi

Pennell. (n.d.). *5 ways to make your Zoom parties feel fresh and exciting again.* TODAY.Com. Retrieved 13 August 2022, from https://www.today.com/tmrw/zoom-party-ideas-make-virtual-parties-feel-fresh-again-t207999

Perez, S. (2018). Apple to Launch its Own 'Digital Health' Features in iOS 12. *TechCrunch.* https://techcrunch.com/2018/06/01/apple-to-launch-its-owndigital-health-features-in- ios-12-says-report/

Pesole, A., Brancati, U., Fernández-Macías, E., Biagi, F., & Gonzalez Vazquez, I. (2018). *Platform workers in Europe.* Publications Office of the European Union.

Pestle Analysis. (2015). *How CATWOE Helps in Business Analysis and Decision Making.* https://pestleanalysis.com/catwoe/

Peters, P., Blomme, R., De Jager, W., & Van Der Heijden, B. (2020). The impact of work-related values and work control on the career satisfaction of female freelancers. *Small Business Economics, 55*(2), 493–506. doi:10.100711187-019-00247-5

Pg Abd Hamid, A. A. A. A. (n.d.). *News 2021—Zakat Payments Online*. Retrieved 4 November 2021, from http://www.rtbnews.rtb.gov.bn/Lists/News%202018/DispForm.aspx?ID=26031&C ontentTypeId=0x010009BBE23B3840184D80AE8D8DEA617660

Pistone, M. (2015). *Law Schools and Technology: Where We Are and Where We Are Heading*. Public Law and Legal Theory Working Paper Series.

Pitichat, T. (2013). Smartphones in the workplace: Changing organizational behavior, transforming the future. *LUX: A Journal of Transdisciplinary Writing and Research, 3*(1).

Poe, M. T. (2014) Contact history. Islık.

Polichka, A. E., Malykhina, O. A., Karpova, I. V., & Tabachuk, N. P. (2020). *Modern Problems of Education in IT and Mathematics: Scientific and Methodological Bases of Improving the Professional Competence of Mathematics Teachers*. Publishing house of Pacific National University.

Polkowska, D. (2020). Platform work during the COVID-19 pandemic: a case study of Glovo couriers in Poland. *European Societies, 23*(sup1), S321–S331. doi:10.1080/14616696.2020.18 26554

Prawirasasra, K. P. (2018). Financial Technology in Indonesia: Disruptive or Collaborative? *Reports on Economics and Finance, 4*(2), 83 – 90. www.m-hikari.com

Prensky, M. (2001). Digital Natives, Digital Immigrants Part 1. *On the Horizon, 9*(5), 1–6. doi:10.1108/10748120110424816

Priyadarshini & Zinna. (n.d.). Exploring The Relationship Between Gaming Addiction, Depression, Anxiety And Stress In Young Males. *International Journal of Research and Analytical Reviews, 6*(1), 40-46.

Purfitasari, S., Masrukhi, Prihatin, T., & Mulyono, S. E. (2019). Digital Pedagogy sebagai Pendekatan Pembelajaran di Era Industri 4.0. *Prosiding Seminar Nasional Pascasarjana (PROSNAMPAS), 2*(1), 806–811. https://proceeding.unnes.ac.id/index.php/snpasca/article/view/374/225

Puri, Y., & Shukla, A. (2021). How Social Media Is Affecting The Youth. *Journal of Emerging Technologies and Innovative Research, 8*(9), 192–201.

Quran.com. (n.d.) *Chapter 6 Surah Al-Anam, Verse 162*. Retrieved 3 November 2022, from https://quran.com/6/162

Rachmayanti, W., & Arumsari, P. (2021). Risk factors analysis affecting project time delay in construction projects using CATWOE analysis. *IOP Conf. Ser.: Earth Environ Sci., 794*. https://iopscience.iop.org/article/10.1088/1755-1315/794/1/012010/pdf

Rahimi, I. D. (2022). Ambient Intelligence in Learning Management System (LMS). In *Science and Information Conference* (pp. 379-387). Springer, Cham. 10.1007/978-3-031-10467-1_24

Rahy, S., & Bass, J. M. (2022). Managing non-functional requirements in agile software development. *IET Software*, *16*(1), 60–72. doi:10.1049fw2.12037

Raja, A. G., Sharma, N., Jenitha, S., & Ranjan, C. (2017). Efficacy of Heartfulness Meditation in Moderating Vital Parameters –A Comparison Study of Experienced and New Meditators. *International Journal of Medical Research and Health Sciences*, *6*(7), 70–78.

Raksnys, A. V., Valickas, A., & Valickiene, R. P. (2015). Transformation of career concept and its effect on career management in organizations. *Human Resources Management & Ergonomics*, *9*(2), 117–128.

Rasdi, R. M., Ismail, M., Uli, J., & Noah, S. M. (2009). Career aspirations and career success among managers in the Malaysian public sector. *Research Journal of International Studies*, *9*(3), 21–35.

Rasdi, R. M., Zaremohzzabieh, Z., & Ahrari, S. (2021). Financial Insecurity During the COVID-19 Pandemic: Spillover Effects on Burnout–Disengagement Relationships and Performance of Employees Who Moonlight. *Frontiers in Psychology*, *12*, 610138. doi:10.3389/fpsyg.2021.610138 PMID:33679526

Ratan, Z. A., Zaman, S. B., Islam, S. M. S., & Hosseinzadeh, H. (2021). Smartphone overuse: A hidden crisis in COVID-19. *Health policy and technology*.

Rathore, H. S. (2016, April). Adoption of Digital Wallet by Consumers. *BVIMSR's Journal of Management Research*, *8*(1), 69–76.

Razzaq, A., Samiha, Y. T., & Anshari, M. (2018). Smartphone habits and behaviors in supporting students self-efficacy. *International Journal of Emerging Technologies in Learning*, *13*(2), 94. doi:10.3991/ijet.v13i02.7685

Rebernik, M. & Širec, K. (2022). *Vzdržljivost podjetniške aktivnosti: GEM Slovenija 2021*. Maribor: Univerzitetna založba. doi:10.18690/um.epf.3.2022

Redekopp, D., Hache, L., & Jarvis, P. (2006). Blueprint for life/work design. National Life/Work Centre, Canada Career Information Partnership & Human Resources Development Canada.

Reed, D. (2017). *Negative Impacts of Social Networking Sites*. https://socialnetworking.lovetoknow.com/Negative_Impact_of_Social_Networking_Sites

Reeves, S., Kuper, A., & Hodges, B. D. (2008). Qualitative research methodologies: Ethnography. *BMJ, 337*(3), a1020–a1020. 1 doi:0.1136/bmj.a1020

Reichmann, W. (2019). The digitalization of the social situation—A sociological exploratory experiment. *Osterreichische Zeitschrift fur Soziologie*, *44*(1), 237–255. doi:10.100711614-019-00355-2

Reid, A., Ronda-Perez, E., & Schenker, M. B. (2020). Migrant workers, essential work, and COVID-19. *American Journal of Industrial Medicine*, *64*(2), 73–77. doi:10.1002/ajim.23209 PMID:33355943

Religions show faith in power of technology. (2019, December 4). *Financial Times.*

Reuschke, D. (2019). The subjective well-being of homeworkers across life domains. *Environment and Planning A. Economy and Space, 51*(6), 1326–1349.

Rhein, T. and Walwei, U. (2018). Forms of Employment in European Comparison. *IAB-Forum.* https://www.iabhttps://www.iab-forum.de/en/forms-of-employment-in-european-comparison/forum.de/en/forms-of-employment-in-european-comparison/.

Right, O. G. S. (2016). *Assessing and Anticipating Changing Skill Needs.* Organisation for Economic Co-Operation and Development OECD.

Riva, G., Calvo, R. A., & Lisetti, C. (2015). Cyberpsychology and affective computing. The Oxford Handbook of Affective Computing, 547-558. Oxford. doi:10.1093/oxfordhb/9780199942237.013.017

Riyanto, S., Ariyanto, E., & Lukertina, L. (2019). WORK LIFE BALANCE AND ITS INFLUENCE ON EMPLOYEE ENGAGEMENT "Y" GENERATION IN COURIER SERVICE INDUSTRY. *International Review of Management and Marketing, 9*(6), 25–31. doi:10.32479/irmm.8499

Roa, A. (2012, October 5). One of 3 Filipinos can't live without cell phones–survey. *The Inquirer.* http://technology.inquirer.net/18168/one-of-3-filipinos-cant-live-without-cell-phones-survey#ixzz5JLeeJKWO/

Robert, I. V. (2020). Axiological Approach to the Development of Education in Conditions of the Digital Paradigm. *Pedagogical Informatics, 2.*

Rodríguez-García, A. M., Moreno-Guerrero, A. J., & Lopez Belmonte, J. (2020). Nomophobia: An individual's growing fear of being without a smartphone—a systematic literature review. *International Journal of Environmental Research and Public Health, 17*(2), 580. doi:10.3390/ijerph17020580 PMID:31963208

Roggeveen, A. L., & Sethuraman, R. (2020). How the COVID-19 Pandemic May Change the World of Retailing. *Journal of Retailing, 96*(2), 169–171. doi:10.1016/j.jretai.2020.04.002

Romance Scams. (n.d.). Federal Bureau of Investigation. Retrieved 13 August 2022, from https://www.fbi.gov/scams-and-safety/common-scams-and-crimes/romance-scams

Roper, J., Ganesh, S., & Inkson, K. (2010). Neoliberalism and knowledge interests in boundaryless careers discourse. *Work, Employment and Society, 24*(4), 661–679. doi:10.1177/0950017010380630

Rosa, W. E., Schlak, A. E., & Rushton, C. H. (2020). A blueprint for leadership during COVID-19. *Nursing Management, 51*(8), 28–34. doi:10.1097/01.NUMA.0000688940.29231.6f PMID:32665503

Roslan, B. (2021, August 17). Online learning resume for the third term amid pandemic. *The Brunei Post.* https://www.thebruneipost.co/health/covid-19/2021/08/18/online-learning-resume-for-the-third-term-amid-pandemic/

Rosli, S. N., Anshari, M., Almunawar, M. N., & Masri, M. (2022). Digital Wallet Ecosystem in Promoting Financial Inclusion. In *FinTech Development for Financial Inclusiveness* (pp. 31–49). IGI Global. doi:10.4018/978-1-7998-8447-7.ch003

Roundup: Brunei introduces curfew to contain COVID-19 local transmission. (n.d.). Retrieved 12 August 2022, from http://www.news.cn/english/2021-10/01/c_1310222246.htm

Roy, G., & Shrivastava, A. K. (2020). Future of gig economy: Opportunities and challenges. *IMI Konnect*, *9*(1), 14–27.

Rožman, M., Shmeleva, Z., & Tominc, P. (2019). Knowledge Management Components and Their Impact on Work Engagement of Employees. *Naše Gospodarstvo/Our Economy, 65*(1), 40–56. doi:10.2478/ngoe-2019-0004

Ryff, C. D. (1989). Happiness is everything or is it? Explorations on the meaning of psychological well-being. *Journal of Personality and Social Psychology*, *57*(6), 1069–1081. doi:10.1037/0022-3514.57.6.1069

Saim, H. S. H. (2013). Brunei Darussalam in 2012: Towards a Zikir Nation. *Southeast Asian Affairs*, *SEAA13*(1), 63–72. doi:10.1355/aa13-1e

Sai, S. K. G., Padmanabha, B. V., Srilatha, B., & Mukkadan, J. K. (2020). Effectiveness of Heartfulness Meditation On Sleep Quality And Quality Of Life In Patients With Type 2 Diabetes. *MOJ Anat. Physiol.*, *7*(1), 19–21. doi:10.15406/mojap.2020.07.00283

Sait, M. A., & Anshari, M. (2021). Industrial Revolution 4.0: A New Challenge to Brunei Darussalam's Unemployment Issue. *International Journal of Asian Business and Information Management*, *12*(4), 33–44. doi:10.4018/IJABIM.20211001.oa3

Sakkir, G., Dollah, S., & Ahmad, J. (2021). E-Learning in COVID-19 Situation: Students' Perception. *EduLine: Journal of Education and Learning Innovation*, *1*(1). Advance online publication. doi:10.35877/454RI.eduline378

Salkever, A., & Wadhwa, V. (2018). How Tech Companies Can Make Their Products Less Addictive. *Medium*. https://medium.com/s/story/how-tech-companies-can-make-their-products-less-addictive

Sá, M. J., Santos, A. I., Serpa, S., & Miguel Ferreira, C. (2021). Digitainability—Digital competences post-COVID-19 for a sustainable society. *Sustainability*, *13*(17), 9564. doi:10.3390u13179564

Samadi, B., Nogoev, A., & Yazdanifard, A. (2011). *The Evolution and Development of E-Commerce Market and E-Cash*. doi:10.1115/1.859858

Samiha, Y. T., Handayani, T., Razaq, A., Fithriyah, M., Fitri, A., & Anshari, M. (2022, March). Implementation of Education 4.0 as Sustainable Decisions for a Sustainable Development. In *2022 International Conference on Decision Aid Sciences and Applications (DASA)* (pp. 846-850). IEEE. 10.1109/DASA54658.2022.9765080

Samiha, Y. T., Handayani, T., Razzaq, A., Fitri, A., Fithriyah, M., & Anshari, M. (2021, November). Sustainability of Excellence in Education 4.0. In *2021 Sustainable Leadership and Academic Excellence International Conference (SLAE)* (pp. 1-5). IEEE. 10.1109/SLAE54202.2021.9788095

Sandbach, J., & Grimes, R. (2020). *Law School Pro Bono and Clinic Report 2020.* https://drive.google.com/file/d/1GaRpXy7WeID0eJM27VplY-e9ovjme1kd/view

Sandybayev, A. (2020). The Impact of E-Learning Technologies on Students' Motivation: Student Centred Interaction in Business Education. *International Journal of Research in Tourism and Hospitality, 6*, 16–24. doi:10.20431/2455-0043.0601002

Sapsed, J., Camerani, R., Masucci, M., Petermann, M., Rajguru, M., Jones, P., & Sussex, W. (2015). *Brighton fuse 2: Freelancers in the creative, digital, IT economy.* AHRC.

Savickas, M. L. (2011). Reshaping the story of career counselling. In *Shaping the story* (pp. 1–3). Brill Sense.

Saygın, Y., & Arslan, C. (2009). Üniversite öğrencilerinin sosyal destek, benlik saygısı ve öznel iyi oluş düzeylerinin incelenmesi. *Selçuk Üniversitesi Ahmet Keleşoğlu Eğitim Fakültesi, 28*, 207–222.

Schniederjans, D. G., Curado, C., & Khalajhedayati, M. (2020). Supply chain digitisation trends: An integration of knowledge management. *International Journal of Production Economics, 220*, 107439. doi:10.1016/j.ijpe.2019.07.012

Schuller, D., & Schuller, B. W. (2018). The age of artificial emotional intelligence. *Computer, 51*(9), 38–46. doi:10.1109/MC.2018.3620963

Schwab, K. (2016). The fourth industrial revolution. *Cologny: World Economic Forum.*

Schwarzmüller, T., Brosi, P., Duman, D., & Welpe, I. M. (2018). How does the digital transformation affect organizations? Key themes of change in work design and leadership. *Management Review, 29*(2), 114–138. doi:10.5771/0935-9915-2018-2-114

Schwellnus, C., Geva, A., & Pak Mathilde, V. R. (2019). Gig economy platforms: boon or bane? Organisation for Economic Co-operation and Development. *Economics department working papers*, 1550.

Scoop, T. (2022, April 4). *Online romance scams: How to spot the red flags.* The Scoop. https://thescoop.co/2022/04/04/online-romance-scams-how-to-spot-the-red-flags/

Scott, A. W., Bressler, N. M., Ffolkes, S., Wittenborn, J. S., & Jorkasky, J. (2016). *Public Attitudes About Eye and Vision Health, 134*(10), 1111–1118.

Seaman, J. E., Allen, I. E., & Seaman, J. (2018). *Grade Increase : Tracking Distance Education in the United States.* https://files.eric.ed.gov/fulltext/ED580852.pdf

SecurEnvoy. (2012). 66% of the population suffer from Nomophobia the fear of being without their phone. *SecurEnvoy.* http://www.securenvoy.com/blog/2012/02/16/66-of-thepopulation-suffer-from nomophobia-the-fear-of-being-without-their-phone/

Seibert, S. E., & Kraimer, M. L. (2001). The five-factor model of personality and career success. *Journal of Vocational Behavior*, *58*(1), 1–21. doi:10.1006/jvbe.2000.1757

Shabahang, R., Aruguete, M. S., & Shim, H. (2021). Online News Addiction: Future Anxiety, Fear of Missing Out on News, and Interpersonal Trust Contribute to Excessive Online News Consumption. *Online Journal of Communication and Media Technologies*, *11*(2), e202105. doi:10.30935/ojcmt/10822

Shahrill, M., Noorashid, N., & Keasberry, C. (2021). COVID-19: Educational Practices and Responses in Brunei Darussalam. In P. Le Ha, A. Kumpoh, K. Wood, R. Jawawi, & H. Said (Eds.), *Globalisation, Education, and Reform in Brunei Darussalam* (pp. 325–354). Springer International Publishing. doi:10.1007/978-3-030-77119-5_16

Shahroom, A. A., & Hussin, N. (2018). Industrial Revolution 4.0 and Education. *International Journal of Academic Research in Business & Social Sciences*, *8*(9), 314–319. doi:10.6007/IJARBSS/v8-i9/4593

Sharbawi, S., & Mabud, S. A. (2021). Malay, Muslim and Monarchy: An Introduction to Brunei Darussalam and Its National Identity. In P. Le Ha, A. Kumpoh, K. Wood, R. Jawawi, & H. Said (Eds.), *Globalisation, Education, and Reform in Brunei Darussalam* (pp. 45–66). Springer International Publishing. doi:10.1007/978-3-030-77119-5_3

Sharma, J. (2018, Oct 7). *Importance of E-Wallets in Cashless Economy* (A Post Demonetisation Study with Special Reference to Ahmedabad City). Retrieved from: https://globalbizresearch.org/Dubai_Conference_2018_oct2/docs/doc/D818.pdf

Silver, L. (2019, Feb 5). *In emerging economies, smartphone adoption has grown more quickly among younger generations*. Retrieved from: https://www.pewresearch.org/global/2019/02/05/in-emerging-economies-smartphone-adoption-has-grown-more-quickly-among-younger-generations/

Simon Kemp. (2022). *Digital 2022, India*. https://datareportal.com/reports/digital-2022-india#:~:text=Social%20media%20statistics%20for%20India,in%20India%20in%20January%202022

Singh, P., Aulak, D. S., Mangat, S. S., & Aulak, M. S. (2015). Systematic review: Factors contributing to burnout in dentistry. *Occupational Medicine*, *66*(1), 27–31. doi:10.1093/occmed/kqv119 PMID:26443193

Skillshare. (n.d.). Retrieved 12 August 2022, from https://www.skillshare.com/about

Smith, A. (2012). Nearly half of American adults are smartphone owners. *Pew Research Center*. https://www.pewresearch.org/internet/2012/03/01/nearly-half-of-american-adults-are-smartphone-owners/

Sohn, S., Rees, P., Wildridge, B., Kalk, N. J., & Carter, B. (2019). Prevalence of problematic smartphone usage and associated mental health outcomes amongst children and young people: A systematic review, meta-analysis and GRADE of the evidence. *BMC Psychiatry*, *19*(1), 1–10. PMID:30606141

Soltovets, E., Chigisheva, O., & Dubover, D. (2019). Foreign Language E-Course as Informal Learning Tool for Digital Literacy Development. *Dilemas Contemporaneos-Educacion Politica y Valores, 6*(3), Art. 50.

Sommer, P. (1998). *Digital footprints: Assessing computer evidence. Criminal Law Review, 12,* 61-78. Tapscott, D. (2008). *Grown up digital: How the next generation is changing your world.* McGraw-Hill.

Songsom, N., Nilsook, P., & Wannapiroon, P. (2019). The synthesis of the student relationship management system using the internet of things to collect the digital footprint for higher education institutions. *International Journal of Online & Biomedical Engineering*, *15*(6), 99. doi:10.3991/ijoe.v15i06.10173

Spajic, D. J. (2022). The Future of Employment - 30 Telling Gig Economy Statistics. *Small Biz Genius*. https://www.smallbizgenius.net/by-the-numbers/gig-economy-statistics/#gref

Spurk, D., Hirschi, A., & Dries, N. (2019). Antecedents and outcomes of objective versus subjective career success: Competing perspectives and future directions. *Journal of Management*, *45*(1), 35–69. doi:10.1177/0149206318786563

Standard Chartered Brunei. (n.d.). Retrieved 13 August 2022, from https://ne-np.facebook.com/StandardCharteredBrunei/posts/pfbid0uguxqZkb3gbSYPUD3tzNTjgpXNztEnHpJnQzEVAWxkAor5d7mH8Yq2dtfC1YyqCUl

Statista. (2022). Time spent with nonvoice activities on mobile phones every day in the United States from 2019-2023. *Statista*. https://www.statista.com/statistics/1045353/mobile-device-daily-usage-time-in-the- us/

Staying Alert Online | Bank Islam Brunei Darussalam. (n.d.). Retrieved 13 August 2022, from http://www.bibd.com.bn/resource-centre/online-safety/

Steiner, C. (2012). *Automate this: How algorithms took over our markets, our jobs, and the world.* Penguin.

Stolterman, E., Fors, A. C., Truex, D. P., & Wastell, D. (2004). Information technology and the good life. In *Information systems research: Relevant theory and informed practice* (Vol. 143, pp. 687–693). Kluwer Academic Publishers. doi:10.1007/1-4020-8095-6_45

Studies, K. L. (2022a). *23 Online LLB Programs in Asia.* Academic Press.

StudiesK. L. (2022b). *9 Online JD Programs in Asia.* https://www.lawstudies.com/Juris-Doctor/Asia/Online/

Subedi, S., Nayaju, S., Subedi, S., Shah, S. K., & Shah, J. M. (2020). Article. *International Journal of Science and Healthcare Research*, *5*(3).

Sullivan, S. E., & Arthur, M. B. (2006). The evolution of the boundaryless career concept: Examining physical and psychological mobility. *Journal of Vocational Behavior*, *69*(1), 19–29. doi:10.1016/j.jvb.2005.09.001

Susskind, R. (2017). Tomorrow's Lawyers: An Introduction to Your Future (2nd ed.). Oxford University Press. doi:10.1177/1037969X1303800316

Sutherland, J. (2013, October). Employment status and job satisfaction. In *Evidence-based HRM: a Global Forum for Empirical Scholarship* (Vol. 1, pp. 187-216). Emerald Group Publishing Limited. 10.1108/EBHRM-08-2012-0008

Tanyeri, E. M., Koçak, P., & Altıncık, H. (2017). A Comparative Analysis On The Use Of Social Media As A Public Relations Tool: Online Shopping Sites. *The Journal of Academic Social Science*, *5*(60), 523–536.

Tarafdar, M., Gupta, A., & Turel, O. (2013). The dark side of information technology use. *Information Systems Journal*, *23*(3), 269–275. doi:10.1111/isj.12015

Tatlı, H. (2015). Akıllı telefon seçiminin belirleyicileri: üniversite öğrencileri üzerine bir Uygulama [The determinants of smartphone choice: An application on university students]. *Çankırı Karatekin Üniversitesi İktisadi ve İdari Bilimler Fakültesi Dergisi*, 1-19. doi:10.18074/cnuiibf.233

TED-Ed—YouTube. (n.d.). Retrieved 12 August 2022, from https://www.youtube.com/

Tema Hari Kebangsaan. (n.d.). Retrieved 20 November 2021, from http://www.kkbs.gov.bn/Hari%20Kebangsaan/Tema%20Hari%20Kebangsaan.aspx

Temporary closure of child care centre extended | Borneo Bulletin Online. (n.d.). Retrieved 6 August 2022, from https://borneobulletin.com.bn/temporary-closure-of-child-care-centre-extended/

Tenbarge, K. (n.d.). *How to throw a perfect Zoom party with your friends and family*. Business Insider. Retrieved 12 August 2022, from https://www.businessinsider.com/how-to-throw-zoom-party-custom-background-friends-family-2020-3

Thatcher, J. (2014). Big data, big questions| Living on fumes: Digital footprints, data fumes, and the limitations of spatial big data. *International Journal of Communication*, *8*, 19.

the American Bar Association. (2020). *Model Rules of Professional Conduct and Practice*. https://www.americanbar.org/groups/professional_responsibility/publications/model_rules_of_professional_conduct/rule_1_1_competence/comment_on_rule_1_1/

The Financial Diet—YouTube. (n.d.). Retrieved 12 August 2022, from https://www.youtube.com/c/thefinancialdiet/videos

The Scoop. (2018). *Millennials driving e-commerce, says a new report from AITI*. Retrieved from: https://thescoop.co/2018/07/15/millennials-driving-ecommerce-report-aiti/

The Scoop. (2019). *Smart nation initiatives: The foundation of Brunei's digital economy*. Retrieved from: https://thescoop.co/2019/02/27/smart-nation-initiatives-the-foundation-of-bruneis-digital-economy/

The Scoop. (2021a, June 18). *AITI eyes digitalisation of 1,200 MSMEs by 2025.* https://thescoop.co/2021/06/18/aiti-eyes-digitalisation-of-1200-msmes-by-2025/

The Scoop. (2021b, June 26). *AMBD renamed Brunei Darussalam Central Bank.* https://thescoop.co/2021/06/26/ambd-renamed-brunei-darussalam-central-bank/#:~:text=AMBD%20renamed%20Brunei%20Darussalam%20Central%20Bank%20%2D %20The%20Scoop

Thimmapuram, Pargament, Bell, Shurck, & Madhusudan. (2021). Heartfulness Meditation Improves Loneliness and Sleep in Physicians and Advance Practice Providers During Covid 19 Pandemic. *Hospital Practice, 49*(3). 1 doi:0.1080/21548331.2021.1896858

Thimmapuram, J., Pargament, R., Sibliss, K., Grim, R., Risques, R., & Toorens, E. (2017). Effect of heartfulness meditation on burnout, emotional wellness, and telomere length in health care professionals. *Journal of Community Hospital Internal Medicine Perspectives, 7*(1), 21–27. doi:10.1080/20009666.2016.1270806 PMID:28634520

Thimmapuram, J., Yommer, D., Tudor, L., Bell, T., Dumitrescu, C., & Davis, R. (2020). Heartfulness meditation improves sleep in chronic insomnia. *Journal of Community Hospital Internal Medicine Perspectives, 10*(1), 1, 10–15. doi:10.1080/20009666.2019.1710948 PMID:32128052

Think Insights. (2022). *CATWOE - How to assess the influence of stakeholders' viewpoints?* https://thinkinsights.net/consulting/catwoe-technique/

Thorpe, M., & Godwin, S. (2006). Interaction and e-learning: The student experience. *Studies in Continuing Education, 28*(3), 203–221. doi:10.1080/01580370600947330

Thumim, N. (2012). *Self-representation and digital culture.* Springer. doi:10.1057/9781137265135

Tinder | Dating, make friends & meet new people. (n.d.). Retrieved 12 August 2022, from https://tinder.com/

Torode, C. (2011). The realities of consumerization: Christina Torode takes a shop-floor look at Ford's bring-your-own-device programme. *Computer Weekly*, 1.

Tosini, G., Ferguson, I., & Tsubota, K. (2016), Effects of blue light on the circadian system and eye physiology. NCBI. https://www.ncbi.nlm.nih.gov/pmc/articles/PMC4734149/

Tran, M., & Sokas, R. K. (2017). The gig economy and contingent work: An occupational health assessment. *Journal of Occupational and Environmental Medicine, 59*(4), e63–e66. doi:10.1097/JOM.0000000000000977 PMID:28244887

Tran, V. A., Nguyen, H. T. T., & Nguyen, T. M. L. (2019). Digital Transformation: A Digital Learning Case Study. *Proceedings of the 2019 The World Symposium on Software Engineering - WSSE 2019*, 119-124. 10.1145/3362125.3362135

Turel, O., & Serenko, A. (2012). The benefits and dangers of enjoyment with social networking websites. *European Journal of Information Systems*, *21*(5), 512–528. doi:10.1057/ejis.2012.1

Turnbull, D., Chugh, R., & Luck, J. (2021). Transitioning to E-Learning during the COVID-19 pandemic: How have Higher Education Institutions responded to the challenge? *Education and Information Technologies*, *26*(5), 4601–4619. doi:10.100710639-021-10633-w PMID:34177349

Types of scams | Cyber.gov.au. (n.d.). Retrieved 13 August 2022, from https://www.cyber.gov.au/learn/threats/types-of-scams

Undavalli, V. K., Rani, G. S., & Kumar, J. R. (2020). Prevalence Of Internet Gaming Disorder In India: A Technological Hazard Among Adolescents. *International Journal of Community Medicine and Public Health*, *7*(2), 688–693. doi:10.18203/2394-6040.ijcmph20200450

Underberg, N. M., & Zorn, E. (2013). *Digital Ethnography: Anthropology, Narrative, and New Media*. University of Texas Press., doi:10.7560/744332

United Nations. (2021). *Digitally enabled new forms of work and policy implications for labor regulation frameworks and social protection systems*. UN. https://www.un.org/development/desa/dspd/2021/09/digitally-enabled-new-forms-of-work-and-policy-implications-for-labor-regulation-frameworks-and-social-protection-systems/

University of Essex. (2022). *LLB (Hons) Law*. https://online.essex.ac.uk/courses/llb-hons-law/

Upwork. (2019). Sixth annual "Freelancing in America" study finds that more people than ever see freelancing as a long-term career path. *Upwork*. https://www.upwork.com/press/releases/freelancing-in-america-2019

Upwork. (2021). Upwork Study Finds 59 Million Americans Freelancing Amid Turbulent Labor Market. *Upwork*. https://www.upwork.com/press/releases/upwork-study-finds-59-million-americans-freelancing-amid-turbulent-labor-market

Urwiler, R., & Frolick, M. (2008). The IT Value Hierarchy: Using Maslow's Hierarchy of Needs as a Metaphor for Gauging the Maturity Level of Information Technology Use within Competitive Organizations. *Information Systems Management*, *25*(1), 83–88. doi:10.1080/10580530701777206

Uzelac, A. (2008). How to understand digital culture: Digital culture- a resource for a knowledge society? A. Uzelac ve B. Cvjeticanin (Ed.) Digital Culture: The Changing Dynamics içinde (7-21). Croatia: Institute for International Relations.

Vaidya, A., Pathak, V., & Vaidya, A. (2016). Mobile Phone Usage Among Youth. *International Journal of Applied Research and Studies, 5*(13). Doi:10.20908/ijars.v5i3.9483

Valcour, M. (2007). Work-based resources as moderators of the relationship between work hours and satisfaction with work-family balance. *The Journal of Applied Psychology*, *92*(6), 1512–1523. doi:10.1037/0021-9010.92.6.1512 PMID:18020793

Van den Born, A., & Van Witteloostuijn, A. (2013). Drivers of freelance career success. *Journal of Organizational Behavior*, *34*(1), 24–46. doi:10.1002/job.1786

Van der Zwan, P., Hessels, J., & Burger, M. (2020). Happy free willies? Investigating the relationship between freelancing and subjective well-being. *Small Business Economics*, *55*(2), 475–491. doi:10.100711187-019-00246-6

Van der Zwan, P., Thurik, R., Verheul, I., & Hessels, J. (2016). Factors influencing the entrepreneurial engagement of opportunity and necessity entrepreneurs. *Eurasian Business Review*, *6*(3), 273–295. doi:10.100740821-016-0065-1

Van Deursen, A.J.A.M., Bolle, C.L., Hegner, S.M. & Kommers, P.A.M. (2015). Modeling Habitual and Addictive Smartphone behaviour: The Role of Smartphone Usage Types, Emotional Intelligence, Social Stress, Self-Regulation, Age, and Gender. *Computers in Human behaviour, 45*(1), pp. 411-420.

Van Stel, A., & Van der Zwan, P. (2020). Analyzing the changing education distributions of solo self-employed workers and employer entrepreneurs in Europe. *Small Business Economics*, *55*(2), 429–445. doi:10.100711187-019-00243-9

Van-Schaik, P., Jeske, D., Onibokun, J., Coventry, L., Jansen, J., & Kusev, P. (2017). Risk perceptions of cyber-security and precautionary behaviour. *Computers in Human Behavior*, *75*, 547–559. doi:10.1016/j.chb.2017.05.038

Van-Zanden, J. L., Baten, J., Mira d'Ercole, M., Rijpma, A., Smith, C., & Timmer, M. (Eds.). (2014). *How Was Life?: Global Well-being since 1820*. OECD Publishing. doi:10.1787/9789264214262-en

Veenhoven, R. (2012). Happiness: Also known as "life satisfaction" and "subjective well-being." In *Handbook of social indicators and quality of life research* (pp. 63–77). Springer. doi:10.1007/978-94-007-2421-1_3

Vieira, T. (2020). The lose-lose dilemmas of Barcelona's platform delivery workers in the age of COVID-19. *Social Sciences & Humanities Open*, *2*(1), 100059. doi:10.1016/j.ssaho.2020.100059 PMID:34173497

Voo, T. C., Senguttuvan, M., & Tam, C. C. (2020). Family Presence for Patients and Separated Relatives During COVID-19: Physical, Virtual, and Surrogate. *Journal of Bioethical Inquiry*, *17*(4), 767–772. doi:10.100711673-020-10009-8 PMID:32840835

Vroom, V.H. (1964). Work and motivation. *Wiley.*

Vural, Z. ve Bat, M. (2010). Social Media as a New Communication Medium: A Research on Ege University Faculty of Communication. *Journal of Yasar University*, *5*(20), 3348–3382.

Warisno, A. (2017). Tradisi Tahlilan Upaya Menyambung Silaturahmi. *Riayah : Jurnal Sosial Dan Keagamaan*, *2*(02), 69–97.

Warner, K. S., & Wäger, M. (2019). Building dynamic capabilities for digital transformation: An ongoing process of strategic renewal. *Long Range Planning*, *52*(3), 326–349. doi:10.1016/j.lrp.2018.12.001

Watch out for phone scams, Bruneians reminded. (n.d.). The Star. Retrieved 13 August 2022, from https://www.thestar.com.my/aseanplus/aseanplus-news/2020/06/12/watch-out-for-phone-scams-bruneians-reminded

We Are Social. (2022, January 26). *Digital 2022: Another year of bumper growth.* We Are Social UK. https://wearesocial.com/uk/blog/2022/01/digital-2022-another-year-of-bumper-growth-2/

What are some common types of scams? (n.d.). Consumer Financial Protection Bureau. Retrieved 13 August 2022, from https://www.consumerfinance.gov/ask-cfpb/what-are-some-common-types-of-scams-en-2092/

Widiger, T. A., and Oltmanns, J. R. (2017). Neuroticism Is A Fundamental Domain of Personality with Enormous Public Health Implications. World Psychiatry; Official Journal of the World Psychiatric Association (WPA), 16(2), 144–145. doi:10.1002/wps.20411

Wiederhold, B. K., & Riva, G. (2013). The quest for active and healthy ageing: What cyberpsychology can offer. Annual Review of Cybertherapy and Telemedicine. *Positive Technology and Health Engagement for Healthy Living and Active Ageing, 191*(3), 444.

Wijaya, B. S. (2019). Dancing with the impropriety of media: How Indonesian consumers think and behave towards the unethical and illogical online news. *Malaysian Journal of Communication, 35*(1), 187–205. doi:10.17576/JKMJC-2019-3501-13

Wilson, J. D. (2017). *Creating Strategic Value Through Financial Technology.* Wiley Finance. doi:10.1002/9781119318682

Windiarti, S., Fadilah, N., Dhermawati, E., & Pratolo, B. W. (2019). Teachers' perception towards the Obstacles of E-Learning Classes. *Journal of Language Teaching and Literature, 6*(2), 117–128. doi:10.30605/25409190.v6.117-128

Wokurka, G., Banschbach, Y., Houlder, D., & Jolly, R. (2017). Digital culture: Why strategy and culture should eat breakfast together. In *Shaping the digital enterprise* (pp. 109–120). Springer. doi:10.1007/978-3-319-40967-2_5

Wong, A. (n.d.). *eKadaiBrunei: Brunei's first online E-commerce directory launched.* https://www.bizbrunei.com/2020/04/ekadaibrunei-bruneis-first-online-E-commerce-directory-launched/

Wood, A. J., Lehdonvirta, V., & Graham, M. (2018). Workers of the Internet unite? Online freelancer organisation among remote gig economy workers in six Asian and African countries. *New Technology, Work and Employment, 33*(2), 95–112. doi:10.1111/ntwe.12112

Wook, T. S. M., Mohamed, H., Noor, S. F. M., Muda, Z., & Zairon, I. Y. (2019). Awareness of digital footprint management in the new media amongst youth. *Jurnal Komunikasi: Malaysian Journal of Communication, 35*(3), 407–421.

Woollaston, V. (2014). How often do you look at your phone? The average user now picks up their device more than 1,500 times a week. *Daily Mail.* http://www. dailymail.co.uk/sciencetech/article-2783677/How-YOU-look-phone-Theaverage-user-picks- device-1-500-times-day.html

World Health Organization. (2017). Pandemic influenza risk management: a WHO guide to inform and harmonize national and international pandemic preparedness and response. *World Health Organization.* https://apps.who.int/iris/handle/10665/259893

World Health Organization. (2020), *Physical activity.* WHO. https://www.who.int/news-room/fact-sheets/detail/physical-activity

World Health Organization. (2020). Coronavirus disease (COVID-2019) situation report, (154). WHO. https://wwwwhoint/emergencies/diseases/novel-coronavirus-2019/ situation-reports/

Wright, B. M. (2017). Blended Learning, Student Perception of Face-to-Face and Online EFL Lessons. *Indonesian Journal of Applied Linguistics, 7*(1), 64–71. doi:10.17509/ijal.v7i1.6859

Xie, Y., Szeto, G. P. Y., Dai, J., & Madeleine, P. (2016). A comparison of muscle activity in using touchscreen smartphone among young people with and without chronic neck– shoulder pain. *Ergonomics, 59*(1), 61–72. doi:10.1080/00140139.2015.1056237 PMID:26218600

Yadav, G. S., Cidral-Filho, F. J., & Iyer, R. B. (2021). Using Heartfulness Meditation and Brainwave Entrainment to Improve Teenage Mental Wellbeing. *Frontiers in Psychology, 12,* 742892. doi:10.3389/fpsyg.2021.742892 PMID:34721219

Yakamoz, Y., Kesgin, C., & Topuzoğlu, A. (2006). Sağlığın tanımı; başa çıkma. *İstanbul Kültür Üniversitesi Dergisi, 3,* 47-49.

Yaman, E. (2010). Teaching staff exposed to mobbing organizational culture and climate perceptions. *Educational Sciences: Theory and Practice, 10*(1), 567–578.

Yan, H., & Xie, S. (2016). How does auditors' work stress affect audit quality? Empirical evidence from the Chinese stock market. *China Journal of Accounting Research, 9*(4), 305–319. doi:10.1016/j.cjar.2016.09.001

Yasmin Mogahed (@yasminmogahed) • Instagram photos and videos. (n.d.). Retrieved 19 August 2022, from https://www.instagram.com/yasminmogahed/

Yildirim, C. (2014). Exploring the dimensions of nomophobia: Developing and validating a questionnaire using mixed methods research [Graduate Thesis]. Graduate Theses and Dissertations, 14005 https://lib.dr.iastate.edu/etd/14005/.

Yıldırım, A., & Şimşek, H. (2006). *Qualitative research methods in the social sciences.* Distinguished Publishing.

Yildirim, C., & Correia, A. P. (2015). Exploring the dimensions of nomophobia: Development and validation of a self-reported questionnaire. *Computers in Human Behavior, 49,* 130–137. doi:10.1016/j.chb.2015.02.059

Yli-Renko, H., Autio, E., & Sapienza, H. J. (2001). Social capital, knowledge acquisition, and knowledge exploitation in young technology-based firms. *Strategic Management Journal, 22*(6-7), 587–613. doi:10.1002mj.183

Yoon, K. H., Lee, C. Y., & Peng, N. L. (2021). Burnout and work engagement among dispatch workers in courier service organizations. *Asia-Pacific Social Science Review, 21*(1), 1–19.

Young, K. S. (1998). Internet addiction: The emergence of a new clinical disorder. *Cyberpsychology & Behavior, 1*(3), 237–244. doi:10.1089/cpb.1998.1.237

Zadros, K. (2021). Employee Satisfaction with the Employer's Health Safety Activities During the SARS-COV-2 Pandemic. *Sciendo. 3(*1), 228 - 238. https://sciendo.com/pdf/10.2478/czoto-2021-0023

Zalat, M. M., Hamed, M. S., & Bolbol, S. A. (2021). The experiences, challenges, and acceptance of e-learning as a tool for teaching during the COVID-19 pandemic among university medical staff. *PLoS One, 16*(3), e0248758. doi:10.1371/journal.pone.0248758 PMID:33770079

Zanetta, L. D., Hakim, M. P., Gastaldi, G. B., Seabra, L. M. J., Rolim, P. M., Nascimento, L. G. P., Medeiros, C. O., & da Cunha, D. T. (2021). The use of food delivery apps during the COVID-19 pandemic in Brazil: The role of solidarity, perceived risk, and regional aspects. *Food Research International, 149*, 110671. doi:10.1016/j.foodres.2021.110671 PMID:34600673

Zhang, D., Guo, B., & Yu, Z. (2011). The emergence of social and community intelligence. *Computer, 44*(7), 21–28. doi:10.1109/MC.2011.65

Zulkarnain, N., & Anshari, M. (2016, November). Big data: Concept, applications, & challenges. In *2016 International Conference on Information Management and Technology (ICIMTech)* (pp. 307-310). IEEE. 10.1109/ICIMTech.2016.7930350

Zulkarnain, N., Anshari, M., Hamdan, M., & Fithriyah, M. (2021, August). Big data in business and ethical challenges. In *2021 International Conference on Information Management and Technology (ICIMTech)* (Vol. 1, pp. 298-303). IEEE. 10.1109/ICIMTech53080.2021.9534963

About the Contributors

Muhammad Anshari is researcher and academic staff at School of Business & Economics, Universiti Brunei Darussalam. His professional experience started when he was IT Business Analyst at Astra International. Research Fellowship from The Government Republic of China (Taiwan) at National Taiwan University (Jan-Dec 2014). Research Fellowship from King Saud University - the Kingdom of Saudi Arabia 2009. Senior Associate Researcher of Informatics Department, Universitas Islam Negeri Yogyakarta, Indonesia.

Akmal Nasri Kamal began his career as a schoolteacher in 2015. A year later, he joined Universiti Brunei Darussalam (UBD) and held the post of Counselling Officer. He spearheaded the transformation agenda of UBD to be amongst the best universities in the world. He is also an accredited Graduate Member of the British Psychological Society, an Associate Member of the American Psychological Association, and a Licensed Master Practitioner of Neuro-Linguistic Programming. Nasri has a wealth of experience in providing training specialising in the areas of leadership, mindfulness, goal setting and many other soft skills. In his free time, Nasri loves to cycle and travel. He is devoted to becoming a "lifelong learner, and continuous and never-ending improvement" mission. In the university, he constantly mentions the importance of taking care of mental health to increase awareness. He hopes to make a difference to future leaders. He believes that small efforts brings great changes.

* * *

Mohammad Nabil Almunawar is currently an associate professor at the School of Business and Economics, Universiti of Brunei Darussalam (UBDSBE), Brunei Darussalam. He was the former dean of UBDSBE. He received his bachelor's degree in 1983 from Bogor Agricultural University, Indonesia, master's degree (MSc) from the Department of Computer Science, University of Western Ontario, London, Canada in 1991, and Ph.D in Computer Science/Information Systems from the University of New South Wales in 1998. Dr. Almunawar has published more than 150 papers in refereed journals, books, book chapters, encyclopedias, and international conference proceedings. He has more than 30 years of teaching experience in the area of information systems. His overall research interests include applications of IT in management, e-business/commerce, digital marketplace/platform, digital business ecosystem, health informatics, information security, and cloud computing. Currently, he focuses his research on digital transformation, digital marketplace, digital platform, and digital business ecosystem.

Nur Hayati Binti Mohd Daud is a graduate student enrolled in the Master of Management program at Universiti Brunei Darussalam. Prior to pursuing a career in management, she graduated from the same institution with a degree in environmental sciences.

Zuhda Fitriana, S.H. Universitas Airlangga, LL.M., UNSW, Australia, is a lecturer at Faculty of Law UPN Veteran Jawa Timur. She has published many articles in national or international journals. Her research areas include public law, business and economic law, and education-issue.

Ivona Huđek is a junior researcher at the Institute for Entrepreneurship and Small Business Management at the Faculty of Economics and Business of the University of Maribor, who actively participates in the Entrepreneurship for Innovative Society research program. She was elected to the habilitation title of assistant in the field of entrepreneurship and participates in the pedagogical process of undergraduate study programs. She is a member of the research team of Slovenian Entrepreneurship Observatory. She is engaged in research in the field of entrepreneurship and the impact of digitalization on the field of work. The results of the research are published in various scientific and professional journals.

Fatma İnce received her Ph.D. degree in Management and Organization. Currently, she is an Associate Professor of Organization at Mersin University in Türkiye, where she teaches Organizational Behavior, Entrepreneurship, Creative Thinking, Leadership, and Teamwork at the undergraduate and graduate levels. Her research interests consist of entrepreneurship, leadership, creativity, synergy, generations, sustainability, and learning organizations. And besides, she serves as Assistant Director at the University Career Center to provide strategic oversight and management for the students' careers as they enhance their skills. However, she performs as the chairman of the faculty internship committee within the scope of the national internship program. In addition, the author gives awareness and mindfulness training so that individuals can concentrate on themselves and experience the beauty and miracles of life.

Awangku Adi Putra is currently a student at Universiti Brunei Darussalam. He is majoring in Cybersecurity and Forensics at UBD School of Digital Science and plans to pursue a career in Cyber Security.

Eka Ravizki, S.H. Universitas Gadjah Mada, LL.M., Universitas Gadjah, is a lecturer at Faculty of Law UPN Veteran Jawa Timur. He has published many articles and worked as a researcher prior joining the university. He currently acts as the head of MBKM curriculum implementation in the faculty.

Anjum Sheikh is working as Assistant Professor in the department of Electronics and Communication Engineering at Rajiv Gandhi College of Engineering Research & Technology, Chandrapur, India. She has complete her PhD from Kalinga Univeristy , Raipur. She has published more than 20 research papers in reputed journals and conference and had completed PG Diploma in Psychological Counseling.

Karin Širec, PhD, is a full-time Professor of Entrepreneurship and Business Economics at the Faculty of Economics and Business (FEB), University of Maribor. She is a Head of Department for Entrepreneurship and Business Economics. As a member of the Institute for Entrepreneurship and Small Business Management she carries out research in the fields of entrepreneurship, business economics, innovations, female entrepreneurship, high-growth entrepreneurship as well as establishment and growth of companies. The findings of her and other Institute members' research are published in the series of scientific monographs 'Slovenian Entrepreneurship Observatory'. Since 2002, the Institute has been implementing the Slovenian part of the world-wide research Global Entrepreneurship Monitor (GEM). Since 2022 she is leading Slovenian GEM team. She is a representative of a Slovenian research group in the international research project DIANA, which specializes in women's entrepreneurship research. Since 2012 she serves as a county expert for the European Commission/OECD project Inclusive Entrepreneurship.

Manisha Urkude works in Chandrapur's Rajiv Gandhi College of Engineering Research & Technology. She has completed her Ph.D. in management and he areas of interest include image processing.

Pelin Yolcu has been working at Dicle University Diyarbakır Technical Sciences Vocational School since 2011. She works as an Instructor. In 2006, she completed her undergraduate education in Radio TV Cinema at Selcuk University, Faculty of

Communication. He graduated from the Institute of Social Sciences of the same university, from the Department of Radio TV Cinema in 2011, and in 2020, he completed his doctorate in the field of Radio TV Cinema with the thesis titled "The use of cultural codes in Turkish cinema after 2000: Derviş Zaim cinema". Yolcu gives trainings in and outside the institution on subjects such as communication, communication with children, diction, cinema history, screenplay, public relations and advertising, editing techniques. The author has international works on semiotics, mise-en-scene analysis, cyberbullying, cold war era cinema, digital citizenship, digital footprint, digital literacy through cartoons, history teaching through cartoons, and migration.

Ida Zaqreen is a Master's degree student in University Brunei Darussalam. She earned her Bachelor of Science (Mathematics) in 2020 at University Brunei Darussalam.

Index

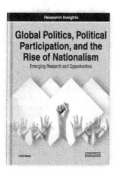

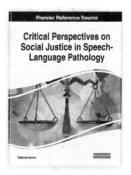

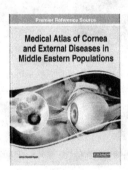

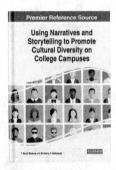

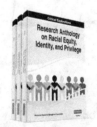

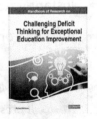

Printed in the United States
by Baker & Taylor Publisher Services